Principles, Procedure, and Justice

Principles, Procedure, and Justice

Essays in Honour of Adrian Zuckerman

Edited by

RABEEA ASSY

ANDREW HIGGINS

OXFORD
UNIVERSITY PRESS

OXFORD
UNIVERSITY PRESS

Great Clarendon Street, Oxford, OX2 6DP,
United Kingdom

Oxford University Press is a department of the University of Oxford.
It furthers the University's objective of excellence in research, scholarship,
and education by publishing worldwide. Oxford is a registered trade mark of
Oxford University Press in the UK and in certain other countries

First Edition published in 2020

Impression: 1

Published in the United States of America by Oxford University Press
198 Madison Avenue, New York, NY 10016, United States of America

British Library Cataloguing in Publication Data
Data available

Library of Congress Control Number: 2019955608

ISBN 978–0–19–885041–0

Printed and bound by
CPI Group (UK) Ltd, Croydon, CR0 4YY

Foreword to Festschrift for Adrian Zuckerman

The Right Honourable Lord Dyson

To have an excellent grasp of legal principles and penetrating analytical skills is a *sine qua non* for an outstanding academic lawyer. Anyone who has read Professor Zuckerman's writings and has had the privilege of discussing legal issues with him knows that he has these qualities in abundance.

But he is no ordinarily excellent academic lawyer. What emerges from his writings (as brought out so clearly in some of the distinguished contributions to this Festschrift) has been his great achievement in persuading the legal community of England and Wales that civil and criminal procedure is of central importance to our system of justice. Procedural justice has for too long been its Cinderella. In this respect, as so often, our jurisdiction has been different from those of other countries, especially those of Europe where it has long been recognized that procedural justice is important and worthy of academic study. Given Professor Zuckerman's international background, it is perhaps not surprising that he has been a powerful champion of the importance of analysing and understanding the principles that underpin procedural justice.

He was exposed to foreign influences in his formative years and he has maintained strong links with academics worldwide throughout his working life. The strength of these links is amply demonstrated by the number of contributions in this volume by overseas academics.

His writings are widely known. They will be his principal legacy. Nor should we overlook his skills as a teacher of law to which the generations of students that he has taught will attest. But before I say a little more about his writings, I should mention one aspect of his work which is less well known. During my years as Deputy Head of Civil Justice (2003–06) and as Master of the Rolls and Head of Civil Justice (2012–16), I had many discussions with him. They were always enjoyably stimulating and rewarding. He was skilled at forging and sustaining links with our senior judiciary. He was adept at persuading judges to participate in his BCL courses at Oxford and his LLM courses at UCL and was not slow to express his views to them, especially on civil justice issues. Some of his ideas found their way into speeches that I gave and possibly into my judgments too.

On occasions, he was also prepared to seek to persuade Government to his point of view. Like myself, he strongly supported the idea of introducing an extensive fixed recoverable costs regime (even more than that advocated by Sir Rupert Jackson in his report). As Head of Civil Justice, I had been trying for approximately three years to persuade the Ministry of Justice to accept the principle that the use of fixed recoverable costs should be expanded. My requests were neither accepted nor rejected. I was repeatedly told that the Government had limited resources and higher priorities. Professor Zuckerman shared my sense of frustration and discussed it with me. I told him that I had no objection to his seeing the Lord Chancellor (The Rt Hon Michael Gove) without me. He met Mr Gove and, no doubt with his usual mix of charm and compelling analysis, succeeded where I had failed. This was no mean achievement. It demonstrated powerfully that he is a man of drive and tenacity who has a politician's sense of the art of the possible. His combination of inter-personal skills, mastery of tactics, and academic scholarship is most unusual.

I should now return to the main piste and say something more about his writings. Although he has written about criminal evidence and procedure and many other topics, his most influential and enduring contribution has surely been in the field of civil procedure. His *magnum opus* is his book *Civil Procedure: Principles of Practice*, first published in 2003 and now in its third edition. It includes a valuable commentary on the most important of our Civil Procedure Rules. It is a *vade mecum* for any sensible judge who has a difficult issue of civil procedure to decide. It has been referred to on numerous occasions in our highest courts as well as in the courts of foreign jurisdictions.

Despite the best efforts of the great Master Jack Jacob, civil procedure was traditionally regarded in England and Wales as rather tedious. Any practitioner had to have a basic knowledge of the rules in order to conduct litigation. But the conventional view was that there were no principles and no law to be found in civil procedure. It was of little or no interest to serious lawyers. Professor Zuckerman saw things very differently. He recognized that procedural rules are, or should be, designed to promote a civil justice system that enables the state (by its judges) to achieve the aim of resolving disputes fairly, efficiently, and at proportionate cost. He was deeply troubled by the fact that under the existing system in England and Wales, the rules were not apt to achieve this aim. He was particularly dismayed to see how costly civil litigation had become in England and Wales. These shortcomings were a serious blot on our legal landscape.

He supported attempts successively by Lord Woolf and Sir Rupert Jackson to overcome the shortcomings. But he made no secret of the fact that in his view the recommendations of the Woolf and Jackson reports were insufficient to solve the problem. He clung steadfastly to his belief that excessive costs were the greatest impediment to a fair and effective system of justice. That is why he believes that fixed recoverable costs are essential. He would go much further than anyone has suggested thus far. But he knows that the vested interests of the legal profession continue to present an obstacle.

Professor Zuckerman has been very influential in promoting the idea that the court should take the lead in managing civil litigation and in allotting to an individual case an appropriate share of the court's resources, while taking into account the need to allot resources to other cases. Lawyers practising only one generation ago would have found these notions strange, not to say fundamentally objectionable.

All his contributions have been marked by rigorous analysis and a search for fundamental principle. Access to justice is his lodestar. Much of his work is directed at explaining how our existing procedural law should be changed to improve access to justice.

Lawyers both here and abroad, whether academic lawyers, judges, or practitioners, have huge respect for him and his work. It should come as no surprise that the editors of this splendid festschrift have attracted contributors and contributions of the highest quality from all over the world. The range of the contributions is very wide. This befits a scholar who is a man of real vision. He is a fine all-round lawyer, always seeking to expose and explain relevant principles. His greatest achievement has been to transform our approach to civil procedure.

Preface

Adrian Zuckerman is a leading authority on English civil procedure and evidence law. His phenomenal work has been very influential and had considerable impact on English law, especially his three-edition book *Zuckerman on Civil Procedure: Principles of Practice*.

This collection of essay contains contributions by friends and colleagues of Adrian, including former students. They cover a wide range of topics that pertain to Adrian's work and ideas, and so provide a fresh evaluation of them. We thank the authors for their invaluable contributions and dedication to this project, and to Harry Stratton and Johannes Kist for copyediting Peter Gottwald's paper on costs in Germany. We are also deeply grateful to Jamie Berezin and the team at Oxford University Press for overseeing this project from start to end.

The breadth and depth of material covered in this book is testament to Adrian's scholarship. For us what stands out about Adrian's work is his ability to take a principled approach to the most practical topics, largely free from the barnacles of voluminous and often conflicting case law. We recall Adrian once describing 'black letter' lawyering as gossip jurisprudence: 'Judge 1 said X and then Judge 2 said Y and then, what would you believe it, Judge 3 said something else altogether!'

Adrian taught us that certainty is a value, and in some cases an institutional imperative (as, for example, in the case of cost and funding rules), but the fact that a judge in 1833 said X, and that many judges since have faithfully reprinted X, says nothing about the intrinsic value of X. Adrian's quest for a principled approach to all matters that come before him, and his endless curiosity in seeking out new matters to examine—the latest being the role of AI in the courtroom—has led to a wealth of material that scholars, students, and judges alike have been able to mine, again and again, to aid their own understanding of procedure and evidence, and in the case of the judiciary, to help them decide difficult cases where the rules provide no clear-cut answer. Many of those he has taught, including us, are still carrying on his work, employing Zuckerman-esque analysis to areas he hasn't yet turned his attention to.

Most of all, however, we want to pay tribute to Az (as he known to his friends) as a mentor and friend. It is safe to say we would not have ended up in academia but for his encouragement and example. Like all good academics he can be intellectually intimidating, but unlike most academics, Az is such a famously charming person you often wouldn't realize he was tearing your work apart, and even if you did, you wouldn't much mind because his company was so entertaining. He has always had a rich life outside law, and even when conducting business, he was keen to discuss the things that mattered most. Many a PhD supervision became a consultation about the state of our love lives. Our partners admire him just as much as we do. So for everything that Az has contributed to scholarship, to the profession, to his students, and to us as friends, we say a very heartfelt thanks.

This book has been a long time coming, partly because we did not want Az to interpret it as a hint to retire, and nor would we let him permanently head to the beach in his beloved Bahamas. Thus it was written with his permission, and on the express understanding that it would simply be a wonderful opportunity for a conference and party with some of his oldest and closest colleagues—an opportunity that Az would never turn down.

Contents

List of Contributors

Rabeea Assy, Associate Professor, Faculty of Law, The University of Haifa

Michael Briggs, Justice of the UK Supreme Court.

Andrew L-T Choo, Professor of Law, Law School, City, University of London

Carla Crifo, Associate Professor, Leicester Law School

Peter Gottwald, Professor, Faculty of Law, University of Regensburg

Andrew Higgins, Associate Professor of Civil Procedure, Faculty of Law and Mansfield College, University of Oxford

Samuel Issacharoff, Reiss Professor of Constitutional Law, NYU School of Law

Sir Rupert Jackson, Arbitrator, 4 New Square Chambers,

Inbar Levy, Lecturer, Melbourne Law School, The University of Melbourne

Thibaut Lienart, Research Associate, Department of Computing, Imperial College London

Andrew Ligertwood, Emeritus Fellow in Law, School of Law, The University of Adelaide, Australia

Paul Roberts, Professor of Criminal Jurisprudence, School of Law, University of Nottingham; Adjunct Professor of Law, China University of Political Science and Law, Beijing

Robert J Sharpe, Distinguished Jurist in Residence at the Faculty of Law, University of Toronto; Visiting Professor, University of Oxford

Stuart Sime, Professor of Law, Programme Director, Bar Professional Training Course; City Law School, City, University of London; Barrister

John Sorabji, Principal Legal Adviser to the Lord Chief Justice and the Master of the Rolls; Senior Teaching Fellow, University College London

Frederick Wilmot-Smith, Fellow of All Souls College; Barrister, Brick Court Chambers

INTRODUCTION

1
A Man for All Processes

Samuel Issacharoff

Sometimes first impressions not only last, but are correct. My first contact with Adrian seems like a lifetime ago, yet informed immediately my appreciation for his work. Back in 1993, I was a very junior professor at the University of Texas School of Law, not even yet tenured. Somehow Adrian had met one of my senior colleagues at a conference in Japan and impressed upon him how wonderful it would be to have an Oxford professor examine a part of America far from the familiar coastal reaches. Although Texans ride high in the saddle and walk with a swagger, there was still the lurking provincial awe at the studied elegance of the British. And even if our visiting British don would carry the accents of the ravages of Middle Europe and the flight to the Middle East, nonetheless we were thrilled to have Adrian in our midst.

In every sense, Adrian offered the New World audience what it would want to hear from the Oxford tradition. As our then frequent visitor Neal MacCormick would comment, the difference between Texas and the United Kingdom was that in the UK there was a belief that 200 miles was a great distance, while in Texas there was the equally parochial view that 200 years is a long time. Certainly Adrian offered the fruits of the long scholarly tradition at Oxford to an American state still debating questions of integration in the American union and demands for local sovereignty. (Perhaps the differences are not as great as might appear.) Adrian was urbane, witty, charming, insightful, and intellectually compelling. But, beyond the clear points for style lay the substance of the presentation, something that proved the foundation of a quarter century of fruitful exchanges and friendship.

The paper Adrian presented covered a distinct feature of British civil procedure known as the *Mareva* injunction,[1] essentially a form of bonding requirement for the harm that may be caused by either the continuation or cessation of a challenged conduct. Under this distinct British procedure, parties may seek an injunction to, in effect, freeze the assets of a defendant in order to offset the risk that funds will be dissipated before a judgment may be enforced. The process arose from court decisions dating only back to the 1970s and were initially presented in the context of foreign defendants in contract disputes who might spirit their holdings out of

[1] The term derives from two cases decided in 1975: *Nippon Yusen Kaisha v Karageorgis* [1975] 1 WLR 1093, and *Mareva Compania Naviera SA v International Bulkcarriers SA* [1975] 2 Lloyd's Rep 509.

Samuel Issacharoff, *A Man for All Processes* In: *Principles, Procedure, and Justice.* Edited by: Rabeea Assy and Andrew Higgins, Oxford University Press (2020). © The editors and several contributors. DOI: 10.1093/oso/9780198850410.003.0001

the country, thereby rendering any subsequent judgment worthless. By the time of Adrian's presentation, these injunctions had taken a life of their own, with pro forma affidavits claiming risk of asset depletion, an *ex parte* hearing, and then a broad injunction against use of the defendant's holdings in which plaintiff claimed no specific right, only the desire to freeze the status quo pending the resolution of a lawsuit.

As presented, and as subsequently published in the *Law Quarterly Review*,[2] the paper was a great success with the audience. It took a wonderful problem of procedure that presented in great relief the ideas of opportunity cost and a sophisticated cost/benefit analysis of the consequences of error both in the grant and in the frustration of immediate injunctive relief. To an American audience, the paper seemed right in keeping with the work that was being developed by a pioneering group of scholars (at the time, I was a very junior member of this cohort) who were applying game theoretic and strategic economic models to the problems of access to justice. The *Mareva* injunction may have been confined to the British system, but corresponding processes were in place in the US as well.

Indeed, only two years before Adrian's presentation, the US Supreme Court had struck down a Connecticut state procedure that allowed a form of prejudgment attachment in contexts even broader than the commercial disputes at issue in the original English cases. As presented in *Connecticut v Doehr*,[3] a bar fight left one participant allegedly injured and suing the other in tort. Upon presentation of an *ex parte* affidavit attesting to a fear of diversion of funds, the claimant was able to secure a lien on the home of the defendant, without any claim to a pre-existing interest in the home or any of the defendant's particular assets. The lien was simply a security in case of a successful tort judgment. The spread of these *ex parte* attachments posed grave risk of strategic misuse, as in the context of *Connecticut v Doehr* itself. Clearly the affidavit could do no more than recite a general grievance and a desire for recovery, not any specifics about the intent of the defendant to sell his home or anything of the like. But knowledge that a disliked neighbour's assets could be tied up in this fashion invited mischievous ends to further disputes outside the legal system, and one could easily slap a lien on a neighbour's home if the neighbour was in need of a second mortgage to pay emergency bills or send a child to college, or any specific need for funds that might put one at the mercy of an invasive local miscreant. Under circumstances of emergency, the only recourse might be to pay off the lienholder, regardless of the merits of the claim. In other words, legalized extortion.

The Supreme Court struck down the Connecticut procedure on analytic grounds that tracked many of the concerns in Adrian's paper on the *Mareva* injunction. The

[2] A Zuckerman, 'Mareva Injunctions and Security for Judgment in a Framework of Interlocutory Remedies' (1993) 109 LQR 432.

[3] (1991) 501 US 1.

American case law, however, provided a formal doctrinal grounding that was absent in British law. Some fifteen years earlier, the Supreme Court undertook to ground American due process law into a balancing of competing interests and the risk of both harm to the defendant and error in the judgment that might ensue from too little or too much process. In the landmark case of *Mathews v Eldridge*,[4] the Court found that a prejudgment attachment over property in which the plaintiff had no pre-existing entitlement posed too great a risk of error and that the procedures in place to dissuade misuse (such as a bonding requirement and high damages for erroneous claims) were insufficient to protect a constitutionally-recognized property interest. As the case law under *Mathews v Eldridge* would develop, and in the inestimable words of former Judge Richard Posner, the result was a form of constitutional balancing in which the 'less that is at stake, other things being equal, the less process is due', and vice versa.[5]

What set *Connecticut v Doehr* apart from the British case law, and indeed the British scholarship, was precisely the development of a well-honed constitutional due process tradition in the US that could assess the corresponding risks in various procedural devices in the nuanced setting of their application. Adrian's paper was elegant and sophisticated, but it seemed to be written without the background conceptual grounding that similar problems would have received in the United States.

After the presentation, I had the pleasure to dine with Adrian and a few other colleagues from Texas. As the dinner progressed and after a few drinks, I decided to confront Adrian with what I took to be a failing of the paper. I might have been junior, and he might have been a distinguished visitor, but what is the point of scholarly exchange if not to raise the stakes of the challenge? And, certainly, what is the role of alcohol if not to raise the willingness to engage in such challenges—as Mr Doehr's Connecticut neighbour had apparently discovered.

So began the exchange that marked many years of engagement. For all the discussion of the theories of law and the practical applications as revealed in contemporary cases, I noted, there was virtually no discussion of the academic debates surrounding the Mareva injunctions or similar areas in which procedural norms had to confront the difficult trade-off between equity and efficiency. Indeed, the references to the academic debates in the paper were to some American academic sources but mostly to Bentham. I was quick to note that I was a great admirer of Bentham and that his writings on the procedural dimensions of the law continue to inform. But a rumour was sweeping our side of the Atlantic that Bentham, notwithstanding occasional sightings at University College, had actually died some time over a century ago. Was there not possibly something more current that might be worth engaging in the British debates over the functioning and the aspirations

[4] (1976) 424 US 319.
[5] *Van Harken v City of Chicago* (1997) 103 F 3d 1346 (7th Cir).

of a legal system? That night for the first time I got an inkling that in fact there might not be.

Thus, when I first encountered Mr Zuckerman's authoritative and magisterial treatise, *Civil Procedure*, my sense of its accomplishment was all the richer. I have the same respect for this work that I have for the pioneering efforts in this country of my late Texas colleague, Charles Alan Wright, and my current NYU colleague Arthur Miller. Together they created the modern field of procedure in the US by force of intellect and through a synthetic understanding of the difficulties in organizing a system of procedural justice. The great Wright & Miller treatise on federal courts drew from the experience of the courts an aspiration towards the proper blend of finality, correctness in adjudication, and reasonable economy. When understood in that light, the experience of the courts could be integrated and examined critically. In Mr Zuckerman's many articles on the related fields of criminal and civil procedure and evidence, and in his work on law reform, including his indispensable intellectual contributions to the Commission headed by Lord Woolf, the same analytic power that Wright and Miller brought to American law has been delivered to British jurisprudence.

What I did not appreciate in 1993 and have since come to value with a respect bordering on awe, is the effect that one individual can have on rekindling an intellectual tradition. Adrian's aim was not the classic debates between Bentham and Blackstone, but the growing perception that British procedure was askew, leading up to the dramatically amended Civil Procedure Rules of 1998, and to the intellectual forebearer of those reforms, the 1995 Lord Woolf report, *Access to Justice*. In Adrian's able hands, *Civil Procedure* imposes from the very first page an analytic template on the rules, a move which joins his work to the best of the American tradition in Wright & Miller. The book begins, as does all the best work in this field, by interpreting the goals of a system of procedural justice in terms of fairness to the litigants, the societal aims of economic resolution of disputes, the integrity of judgments, and the need for costs to be commensurate with the ability of disputants to seek meaningful resolution within the justice system. For Adrian, the role of procedural law is to allow the enforcement of entitlements upon whose vitality the society depends. The political theory underlying this intuition is rich and diverse. We can trace back to Hobbes, for example, the concern with security in entitlements as a precondition for enterprise, investment, and the ability to ward off the dreaded war of all against all. Adrian harnesses political theory to create an analytic framework in which a procedural system is measured not in terms of its formal structures, but in its ability to secure dependable justice that promotes the rights and responsibilities assigned by the society.

This last point is critical and it is Adrian's most distinctive and influential contribution to British law. From an American perspective, one of the most striking features about British procedural law and the limited academic commentary on it was its astonishing formalism. Everything seemed to operate at the level of best practices, with an odd assumption that additional layers of procedure would add only benefit, with costs considered an almost vulgar topic not to be mentioned in polite company. The inattention to costs meant that there was no sustained engagement with the ability of the British legal system to deliver justice not only at the level of the ideal, but at the level of social reality. The inattention to costs seemed all the more perplexing since everyday conversations in Britain revealed exquisite frustration over the fact that the disputes that naturally arise (eg, a road accident, a contractual disagreement with a builder, the delivery of nonconforming goods) were effectively not subject to redress through the legal system. Except for those eligible for legal aid at one extreme, and the very wealthy at the other, the rapidly escalating cost structure of British legal practice made resort to the courts prohibitively expensive.

Again the contrast to America is instructive. American procedural law had moved overwhelmingly to a balancing approach that tried to peg the level of procedural rigor to the stakes in the dispute and the risk and consequences of error; more procedure when there were extraordinary consequences (as with the extreme example of capital punishment), informal and inexpensive procedure for matters of low consequence (with examples in our small claims courts and traffic courts, for example). This is not, by any account, meant to imply the perfection of American law. This is just an indication of the difference in how far the different systems had moved in their departure from the shared origins in the extreme formalism of the British common law pleading systems of many centuries ago.

Adrian simply transformed the debate in Britain and was a pivotal force in changing the institutional practice of law as well. From his work on the *Mareva* injunctions to the critical commentaries on cost structures to his forceful interjections into the work of the Woolf Commission to his compendious study in *Civil Procedure*, and including the many intervening articles and his stewardship of *Civil Justice Quarterly*, the central feature of Adrian's work in civil procedure has been his ability to analyse the complex issues of procedure in a way that is both institutionally rich and theoretically sophisticated. This is work that had to be undertaken from a perch slightly above the world of practice. For judges and lawyers immersed in the details of a system as it presents itself in a particular case, the systemic overview is both frustrating and almost an indulgence that does not produce immediate results for the problem at hand. On the other hand, to be effective, this work had to be informed by extensive study of the world of law in practice as applied to the myriad details of bringing a generalized social commitment to justice to fruition. Just as the pressures of time and focus tended to keep judges and practicing lawyers from the ability to abstract effectively from their day-to-day observations, so too did the distance of the British academy from the bar dissuade serious study of how law was actually practiced in Britain. This was the void that Adrian so ably filled.

The basic thesis of this work is that an economic analysis of the incentives at work in the system, largely driven by the financial rewards to those inside the game, shows the need for reform to achieve the ultimate objective of affordable justice. This is a highly controversial proposition for it admits of circumstances when the justice system overall and the litigants themselves all have an interest in cheaper, less certain, and oftentimes less accurate dispute resolution. When Adrian began to critique systematically the various levers of the British civil justice system as frustrating litigant rights by denying them affordable justice, it was a strikingly discordant voice in British legal commentary. Moreover, coming from the pinnacle of the academic elite it was hard to say which was more jarring, the message or the fact that it came from an academic voice at Oxford. In article after article dealing with the cost structure of legal representation, the consequences of delay, the failure to enforce procedural obligations of timely filings and temperance in document production, a sustained critique emerged of a procedural systems increasingly shorn of its moorings.

I corresponded frequently with Adrian during the period in the mid-1990s when he was turning his academic attention squarely to an economic analysis of the procedural system. But it is clear that I was not the only such correspondent. Recognizing the limitations of the British treatment of these issues, Adrian began a systematic investigation of a number of national systems as well as of the state of the art academic analysis in those countries. To the best of my knowledge, these efforts were unprecedented in the modern era of the British academy. The field had fallen from favour long before and there was little or no disciplined academic work being done. It is ironic that the great early works in this area were from jurists such as Blackstone and Bentham, but that the tradition had largely dried up.

This renewed scholarly effort to overhaul the British academic treatment of procedural justice coincided with mounting public concern over the British legal system. By extraordinary good fortune, Adrian's academic breakthroughs of the early to mid-1990s coincided with the commissioning of the inquiry headed by Lord Woolf. This led to the publication of two books that cemented Adrian's international reputation as a recognized authority on procedural justice, British or otherwise. His two edited volumes on these themes, with his own contributions included, are now the standard fare of anyone who wants to seriously engage these issues in any national setting. (I refer to the 1995 OUP book *Reform of Civil Procedure* and the 1999 OUP book *Civil Justice in Crisis*.) The first of these books gave a deeper theoretical grounding to the draft proposals of the Woolf Commission, attempting both to shore up the suggested revisions against the predictable consternation of the bar while at the same time exposing some of the shortcomings of the initial reform proposals. The second book allowed a systematic cross-national comparison of how the same issues were coming to plague inherited procedural systems in increasingly fluid and complex legal systems.

This led to a direct confrontation with the inevitable caution or conservatism that accompanies settled institutional practices. The first impulse of the Woolf Commission was to address some features of complexity in British procedure without tackling forthrightly the economic incentives towards cost escalation that had compromised the effectiveness of British civil justice. Adrian was a forceful critic of this approach and produced a highly publicized set of recommendations for cost constraints. This led to a second front when the bar responded. Here again the result was a set of highly visible reform proposals and comparisons to other practices, most notably from Germany, that could be used to rationalize British procedure. Ultimately, this led to an academic examination of the core economic structure of British litigation, focusing on what is known as the English rule of fee shifting. Under this rule, the loser bears the costs of litigation not only for himself, but for the victor as well. This creates a tremendous moral hazard by which parties who do not internalize the full costs of their endeavours do not exhibit the constraints of properly weighing the costs against the benefits of additional expenditures. (For example, if a litigant has a 50 per cent chance of prevailing, then each incremental unit of expenditure is discounted 50 per cent on the chance that the opponent might be forced to absorb the costs.) The question of how to fund litigation and the consequences that this may have on party incentives is a topic of great interest in the US and among economists in Britain and around the world. But until this inquiry, there was no one in the British legal academy giving this serious thought. This too proved to be an area where Adrian's academic inquiries will run up against the inherited patterns of the British legal system. It has long been thought that the strength of the academy lies in the ability to speak truth to power. One need look no further.

A truly remarkable feature of these efforts is that they not only changed the terms of academic discussion in Britain, but they came to dominate debates in the broader world of British law. The final version of the Woolf proposals bears the unmistakable imprint of Adrian's efforts, particularly in the unprecedented efforts to move litigation into mandatory tracks limiting the extent of factual inquiry and capping costs to keep access to the legal system affordable. Although the significance of this shift in perspective may be difficult to appreciate outside the world of law, this marks a sea change in the British conception of how to think about procedural justice. Nor is Adrian's role in bringing this about not appreciated. It is by now commonplace to read opinions of British courts addressing novel issues of procedure by reference to Adrian's work, most notably his treatise of civil procedure and the shaping essays he has brought to public attention through his editorship of *Civil Justice Quarterly*. What I find even more striking are the judicial opinions I have read that *reject* Adrian's approach but nonetheless feel compelled to justify the reasons for doing so. These opinions well attest to the pivotal role that his scholarship plays in British legal discourse.

I have seen this role play out in other ways, during visits to Oxford with leading English jurists, and most notably when I was invited a few years back for a private meeting with High Court judges to discuss developments in American treatment of complex litigation. The English may have pioneered many methods of aggregate claim resolution, from the early forms of the class action to the Prize Courts of the admiralty. But the newer forms of consumer claims and mass torts has proved a challenge in Britain as in all countries. I was asked to give a talk of developments in the American handling of multiparty, multijurisdictional lawsuits that tend to tax the administrative capabilities of courts in any national setting. I was honoured and impressed by this form of judicial gathering organized not under the normal common law setting of specific case resolution, but under the institutional authority of the courts as having to examine a pressing problem. As best anyone could tell, this was the first such informal gathering of these British judges for a tutorial on how to think about efficiencies in the handling of complex cases. And, it was noteworthy that the person to whom they turned to organize these gatherings was of course Adrian.

The focus on civil procedure should not be taken to slight Adrian's serious academic contributions to the study of criminal procedure and evidence. The same analytic tools and disciplined inquiry are on view in those areas as well, as is the insistence on moving legal inquiry away from a formalistic recounting of the rules, their applications, and their exceptions. In each area, Adrian lays out a functional account of both evidence and criminal procedure as setting out an institutional commitment to broader objectives of security and integrity in judgments. Each of these areas of his work show off the same tools of measuring the success of legal rules against a metric of efficient realization of broader society objectives. Nonetheless, I focus on civil procedure for two reasons. First, this is an area of my expertise in which my views are most informed and in which I have the greatest familiarity with the British experience. Second, it is a rare achievement for a legal academic to have played such a great role in changing the terms of a national debate. That happens infrequently and ought to be highlighted when it does.

Further, it in the academic setting that I have seen the impact of the changed agenda. My first trip to Oxford came in 1994, invited by Adrian to speak to a graduate class in procedure. Although the students came from far and wide, the effect of the academic disregard of procedure could be felt. Evidence was a topic taught in traditional legal education, but procedure was not. It was assumed that the internal workings of a legal system were a matter for apprenticeship-style integration into the profession, not for intellectual discourse. I had chosen to present a recent paper of mine that used reforms in summary judgment to challenge the early law and economics accounts of procedural rules. This paper was part of what may be termed a second generation critique of the first generation of law and economics scholarship on procedure. (The basic divide is between the first generation's use of a static model that analyses the incentives operating on parties independently and the second generation's use of a strategic model that examines the interactive and behavioural incentives that may complicate the analysis.) I made some early comment in presenting the paper that not only summarized what I was critiquing but then moved on based on the assumption that the audience already understood the first generation moves. The sea of blank faces quickly dispelled that notion. Fortunately, I had the wherewithal to stop the lecture and ask, pretty much point blank, whether the students had any understanding of the basic approaches to the economic analysis of law that I proposed to critique. No one had any such understanding. I then asked whether any of them could tell me how litigation was financed and on what terms in their home country. Again, blank responses.

I realized that there was such inattention to how legal systems actually functioned that the students, many of whom were formally admitted to legal practice and were now returning for a graduate degree, simply had never been exposed to the idea of the legal system as a subject for serious analytic inquiry. I rapidly jettisoned increasing portions of my presentation in favour of a rudimentary exposition of the basics of an economic analysis of a legal system. By the end, I had entirely abandoned my planned lecture and instead presented a basic primer on the economic assessment of basic civil procedure. An insight into Oxford, but quite fascinating.

In the twenty years that followed, I had a number of occasions to speak at Oxford or elsewhere in England, and invariably would take the opportunity to present in Adrian's graduate courses, so long as dates accommodated. The change over time has been dramatic. In subsequent years I would find the students well prepared for the topics I presented, engaged in high level analysis, and familiar with a range of academic debates on sophisticated procedural issues both in Britain and abroad. The renewed focus on civil procedure teaching had not only taken hold as a core part of the curriculum but the interest in process would prove to draw top students from Britain and beyond.

The effect has been transformative of the British legal academy. Adrian has revitalized the areas of law concerning the procedural forms of justice. His work has introduced a measure of analytic rigor that had been sorely lacking for many generations, perhaps even longer. And, his work has had a galvanizing effect on the reform of British justice and the way in which procedural fairness is evaluated in Britain and beyond. In short, he has taken a field that had basically (and unfortunately) fallen from favour, revitalized it in the academy, and by force of will and analytic prowess convinced the leading jurists of Britain that the world of British courts had to be remade. This is an extraordinary record, fully meriting the highest of academic honours that have been accorded.

Over the course of these decades, the insights have decidedly swung in both directions. Not only did I have many opportunities to visit Oxford, but Adrian has been a much cherished regular visitor to NYU to speak in classes on complex litigation. He most often addresses the questions of the funding of litigation, the access implications of different legal regimes, and the cost boundaries of different rules of paying for litigation. He easily wins over the class each year with the combination of charm, wit, and rigorous analytic presentation.

As much as anything, however, students are struck by the similarities in problems and consequences even in legal systems with strikingly different forms of organization. It is reassuring that problems can be addressed productively based on a shared analytic effort, even for countries separated by expanses of water. (Perhaps we should try our hand at Brexit.)

PART I

THE CHANGING FACE OF EVIDENCE LAW

2

Defining the Scope of the Hearsay Rule in Criminal Cases: A Comparative Perspective

*Andrew L-T Choo**

Introduction

As with much else in the field of criminal evidence, hearsay doctrine in England and Wales has changed considerably since Adrian Zuckerman's *The Principles of Criminal Evidence* was published in 1989.[1] Roughly half way between 1989 and now, the law of criminal hearsay became embedded in provisions of the Criminal Justice Act 2003.[2] While it is axiomatic that a witness's oral testimony in court about an event allegedly witnessed may be unreliable because of defects in the witness's perception, memory, sincerity, or ability to communicate clearly, the traditional assumption has been that such testimony will be able to be 'tested' through observation of the witness's demeanour and through contemporaneous cross-examination. These 'tests' being unavailable where evidence of words spoken or written, or non-verbal conduct engaged in, out of court is later introduced in court as evidence of the truth of its contents, there is good reason, it is said, to be cautious about the reliability of such evidence.[3] In more contemporary times, however, scepticism about the effectiveness of the 'tests' of observation of demeanour[4] and contemporaneous cross-examination,[5] and empirical evidence

* I thank Richard Glover, Paul McKeown, Abenaa Owusu-Bempah, and Andy Roberts for helpful discussions, and the anonymous reviewer of the chapter for constructive comments and for saving me from a number of infelicities.

[1] AAS Zuckerman, *The Principles of Criminal Evidence* (Clarendon Press 1989). This book, which Zuckerman completed while I was his doctoral student, later formed the basis of a co-written (with Paul Roberts) and more comprehensive treatment of criminal evidence: P Roberts and AAS Zuckerman, *Criminal Evidence* (OUP 2004); P Roberts and AAS Zuckerman, *Criminal Evidence* (2nd edn, OUP 2010).

[2] The hearsay provisions of this Act came into force on 4 April 2005.

[3] 'The truthfulness and accuracy of the person whose words are spoken to by another witness cannot be tested by cross-examination, and the light which his demeanour would throw on his testimony is lost': *Teper v R* [1952] AC 480 (PC) 486 (Lord Normand).

[4] See AL-T Choo, *Evidence* (5th edn, OUP 2018) 60–61.

[5] See ibid 265.

Andrew L-T Choo, *Defining the Scope of the Hearsay Rule in Criminal Cases* In: *Principles, Procedure, and Justice.* Edited by: Rabeea Assy and Andrew Higgins, Oxford University Press (2020). © The editors and several contributors.
DOI: 10.1093/oso/9780198850410.003.0002

questioning the assumption that juries in serious criminal cases are incapable of assessing the reliability of hearsay evidence competently,[6] have raised the possibility that, as a class, first-hand evidence may not be far superior to hearsay evidence. Thus the question is raised whether a more contextual approach to the admissibility of hearsay evidence—one that distances itself somewhat from the traditional suspicion with which such evidence was approached—might be appropriate.

Zuckerman argued persuasively for a less rigid and more nuanced approach to criminal hearsay which accommodates contemporary thinking of this nature,[7] and to some extent his wishes have been realized. One of the key features of the hearsay provisions of the Criminal Justice Act 2003 is a more liberalized régime for the admissibility of hearsay evidence, notably including a broad 'interests of justice' exception[8] to the rule against hearsay. More recently, courts[9] and academic commentators[10] have paid increasing attention to the implications of European human rights norms[11] for the admissibility of hearsay evidence.

This chapter considers an issue which has been somewhat neglected in academic commentary on criminal hearsay in the 2003 Act era: how the rule against hearsay is defined (or ought to be defined) in the first place. The importance of this issue as a matter of principle is self-evident, as the definition of the rule provides the starting point for consideration of the admissibility of particular evidence: depending on the precise definition of the rule adopted, the role for exceptions to it might be enhanced or diminished. Practically, the statutory definition of the rule has, as will be demonstrated, generated some apparent difficulty for the courts. Consideration of the issue is also of particular contemporary interest from a comparative perspective; we shall see later in this chapter (in the section entitled 'Canada: Defending *R v Kearley*') that, aftera period of uncertainty, Canada has opted for an approach that fundamentally differs from that taken in other major common law jurisdictions. Which of the competing approaches is preferable will form the basis of the discussion in this chapter.

[6] See generally, for discussions of empirical evidence concerning the hearsay rule, RC Park, 'Empirical Evaluation of the Hearsay Rule' in P Mirfield and R Smith (eds), *Essays for Colin Tapper* (OUP 2003); RC Park, 'Visions of Applying the Scientific Method to the Hearsay Rule' [2003] Mich St L Rev 1149; J Sevier, 'Popularizing Hearsay' (2016) 104 Georgetown LJ 643.

[7] Zuckerman (n 1) ch 11.

[8] Sections 114(1)(d) and 121(1)(c).

[9] See *Al-Khawaja and Tahery v UK*, App nos 26766/05 and 22228/06 (ECtHR, 15 December 2011); *Schatschaschwili v Germany*, App no 9154/10 (ECtHR, 15 December 2015); *Blokhin v Russia*, App no 47152/06 (ECtHR, 23 March 2016).

[10] See eg AL-T Choo, 'Criminal Hearsay in England and Wales: Pragmatism, Comparativism, and Human Rights' (2013) 17 Can Crim L Rev 227.

[11] The general right of a person charged to a fair trial (European Convention on Human Rights, art 6(1)), and the right of such a person 'to examine or have examined witnesses against him' (European Convention on Human Rights, art 6(3)(d)).

R v Kearley: Where it all supposedly went wrong

The much-criticized decision of the House of Lords in *R v Kearley*[12] illustrates neatly the state of hearsay doctrine prior to the 2003 Act. Kearley was charged with possession of a controlled drug with intent to supply. At issue was evidence that, following his arrest and while his house was being searched by the police, a number of telephone calls had been made to the house in which the callers requested to speak to him and asked to be supplied with drugs; and that a number of individuals had called at the house asking to be supplied with drugs. The following point of law of general public importance was certified for consideration by the House of Lords:

> Whether evidence may be adduced at a trial of words spoken (namely a request for drugs to be supplied by the defendant), not spoken in the presence or hearing of the defendant, by a person not called as a witness, for the purpose not of establishing the truth of any fact narrated by the words, but of inviting the jury to draw an inference from the fact that the words were spoken (namely that the defendant was a supplier of drugs).

The House of Lords split 3:2, the majority answering the above question in the negative. Lord Bridge, in the majority, stated:

> The sole possible relevance of the words spoken is that by manifesting the speaker's belief that the defendant is a supplier they impliedly assert that fact. This is most clearly exemplified by two of the requests made to police officers in the instant case by callers requesting drugs from the defendant where the speaker asked for a supply of his 'usual amount'. The speaker was impliedly asserting that he had been supplied by the defendant with drugs in the past. If the speaker had expressly said to the police officer that the defendant had supplied him with drugs in the past, this would clearly have been inadmissible as hearsay. When the only relevance of the words spoken lies in their implied assertion that the defendant is a supplier of drugs, must this equally be excluded as hearsay?[13]

The 'clear and unequivocal'[14] answer to this question was held to be 'yes', the applicable principle being that 'evidence of words spoken by a person not called as a witness which are said to assert a relevant fact by necessary implication [is] inadmissible as hearsay just as evidence of an express statement made by the speaker asserting the same fact would be'.[15] As the evidence at issue in this case

[12] [1992] 2 AC 228 (HL).
[13] ibid 243.
[14] ibid 243.
[15] ibid 245.

was hearsay evidence to which no exception applied, it had to be excluded. While 'fully appreciat[ing] the cogency of the reasons advanced in favour of a limitation or exception to the operation of the hearsay rule which would allow the admission of implied assertions of the kind in question',[16] Lord Bridge considered it an established principle that any modification of hearsay doctrine could not be effected judicially.[17]

Kearley demonstrated that the spirit of *Wright v Doe d Tatham*[18] continued to live on more than a century and a half later. At issue in *Wright* was whether one Marsden had testamentary capacity, and the question arose whether three letters to him, written in such a manner as to suggest that the writers believed they were dealing with a person of reasonable understanding, were admissible in evidence. Representing the majority position, Parke B stated that

> proof of a particular fact … which is relevant … as implying a statement or opinion of a third person on [a] matter in issue … is inadmissible …; and, therefore, in this case the letters which are offered only to prove the competence of the testator, that is the truth of the implied statements therein contained, were properly rejected …[19]

Parke B provided further examples of evidence which, by analogy, would also be excluded under the hearsay rule as implied assertions:

> (a) Evidence of a letter demanding a debt and treating the addressee as a debtor, to establish that the debt was really due.
> (b) Evidence of a note congratulating someone 'on his high state of bodily vigour', to establish that that person was in good health.
> (c) Evidence of the supposed conduct of the family or relations of a testator, taking the same precautions in his absence as if he were a lunatic; his election, in his absence, to some high and responsible office; the conduct of a physician who permitted a will to be executed by a sick testator; the conduct of a deceased captain on a question of seaworthiness, who, after examining every part of the vessel, embarked in it with his family; all these, when deliberately considered, are, with reference to the matter in issue in each case, mere instances of hearsay evidence, mere statements, not on oath, but implied in or vouched by the actual conduct of persons by whose acts the litigant parties are not to be bound.[20]

[16] ibid 249.
[17] ibid 249–51.
[18] (1837) 7 Ad & E 313, 112 ER 488.
[19] (1837) 7 Ad & E 313, 388–89, 112 ER 488, 516–17.
[20] (1837) 7 Ad & E 313, 388, 112 ER 488, 516.

The above examples, especially the instances of evidence of non-verbal *conduct* provided in (c),[21] illustrate how potentially far reaching the decision of the House of Lords in *Kearley* was to cling steadfastly to the position in *Wright*. Controversial enough in the context of the result reached in the case, *Kearley* further confirmed the inadmissibility of a large swathe of evidence, unless an available exception to the rule could come to the rescue in a particular case. Fundamental reform was finally implemented by the Criminal Justice Act 2003.

The Criminal Justice Act 2003: Was it a purpose of the maker of the statement to cause another person to believe the matter or to cause another person to act on the basis that the matter is as stated?

In England and Wales, section 114(1) of the Criminal Justice Act 2003 provides that, in criminal proceedings, 'a statement not made in oral evidence in the proceedings is admissible as evidence of any matter stated' only in specified circumstances. Section 115(2) clarifies that a statement may be made by words or by non-verbal conduct: 'A statement is any representation of fact or opinion made by a person by whatever means; and it includes a representation made in a sketch, photofit or other pictorial form.' Crucially, in terms of the focus of this chapter, section 115(3) provides: 'A matter stated is one to which this Chapter applies if (and only if) the purpose, or one of the purposes, of the person making the statement appears to the court to have been (a) to cause another person to believe the matter, or (b) to cause another person to act... on the basis that the matter is as stated.'

The rationale for the focus on the state of mind of the maker of the statement is that the danger of insincerity will be reduced if the person responsible for the out-of-court words or actions did not consciously turn his or her mind to the matter in question. It is thought therefore that there is no need for evidence of such words or actions to be caught by any presumptive rule of inadmissibility. In the words of the Law Commission of England and Wales, whose recommendations formed the basis for the relevant provisions of the 2003 Act:

> Where there is a substantial risk that an out-of-court assertion may have been deliberately fabricated, ... we think it right that the assertion should fall within the hearsay rule—whether it is express or implied. It follows that the rule should extend to any conduct which is intended to give the impression that a particular fact is true, and is adduced as evidence of that fact. But where that risk is not

[21] Another hypothetical illustration commonly offered is that of the inadmissibility, as hearsay, of evidence that people were carrying opened umbrellas or wearing raincoats to establish that it was raining.

> present—in other words, where the person from whose conduct a fact is to be inferred can safely be assumed to have believed that fact to be true—we do not think a court should be precluded from inferring that fact merely because that person may have been mistaken in believing it. And if that person did not intend anyone to infer it, it follows that that person cannot have been seeking to mislead anyone about it.[22]

This strategy was influenced by the approach that by then had been adopted in the Federal Rules of Evidence in the United States and by statute in parts of Australia, examined in the next two sections of this chapter.

The choice of 'purpose' rather than the perhaps more orthodox concept of 'intention' as the relevant requirement may be traced to the recommendations of the Law Commission of England and Wales, which reasoned by first noting that

> the word 'intention' is ambiguous[,] [i]n some contexts ... refer[ring] only to the *purpose* with which a person acts—the objective that that person hopes to achieve by acting as he or she does. In others, it includes not only purpose but also what is sometimes called 'oblique' intention. In this wider sense, a person 'intends' not only the consequences that he or she *wishes* to bring about, but also those that he or she knows to be an inevitable side-effect of the consequences that he or she desires.[23]

This, of course, is unanswerable: where intention is an element of a criminal offence in England and Wales, it is well established that the requirement may be satisfied by proof of intention in either the narrower or wider sense.[24] The width and, it is true, the ambiguity of the concept of intention are not therefore matters of much contemporary concern in that jurisdiction. The Commission continued:

> The point is perhaps unlikely to be of great practical importance, but we have considered whether the applicability of the hearsay rule to a particular statement should depend on the *intention* (in our wider sense) or only on the *purpose* with which the statement is made. Should a person's words or conduct count as a hearsay statement of a fact if that person does not positively desire that another should thereby be caused to believe that fact (or that another should be caused to act ... on the basis that it is true), but knows that this will inevitably occur?
>
> [The argument] that, if [a] person is not seeking to convey a particular impression, it follows that he or she cannot be seeking to convey a *misleading*

[22] Law Commission, *Evidence in Criminal Proceedings: Hearsay and Related Topics* (Law Com No 245, 1997) para 7.20.
[23] ibid para 7.36 (emphasis in original).
[24] *R v Woollin* [1999] AC 82 (HL).

> impression[,] ... [and] the possibility of deliberate fabrication is thus ruled out[,] ... seems equally applicable where, although he or she knows that a particular inference will inevitably be drawn, that is not his or her purpose. Moreover, if we were to include within the hearsay rule the case where he or she knows that a particular inference *will* be drawn, it is hard to see any rational basis for excluding the case where he or she knows that it *may* be drawn. We believe that the most defensible place to draw the line is between those consequences that it is the putative declarant's *purpose* to bring about, and those that it is not.[25]

This somewhat lightly argued rationalization suggests that the choice of 'purpose' was driven more by what appear to have been considerations of practicality than by considerations of principle. It may well also have been motivated by a desire to see the scope of the hearsay rule being confined as tightly as possible.

More fundamentally, the very notion of ascertaining the state of mind of the person responsible for the words or non-verbal conduct in question may be regarded as problematic, in essence 'requir[ing] the court to speculate on whether the declarant meant one thing when he said another—to search inside the declarant's head for what he really had "in mind"'.[26] This will by its nature be no straightforward task, and indeed it is one which, as will be seen, has generated difficulties across jurisdictions.

Not long after the relevant provisions of the Criminal Justice Act 2003 came in force, the Court of Appeal confirmed that '[t]he view of the majority in *R v Kearley*, in relation to hearsay, has been set aside by the Act'.[27] The wording of the legislation, notably, suggests the necessity for a purpose to *communicate or relay* a message, or information, *to another*, rather than a purpose simply to articulate it. Thus in *R v Twist*,[28] the Court of Appeal provided the following rationalization of the earlier decision in *R v Singh*:[29]

> The court [in *Singh*] was ... not considering a communication at all, but rather the note for himself that a mobile telephone user makes when he enters in the memory of his telephone the number of a contact. This was [a] similar case to a private diary entry which is written for oneself and no one else; the maker of the entry has no purpose to cause anyone else to believe or act upon the truth of the entry—it is entirely for his own use and for that reason is not hearsay. It was therefore

25 Law Commission (n 22) paras 7.37–7.38 (emphasis in original).

26 PS Milich, 'Hearsay Antinomies: The Case for Abolishing the Rule and Starting Over' (1992) 71 Or L Rev 723, 729.

27 *R v Singh* [2006] EWCA Crim 660, [2006] 1 WLR 1564 [14].

28 [2011] EWCA Crim 1143, [2011] 3 All ER 1055. See generally P Mirfield, 'A Final Farewell to *Kearley*' (2012) 128 LQR 331.

29 [2006] EWCA Crim 660, [2006] 1 WLR 1564.

admissible evidence to tend to prove that the telephone number in question was used by the defendant, the person to whom the entry was attributed.[30]

The landmark decision on the interpretation of section 115(3) is undeniably *R v Twist*,[31] where the Court of Appeal articulated the following approach:

> Generally, . . . it is likely to be helpful to approach the question whether the hearsay rules apply in this way: (i) identify what relevant fact (matter) it is sought to prove; (ii) ask whether there is a statement of *that matter* in the communication. If no, then no question of hearsay arises (whatever other matters may be contained in the communication); (iii) if yes, ask whether it was one of the purposes (not necessarily the only or dominant purpose) of the maker of the communication that the recipient, or any other person, should believe *that matter* or act upon it as true? If yes, it is hearsay. If no, it is not.[32]

In *R v Midmore*[33] the defendant and a co-defendant, his half-brother, were charged with causing grievous bodily harm using sulphuric acid. The defendant contended that the acid had been purchased to unblock a drain. At issue was a WhatsApp message, sent by the co-defendant to his girlfriend, containing a picture of a box of One Shot sulphuric acid accompanied by the caption 'This is the one face melter'. The Court of Appeal held:

> The specific question in this case is whether the message was a statement of the current intention of the defendant's half-brother which he shared with the defendant. In other words, was the message itself evidence of the matter sought to be proved, namely that the purchase was made with the intention to use the product to cause harm to the complainant or was the message merely a comment and therefore only evidence from which the matter sought to be proved, the purchase with that intention, could be inferred?
>
> This is a short point on which views can differ. On balance, we think the better view is that it was an implied representation of the intention, not simply a

[30] [2011] EWCA Crim 1143, [2011] 3 All ER 1055 [23].

[31] ibid. Shortly after the decision in *Twist* the Court of Appeal stated in *R v Mateza* [2011] EWCA Crim 2587 [23]: 'It seems to us for the future it is entirely unnecessary for any court to look at cases earlier than *Twist* because *Twist* sets out all of the relevant considerations and the correct approach. It is therefore unnecessary for us . . . to set out any further reasons why we consider that *Twist* is the case to be followed. We cannot in any way improve upon that analysis, but would merely commend it to the courts of the future.'

[32] [2011] EWCA Crim 1143, [2011] 3 All ER 1055 [17] (emphasis in original). The Court discussed the earlier cases of *R v Singh* [2006] EWCA Crim 660, [2006] 1 WLR 1564; *R v K* [2007] EWCA Crim 3150, (2007) 172 JP 538; *R v Leonard* [2009] EWCA Crim 1251, (2009) 173 JP 366; *R v Bains* [2010] EWCA Crim 873; *R v Chrysostomou* [2010] EWCA Crim 1403, (2010) 175 JP 112; *R v Elliott* [2010] EWCA Crim 2378, (2010) 175 JP 39.

[33] [2017] EWCA Crim 533, [2017] 4 WLR 107.

> comment from which the intention could be inferred. It therefore fell within the definition in section 115(2) as it was a statement of the matter intended to be proved.[34]

Such judicial musings on whether particular words might constitute a 'statement' in the first place present an unfortunate distraction from the key issues at hand. It would surely be more straightforward simply to acknowledge that the form of words used is irrelevant and that a 'statement' by words of any matter may be made expressly or impliedly (in the latter case constituting an implied assertion); there will be a statement so long as the relevant words can be interpreted as a representation, however indirect, of the matter in question. On this basis, there should have been no doubt that there was a relevant statement here.

The Court continued:

> However, even though the message fell within the definition in section 115(2) on the basis it was evidence of the intention to use it to cause harm and not merely a comment from which the intention could be inferred, we are firmly of the view that the statement or representation was not made to cause the girlfriend to believe the statement or to act on it as true. Nothing in the message could possibly suggest that it was sent to cause the girl friend to believe One Shot would actually melt a face or to cause her to act on that basis or to believe that it was his intention so to use it or to act on that basis. Thus even if the terms of section 115(2) were satisfied in that it was a representation of fact, the message did not in any event therefore satisfy the provisions of section 115(3) of the 2003 Act. It was not therefore hearsay.[35]

In conclusion, the Court resolved the appeal as follows:

> As the message was not hearsay within the meaning of the ... 2003 [Act], the message was admissible provided it was relevant and not subject to the discretionary exclusion. In our judgment the message was plainly relevant evidence and the judge was entirely correct in his decision not to exclude it under section 78 of the Police and Criminal Evidence Act 1984.[36]

[34] [2017] EWCA Crim 533, [2017] 4 WLR 107 [38]–[39].

[35] [2017] EWCA Crim 533, [2017] 4 WLR 107 [40]. *R v Twist* [2011] EWCA Crim 1143, [2011] 3 All ER 1055 also provides an illustration of the Court's fixation with the issue of what precisely constitutes a 'statement', before similarly concluding that the issue was ultimately academic in the light of s 115(3) ([15]): 'Some communications may contain no statement at all. If, for example, the communication does no more than ask a question, it is difficult to see how it contains any statement. A text message to someone asking "Will you have any crack tomorrow?" seems to us to contain no statement at all. But even if it be analysed as containing an "implied assertion" that the recipient is a drug dealer, that fact is still not a "matter stated" for the purposes of ss 114 and 115(3) because the sender does not have any purpose to cause the recipient to believe that fact or to act upon the basis that it is true. They both know it, and it is the common basis of their communication.'

[36] [2017] EWCA Crim 533, [2017] 4 WLR 107 [41].

The difficulties inherent in determining the purpose of the maker of the statement[37] are brought out very clearly by the facts of this case. Contrary to the decision of the Court, it would be a very plausible conclusion that the co-defendant's precise purpose had been to cause the recipient of the message, his girlfriend, to believe that his intention was to use One Shot to melt a face. McKeown notes succinctly that, while 'the court concluded that there was nothing in the representation which suggested [the co-defendant] intended to cause his girlfriend to believe *One Shot* would actually melt a face', '[w]ith respect, it is hard to see what else his intention could have been'. It is also interesting to speculate whether, had it been held to be hearsay, the evidence would have been considered a suitable candidate for admission under section 114(1)(d) of the Criminal Justice Act 2003, on the basis 'that it [was] in the interests of justice for it to be admissible'.[38]

It is worth noting that the phrase 'on the basis that the matter is as stated' may be regarded as somewhat ambiguous, even if it appears not to have troubled the courts to date. Consider *R v Twist* and some of the cases conjoined with it for consideration by the Court of Appeal. In both *Twist* and *Boothman* the prosecution sought to prove intent to supply drugs, and at issue in each case were messages received by the defendant containing requests that he supply drugs. The Court of Appeal held in *Twist*:

> In our view these messages were not hearsay. The matter sought to be proved was that the defendant was a supplier of drugs ... Even if [the messages] could be said to amount to an implied assertion that he was, the purpose of the senders did not include causing him or anyone else to believe that he was.[39]

And in *Boothman*:

> In our view these messages were not hearsay, for reasons largely the same as in the case of *Twist*. The fact sought to be proved was that the defendant was dealing in cocaine, as well as in cannabis ... [I]n none of the messages did the sender have it as one of his purposes to make the defendant believe that he was a supplier of cocaine, or to act on the basis that that representation was true. They no doubt wanted him to act on their orders, but that, for the reasons explained, is not the same thing as wanting him to accept the truth of their references to his cocaine dealing. The distinction ... between express representations and those which are not express was relevant under *R v Kearley* ... but is no longer so.[40]

[37] In *R v Lam Hai Vo* [2013] EWCA Crim 2292 the Court of Appeal managed to avoid the need to engage with the issue, while somewhat confidently asserting that it was 'plain' ([14]) that evidence of the text message in question did constitute hearsay.

[38] Considered, as required, in conjunction with s 114(2).

[39] [2011] EWCA Crim 1143, [2011] 3 All ER 1055 [29].

[40] ibid [32].

In *Tomlinson and Kelly*, which concerned a prosecution for robbery, a crucial question for determination was whether the defendants had a gun in their possession at a particular time, and at issue was a message received by one of the defendants containing a request for a gun to be delivered to the sender. The Court of Appeal held:

> In our view, the message was not hearsay. The matter which it was sought to prove was that the defendants were in possession of a gun ... [I]t was not one of the purposes of the sender to cause Tomlinson, or anyone else, to believe that Tomlinson had a gun in his possession. That was simply the common understanding of sender and recipient underlying the communication. Therefore the message was not within the 2003 Act's concept of hearsay.[41]

Applied to *Kearley* itself, this approach to interpreting the provisions of the 2003 Act would clearly yield a different result from that reached by the House of Lords, because the purpose of the callers would not be deemed to have been either to cause the recipients of the calls to believe that Kearley was a drug supplier, *or* to cause them to act on the basis that Kearley was a drug supplier. Yet an entirely plausible alternative view is that it *was* their very purpose to cause the recipients of the calls to act on the basis that Kearley was a drug supplier. Adopting this interpretation would mean that, completely contrary to what it intended, Parliament would have failed to overturn *Kearley*. It is perhaps of no surprise then that this interpretation has not received a great deal of airing. Such academic discussions as have touched on it have tended to shy away from endorsing it.[42]

US Federal Rules of Evidence: Were the words or was the non-verbal conduct intended as an assertion?

As the basis for recognizing a general rule against hearsay,[43] the US Federal Rules of Evidence define hearsay as any out-of-court statement 'offer[ed] in evidence to prove the truth of the matter asserted in the statement',[44] with a 'statement', in turn,

[41] ibid [37].

[42] Mirfield observes in relation to *R v Twist* [2011] EWCA Crim 1143, [2011] 3 All ER 1055 (P Mirfield, 'A Final Farewell to *Kearley*' (2012) 128 LQR 331, 335 (emphasis in original)): 'In the drugs case ... the argument [accepted] is that all that matters to the caller is that the receiver *act* on the message, whether or not it be true, not that he does so *because it is true*, nor because he *assumes it to be true*. Looked at another way, the callers to Boothman's number might, by chance, have reached someone other than the previous supplier, but the receiver might still supply them with drugs ... Similarly, in the gun case, all that mattered to the caller was that the gun be returned to him, not who truly possessed it, or was assumed to do so. Still, the distinction is a close one, which may very well have the capacity to result in further difficulty for the courts.' See also IH Dennis, *The Law of Evidence* (6th edn, Sweet & Maxwell 2017) 725.

[43] US Federal Rules of Evidence, rule 802.

[44] Rule 801(c).

'mean[ing] a person's oral assertion, written assertion, or nonverbal conduct, if the person intended it as an assertion'.[45] There is a subtle difference between this terminology and that used in the Criminal Justice Act 2003 in England and Wales; under the US Federal Rules, words or non-verbal conduct will qualify as a 'statement' in the first place only if there was an intention to assert.

Another point of distinction is that, beyond an intention to assert, there is in the US Federal Rules no further requirement that the assertion have been intended to be communicated or relayed to some other person. Thus evidence of an entry in a private diary, which would not constitute hearsay in England and Wales, would be so under the US Federal Rules. Reservations about such an outcome in England and Wales have been expressed by at least one US commentator.[46] In response, it might be suggested that, if the underlying concern of the focus on state of mind is the potential danger of insincerity, then the fact that insincerity typically connotes an outward-facing act must be acknowledged; as one might not be expected to lie to oneself, the approach in England and Wales is entirely justified in requiring foresight in relation to communication to another person. Yet this argument misses the point that, in reality, '[s]elf-deception is a defining part of our human nature'.[47]

The approach adopted in the US Federal Rules has formed the basis for all the other statutory approaches considered in this chapter. There appears to have been ready acceptance in the jurisdictions in question of that basic approach, as the following observations made in Australia, in a joint report of the Australian Law Reform Commission, New South Wales Law Reform Commission, and Victorian Law Reform Commission, illustrate:

> In the United States, the distinction between intended and unintended assertions has been codified in the *Federal Evidence Code* since 1975, and built on similar provisions in the *California Evidence Code* enacted in 1965. While the matter has not been free of controversy, a survey of the American case law and commentary leads the Commissions to the view that the United States provisions have operated satisfactorily and are conceptually sound.[48]

This may be too sanguine a perception, as *US v Torres*[49] illustrates. Torres was accused of knowingly transporting cocaine across the United States-Mexico border concealed in a specially constructed compartment of his pickup truck. He sought

[45] Rule 801(a).

[46] Panel Discussion, 'The Philip D Reed Lecture Series: Symposium on Hearsay Reform' (2016) 84 Fordham L Rev 1323, 1348–49; MS Brodin, 'The British Experience with Hearsay Reform: A Cautionary Tale' (2016) 84 Fordham L Rev 1417, 1424–25.

[47] N Burton, *Hide and Seek: The Psychology of Self-Deception* (Acheron Press 2012) 223.

[48] Australian Law Reform Commission, New South Wales Law Reform Commission, and Victorian Law Reform Commission, *Uniform Evidence Law: Report* (ALRC Report 102, NSWLRC Report 112, VLRC Final Report, 2005) para 7.33.

[49] 794 F 3d 1053 (9th Cir 2015).

to testify about requests made to him by a friend, Fernando Griese, who he contended had manipulated him into unknowingly bringing drugs in his truck across the border by asking him for favours involving running errands in San Diego. The question for the US Court of Appeals for the Ninth Circuit was whether evidence of these requests constituted hearsay. Of interest—especially in the light of the perception that the hearsay provisions of the US Federal Rules are well established and that their operation has had a considerable time in which to 'bed in' properly—are the Court's preliminary observations that 'we have not previously addressed whether questions constitute hearsay',[50] and that there was a lack of consensus among the different circuits about such evidence: 'Some of our sister circuits have held that questions or requests are admissible as non-hearsay because questions are not intended to assert anything.'[51] The Court rightly regarded such an approach as unduly dogmatic: 'we think the issue is more nuanced and context specific. It is widely recognized that the grammatical form of a verbal utterance does not govern whether it fits within the definition of hearsay.'[52] Indeed, '[o]ther circuits have not foreclosed the possibility that questions can be classified as hearsay',[53] and this too was the approach that the Court thought should be taken: 'Because there may be instances where a party attempts to admit hearsay by cloaking statements under the guise of a question, the focus of the inquiry should be on what the declarant intended to say, whether implied or directly asserted.'[54] The Court concluded:

> Fernando asked: Can you take my friend to the DMV [Department of Motor Vehicles]? Torres said no. Fernando asked a second time: Can you take my friend to the DMV? Torres said no. Fernando asked a third time: Can you take my friend to a tire shop? Torres said no. Fernando's intent in asking for Torres's truck on three separate occasions in the span of a week and a half is apparent: Fernando wanted control of Torres's truck on the US-side of the border. In other words, Fernando intended the implied assertion rather than the express one, and Torres offered the questions for this intended implied message to show it was Fernando who was calling the shots and who unknowingly set him up on the drug importation scheme. Thus, Torres offered the statements for the truth of the defense asserted. We hold the district court did not abuse its discretion in finding that Torres offered Fernando's inquiries for the truth of the matter asserted to prove his third-party culpability defense. Thus, the objections were properly sustained on hearsay grounds.[55]

[50] ibid 1061.
[51] ibid 1059.
[52] ibid 1060.
[53] ibid 1060.
[54] ibid 1061.
[55] ibid 1061.

It seems somewhat surprising that the relatively straightforward issues raised by this case appeared to exercise the Court to the extent that they did.

Australian uniform evidence legislation: Was it the intention of the maker of the representation to assert the fact?

Like the Criminal Justice Act 2003 in England and Wales, the approach of the Australian uniform evidence legislation[56] to the definition of hearsay derives from the US Federal Rules of Evidence. Section 59(1) of the Australian uniform legislation[57] originally provided: 'Evidence of a previous representation made by a person is not admissible to prove the existence of a fact that the person intended to assert by the representation.' In *Lee v R* the High Court of Australia observed of the effect of this provision:

> The [hearsay] rule's operation requires consideration first of why it is sought to lead evidence of something said or done out of court (a previous representation). What is it that that 'previous representation' is led to prove? In particular, is it sought to lead it to prove the existence of a fact that the person who made the representation intended to assert by it? The fact that the statement or the conduct concerned might unintendedly convey some assertion is not to the point. The inquiry is about what the person who made the representation intended to assert by it.[58]

In *R v Hannes*,[59] however, statements were made in the New South Wales Court of Criminal Appeal that appeared to endorse the widest possible approach to determining intention, such that 'intention' would very readily be inferred. The foundation of such an approach, in the words of Spigelman CJ, is 'that a person intends the natural consequences of his or her acts'.[60] 'If the word "intended" in s 59(1)

[56] This legislation applies in the Commonwealth jurisdiction (Evidence Act 1995 (Commonwealth)) and in New South Wales (Evidence Act 1995 (New South Wales)), Tasmania (Evidence Act 2001 (Tasmania)), Victoria (Evidence Act 2008 (Victoria)), the Australian Capital Territory (Evidence Act 2011 (Australian Capital Territory)), and the Northern Territory (Evidence (National Uniform Legislation) Act 2011 (Northern Territory)). See generally JD Heydon, *Cross on Evidence* (11th Australian edn, LexisNexis Butterworths 2017); A Ligertwood and G Edmond, *Australian Evidence: A Principled Approach to the Common Law and Uniform Acts* (6th edn, LexisNexis Butterworths 2017); S Odgers, *Uniform Evidence Law* (13th edn, Thomson Reuters (Professional) Australia Ltd 2018); N Williams and others, *Uniform Evidence in Australia* (2nd edn, LexisNexis Butterworths 2018); J Gans, A Palmer, and A Roberts, *Uniform Evidence* (3rd edn, OUP 2019); F Hum and others, *Australian Uniform Evidence Law* (CUP 2019).

[57] The legislation is not in fact fully uniform, and quotations provided in this chapter will be from the Commonwealth legislation.

[58] [1998] HCA 60 [22].

[59] [2000] NSWCCA 503.

[60] ibid [357].

requires some form of specific conscious advertence on the part of the assertor', '[t]he application of s 59 to implied assertions would be restricted to cases of deliberate allusion or hints'.[61] 'Nothing in ... the text of the *Evidence Act* suggests so restricted an operation for the hearsay rule under that Act.'[62] On Spigelman CJ's approach:

> It is arguable that the scope of the word 'intended' in s 59(1) goes beyond the specific fact subjectively adverted to by the author as being asserted by the words used. It may encompass any fact which is a necessary assumption underlying the fact that the assertor does subjectively advert to. The Court was not addressed on the proper construction of the word 'intended' in s 59 and it is not necessary to express a final view.[63]

In a similar vein, Studdert J observed in relation to the facts at hand: 'Absent evidence to the contrary, it could not be inferred that the appellant did not intend to assert by what he wrote the very matters which the appellant contends emerged from a reading of the document.'[64]

Taken to its logical conclusion, such an 'objective' approach to the interpretation of section 59(1)[65] would appear to undermine substantially, if not completely, the very point of requiring an investigation into the (subjective) state of mind of the maker of the statement in the first place.[66] Consideration was given to the matter in the joint report by the Australian Law Reform Commission, New South Wales Law Reform Commission, and Victorian Law Reform Commission on the operation of the uniform evidence legislation, in which it was observed:

> On one view, Spigelman CJ's approach has no limitations[:] ... a person making a simple representation in the form of an oral communication would be taken to intend to assert a very large number of facts. This is because the necessary assumptions of a simple oral representation include:

[61] ibid [359].
[62] ibid [360].
[63] ibid [361].
[64] ibid [477].
[65] Similar approaches to the interpretation of the US Federal Rules of Evidence have also been advocated on occasion. Writing in the context of a discussion of evidence of non-verbal conduct, Schaitkin notes (KA Schaitkin, '"Negative Hearsay"—The Sounds of Silence' (1979–80) 84 Dickinson L Rev 605, 612): 'Intent to communicate exists when a reasonable person in the position of the actor at the time and place under consideration would intend his conduct to be communicative. A subjective standard, based on the actual intent of the actor, seems unworkable since the primary source of establishing that intent, the testimony of the actor, is unavailable.'
[66] To 'treat[] a person as intending all the reasonably likely consequences of his acts, whether or not he desired them or even thought about them[,] ... reduces intent to a fiction': OG Wellborn III, 'Definition of Hearsay in the Federal Rules of Evidence' (1982) 61 Texas L Rev 49, 76–77.

- that the assumption is capable of being understood;
- that other persons exist who have knowledge of the linguistic, social and other 'public conventions' relied on by the representor in making the oral assertion; and
- that consequences will follow from breach of those norms, whatever those consequences may be.[67]

The undesirability of such a potentially 'limitless' judicial interpretation led to the recommendation in the report that '[t]he prospect of courts adopting a[n] ... approach to "intention" ... such as the approaches explored in *Hannes* ... should be foreclosed' by way of amendment to the legislation.[68] This recommendation was implemented, so that the amended section 59(1) now provides: 'Evidence of a previous representation made by a person is not admissible to prove the existence of a fact that it can reasonably be supposed that the person intended to assert by the representation.' Further, a new subsection, subsection (2A), has been added to section 59: 'For the purposes of determining under subsection (1) whether it can reasonably be supposed that the person intended to assert a particular fact by the representation, the court may have regard to the circumstances in which the representation was made.' One commentator has noted witheringly that 'the concept of what "may reasonably be supposed" to have been intended makes no sense in the law of evidence'.[69] As regards its interpretation, it is hard to disagree with the observation of Gans, Palmer, and Roberts that 'the reasons why [the amendment] would prevent a court from taking the approach taken in *Hannes* are not immediately obvious'.[70] Indeed, the Victorian Court of Appeal remarked in *Karam v The Queen* that 'the expression "it can reasonably be supposed that the person intended to assert" in s 59(1) ... carries with it the prospect that intention may properly be inferred objectively, thereby expanding the scope of the hearsay rule into the realm of implied assertions'.[71] In the same court in a subsequent case, *Fletcher v The Queen*, Priest JA, clearly no fan of the wording of section 59(1), went so far as to describe it as being 'expressed in terms that would make Sir Humphrey Appleby proud'.[72]

[67] Australian Law Reform Commission, New South Wales Law Reform Commission, and Victorian Law Reform Commission, *Uniform Evidence Law: Report* (ALRC Report 102, NSWLRC Report 112, VLRC Final Report, 2005) para 7.43.

[68] ibid para 7.62.

[69] G Taylor, '"Let Them Say More That Like of Hearsay Well": Implied Assertions under the Hearsay Rule as Expressed in the Uniform Evidence Legislation' (2011) 35 Aust Bar Rev 270, 271.

[70] J Gans, A Palmer, and A Roberts, *Uniform Evidence* (3rd edn, OUP 2019) 130. See also J Hunter and others, *The Trial: Principles, Process and Evidence* (Federation Press 2015) 318: 'it is not clear how [the amendment] displaces the decision in *Hannes*'.

[71] [2015] VSCA 50 [62] fn 16.

[72] [2015] VSCA 146 [9] fn 5. An expert in verbal obfuscation, Sir Humphrey was the fictional Permanent Secretary and later Cabinet Secretary in the television series *Yes, Minister* and *Yes, Prime Minister*: see <https://www.bbc.co.uk/programmes/b006xtc5>; <https://www.bbc.co.uk/programmes/

While the Australian experience itself has not been entirely straightforward, on one issue at least there appears to be greater clarity than in England and Wales. The Dictionary accompanying the Australian legislation specifically provides that the word 'representation' is to be taken to include 'an express or implied representation (whether oral or in writing)' and 'a representation to be inferred from conduct'. This is welcome, as it forestalls speculation about the status of particular implied oral representations of the type in which the Court of Appeal of England and Wales has engaged, allowing attention to be focused instead on the crucial question of the intention of the maker of the representation.

That the requirement in England and Wales for some communication to another to be envisaged by the maker of the statement is—as in the US Federal Rules of Evidence—absent in the Australian uniform evidence legislation is made plain by the definition of a representation as including 'a representation not intended by its maker to be communicated to or seen by another person'.[73] All that is required to bring evidence of out-of-court words or non-verbal conduct within the definition of hearsay is an intention to assert.

New Zealand: Was it a spoken or written assertion, or non-verbal conduct intended as an assertion?

As the basis for recognizing a general rule against hearsay,[74] the Evidence Act 2006 of New Zealand defines a hearsay statement as an out-of court statement 'offered in evidence ... to prove the truth of its contents', with a statement in turn 'mean[ing] (a) a spoken or written assertion by a person of any matter; or (b) non-verbal conduct of a person that is intended by that person as an assertion of any matter'.[75] In common with the US Federal Rules of Evidence and the Australian uniform evidence legislation, the requirement in England and Wales for foresight of some communication to another is absent here. What is immediately noteworthy on a reading of the New Zealand provisions is that the requirement of intention formally attaches only to non-verbal conduct and does not cover words. Interpreted literally, then, the effect of the provisions is that unintended assertions by words are caught by the hearsay rule, so that evidence such as that at issue in *Kearley* and similar cases would be hearsay. The New Zealand High Court gave extensive consideration to the point in *R v Holtham*.[76] Noting that '[a]ssertion is not

b00lplrt>; <https://www.bbc.co.uk/programmes/b00ltsml>; <https://www.bbc.co.uk/programmes/b00m01h7>; <https://www.bbc.co.uk/programmes/b00m01jl> all accessed 13 February 2020.

[73] Dictionary accompanying the uniform evidence legislation.
[74] Evidence Act 2006 (NZ), s 17.
[75] Section 4, which deals with matters of interpretation.
[76] [2007] NZHC 2153, [2008] 2 NZLR 758.

defined in the Act',[77] the Court, after quoting three dictionary definitions of the word,[78] concluded:

> The consistent inference from these definitions is that an essential characteristic of an assertion is that the person asserting is intending to make a statement, or assert a fact or opinion.
>
> [A]n intention to assert something is [therefore] seen as an integral part of the concept of 'assertion' ... Once para (a) of the definition is read in this way, para (b) can be seen as inclusory. Its role is to make it clear that conduct can also be a statement as long as the person doing the conduct is intending to assert. Paragraph (b) therefore confirms that the essence of a statement, be it verbal or by conduct, is the intention to assert.[79]

Such an interpretation, the Court thought, was consistent with the senses in which the word 'statement' was used elsewhere in the Evidence Act 2006; a 'review of the Act suggests that there is no obvious place where interpreting statement to mean "intentional assertion" would make the Act unworkable or unintelligible'.[80] The New Zealand Court of Appeal has subsequently endorsed this interpretation.[81] As under the US Federal Rules of Evidence, but unlike in England and Wales, therefore, particular words or non-verbal conduct will qualify in New Zealand as a 'statement' in the first place only if the person responsible had the relevant intention.

Canada: Defending *R v Kearley*

The rule against hearsay is not defined legislatively in Canada. *R v Baldree*[82] provided the Supreme Court of Canada with the opportunity of finally addressing in

[77] ibid [41].

[78] These were: 'a confident statement of fact or belief', in *The Concise Oxford Dictionary* (ibid [41]); 'the act of asserting; a positive or definite statement or affirmation concerning some particular thing, advanced without accompanying proof; declaration', in *Funk and Wagnall's New Standard Dictionary of the English Language* (1924) (ibid (42]); and 'a declaration; a forthright statement', in *The New Zealand Oxford Dictionary* (ibid [43]).

[79] ibid [44]–[45].

[80] ibid [49].

[81] *McKenzie v R* [2013] NZCA 378 [22] (application for leave to appeal to New Zealand Supreme Court declined: *McKenzie v The Queen* [2013] NZSC 109); *Preston v R* [2016] NZCA 568, [2017] 2 NZLR 358 [43] ('An assertion requires an intention to assert. If the speaker intended to convey the meaning relied upon, the statement falls within the definition. If the speaker did not so intend but reliance is nevertheless sought to be placed upon the inferences sought to be drawn from the statement, the statement will fall outside the definition').

[82] [2013] 2 SCR 520, 2013 SCC 35. See generally G Ferguson and BL Berger, 'Recent Developments in Canadian Criminal Law' (2013) 37 Crim LJ 315; C Hunt and M Rankin, 'Hearsay by Implication: *R v*

detail the issue of implied assertions, on the basis of facts which it recognized to be similar to those of *R v Kearley*[83] in the sense that a request to purchase drugs was involved, albeit that there was only a single telephone call at issue here. The Court noted:

> Had the caller stated that he wanted to buy drugs from Mr Baldree because *Mr Baldree sells drugs*, this would have amounted to an express assertion that Mr Baldree is a drug dealer. Thus framed, the caller's assertion would doubtless have constituted hearsay.
>
> But the caller stated instead that he was calling because he wished to *purchase drugs from Mr Baldree*. His assertion that Mr Baldree is a drug dealer was no less manifest in substance, though implicit rather than explicit in form.[84]

In the Court's view,

> the hearsay nature of this evidence cannot be made to depend on how the declarant framed his request ...
>
> There is no principled or meaningful distinction between (a) 'I am calling Mr Baldree because I want to purchase drugs from him' and (b) 'I am calling Mr Baldree because he sells drugs'. In either form, this out-of-court statement is being offered for an identical purpose: to prove the truth of the declarant's assertion that Mr Baldree sells drugs. No trier of fact would need to be a grammarian in order to understand the import of this evidence ...
>
> Accordingly, there is no principled reason, in determining their admissibility, to distinguish between express and implied assertions adduced for the truth of their contents. Both function in precisely the same way. And the benefits of cross-examining the declarant are not appreciably different when dealing with one form of testimony than the other. If an out-of-court statement implicates the traditional hearsay dangers, it constitutes hearsay and must be dealt with accordingly.[85]

The Court justified its conclusion that the evidence at issue should be treated as hearsay in Canada, *irrespective of what the caller might have intended*, by refuting the arguments commonly put forward in support of the opposing view.

Baldree' (2014) 18 IJEP 181; C de Sa, 'Revisiting *Baldree*: Analyzing the Underlying Basis for the Admission of Implied Assertions' (2017) 22 Can Crim L Rev 121.

83 [2013] 2 SCR 520, 2013 SCC 35 [57].
84 ibid [40]–[41] (emphasis in original).
85 ibid [42]–[43], [48].

Refuting the argument that 'the danger of lack of sincerity is sometimes diminished for implied assertions'

The Court noted that this will not necessarily be the case, quoting Rice's view that[86]

> [i]t is illogical to conclude that the question of sincerity is eliminated and that the problem of unreliability is reduced for unintended implications of speech if that speech might have been insincere in the first instance ... If potential insincerity is injected into the utterance of words that form the basis for the implied communication, the implication from the speech is as untrustworthy as the utterance upon which it is based.[87]

An illustration of this point may be provided with reference to *Wright v Doe d Tatham*. Even if the writers of the letters to Marsden had not intended to assert that he was a person of reasonable understanding, the danger of insincerity on their part might still have been considerable, if rather subtle: the writers may well have been aware that Marsden was not a person of reasonable understanding, but have decided to write in the manner in which they did because of a desire to act kindly and spare his feelings, or simply because of social convention.[88] Further, the Court in *Baldree* noted that, regardless of any considerations of insincerity, 'the other hearsay dangers clearly remain operative, and may in fact increase when an individual "states" something by implication'.[89] It will be recalled that the Law Commission of England and Wales was somewhat dismissive about any potential danger of mistake ('we do not think a court should be precluded from inferring [a] fact merely because th[e] person may have been mistaken in believing it'[90]). As a warning of the potential hearsay dangers inherent in implied assertions, the following two illustrations offered by Zuckerman are instructive:

> A much-discussed example is the utterance 'Hello, Mr Smith' adduced to support a conclusion that Smith was present at the time and place where the words were spoken. In this kind of situation the risk of misinterpretation is particularly serious because, first, it is easier to mishear or misinterpret short exclamations than long utterances that are made in some explanatory context, and, secondly, the

[86] ibid [45].
[87] PR Rice, 'Should Unintended Implications of Speech Be Considered Nonhearsay? The Assertive/Nonassertive Distinction under Rule 801(a) of the Federal Rules of Evidence' (1992) 65 Temple L Rev 529, 534.
[88] See AL-T Choo, *Hearsay and Confrontation in Criminal Trials* (OUP 1996) 85.
[89] [2013] 2 SCR 520, 2013 SCC 35 [46].
[90] Law Commission (n 22) para 7.20.

> evidential value of greetings and the like depends on the degree of acquaintance between the persons involved and on the circumstances of the greeting. In the absence of cross-examination it is very difficult to assess these factors and to place much reliance on such utterances.[91]

Secondly, in addressing the ship captain hypothetical scenario from *Wright v Doe d Tatham*, Zuckerman observes that

> the danger of misinterpretation [of the evidence] is very considerable. The captain may have examined his ship for some reason other than to determine its seaworthiness. Since the inference from such conduct entails an inference about the captain's state of belief an inference has to rely on his powers of perception, judgment, and memory . . .[92]

In the light of such considerations, the Supreme Court of Canada was clearly right in not being swayed by what has become the prevailing legislative approach in other jurisdictions of treating unintended implied assertions as constituting a *class* of evidence presumptively raising fewer hearsay concerns.[93]

Refuting the 'too much evidence would be caught by the hearsay rule' argument

In responding to the argument that treating all implied assertions as subject to the hearsay rule would result in the presumptive exclusion of too much evidence, the Supreme Court noted, without deciding the matter, that it might be appropriate to confine its holding to evidence of *words* alone:

[91] Zuckerman (n 1) 198 fn 76. Zuckerman goes on in the same footnote to observe: 'Situations are, however, likely to arise where the utterance is of such compelling probative force that the courts would find admissibility irresistible.'

[92] ibid 199.

[93] This prevailing approach has been (somewhat optimistically) defended on the ground that it is sufficient for the presence of any 'dangers' other than insincerity to be left to be detected on a case-by-case basis, leading to the exclusion of the evidence where appropriate. Writing of evidence of the type at issue in *Kearley*, Mueller notes (CB Mueller, 'Incoming Drug Calls and Performative Words: They're Not Just Talking about It, Baron Parke!' (1995) 16 Miss C L Rev 117, 123 (emphasis in original)): 'Nonhearsay treatment does not mean throwing caution to the wind. Exclusion may be justified even if the incoming calls are *not* hearsay. Callers or visitors may lack reliable knowledge, having been misinformed or misled. This risk can be addressed by argument or cautionary instructions. It could also be addressed by requiring proof of knowledge as a matter of conditional relevance. Calls could be excluded unless knowledge were shown or circumstances, such as repetition by numerous callers, suggest the knowledge was there because too much baseless coincidence is implausible. (The jury could resolve this issue if facts or circumstances justify a positive finding but leave room for the opposite conclusion too.) And calls could be excluded under Federal Rule of Evidence 403 as confusing or misleading.'

> [W]e are not concerned on this appeal with the application of the hearsay rule to assertions implied through non-verbal conduct. Our concern, rather, is with a quintessentially *verbal* statement.
>
> The issue of the applicability of the hearsay rule to inferences that can be drawn from non-verbal conduct is best left for another day.[94]

In a case involving evidence of non-verbal conduct the following year, the Ontario Court of Appeal was equally evasive, noting that, '[f]or the purposes of this case, it is unnecessary to state a general principle as to whether inferences from non-verbal conduct should be treated as hearsay',[95] but then proceeding to apply to the evidence precisely the type of analysis that would be applied if it were to be classified as hearsay.

Further, the Supreme Court in *Baldree* noted that, while automatic exclusion of the evidence in *R v Kearley* followed from the treatment by the House of Lords of the evidence as hearsay, this would not be the case in Canada, where hearsay evidence might be admitted if it did not fall within a traditional exception but nonetheless satisfied the criteria of necessity and reliability. On this basis, 'implied assertions that are necessary and reliable may be admitted while those that are unreliable or unnecessary will be excluded'.[96] Of course, the observation that the law in Canada would not necessarily require the evidence in *Kearley* ultimately to be excluded, even if the conception of hearsay in *Kearley* were adopted, is also true now of England and Wales and other jurisdictions. More liberal admissibility of hearsay evidence is hardly a phenomenon that remains unique to Canada.

The holding on the facts

The Supreme Court found the evidence of the single telephone call in this case to be insufficiently reliable,[97] but cautioned that this holding was one confined to the facts. Thus, '[f]or example, where the police intercept not one but several drug purchase calls, the quantity of the calls might well suffice in some circumstances to establish reliability'.[98] Indeed, this consideration has proved crucial in decisions of provincial Courts of Appeal in subsequent cases. In *R v Gerrior*, Beveridge JA, giving judgment for the Nova Scotia Court of Appeal, held:

[94] [2013] 2 SCR 520, 2013 SCC 35 [62]–[63] (emphasis in original).
[95] *R v Badgerow* 2014 ONCA 272 [134].
[96] [2013] 2 SCR 520, 2013 SCC 35 [66].
[97] ibid [69]. The Court also found that the criterion of necessity had not been established: 'the police *made no effort at all* to secure the evidence of the declarant: they never sought to interview or even find him, though *he gave them his address*. Moreover, there was no explanation offered as to why no efforts were made to locate the declarant' ([68] (emphasis in original)). Moldaver J dissented on this point: [109].
[98] ibid [71].

> [I]n the case at bar, there was not just one call, but three coded conversations, which … were about obtaining cocaine from the appellant. Does this make a difference? In these circumstances, I find that it does …
>
> Here, two of the out-of-court statements were recorded by the mobile service provider, and reproduced by means of a production order. There could be no dispute about the completeness of the communications or the absent declarant having misperceived the actual exchange of information contained in the text messages, nor accurately recalling what was said. In my opinion, this goes a long way towards satisfying the threshold requirement of reliability …
>
> [T]he Crown points to the evidence within the text messages themselves, and to the considerable body of other circumstantial evidence, including a number of pre-arrest texts for commerce in cocaine, all of which tend to support the reliability of the implied assertion that the appellant was an individual who trafficked in cocaine. I agree.[99]

Again, the Ontario Court of Appeal in *R v Malcolm-Evans* distinguished *Baldree* as follows:

> Unlike the circumstances in *Baldree*, which involved evidence of a single drug purchase call and no other evidence connecting the accused to drug dealing, in this case there were multiple calls, which the *Baldree* court … recognized may establish reliability. In addition, in this case, there was significant confirmatory evidence that the appellant was a drug dealer.[100]

Any future developments in the Supreme Court of Canada on matters relating to implied assertions will clearly be watched with interest.

Ireland

In 2016, the Law Reform Commission of Ireland, noting that there had been 'scant discussion of implied assertions in this jurisdiction',[101] was able to examine the issue with the benefit of consideration of the experience of other jurisdictions.

[99] 2014 NSCA 76 [44], [46], [48].

[100] 2016 ONCA 28 [7].

[101] Law Reform Commission, *Report: Consolidation and Reform of Aspects of the Law of Evidence* (LRC 117-2016) para 2.36. The judgment of Kingsmill Moore J in *Cullen v Clarke* [1963] IR 368, 378, was interpreted as apparently favouring the view that the *Kearley* approach did not represent the law in Ireland. For the position in Scotland (which also appears to be characterized by uncertainty) see P Duff, 'Hearsay Issues: A Scottish Perspective' [2005] Crim L Rev 525; P Duff, 'The Uncertain Scope of Hearsay in Scots Criminal Evidence: Implied Assertions and Evidence of Prior Identification' [2005] Juridical Rev 1. For discussions of the position in Hong Kong and Singapore respectively, see EYN Hong, CJ Yao,

The Commission ultimately 'recommend[ed] that implied assertions be allowed in evidence, save where it can reasonably be supposed that the purpose of making the statement was to cause another person to believe the matter implied',[102] thus favouring an approach in line with that of England and Wales. In doing so, the Commission appears to have been persuaded by the orthodox justifications for such an approach:

> Submissions received by the Commission generally favoured the admissibility of implied assertions, noting that while hearsay dangers are not entirely absent from implied assertions, they are much reduced.
>
> However, one submission argued strongly against their admission in evidence. It was argued that 'logically there is little difference between classic hearsay and an implied assertion.' The view was expressed that the same reliability dangers present themselves in the case of an implied assertion; it is an out-of-court statement which cannot be tested which is relied upon to prove that which is asserted, even though the assertion is indirect. This analysis is surely correct. The same barrier to the interrogation of the evidence presents itself in the case of implied assertion; there is no way to challenge the assertion in the absence of the declarant.
>
> However the argument in favour of their admission asserts that fabrication in such a situation is so unlikely as to warrant a general rule in favour of their admission, even in the absence of the opportunity to cross-examine. It is also … very difficult to square implied assertions with any existing definition of hearsay.[103]

It is disappointing that the Commission did not explain more thoroughly why it considered the arguments advanced in the one 'dissenting' submission, which it appeared to think had considerable merit, to be ultimately outweighed by the opposing arguments. The final sentence of the quotation, referring to the difficulty of aligning implied assertions with any established definition of hearsay, is also obscure. Certainly the standard legislative definition of hearsay across the major common law jurisdictions removes 'unintended' implied assertions from the scope of the hearsay rule, but it would be misguided to allow the weight of numbers alone to justify emulating this approach. A hearsay rule that does not account specially for implied assertions would be entirely straightforward to define. But above all else, it appears to be a fundamental omission that the Commission's trawl through the approaches of other jurisdictions had failed to uncover the radically different position adopted in Canada.

and AL Yang, 'Rethinking the Admissibility of Implied Assertions as Evidence in Hong Kong's Criminal Cases' (2017) 8 Queen Mary LJ 51; TY Chin, 'Hearsay Reforms: Simplicity in Statute, Pragmatism in Practice?' (2014) 26 SAcLJ 398.

[102] Law Reform Commission (n 101) para 2.48.
[103] ibid paras 2.45–2.47.

Conclusion: A return to *R v Kearley*

One of the central themes developed by Adrian Zuckerman in *The Principles of Criminal Evidence* was that evidence law should be characterized by greater flexibility which better reflected the rationale(s) for treating particular evidence with caution. The hearsay provisions of the Criminal Justice Act 2003 have partially achieved this by allowing, through the operation of revised and liberalized exceptions to the hearsay rule, freer admissibility of hearsay evidence that appears sufficiently reliable for the trier of fact to be trusted to evaluate. The provisions of the 2003 Act provide, as the starting point for analysing non-first-hand evidence, what is perhaps the most sophisticated of the legislative definitions of hearsay examined in this chapter; and this definition may also be the most far-reaching in the sense that it has the potential to shield the greatest amount of evidence from the hearsay prohibition. The definition, we have seen, raises two broad issues of concern. First, the definition, close variants of which are to be found in the US Federal Rules of Evidence, in the Australian uniform evidence legislation, and in New Zealand, fails properly to reflect the rationale(s) for treating non-first-hand evidence with caution; it is focused on only one of the four 'hearsay dangers', and even then may not address that danger adequately. The purpose or intent of the person responsible for the words or non-verbal conduct in question is elevated to a status it does not deserve. The second issue is practical: there appear to be considerable difficulties involved in successfully encapsulating, in statutory wording that the courts can easily work with, the crucial essence of such purpose or intent.[104] To put it simply, the hearsay provisions of the 2003 Act may be viewed as the proverbial sledgehammer being deployed to crack the nut, but then, in this instance, succeeding in cracking it only partially: while the decision of the House of Lords in *R v Kearley* clearly demonstrated that hearsay doctrine was in need of reform, the strategy of *both* liberalizing the exceptions régime *and* confining the scope of the rule itself smacks of overreaching. The result in *R v Kearley* may well have been unjustifiable, but simply adopting the former strategy would have sufficed to address the underlying problem. In essence, this is the reasoning of the Supreme Court of Canada in *R v Baldree*. Here again, though, the experience of England and Wales has not exactly been unique, as the US Federal Rules of Evidence, Australian uniform evidence legislation, and Evidence Act 2006 of New Zealand have attempted a broadly similar strategy.

All this points to the 'outlier' approach adopted by the Supreme Court of Canada as providing the most sensible basis for the way forward. The precise route by which reform of the position in England and Wales should be achieved,

[104] Spencer (JR Spencer, *Hearsay Evidence in Criminal Proceedings* (2nd edn, Hart Publishing 2014) 92) writes that 'the new definition of hearsay, if better than the old one, is neither sound as a discriminator between statements that are reliable and unreliable, nor easy to apply'.

however, requires careful thought. Some might argue, for example, that simply to revert to the *Kearley* position on implied assertions that prevailed prior to the 2003 Act would result in too much evidence being categorized as presumptively inadmissible as hearsay, especially in the light of the requirements imposed on a party to provide notice of its intention to introduce such evidence.[105] In response to this, it would be possible to offer solutions that seek to address any such concern.

One strategy might be to treat words and non-verbal conduct differently. Where words are concerned, the above discussion has pointed already to the conclusion that there is no justification for distinguishing between express assertions and implied assertions; both should be covered by the hearsay rule without any investigation into the intent or purpose of the source of the words. In the case of non-verbal conduct, however, the reach of the hearsay rule might be able to be restricted to any such conduct as appears to the court to assert the matter in question *expressly*—for instance, the act of pointing out something or someone. Notably, the Court of Appeal appeared in no doubt in *R v Twist* that an implied assertion inferred from non-verbal conduct, as opposed to words, could never constitute a 'statement' in the first place:

> If there is a queue of young people outside a building at midnight, obviously waiting for an evening out, that is some evidence tending to prove that the building is being operated as a club, which may be the matter which it is sought to prove, perhaps in licensing proceedings. There is no statement of that matter for the purposes of the 2003 Act.[106]

Such an approach would seem to flow logically from acceptance of the reality that, in Zuckerman's words, '[m]uch proof in criminal cases depends on drawing inferences from conduct which is relevant because it displays the actor's belief in the fact in issue'.[107] Excluding from the definition of a 'statement' non-verbal conduct such as that discussed in the hypothetical scenario offered in *Twist*—the action of simply queuing outside particular premises—would mean that the necessity of ascertaining the purpose of the actor would not arise.[108] Building on this, it is worth pondering whether it might not in fact be too large or radical a step to take to argue that evidence of *any* non-verbal conduct—including that which expressly asserts a fact—should be excluded entirely from the reach of the hearsay rule. We might say, putting it another way, that the consequence of such an approach is that 'see-do'

[105] Criminal Procedure Rules, rule 34.

[106] [2011] EWCA Crim 1143, [2011] 3 All ER 1055 [14].

[107] Zuckerman (n 1) 200. See also CR Callen, 'Interdisciplinary and Comparative Perspectives on Hearsay and Confrontation' in P Roberts and M Redmayne (eds), *Innovations in Evidence and Proof: Integrating Theory, Research and Teaching* (Hart Publishing 2007).

[108] See also CR Williams, 'Implied Assertions in Criminal Cases' (2006) 32 Monash U L Rev 47.

evidence[109] would never constitute hearsay evidence. The potential difficulty of determining whether an assertion by non-verbal conduct is express or merely implied is avoided.

Again, it might specifically be provided that any 'revised' hearsay rule would cover prosecution evidence only,[110] leaving non-first-hand evidence sought to be introduced by the defence outside the reach of the rule. The provisions of the Civil Evidence Act 1995 abolishing the hearsay rule in civil cases, but offering guidelines on the weight to be attached to particular evidence, could provide a model here. More specifically, consideration could be given to restricting the reach of the hearsay rule to a particular *type* of prosecution evidence, along the lines suggested, if not entirely enthusiastically, by Spencer as follows:

> If it was really necessary to draw a line between out-of-court statements which are prima facie excluded and only exceptionally admitted and those that are admitted automatically, the proper distinction to have drawn, I believe, would have been between statements made to the authorities in the course of their investigations, and everything else ... [It is] once a crime has been committed, and the police are investigating it, [that] risks of invention and distortion start to become important, and from that point on, it is right and proper for the law to expect the maker of the statement to come to court to give his evidence again orally, so that the defendant can dispute it.[111]

The underlying premise of this would appear already to be established in the law: in addition to the standard requirements to be satisfied for the admissibility in evidence of statements in what might broadly be termed 'business documents', section 117 of the Criminal Justice Act 2003 imposes additional requirements for any statement 'prepared for the purposes of pending or contemplated criminal proceedings, or for a criminal investigation'.[112] There is also an analogy to be drawn here with the US Supreme Court's conception of a 'testimonial statement'. Such a statement is described by the Court as one that is 'procured with a primary purpose of creating an out-of-court substitute for trial testimony',[113] in the context of the Court's interpretation of the so-called 'Confrontation Clause' of the Sixth Amendment to the US Constitution[114] as operating to prevent the 'admission of testimonial statements of

[109] See JF Falknor, 'The "Hear-Say" Rule as a "See-Do" Rule: Evidence of Conduct' (1961) 33 Rocky Mt L Rev 133.

[110] This might bring hearsay doctrine in closer alignment with the requirements of art 6 of the European Convention on Human Rights.

[111] Spencer (n 104) 92.

[112] Section 117(4)(a).

[113] *Michigan v Bryant* (2011) 562 US 344, 358. See generally WE O'Brian Jr, 'Confrontation and Ongoing Emergencies: *Michigan v Bryant*' (2011) 15 IJEP 357.

[114] This guarantees the accused the right 'to be confronted with the witnesses against him'.

a witness who [does] not appear at trial unless he [is] unavailable to testify, and the defendant [has] had a prior opportunity for cross-examination.'[115]

Which of these (or which combination of these) possible paths to reform is preferable would require a more thoroughgoing review of hearsay doctrine than is possible in this chapter.[116]

Earlier in his career, Adrian Zuckerman was one of the pioneers of a more contemporary, more reflective, and less rigid approach to evidence scholarship in England and Wales. Such an approach has proved influential in subsequent years in shaping the development of the law and of academic thinking. The hearsay provisions of the 2003 Act may be said to reflect this influence, but only partially. It is my hope that Zuckerman would broadly approve of the arguments made in this chapter.

[115] *Crawford v Washington* (2004) 541 US 36, 53–54. See generally AL-T Choo, '*Crawford v Washington*: A View from Across the Atlantic' (2004) 2(1) ICE; HL Ho, 'Confrontation and Hearsay: A Critique of *Crawford*' (2004) 8 IJEP 147; RM Cassidy, 'Reconsidering Spousal Privileges after *Crawford*' (2006) 33 Am J Crim L 339.

[116] For sustained treatments of criminal hearsay, the former now very dated, see Choo (n 88); Spencer (n 104).

3

Common Law Principles and the Expression and Use of Forensic Evidence in Criminal Cases

Andrew Ligertwood

Introduction

Interest in evidential scholarship at Oxford was rekindled by Zelman Cowan and Peter Carter[1] and given focus by the teaching and consequent treatise of Rupert Cross.[2] Cross brought great clarity to the subject and also a broad notion of 'common sense' which he used to criticize the arcane approach taken to many evidential rules by lawyers. At that time Evidence was not taught as an undergraduate course at Oxford but was available to graduate students as an optional subject in the BCL. Many of those students had already taken Evidence as part of undergraduate degrees completed outside England. Evidence was generally regarded as a practitioner's subject, suitable for Bar Examinations but not academic institutions. Facts could simply be stipulated in teaching the law. How facts were discovered and determined in courts was regarded either as of no academic interest or simply beyond the scope of a 'legal' education.[3] One might comment that given every potentially precedential common law case turns upon its facts it is extraordinary that forensic fact-finding should not have been regarded as pivotal to a law course teaching the case by case (trial by trial) evolution of the common law.[4]

[1] Z Cowan and PB Carter, *Essays on the Law of Evidence* (OUP 1956).

[2] R Cross, *The Law of Evidence* (OUP 1958). *Cross on Evidence* has since become the leading practitioner text in England (13th edn, OUP 2018) (edited by R Munday), Australia (12th edn, LexisNexis Butterworths 2017 and on line) (edited by JD Heydon) and in New Zealand (10th edn, LexisNexis Butterworths 2017 and on line) (edited by Justice M Downs).

[3] DJ Nicolson, 'Facing Facts: The Teaching of Fact Construction in University Law Schools' (1997) 1 E & P 139 at 139; '[t]he crusade to persuade university law schools to devote more time to facts and fact-finding has a long and sorry history.'; W Twining, *Rethinking Evidence* (Blackwell 1990) 15 comparing this task of persuasion to Sisyphus condemned to push the rock.

[4] The central importance of facts and their discovery in the process of justice is analysed and confirmed in the many publications of William Twining: see for example his early essay W Twining, 'The Rationalist Tradition of Evidence Scholarship', first published in E Campbell and PL Waller (eds), *Well and Truly Tried* (Melbourne University Press 1982), and republished, with some additions, and together with other of his significant essays, in W Twining, *Rethinking Evidence* (first published by Blackwell, Oxford, 1990, and later by CUP 2006).

Andrew Ligertwood, *Common Law Principles and the Expression and Use of Forensic Evidence in Criminal Cases* In: *Principles, Procedure, and Justice.* Edited by: Rabeea Assy and Andrew Higgins, Oxford University Press (2020).
 DOI: 10.1093/oso/9780198850410.003.0003

Cross was influential in giving The Law of Evidence respectability in 'modern' English academe. His late start in 1958 when the first edition of his treatise was published might be seen in contrast to the situation in the United States where Thayer[5] and his sometime student Wigmore[6] had brought the subject into modernity at the turn of the nineteenth century. But Cross did not seek to develop an over-arching theoretical basis to the subject, rather preferring to justify his analysis of the subject on the basis of his very practical and perceptive notion of 'common sense'. Again by way of contrast, Thayer emphasized the notions of relevance and proof as fundamental to evidence laws and Wigmore went further in attempting to analyse the logic of proof in his *Science of Judicial Proof*.[7]

Adrian Zuckerman enrolled as a graduate student at Oxford with Cross appointed as his supervisor. His research manifested itself in his appointment as a Fellow of University College ('Univ') and in the subsequent publication of his book *The Principles of Criminal Evidence*.[8] This work was ground-breaking in that it sought to give unity to rules of evidence in criminal cases by isolating and emphasizing those principles, epistemological and ontological, which provide their very rationale. His overarching thesis emphasized the importance in criminal cases of factual rectitude consequent upon the application of those normative principles constituting fair trial. Evidential rules are clearly and elegantly analysed in this principled context. While what constitutes rectitude is not independently analysed it does come under scrutiny when the importance of the presumption of innocence and the use of lay juries is under discussion. His conclusion, as stressed in the second edition of his book co-authored with Paul Roberts, is that courts 'remain the final arbiters *as a matter of law* of forensically contested facts'.[9] And as with Cross (and indeed Thayer), the difficult notions of relevance and proof, which form the very rationale for the tender and use of evidence in search of rectitude, are left to, and justified by, 'common sense':

> 'The ultimate form of validation is internal to the process itself, a form of self-referential validation based upon trusted methodologies of enquiry and the persuasive power of the narratives which the process is able to reconstruct. It follows that public confidence in the criminal verdict has to be generated by confidence in the procedures adopted at trial. In this, the jury system, and to a lesser extent lay

[5] J Thayer, *Preliminary Treatise on the Law of Evidence at Common Law* (Little, Brown & Co 1898).

[6] His *Treatise on the Anglo-American System of Evidence in Trials at Common Law* was first published in 1904.

[7] JH Wigmore, *The Principles of Judicial Proof as Given by Logic, Psychology, and General Experience and Illustrated in Judicial Trials* (Little, Brown & Co 1913), republished as *The Science of Judicial Proof* (3rd edn, Little, Brown & Co 1937). See also JH Wigmore 'The Problem of Proof' (1913) 8 Ill L Rev 77.

[8] AAS Zuckerman, *The Principles of Criminal Evidence* (OUP 1989).

[9] P Roberts and A Zuckerman, *Criminal Evidence* (OUP 2004) ch 1 n 61 (hereinafter referred to as *Criminal Evidence*).

magistrates, have an important part to play. The space reserved for lay fact-finders in modern criminal proceedings is meant to ensure that factual decisions ... are in touch with the ordinary citizen's view of the world.'[10]

I met Adrian Zuckerman in 1973 when I spent time at 'Univ' on study-leave. We had a common interest—to write a treatise that sought to explain evidence laws by reference to fundamental and overarching principles. But whereas his focus was upon the normative principles of criminal evidence particularly upon those underlying the notion of a fair trial, mine was prompted by the need to understand further the epistemological basis of that rectitude sought through the adversarial process of the common law. With this notion apparently underlying both criminal and civil cases my interest extended to both. This was not to deny that in criminal cases rules are influenced by the accusatorial nature of the adversarial criminal trial, nor that there are also other evidential rules that seek to recognize values external to the quest for rectitude in both civil and criminal cases. But I saw the starting point in any treatise on evidence as requiring analysis of the very notion of epistemological rectitude.[11] In particular my initial interest was whether the rectitude sought in courts could find justification in the logic of the probability calculus.[12]

The importance of grappling with the nature of this fundamental task has now been highlighted not only by the debate between those who contend that the logic of a mathematical theorem (Bayes' Theorem) necessarily applies and those who regard the logic practised in courts as a different but rational and necessary complement to that mathematical logic,[13] but also by the increasing presentation of evidence in statistical terms, now most prominently in the case of what is reverently called 'DNA evidence'. Furthermore, the apparent statistical rigor with which DNA evidence can be empirically justified contrasts with, and has called into question, the very reliability of the evidence of other forensic experts who seek to match other trace materials with the accused (visual images, fingerprints, bite marks, gait, ballistic residues, etc), evidence which until recently has been simply accepted by

[10] ibid 16. See also their conclusions following a discussion of the use of Bayes' Theorem at 131.

[11] Ultimately my treatise on Evidence (ALC Ligertwood, *Australian Evidence*, Butterworths, Sydney, 1988) was published in 1988 and Adrian Zuckerman's the next year. In the first chapter of my treatise, now in its sixth edition and co-authored with Gary Edmond (A Ligertwood and G Edmond, *Australian Evidence: A Principled Approach to the Common Law and Uniform Acts* (6th edn, LexisNexis Butterworths 2017)), the very notions of relevance and proof are analysed.

[12] Prompted by the discussion of the case of *Collins* in the article of MO Finkelstein and WB Fairley, 'A Bayesian Approach to Identification Evidence' (1970) 83 Harv L Rev 489 and the response of LH Tribe,'Trial by Mathematics: Precision and Ritual in the Legal Process' (1971) 84 Harv L Rev 1329. See A Ligertwood, 'The Uncertainty of Proof' (1976) 10 Melbourne U LRev 367.

[13] Symposia held at the height of the controversy can be found in (1986) 66 Boston ULR Pts 3 and 4; and (1991) 13 Cardozo LR Pts 2 and 3. A clear and simple exposition of the nature of the debate can be found in MS Pardo, 'Juridical Proof, Evidence, and Pragmatic Meaning: Toward Evidentiary Holism' (2000) 95 Northwestern U L Rev 399.

lawyers, judges, and juries, but is now being questioned for not having a demonstrable empirical basis capable of being statistically expressed.

But once received in statistical terms by what rational process can a fact-finder use this evidence to find the matters in issue proved? Can this simply be left to the 'common sense' of fact-finders or should the law provide further guidance to them about how they should reason in applying standards of proof? Should guidance extend to demanding that witnesses who give statistical evidence express that evidence in a particular form? With these issues now of vital importance in criminal cases, particularly where forensic witnesses testify, and with Zuckerman having refocused his insights to Civil Procedure, I write this piece which, having regard to the principles expressed in his work on criminal evidence, suggests how statistical forensic evidence might in principle be expressed and then used by the trier of fact to decide whether or not an accused is guilty of a criminal offence.

The nature of common law fact-finding

The argument proceeds upon the basis of three starting assumptions:[14] that ultimately justice must be administered according to law by human beings (not by computers); that the application of law necessarily requires determination of those facts (generally past events) which give rise to the law's application; and that the determination of those facts is made upon the basis of evidence—those remnants left in the world from which past events can be rationally determined. The question is how should those decision-makers reason from evidence to proof in order to achieve that factual rectitude sufficient for application of the law. As Roberts and Zuckerman explain in the quote above, this is ultimately a normative issue, in the sense that it is the law that determines when sufficient rectitude from evidence is achieved. But while their quoted conclusion might suggest that the law simply leaves the issue to the 'common sense' of lay fact-finders this is not the whole story. Trial judges can dismiss claims or accusations if of the view that the evidence is obviously insufficient, appellate courts can overturn the verdicts of lay fact-finders, and besides, in many cases, criminal and civil, juries are not employed, and, unlike juries, judges do not simply determine facts without explanation but must provide reasons for their decisions. These reasons assume an epistemological task that can be rationally justified.

It appears that there are two epistemological approaches to the rational determination of rectitude. The one, what I will call the atomistic probabilistic approach,

[14] These assumptions are not necessarily central to the idea of justice (consider for example trial by ordeal or calls to the supernatural) but it is assumed that, at least at the time of writing, they are central to justice in the common law legal systems under discussion.

seeks to isolate the many inferences and their relationship required from the evidence before the court to reach a conclusion that an event occurred.[15] By allotting values to the probability of each and every inference, mathematical equations can then be used to calculate a conclusion about the probability of the occurrence of the event in issue.

In this way statisticians and mathematicians can provide a rational logic for reasoning from evidence to sufficient rectitude. But even accepting the logic, the problem is its practical empirical application. While individual inferences determinative of the facts (past events) to which this logic must be applied are many, the isolation and the strength (probability) of each and every inference demands empirical justification.[16] Sometimes experts can provide empirical justification for an individual inference (eg the statistical possibility of a DNA match occurring at random), but the match can only be acted upon following determination of where and how the particular samples used for the match were collected and analysed, questions that in turn can only be answered after listening to witnesses and determining their credibility, answers provided by fact-finders using their own general experiences. So, as evidence is broken down into the individual inferences it might support, the empirical basis of the generalization supporting each inference becomes more individually experiential. While numerical subjective probabilities can in theory be placed upon these inferences to show their logical mathematical relationship, in practice this is highly problematical. Ultimately isolating the many possible individual inferences and providing precise empirical or subjective weight to them becomes not just difficult but impossible for mere mortals.[17] Furthermore, even if numerical probabilities could be calculated the issue of what overall value equates to rectitude must also be faced. This creates particular difficulties in criminal cases where the statistical possibility of innocence would be revealed. Probabilities are by definition generated within ranges that include, but can never isolate, the individual case.

Lay fact-finders do not take this atomistic probabilistic approach to the determination of past events. In practice evidence is looked at holistically to provide

[15] The charting of Wigmore might be seen as a precursor to this approach.

[16] Probabilities of inference are developed in chosen generalizations, with various degrees of specificity (but never individual). The problem is that of isolating the generalization (reference class) determining the probability of each inference: See RJ Allen and MS Pardo, 'The Problematic Value of Mathematical Models of Evidence' (2007) 36 J Legal Stud 107 and the symposium entitled 'The Reference Class Problem' in (2007) 11 E & P 243. See also J Franklin, 'The Objective Bayesian Conception of Proof and Reference Class Problems' (2011) 33 Sydney L Rev 545.

[17] See CR Callen, 'Notes on a Grand Illusion: Some Limits on the Use of a Bayesian Theory in Evidence Law' (1982) 57 Ind LJ 1 at 10–15; CR Callen, 'Second Order Considerations, Weight, Sufficiency and Schema Theory: A Comment on Professor Brilmayer's Theory' (1986) 66 Boston ULR 715 at 726, n 72: '[F]or the consistent use of Bayesian theory for the updating of probabilities by conditionalization, where thirty items of evidence are introduced relevant to an inference, one must record a billion probabilities.'

a basis for applying their experience in determining whether the evidence justifies the conclusion sought. Justification will be through an over-arching hypothesis, generally an individual story or narrative, that best explains the existence of all the evidence.[18] Indeed the adversarial trial[19] provides this structure, with parties having the opportunity to present that particular story or narrative justifying the claim to justice sought (although in criminal cases normative principles ensure there is no obligation upon an accused to provide an explanation consistent with innocence). In turn evidence consistent with this story or narrative will be presented which, it will then be argued, is inconsistent with other stories or narratives also before the court. The story or narrative that produces the best, the most plausible, explanation of all the evidence will then be left to the court to be acted upon (or not).

This does not mean that any explanation put forward does not demand rigorous analysis having regard to the evidence. Explanations of individual items of evidence and their inferential relationship to and dependence upon other evidence must be given. In this respect the inferential charting of Wigmore remains of assistance,[20] although the analysis of evidence in relation to an hypothesis/story/narrative will ultimately be expressed orally to the court.

This approach does not reject consideration of evidence put in probabilistic terms. Such evidence may be taken into account in determining the weight of individual inferences but ultimately requires consideration in seeking the best explanation of all the evidence in the case.[21] And it may be of such crucial weight that it becomes decisive of the 'best explanation' in the absence of contradicting evidence. But the best explanation theory rejects expressing ultimate conclusions as a calculation following the application of the equations of probability.

While the justification for this 'best explanation' approach appears to lie in practice (in the 'positive') rather than in theory (the 'normative'),[22] that suggests this

[18] This story model was empirically confirmed by N Pennington and R Hastie, 'A Cognitive Model of Juror Decision Making: The Story Model' (1991) 13 Cardozo L Rev 519. The model and its acceptance in US courts is explained by Pardo (n 13) at 402ff.

[19] Similarly in non-common law jurisdictions party involvement results in stories and narratives being put to the court that may be justified by the evidence before it.

[20] For an up-to-date exposition of inferential reasoning based upon Wigmore's work see P Roberts and C Aitken, Royal Statistical Society, Communicating and Interpreting Statistical Evidence in the Administration of Justice, Practitioner Guide No 3, The Logic of Forensic Proof: Inferential Reasoning in Criminal Evidence and Forensic Science (2014) Part 3 'Neo-Wigmorean Analysis'.

[21] See Pardo (n 13) at 421–22.

[22] The founding and principal advocate for the 'best explanation' justification of forensic proof is Professor Ronald J Allen: see for example 'A Reconceptualisation of Civil Trials' (1986) 66 Buffalo U L Rev 401; 'Factual Ambiguity and a Theory of Evidence' (1994) 88 Northwestern U L Rev 604; 'The Nature of Juridical Proof' (1991) 13 Cardozo L Rev 373; 'Rationality, Algorithms and Juridical Proof' (1997) 1 E & P 254. Forceful arguments in favour of Allen's approach are summarized in Pardo (n 13) above at 415ff. See most recently RJ Allen and MS Pardo, 'Relative Plausibility and its Critics' (2019) 23 E & P 5 (and other articles in this volume).

approach will continue until the unlikely (?) situation arises where indisputable empirical evidence exists for each and every probabilistic inference required in reaching decisions of fact and computers can be programmed to process their logical relationship.[23]

Standards of proof

The holistic non-probabilistic approach underlies the approach taken to evidence and proof in courts in both civil and criminal cases. It is an approach that is reflected in the very formulation of the standards of proof. These standards are not formulated numerically. Moreover courts have made it clear that, in both civil and criminal cases, they refuse to act upon a bare statistical probability and require more direct evidence concerning the individual event before the court.

The standard in a civil case is 'satisfaction on the balance of probabilities'; the standard in a criminal case is 'satisfaction beyond reasonable doubt'. The human nature of the process is emphasized by the requirement of 'satisfaction'. That is ultimately a subjective process. This suggests the standards are never definitive; but their application does require justification having regard to the evidence before the court. Despite juries not being required to give reasons for their decisions judges must reject claims and accusations altogether where of the opinion that the evidence does not justify an answer, and following verdict parties may seek another opinion on appeal—and even afterwards if fresh and compelling evidence becomes available—if they think justification of that verdict cannot be sustained.

The civil standard

It might be argued persuasively that given the nature of civil cases there could be no objection in principle to the notion of rectitude being openly statistically

[23] Probabilistic values can be computed for some items of evidence: cf comments in P Roberts and CGG Aitken, Royal Statistical Society, Communicating and Interpreting Statistical Evidence in the Administration of Justice, Practitioner Guide No 3, The Logic of Forensic Proof: Inferential Reasoning in Criminal Evidence and Forensic Science (2014) at 1.22 and 4.2. Research into developing Software for the Analysis and Implementation of Likelihood Ratios (SAILR) has been funded by the European Network of Forensic Science Institutes through their Monopoly programme. See CGG Aitken, 'Bayesian Hierarchical Random Effects Models in Forensic Science' (2018) 9 Front Genet 126. doi: 10.3389/fgene.2018.00126. Software has been developed to express those likelihood ratios necessary for the application of Bayesian analysis to DNA matches where DNA samples are incomplete or mixed because from more than one contributor. The use of a computer program (named STRmix) to provide likelihood ratios for a match given a mixed sample was approved in *Tuite v The Queen* [2015] VSCA 148; (2015) 49 VR 196.

probabilistic, this being an appropriate conceptualization for the purpose of solving a civil dispute where the risks of error fall (often equally) upon the disputants. And the numerical degree of probability required for proof might even then be varied depending upon the seriousness of the allegations made and their more serious consequences for the opponent.

The practical difficulties of implementing in practice such an atomistic approach have been discussed above. Even in cases where inferential strength of some evidence is presented statistically from an empirical basis triers of fact must somehow combine the atomistic with the holistic, giving one or other of these approaches preference. Perhaps in a civil case an atomistic probabilistic approach could be given preference where the decisive evidence is an empirically based numerical probability within a class that appropriately embraces the very facts in issue; for example where epidemiological studies show increased rates of injury or disease in persons exposed to certain chemicals. But then the exposure and its level would have to be undisputed for the statistic to be decisive, so that even in these cases courts refuse to accept bare statistical conclusions as proof.[24]

The criminal standard

While an atomistic probabilistic approach might be advocated in theory as having a role to play in the settlement of civil disputes it is highly problematic to suggest that such an approach can be advocated in criminal cases. As Roberts and Zuckerman show there is a clear distinction in principle between objectives in civil as opposed to criminal cases.[25] Whereas the former involve private disputants, the latter involve accusations of wrongfulness by the State against citizens. And whereas the risks of reaching an erroneous decision of fact may fall equally upon private disputants, in the case of a criminal accusation the party with the most to lose is the wrongfully convicted accused. Given the assumptions of a liberal-democratic society, the risk of avoiding wrongful conviction and the consequent punishment of an innocent accused is regarded as paramount.[26] The criminal standard finds principled justification in the presumption of innocence principle and Roberts and Zuckerman discuss it in that context.[27]

[24] See, for example, *Seltsam Pty Ltd v McGuiness* (2000) 49 NSWLR 262 at [122], [123], [130] (Spigelman CJ); *Amaca Pty Ltd (formerly James Hardie & Co Pty Ltd) v Hannell* [2007] WASCA 158; *Cowan v Bunnings Group Ltd* [2014] QSC 301.

[25] *Criminal Evidence* (n 9) Section 1.2.

[26] Other evidential rules exist to mitigate the risk of wrongful conviction: for example, rules relating to the admissibility of confessional evidence, rules controlling the disclosure of the accused's character and other misconduct, and rules requiring supporting evidence for some categories of prosecution evidence.

[27] *Criminal Evidence* (n 9) ch 8, parts 8.4 and 8.5.

As a consequence the standard of satisfaction for concluding rectitude in a criminal case cannot be mere likelihood as in civil cases but demands satisfaction beyond reasonable doubt.[28] This standard strives for an individualized justice rather than a generalized justice that recognizes other reasonable explanations for the evidence may remain.

Mere statistical probabilities, in that they recognize expressly the numerical possibility of error, are regarded as unacceptable as a sufficient basis for rectitude in a criminal case. For as long as a numerical possibility of innocence remains, the risk of convicting an innocent person remains. What must be shown is that any statistical possibility of error can be ignored altogether and the only way of achieving this is for the prosecution to convince the trier of fact that, having regard to all the evidence before the court, any explanation based upon that statistical possibility of error would be 'unreasonable'.

Consequently, taking practice and principle[29] as the starting point, the criminal standard of proof is not expressed numerically. Rather proof is expressed in terms that seek to exclude the risk of wrongful conviction by ensuring that, on the evidence before the court, the trier of fact believes that no reasonably possible innocent explanation remains. Certainty being unobtainable, this creates a standard of rectitude as high as can be conceptualized by the courts. In so doing, as Roberts and Zuckerman conclude, it demands a procedure for reasoning,[30] a procedure that does not seek expression as a statistical probability. Furthermore this procedure for reasoning is assumed instinctive to those lay fact-finders (including judges) that lie at the heart of the process of justice.

It is important to emphasize that the presumption of innocence demands that throughout the accusatorial trial the prosecution bears the burden of proving its case beyond reasonable doubt. There is no obligation upon the accused to provide an innocent explanation. So that, for example, where prosecution evidence is regarded by the trier of fact as simply inherently unreliable and therefore incapable of eliminating doubt, it cannot convict despite absence of explanation from the accused. The very unreliability of the evidence gives rise to explanations of reasonable doubt that undermine satisfaction of the prosecution's burden of proof.

[28] The acceptance of this common law notion is regarded as fundamental to common law criminal justice, despite attempts in England to give it different expression by direction to the jury to be 'sure'. Although English trial judges need not refer to the traditional standard, if they do they should explain that it means the same as 'sure': *Criminal Evidence* (n 9) 363; see also F Picinali, 'The Threshold Lies in the Method: Instructing Jurors About Reasoning Beyond Reasonable Doubt' (2015) 19 E & P 139 at 139–40. An in-depth discussion of the in principle justifications for this high standard can be found in F Picinali, 'Can the Reasonable Doubt Standard be Justified? A Reconstructed Dialogue' (2018) 31 Can J Law Juris 365.

[29] The principled justifications for the procedure are encapsulated in the quote from *Criminal Evidence* (n 9).

[30] *Criminal Evidence* (n 9) 366ff, Part 8.5 headed 'The Criminal Standard as Reasoning Procedure'.

Using probabilistic forensic science evidence in criminal cases

The discussion above does not reject the logic of the probability equations.[31] For what may ultimately be practical reasons, they are not permitted to define what constitutes rectitude in a criminal trial. However, statistical probabilities generated empirically may be tendered, and, if so, their logical influence upon the accused's guilt requires explanation to ensure that they are not given illogical and undue weight.[32] The logic of probability remains important in informing the process of forensic reasoning adopted in courts.

Expressing forensic science evidence

This conclusion is important because increasingly forensic scientists are justifying their evidence through empirical statistical research, and consequently prosecutors are tendering, and courts are accepting as admissible, forensic science evidence so expressed. This approach has not always been demanded. Forensic experts, regarding their primary role as assisting in the investigation and conviction of wrongdoers, have historically presented their opinions in definitive verbal terms, for example, using their experiences to assert that items examined by them had unique patterns that enabled them to be traced to the accused with absolute certainty (for example fingerprints). But now, with the concept of uniqueness having been shown to produce a false certainty, forensic scientists are obliged to seek expression of their opinions in probabilistic terms,[33] preferably, but not necessarily,[34] generated scientifically rather than based simply upon experience.

Experts play an influential role in court proceedings. There is always the risk that their evidence will be given more probative weight than it deserves, particularly when it is technical and beyond the knowledge of lay-persons. With probabilistic conclusions capable of expression in various ways, that expression should be

[31] cf SP Lund and H Iyer, 'Likelihood Ratio as Weight of Forensic Evidence: A Closer Look' (2017) 122 J Res Nat Inst Standards Tech Article 27 and response from C Aitken, A Norgard, F Taroni, and A Biedermann, Front Genet, 22 June 2018 <https://doi.org/10.3389/fgene.2018.00224|> (accessed 4 February 2020).

[32] Graham Jackson, Colin Aitken, and Paul Roberts: Royal Statistical Society, Practitioner Guide No 2, Part 7 'Presenting DNA Evidence in the Courtroom,' 7.2.

[33] See MJ Saks and J Koehler, 'The Individualization Fallacy in Forensic Science Evidence' (2008) 61 Vand L Rev 199; DH Kaye, 'Probability, Individualization, and Uniqueness in Forensic Science Evidence' (2009) 75 Brook L Rev 1163; MJ Saks and J Koehler, 'Individualization Claims in Forensic Science: Still Unwarranted' (2009) 75 Brook L Rev 1187; SA Cole, 'Forensics without Uniqueness, Conclusions without Individualization: The New Epistemology of Forensic Identification' (2009) 8 Law Probab Risk 233; WC Thomson, J Vuille, F Taroni, and A Biedermann, 'After Uniqueness: The Evolution of Forensic Science Opinions' (2018) 102(1) Judicature 18.

[34] See for example *R v Dlugosz* [2013] EWCA Crim 2, [2013] 1 Cr App R 32 where absence of statistical conclusions did not prevent tender of an expert opinion relating to analysis of a mixed sample of DNA.

used that is most capable of being understood and used when juries and judges are undertaking their holistic fact-finding task.[35]

Where forensic evidence does not have a scientific or otherwise measured empirical basis, but is an opinion based only upon the experience of the witness, it must of necessity be expressed verbally. In *Atkins v R*[36] the court approved a verbal expression of support from an expert (an experienced medical artist identifying the accused from a CCTV image) in terms of a six-stage scale from 'Lends no support' to 'Lends strong support'. But the court disapproved of testimony based on that same scale being expressed numerically (support from zero to five)—the numerical scale perhaps suggesting a more definitive empirical basis for the opinion and being less able to be accommodated into the overall assessment of guilt. Perhaps also a rejection of reasoning that might give rise to mathematical calculation.

But where forensic evidence does have a scientific or an empirical statistical foundation courts do permit probabilistic expression in numerical terms.[37] However numerical probabilistic conclusions can be accurately expressed in a variety of ways.[38] And there is psychological evidence suggesting that laypersons assess the probative weight of equivalent statistical expressions differently.[39] The question is which expressions are of most assistance to the jury's holistic task?

The expression forensic scientists prefer to use in explaining the probabilistic weight of their evidence is the likelihood ratio.[40] This is the ratio between the likelihood of the evidence being found assuming the guilty hypothesis and the likelihood of the evidence being found assuming an innocent hypothesis. What is here of interest is that this expression then requires the use of Bayes' Theorem to take the next logical step to calculate how this probability of *finding the evidence* affects

[35] For a sceptical view of their ability to do this rationally given the way forensic science evidence is currently presented see G Edmond, 'Forensic Science Evidence and the Conditions for Rational (Jury) Evaluation' (2015) 39 Melbourne U L Rev 77.

[36] [2009] EWCA Crim 1876.

[37] DNA evidence is the obvious example of this. Where DNA experts are unable to provide statistical support their opinions, if otherwise justified as sufficiently reliable, may, as with other experts, be given using a verbal scale: see for example *R v Dlugosz* [2013] EWCA Crim 2, [2013] 1 Cr App R 32,.

[38] See *Aytugrul v R* [2010] NSWCCA 272 at [86]–[87] where McClellan CJ distinguishes six different but accurate expressions of the evidence before him. The majority held that the expression used (the high percentage of persons *not matching* the DNA trace found) was accurate and would not have misled the jury. In a strong dissent McClellan CJ argued that expression as a 'random occurrence match as a frequency' should have been used (appeal to the High Court dismissed: (2012) 247 CLR 170). Case discussed in A Ligertwood, 'Can DNA Evidence Alone Convict an Accused?' (2011) 33 Sydney L Rev 487 and A Ligertwood, 'Forensic Science Expressions and Legal Proof' (2013) 45 Aust J Forensic Sci 263.

[39] See for example, J Koehler, 'On Conveying the Probative Value of DNA Evidence: Frequencies, Likelihood Ratios, and Error Rates' (1996) 67 U Col L Rev 859; J Koehler, '*The Psychology of Numbers in the Courtroom;* How to Make DNA-Match Statistics Seem Impressive or Insufficient' (2001) 74 S Cal L Rev 1275 and discussion of RK Helm, VP Hans, and VF Reyna, 'Trial by Numbers' (2017) 27 Cornell J L & Public Policy 107 at 112–16.

[40] Guest Editorial, 'Expressing Evaluative Opinions: A Position Statement' (2011) 51 Sci & Justice 1. See also WC Thomson, J Vuille, F Taroni, and A Biedermann, 'After Uniqueness: The Evolution of Forensic Science Opinions' (2018) 102 Judicature 18; M Redmayne, P Roberts, C Aitken, and G Jackson, 'Forensic Science Evidence in Court' [2011] Crim L Rev 347, European Network of Forensic Science Institute (ENFSI), Guidelines for Evaluating Reporting in Forensic Science, 2015, para 2.4; and n 23 above.

the prior probability of the accused's *guilt*. This creates problems as lay fact-finders generally have no knowledge of this theorem and the risk is that they will simply equate the likelihood of *finding the evidence* with the likelihood of *guilt* (the so-called 'prosecutors' fallacy'). Such psychological evidence as exists[41] suggests lay fact-finders have difficulty in understanding a likelihood ratio whereas they are more likely to understand a simple statement of the probability of a random match within a population. This can more easily be converted to understand how many other persons other than the accused in reasonable proximity of the crime might satisfy that match. In *R v Doheny and Adams*[42] the court endorsed the expression of DNA in these terms. And with the random match probability (RMP) of DNA capable of assessment in many cases at over a billion this makes such a statistic extremely compelling if guilt turns upon its acceptance alone.

However, while a RMP may remain a possible expression in the case of the analysis of a sample of DNA from a single donor, in the case of samples containing DNA from a number of donors sophisticated Bayesian analysis is now available, with computing assistance, to disentangle a mixed DNA sample and to express the likelihood of finding such evidence if the suspect is a contributor. In *Tuite v The Queen*[43] the Court of Criminal Appeal in Victoria accepted such analysis through use of a computer program called STRmix and the necessary expression of the results as a likelihood ratio. Thus expression in terms of a likelihood ratio will continue and must somehow be understood and assimilated by triers of fact.

Does the law assist juries in understanding statistical expressions?

As emphasized above the common law's reasoning process to proof is expressed in the criminal standard of proof and courts are agreed that this is not a mathematical standard. Courts are further of the view that it should not be elaborated in any way. There is no obligation to emphasize the exclusionary nature of the standard[44] nor to elaborate what constitutes a reasonable doubt. The investigation into the nature of reasonableness would certainly be counter-productive, and aside some

[41] J Koehler, 'On Conveying the Probative Value of DNA Evidence: Frequencies, Likelihood Ratios, and Error Rates' (1996) 67 U Col L Rev 859 at 878–79 and 880ff (Reporting on his experiment: 'Likelihood Ratios vs Frequencies'); Graham Jackson, Colin Aitken, and Paul Roberts: Royal Statistical Society, Practitioner Guide No 2, 2014, Part 7.3 'Presenting DNA Evidence in the Courtroom'. Cf WC Thompson and EJ Newman, 'Lay Understanding of Forensic Statistics, Evaluation of Random Match Probabilities, Likelihood Ratios, and Verbal Equivalents' (2015) 39(4) Law Human Behav 332–49.

[42] [1997] 1 Cr App R 369. See also *R v Reed and Reed; R v Garmson* [2009] EWCA Crim 2698, [2010] 1 Cr App R 23 [53]–[55].

[43] [2015] VSCA 148, (2015) 49 VR 196.

[44] Although a direction on the need to eliminate innocent explanations may be appropriate in cases relying upon circumstantial evidence: *R v Hodge* (1838) 2 Lew CC 227 at 228; *R v Bracewell* (1979) 68 Cr App R 44 at 49. Failure to give a 'Hodge direction' is not necessarily productive of a miscarriage of justice.

platitudinous direction to the effect that absolute certainty is impossible to attain and that reasonable doubts are not 'fanciful' or 'theoretical' or 'imaginary' doubts, reasonable doubts remain those doubts held by a (reasonable) jury. In England the exclusionary nature of the direction appears to have got lost in the direction that it is enough for the jury to be 'sure' of guilt before convicting.[45] This approach is difficult to understand,[46] particularly where statistics are put before the court in terms of probabilities generated in defined ranges. What such statistics are able to immediately show is the capacity for the evidence to be consistent with an innocent account. The task of the jury is to consider such innocent accounts and if, having regard to all the evidence before the court, one is regarded as reasonable, it must acquit. To emphasize this exclusionary nature of the criminal standard is consistent with that principle demanded at common law that excludes the reasonable risk of convicting an innocent person.

Emphasizing this standard also demonstrates the problem with a likelihood ratio. This ratio expresses the likelihood of finding evidence (eg DNA) if the accused is guilty (the contributor) as opposed to finding it if not guilty (not the contributor). Leaving aside the difficulties of the fact-finder understanding and using this ratio, it might be said that the criminal standard is not ever satisfied by mere likelihood; it requires the exclusion of all other reasonable explanations of the evidence. What the jury requires is an expression that more directly demonstrates the degree to which statistical evidence might be consistent with innocent explanations so it can go ahead with its task of determining whether these explanations can be rejected on consideration of other evidence before the court.

The likelihood ratio can logically be used to calculate the effect of evidence upon the probability of the accused's guilt, which in turn will reveal the extent to which innocent explanations are open. But this requires the application of Bayes' Theorem. For this a numerical prior probability must be determined. This would have to be determined by each member of the jury. The law might approach this problem by requiring juries to receive sufficient instruction about the application of the theorem so each member could make the appropriate calculation. Or, to illustrate the probative value of the evidence, the expert could make the calculation on the basis of a range of prior probabilities. But judges steer clear of these approaches for fear of confusing juries and diverting them from their holistic task.[47]

[45] In Canada the word 'sure' is used in the National Judicial Institute model direction in the context of emphasizing that absolute certainty is unattainable and that juries can go no further than have a belief in guilt beyond reasonable doubt: see the Model Jury Instructions published by the Institute (at <https://www.nji-inm.ca/index.cfm/publications/> last accessed 4 February 2020) in particular those instructions in Part A Preliminary Instructions, 5 Fundamental Principles.

[46] The use of 'sure' in England is critiqued by F Picinali, 'The Threshold Lies in the Method: Instructing Jurors About Reasoning Beyond Reasonable Doubt' (2015) 19 E & P 139 at 139–40. The use is also discussed in *Criminal Evidence* (n 9) 362–64.

[47] *R v Dennis Adams* [1996] EWCA 222, [1996] 2 Cr App R 467; *R v Doheny and Adams* [1996] EWCA 728, [1997] 1 Cr App R 369; *R v Dennis Adams (No 2)* [1998] 1 Cr App R 377 at 384.

Nevertheless, if evidence is accepted as a likelihood ratio some explanation is required.

Alternatively forensic witnesses may find an expression more conducive to the way jurors are asked to reason. Hence in *R v Doheny and Adams*[48] presentation as a RMP and application of this to a suspect population indicated there were twenty persons likely to have this DNA. Thus the jury's attention was focused upon eliminating the reasonable possibility that one of these other persons committed the crime against the accused.

This approach makes even very powerful statistical evidence accessible to the jury by directing the jury to consider other explanations of the evidence consistent with the accused's innocence. Of course, with the RMP now being 1 in over a billion there may only be six people in the world who might match the DNA in question and eventually the RMP will include a figure that exceeds the world's population. Nevertheless, while it remains a statistic short of absolute certainty the remote possibility of another random match remains, even though it is unlikely to give rise to a reasonable doubt in the absence of other evidence. With this development accused who wish to contest DNA evidence will find other avenues, which do not necessarily involve empirical statistical issues—systemic and human errors that may arise in the process of collecting and analysing forensic samples. This change in focus is already occurring as challenges to apparently implicating DNA are made on grounds of indirect transfer.[49] These avenues are much more likely to give rise to reasonable explanations consistent with innocence.

Error rates

The approach here advocated has serious ramifications for the presentation of forensic evidence generally in that it requires forensic scientists to be candid about what might broadly be described as 'error rates', that is, in the context of this discussion, the possibility of their evidence being consistent with innocent explanations. If it is possible to collect empirical statistical evidence this should be done. Where processes and procedures for analysis exist these can be tested for systemic error rates. The competency of examiners generally and individually can be calculated. Evidence of statistics gathered can then be tendered which demonstrate rates of error that can be expected. These statistics can then be presented to reveal not just overall reliability but also the possibility of the evidence being consistent with an innocent explanation.

In cases where the expert testifies to an opinion based only upon experience the 'error rates' are individual and can be assessed only through examination and

[48] [1997] 1 Cr App R 369.

[49] See for example *Fitzgerald v The Queen* [2014] HCA 20, (2014) 88 ALJR 779.

cross-examination. Courts remain willing to admit evidence from witnesses experienced in identifying matching features that a lay-person would not observe (for example in fingerprints and video images). This evidence remains often presented without a scientific probabilistic justification, just as lay witnesses identify persons simply upon the basis of their past observations. While empirically based statistics can now be gathered in the case of some of these experts (for example, fingerprint examiners), in the case of others (for example, facial mappers), assuming a challenge to the unreliability of their evidence does not lead to exclusion of their evidence, then fact-finders must determine probative weight as best they can. In some jurisdictions such evidence is restricted to describing similarities rather than extending to an opinion of a positive identification.[50]

But what remains important is the principled approach that courts should take to forensic evidence generally. With few disciplines qualifying as sciences there are many reasons to suspect the reliability of forensic evidence. Assuming that the evidence is adjudged as of sufficient reliability to allow its admissibility,[51] if the exclusionary reasoning of the standard of proof is to be applied, remaining risks of error, if possible empirically quantified, should be disclosed in the testimony of the forensic witness. Empirical research needs to be conducted to classify and quantify, where possible, the reliability of evidence given by practitioners in the traditional forensic science disciplines. And courts must insist that forensic experts be transparent when testifying about possible risks of error.[52]

This emphasizes that the primary duty of the forensic expert is not to the prosecution but to the court. It can also be argued that prosecutors already have a duty to ensure full and complete disclosure of expert evidence as part of their primary duties to the court.[53] Indeed practice in many jurisdictions has achieved or is seeking to achieve these best practices.[54] The traditional assumption that the adversary trial will result in the disclosure of any risks of unreliability is of doubtful

[50] See, for example, *R v Tang* (2006) 65 NSWLR 681 (where the appeal succeeded because the testimony went beyond describing similarities). But cf *Atkins v R* [2009] EWCA Crim 1876 discussed at n 36 above.

[51] Error rates are also important where admissibility can be contested on grounds of unreliability: see for example, *Daubert v Merrell Dow Pharmaceuticals, Inc* (1993) 509 US 579 and in England (Criminal Procedure Rules Part 19(4)(h) based on the common law). In most Australian jurisdictions reliability is not considered in determining the admissibility of expert evidence (see s 79 Uniform Evidence Act where only 'specialized knowledge' is required cf *Honeysett v The Queen* (2014) 253 CLR 122 at [23]).

[52] Court rules now exist in many jurisdictions emphasizing the duty of the expert to the court and demanding candid disclosure of their opinions and their basis prior to trial: see for example, Criminal Procedure Rules 2015 Part 19 (at justice.gov.uk).

[53] See G Edmond, '(Ad)Ministering Justice: Expert Evidence and the Professional Responsibilities of Prosecutors' (2013) 36 UNSW L Rev 921. And see, for example, National Streamlined Forensic Reporting Guidelines for Providers of Forensic Science and a Practical Step Guide issued by the Crown Prosecution Service (at cps.gov.uk).

[54] In the UK through the Forensic Science Regulator (Gillian Tully): see generally G Tully, Regulating Forensic Science, in P Roberts and M Stockdale (eds), *Forensic Science Evidence and Expert Witness Testimony* (Elgar, 2018) ch 4.

effectiveness,[55] there being increasing evidence that unreliable forensic evidence has been influential in innocent persons having been wrongly convicted.[56]

Conclusions

There is much progress to be made in ensuring the sufficient reliability of forensic evidence but it is important to keep in mind that the discipline exists to further the administration of justice. While forensic investigators assist the State in its gathering of evidence, when it comes to presenting their evidence in court their role must be understood. This article has sought to show that the very reasoning process employed by courts in determining proof is not simply the probabilistic exercise employed by the forensic scientist. While forensic witnesses are concerned only with the probative weight of a single item of evidence, courts are involved in determining the guilt of the accused beyond reasonable doubt upon the basis of all the evidence before the court. This process ultimately demands not mathematical computation but consideration of the consistency of the evidence with all those explanatory stories/narratives/hypotheses to which the evidence may give rise, and the exclusion of those reasonably consistent with innocence. This holistic process is instinctively taken by lay fact-finders (jurors and judges), designated by the common law as responsible for determining rectitude in a court of law. All evidence, including statistical evidence, requires expression and use complementary to this process. A conclusion supported by common law principles of criminal evidence advocated by Adrian Zuckerman.

[55] G Edmond and M San Roque, 'The Cool Crucible: Forensic Evidence and the Frailty of the Criminal Trial' (2012) 24 Current Issues Crim Just 51. See also G Edmond and others, 'How to Cross-examine Forensic Scientists: A Guide for Lawyers' (2014) 39 Aust Bar Rev 174.

[56] See for example: BL Garrett and PJ Neufeld, 'Invalid Forensic Science Testimony and Wrongful Convictions' (2009) 95 Virginia L Rev 1; G Edmond, 'What Lawyers Should Know' (2015) 36 Adelaide L Rev 33 at 38; and 'innocence projects' that now exist in many jurisdictions.

4

Adrian Zuckerman's New Evidence Scholarship

Paul Roberts

Introduction: A tale of two Zuckermans

It is barely contentious to say that Adrian Zuckerman has exerted a profound and lasting influence on the procedural law and scholarship of his adopted jurisdiction, England and Wales. Searching Westlaw UK by his full name produces 183 hits, including eighteen judicial citations. Impressive enough, you might think—and they are all him (Google, incidentally, is not so discriminating). But refine the search to 'Zuckerman on', and you will need to sift through 3,465 hits, including 3,376 case-related mentions, mostly in commentaries. In terms of direct citation, Zuckerman's arguments and analysis have been recognized as authoritative by the UK Supreme Court,[1] the House of Lords (the UKSC's judicial predecessor),[2] the Court of Appeal (Civil Division),[3] and the English High Court.[4] Counsel have leveraged their submissions with citations to what Cranston J, in the Commercial Court, recently hailed as 'Professor Adrian Zuckerman's well-recognised book'.[5] In one judgment the Court of Appeal scrutinized 'a bold passage in Chapter 4 of his book [where] Mr Zuckerman suggests that Denning LJ got things wrong',[6] but on

[1] *Financial Services Authority v Sinaloa Gold Plc* [2013] UKSC 11, [2013] 2 AC 28 [18] (Lord Mance JSC, Lord Neuberger, Baroness Hale, Lord Clarke, and Lord Sumption concurring).

[2] *Somerville v Scottish Ministers (No 2)* [2007] UKHL 44, 2008 SC (HL) 45 [205] (Lord Mance); *Three Rivers DC v Bank of England (No 6)* [2004] UKHL 48, [2005] 1 AC 610 [34] (Lord Scott observing that Zuckerman 'refers to the rationale underlying legal advice privilege as "the rule of law rationale" ... I, for my part, subscribe to this idea. It justifies, in my opinion, the retention of legal advice privilege in our law, notwithstanding that as a result cases may sometimes have to be decided in ignorance of relevant probative material').

[3] *Collier v Williams* [2006] EWCA Civ 20, [2006] 1 WLR 1945 [19]; *Hashtroodi v Hancock* [2004] 1 WLR 3206, [2004] EWCA Civ 652 [10]; *C Plc v P* [2008] Ch 1, [36] (Longmore LJ finding that 'there is no privilege in the offending material itself, which is material which existed independently of the order. This is essentially the position maintained by Professor Adrian Zuckerman').

[4] *Winterthur Swiss Insurance Co v AG (Manchester) Ltd (In Liquidation)* [2006] EWHC 839 (Comm) [69], n 31.

[5] *Hutchison 3G UK Ltd v EE Ltd*, High Court of Justice Commercial Court, 6 October 2017, 2017 WL 04477790 [24]. Also see *Bidgood v Barclays Bank Plc* [2017] EWHC 2942 (QB) [35]; *Harley Street Capital Ltd v Tchigirinsky (No 2)* [2005] EWHC 1897 (Ch) [71].

[6] *Akram v Adam* [2004] EWCA Civ 1601, [2005] 1 WLR 2762 [37].

Paul Roberts, *Adrian Zuckerman's New Evidence Scholarship* In: *Principles, Procedure, and Justice.* Edited by: Rabeea Assy and Andrew Higgins, Oxford University Press (2020). © The editors and several contributors.
DOI: 10.1093/oso/9780198850410.003.0004

that occasion Denning trumped Zuckerman:[7] albeit without the benefit of full submissions, Brooke LJ concluded that 'the point is without substance' and could not 'see anything in the new [Civil Procedure Rules] which contravenes Article 6 of the European Convention on Human Rights in the way which Mr Zuckerman suggests'.[8] Nobody can win them all. Zuckerman may be quoted at length as the only relevant commentator on a contested issue before the court.[9] The Court of Appeal has commended his 'valuable discussion of the principles' pertaining to striking out misbehaving claimants[10] and acknowledged 'the very interesting discussion by Professor Zuckerman' on judicial sanctions for non-disclosure of witness statements.[11] It is thought to count against the authority of a putative precedent, notwithstanding that 'the Civil Appeals Office has been accustomed to act on the faith of it', that Zuckerman no longer cites it.[12] Even a Zuckerman footnote may attract judicial attention and adversarial argument.[13] Zuckerman's influence further extends geographically, north of the border to Scottish civil litigation,[14] and all the way to Strasbourg.[15]

Attentive readers will have noticed that all of these judicial sightings and notices relate to points of civil procedure, and 'the well-recognised' book in question is, of course, *Zuckerman on Civil Procedure: Principles of Practice* (as the third edition is titled).[16] This is the harvest of what we might describe as Zuckerman's second career in procedural scholarship and teaching. In this festschrift essay, however, I want to celebrate an earlier phase of Zuckerman's intellectual journey, in which his central—albeit never exclusive[17]—focus was criminal rather than civil procedure. And my principal claim will be that Zuckerman's influence on British evidentiary scholarship would still have been profound and lasting even if he had

[7] Contrary to form, one might think, on points of procedure, where Denning was characteristically unorthodox. According to Denning LJ in *Bater v Bater* [1951] P 35 (CA) 36–37, whilst '[i]t is of course true that by our law a higher standard of proof is required in criminal cases than in civil cases... this is subject to the qualification that there is no absolute standard in either case. In criminal cases the charge must be proved beyond reasonable doubt, but there may be degrees of proof within that standard'. Also see *Hornal v Neuberger Products Ltd* [1957] 1 QB 247 (CA) 258 ('[T]he standard of proof depends on the nature of the issue. The more serious the allegation the higher the degree of probability that is required'). Denning's 'floating standard' heresy (albeit an historically plausible interpretation of a common law maxim) was authoritatively rejected by the House of Lords in *In re D* [2008] 1 WLR 1499, [2008] UKHL 33 [23]–[28].

[8] ibid [38]–[41] (Jonathan Parker and Keene LJJ agreeing).

[9] *Cape Distribution Ltd v Cape Intermediate Holdings* [2016] EWHC 1786 (QB) [169].

[10] *Masood v Zahoor* [2010] 1 WLR 746, [2009] EWCA Civ 650 [71] (Mummery LJ).

[11] *Chartwell Estate Agents Ltd v Fergies Properties SA* [2014] EWCA Civ 506 [31] (Davis LJ).

[12] *Handley v Lake Jackson Solicitors* [2016] 1 WLR 3138 [42].

[13] *New Century Media Ltd v Makhlay* [2013] EWHC 3556 (QB) [42].

[14] *Prospect Healthcare (Hairmyres) Ltd v Kier Build Ltd* 2018 SLT 815 [27].

[15] *MGN Ltd v United Kingdom* [2011] 1 Costs LO 84 (ECtHR) [113] (quoting the Jackson Costs Review's reference to Zuckerman's 'forceful' submissions).

[16] A Zuckerman, *Zuckerman on Civil Procedure: Principles of Practice* (3rd edn, Sweet & Maxwell 2013). The first edition, which appeared in 2003, was simply titled *Civil Procedure*.

[17] Privilege has been for Zuckerman an abiding specialist subject. A notable early essay is AAS Zuckerman, 'Privilege and Public Interest' in CFH Tapper (ed), *Crime, Proof and Punishment: Essays in Memory of Sir Rupert Cross* (Butterworths 1981).

never had that remarkable second incarnation as a guru of civil litigation practice, and had never written a single word on civil procedure.

The influence I have in mind is not measurable by court citations (with no apology to metrics mongers),[18] and its lasting significance might only be fully appreciated in generational terms over the span of decades (bad luck, then, if you think that the REF cycle marks the horizon of scholarly endeavour). My topic relates to how we think about the disciplinary contours and methodologies, intellectual foundations, and normative value of procedural scholarship. I will suggest, in this essay, that in the earlier phase of his work Zuckerman made three particularly significant conceptual advances which together reconfigure the terrain of common law evidentiary scholarship and pedagogy. These conceptual advances concern the (1) disciplinary domain; (2) institutional context(s); and (3) normative sources of evidence law. This essay elucidates and evaluates each of these three conceptual innovations, which can be summarized in terms of three corresponding dynamic transitions: (1) from 'Law of Evidence' to 'Evidence and Proof'; (2) from transubstantivity to procedural differentiation; and (3) from evidentiary rules to principled discretion. Although this triad comes as an integrated package and should, ultimately, be evaluated holistically, there are interesting and important things to be said about each of its individual components, as we shall see.

Disciplinary domain: From 'Law of Evidence' to 'Evidence and Proof'

Zuckerman's first claim to be regarded as a pivotal figure in evidentiary scholarship is that he was one of the very few UK-based academic lawyers to participate in 'the New Evidence Scholarship', a convenient if not entirely transparent umbrella for theoretical developments in (predominantly US) Evidence law stretching back to the 1970s. On a narrow reading, the New Evidence Scholarship is associated with a specifically American interest in the study of the science of proof, in which formal logic, mathematics, probability, and decision theory feature prominently.[19] Viewed more expansively, New Evidence Scholarship could be stretched to embrace all of the diverse strands of multi-disciplinary interest in the topic of evidence and proof which, aside from doctrinal analysis, might encompass procedural scholarship, sociological or socio-legal studies of legal institutions and processes, the

[18] Cf. R van Gestel, 'Ranking, Peer Review, Bibliometrics and Alternative Ways to Improve the Quality of Doctrinal Legal Scholarship' in R van Gestel, H-W Micklitz, and EL Rubin (eds), *Rethinking Legal Scholarship: A Transatlantic Dialogue* (CUP 2017).

[19] See RO Lempert, 'The New Evidence Scholarship: Analyzing the Process of Proof' (1986) 66 BU L Rev 439; RC Park, 'Evidence Scholarship, Old and New' (1991) 75 Minnesota L Rev 849; JD Jackson, 'Analysing the New Evidence Scholarship: Towards a New Conception of the Law of Evidence' (1996) 16 OJLS 309.

logic of inference, intelligence analysis and 'information science', discourse analysis (including structuralism, deconstruction, semiotics, rhetoric, narrative and phenomenological approaches), psychological research, scientific and technical developments including forensic science, computer applications and expert systems, and historical inquiries relating to all of the foregoing.[20] The New Evidence Scholars were the shock troops in a campaign to reconfigure the disciplinary parameters and methodologies of Evidence law, with potentially far-reaching implications for scholarship, pedagogy, and institutional practice. 'This profusion of theoretical approaches', enthused one of its leading exponents thirty years ago, 'evinces tremendous intellectual ferment. A profound transformation in human thinking about inference and probability is under way'.[21] Zuckerman was a torchbearer and catalyst for British participation and engagement with this ambitious project.

To appreciate what is 'new', and significant, about the New Evidence Scholarship one must view it in contrast with prevailing disciplinary orthodoxy. Since Thayer[22] and then Cross,[23] the widely accepted model of Evidence law envisages a collection of more or less discrete exclusionary exceptions to a threshold relevancy standard. Plainly, only relevant evidence is admissible at trial. This is a principle of logic which any system of adjudication aspiring to rationality must accept. The Law of Evidence, then, comprises a set of 'rules of exclusion' further regulating admissibility. It is an elegant, and in some ways, beguiling model. When the rules—and the exceptions to the rules; and the exceptions to the exceptions to the rules—become complex and wondrously refined through judicial dialectics and sedimentary accretion, common law jurisprudence produces an impressive doctrinal corpus capable of bulking out fearsomely erudite tomes with which to torture law students and keep professors endlessly preoccupied.

The New Evidence Scholarship brought intellectual excitement and theoretical renewal to this bastion of doctrinalism.[24] It rediscovered questions of epistemology, argumentation, inferential reasoning, and proof that had fascinated pioneers such as Bentham, Thayer, and Wigmore,[25] but had somehow been

[20] For accessible entry points into a large and diverse literature, see P Roberts (ed), *Theoretical Foundations of Criminal Trial Procedure* (Ashgate 2014); P Dawid, W Twining, and M Vasilaki (eds), *Evidence, Inference and Enquiry* (OUP 2011); W Twining, *Rethinking Evidence* (2nd edn, CUP 2006); RC Park and MJ Saks, 'Evidence Scholarship Reconsidered: Results of the Interdisciplinary Turn' (2006) 47 Boston C L Rev 1; P Roberts and M Redmayne (eds), *Innovations in Evidence and Proof* (Hart 2007).

[21] P Tillers, 'Introduction' (1986) 66 BU L Rev 381, 383.

[22] JB Thayer, *A Preliminary Treatise on Evidence at the Common Law* (Little, Brown & Co 1898). See E Swift, 'One Hundred Years of Evidence Law Reform: Thayer's Triumph' (2000) 88 Cal L Rev 2437; J Hook, 'A Brief Life of James Bradley Thayer' (1993) 88 Nw U L Rev 1.

[23] The very first page of *Cross on Evidence* begins by addressing 'the law of evidence', and in the very next breath is talking about 'the modern rules of evidence'. This telling elision has been adopted by successive editors and co-authors unchanged, into the recently published thirteenth edition by R Munday, *Cross and Tapper on Evidence* (OUP 2018).

[24] Also see P Roberts, 'Groundwork for A Jurisprudence of Criminal Procedure' in RA Duff and S Green (eds), *Philosophical Foundations of Criminal Law* (OUP 2011).

[25] W Twining, *Theories of Evidence: Bentham and Wigmore* (Weidenfeld & Nicolson 1985).

mislaid after so much effort had been diverted into collecting, organizing, analysing, and synthesizing case law precedents into new doctrinal rules. The New Evidence Scholarship built up enthusiasm and resources for pressing the Law of Evidence *qua* rules of admissibility in the direction of interdisciplinary studies of Evidence and Proof. This might be viewed as a major staging post on the road towards a more fully realized Forensic Science of inquiry, evidence, inference, and proof in criminal adjudication.[26]

Zuckerman contributed an essay titled 'Law, Fact or Justice?'[27] to a symposium on 'Probability and Inference in the Law of Evidence' published in the *Boston University Law Review* in 1986,[28] a landmark event now lionized in the history of the New Evidence Scholarship and an important catalyst for its further development and propagation. The architect and principal dynamo of the project was Peter Tillers, then a Visiting Professor at Cardozo School of Law in New York. He was supported, notably, by 'Adrian Zuckerman, William Twining, and David Schum, who, together with Peter Tillers, saw the need for the symposium and contributed to its organization'.[29] The symposium was said to have 'brought together virtually all the leading scholars concerned with issues of probabilistic and mathematical proof in court',[30] and the roll-call is indeed impressive. Yet most of the recognisable names it contains—Ron Allen, Craig Callen, Richard Friedman, David Kaye, Rick Lempert, Dale Nance, Charles Nesson, David Schum, Peter Tillers—are American.[31] British representation was limited to Twining, Zuckerman, and the Oxford philosopher L Jonathan Cohen.[32]

It is immediately apparent from the first introductory sentences of Eric Green's Foreword that the methodology of inquiry shared by Symposium participants departed radically from the orthodox Thayerite model of evidence law as a system of exclusionary rules:

> The central question in evidence is, 'What does it mean to prove something so that a court will either order a person imprisoned or order a transfer of money or property?' Related issues include the extent to which proof in courts is concerned

[26] See further, J Jackson and P Roberts, 'Beyond Common Law Evidence: Reimagining, and Reinvigorating, Evidence Law as Forensic Science' in DK Brown, JI Turner, and B Weisser (eds), *The Oxford Handbook of Criminal Process* (OUP 2019); P Roberts, 'The New Interdisciplinary Forensic Science' (2016) 43 J Law Soc 647.

[27] AAS Zuckerman, 'Law, Fact or Justice?' (1986) 66 BU L Rev 487.

[28] ED Green, 'Boston University Law Review Symposium: Foreword' (1986) 66 BU L Rev 377. The Symposium occupied two entire issues of volume 66 of the journal, spanning some 580 pages.

[29] ibid 380.

[30] ibid 379.

[31] They are also all male, with the exception of L Brilmayer, 'Second-Order Evidence and Bayesian Logic' (1986) 66 BU L Rev 673; and one of her commentators, AW Martin, 'Comment' (1986) 66 BU L Rev 709. This pronounced gender imbalance was presumably, in part, generational. Now see M Childs and L Ellison (eds), *Feminist Perspectives on Evidence* (Cavendish, 2000).

[32] LJ Cohen, 'The Role of Evidential Weight in Criminal Proof' (1986) 66 BU L Rev 635.

> with finding 'truth' in the abstract (as opposed to some acceptable operational surrogate); the procedural structure of the fact-finding process; the allocation of responsibilities among judge, jury, and advocates and witnesses; the application of rules of evidence to achieve the objectives of the fact-finding system; and the kinds of reasoning to be employed in adjudication ... Because most tried cases involve circumstantial evidence, questions about the nature of proof invariably raise questions about theories of inference and the proper use of mathematical and statistical evidence and probability arguments in courts.[33]

The New Evidence Scholarship was still at that time labouring under the long shadow of the remarkable judgment in *People v Collins*,[34] and many of the contributions to the symposium did indeed concern themselves with questions of probability, Bayes Theorem, and statistics. But the New Evidence Scholarship was never circumscribed or delimited by its fascination with probability theory and the undeniably engrossing 'thought experiments' that go with it (Blue and Green Buses; The Rodeo/Gatecrasher Paradox; Prison Yard, etc).[35] Once the question becomes, not 'What are the doctrinal rules?' but 'What does it mean to prove something ... ?' the entire vista of epistemology, rational inference, forensic argumentation, and the procedural architecture, intellectual frameworks, pedagogy and practical tools to support effective litigation and sound adjudication opens up to the Evidence and Proof research agenda.

Zuckerman's contribution to the Boston symposium set out to reconsider three basic concepts of the Law of Evidence—'law', 'fact', and 'justice'—and to explore their interrelationship. On the face of it, the meaning of these concepts appears reasonably well-defined and their roles discrete. The law allocates legal entitlements and duties and, in trials, issues of law are determined by the judge. Facts relate to 'what happened', the disputed issues in contested litigation, and fact-finding is entrusted to the common law jury or lay magistrates in criminal trials.[36] Legal reasoning, then, is normative, whereas forensic fact-finding concerns empirical

[33] Green (n 28) 377.

[34] *People v Collins* (1968) 68 Cal 2d 319. See LH Tribe, 'Trial by Mathematics: Precision and Ritual in the Legal Process' (1971) 84 Harv L Rev 1329.

[35] As Green (n 28), 378, quipped of *Collins'* direct legacy: 'In the ensuing debate, numerous blue buses have run untold numbers of near-sighted elderly ladies off the road, hundreds of alleged gatecrashers have been collared, dozens of murderous prisoners have been brought to justice, and countless articles, books, and opinions have been written on the subject' (footnotes omitted). Generally, see M Redmayne, 'Exploring the Proof Paradoxes' (2008) 14 Legal Theory 281; SE Fienberg, 'Gatecrashers, Blue Buses, and the Bayesian Representation of Legal Evidence' (1986) 66 BU L Rev 693; DH Kaye, 'The Paradox of the Gate-Crasher and Other Stories' [1979] Ariz St LJ 101.

[36] See eg *Daniel v State of Trinidad and Tobago* [2014] UKPC 3, [2014] AC 1290 [48] ('The general rule for the conduct of a criminal trial is that questions of law are for the judge and questions of fact are for the jury'). But also note *R v Fanning* [2016] EWCA Crim 550, [2016] 1 WLR 4175 [2] (referring to 'the constitutional position of the jury in a criminal trial ... [T]rial by jury developed in a way that, although questions of fact were for the jury and questions of law were for the judge, rules were established which delineated the jury's function to determine issues of fact').

matters and is performed through ordinary processes of inferential reasoning for which lay jurors and magistrates are well-equipped by their accumulated 'common sense' rooted in ordinary, everyday experience. Justice requires faithful application of legal rules to the true facts of the case, ascertained through a rational process of evidence gathering, testing, and proof. Zuckerman's aim was to complicate this overly simplistic picture of conceptual demarcation, and thereby to challenge the assumption that forms of reasoning applicable in other areas of life—including probabilistic and statistical reasoning—could be extrapolated to the forensic context without any major adjustment or contextualization. This misapprehension, Zuckerman argued, rested on a fallacious 'assumption of objectivity; the assumption that the sole function of the judicial process is to search for the objective truth that lies beyond, and is independent of, the law'.[37] Yet this assumption could not survive better and closer acquaintance with the institutional facts: 'present procedural practices denote the existence of a meeting ground between fact-finding and law application, where normative values shape the facts as well as the law ... [L]aw application and fact-finding converge in adjudication'.[38]

Legal disputes are framed by distinctively *legal* conceptions of materiality indexed to the applicable substantive law. This implies not only that the law stipulates 'the issues in the case' which define the subject matter of any contested trial, and by extension supply (legal) criteria of evidential relevancy; more fundamentally, it is not even possible to describe 'the facts of the case' without reference to legal concepts and categories. For example, the question whether the accused 'occasioned' a particular level of injury ('actual bodily harm', 'grievous bodily harm', 'wounding', etc) as much concerns legal tests of 'occasioning'[39] and classifications of injury as it does the metaphysics of action or the physical state of bodies: the 'brute facts',[40] so to speak, of 'what the accused did'. Interestingly, though, these juridical questions of legal classification are often in practice left to juries to determine. Is this conceptual seepage some kind of oversight or deficiency in legal process? Zuckerman argued, to the contrary, that the policy was calculated and deliberate: 'The assimilation, for the purpose of adjudication, of fact-finding and law application is vital for the role that we expect adjudication to fulfil.'[41] This blending flows from the twin imperatives of securing social approval for verdicts and maintaining public confidence in the administration of justice, especially in criminal adjudication, which in turn presuppose and leverage the *normative* (moral) quality of forensic fact-finding. Juries are prized precisely because, not in spite of, their ability to inject prevailing social morality into criminal verdicts. A procedural

[37] AAS Zuckerman, 'Law, Fact or Justice?' (1986) 66 BU L Rev 488.

[38] ibid 489.

[39] Section 47 of the Offences Against the Person Act 1861 (still in force and routine use in England and Wales) proscribes 'assault occasioning actual bodily harm'.

[40] Zuckerman was here following GEM Anscombe, 'On Brute Facts' (1958) 18 Analysis 69.

[41] AAS Zuckerman, 'Law, Fact or Justice?' (1986) 66 BU L Rev 494.

system orientated towards moral legitimacy will predictably invest considerable institutional capital in individualized justice on the merits, through which empirical truths are subjected to moral appraisal. This rationale, suggested Zuckerman, goes a long way towards explaining the law's traditional hostility to (overt) probabilistic reasoning and illuminates the intuition that 'naked statistical evidence' should never be sufficient to establish proof to the criminal standard. In the end, however, we face an unresolved tension which takes us to the limit of the human epistemic condition:

> The debate about the introduction of probabilistic assessment into the judicial process reflects much of th[e] age old conflict between our deeply rooted attitudes concerning fact-finding. On the one hand, the doubts that we entertain regarding our ability to arrive at the truth would seem to argue for the adoption of mathematical methods which would at least maximize the number of correct decisions in the long run. On the other hand, such a step would involve us in giving up, to a considerable extent, the hope of seeing justice supervene in individual trials.[42]

Having been energized by first wave New Evidence Scholarship, debates about the role of probability and statistical information in legal proceedings have raged on unabated.[43] They have lately been infused with even greater theoretical significance and practical urgency by the dawning realisation that all scientific evidence is probabilistic and, in principle, probatively quantifiable.[44] DNA profiling has inaugurated a new era of statistically-based forensics generating quantified measures of (estimated)[45] probative value.[46] Zuckerman's qualified scepticism about forensic

[42] ibid 508.

[43] See eg C Aitken, 'An Introduction to a Debate' (2012) 11 Law, Prob & Risk 255; M Redmayne, P Roberts, C Aitken, and G Jackson, 'Forensic Science Evidence in Question' [2011] Crim L Rev 347; B Robertson, G A Vignaux, and CEH Berger, 'Extending the Confusion about Bayes' (2011) 74 MLR 444; C Aitken, P Roberts, and G Jackson, *Fundamentals of Probability and Statistical Evidence in Criminal Proceedings* (Royal Statistical Society, 2010); RJ Allen and MS Pardo, 'The Problematic Value of Mathematical Models of Evidence' (2007) 36 JLS 107; M Redmayne, *Expert Evidence and Criminal Justice* (OUP 2001); M Redmayne and R Allen (eds), 'Bayesianism and Juridical Proof' (1997) 1(5) IJEP 253; B Robertson and GA Vignaux, 'Probability—The Logic of the Law' (1993) 13 OJLS 457; CR Callen, 'Notes on a Grand Illusion: Some Limits on the Use of Bayesian Theory in Evidence Law' (1982) 57 Ind LJ 1.

[44] MJ Saks and JJ Koehler, 'The Coming Paradigm Shift in Forensic Identification Science' (2005) 309 Science 892; I Evett, 'The Logical Foundations of Forensic Science: Towards Reliable Knowledge' (2015) 370 Phil Trans R Soc B Article 20140263; G Jackson, C Aitken, and P Roberts, *Case Assessment and Interpretation of Expert Evidence* (Royal Statistical Society 2014).

[45] An important qualification, because forensic scientists invariably work with factual assumptions over which the jury has the final decisive authority to accept or reject: cf CEH Berger and K Slooten, 'The LR Does Not Exist' (2016) 56 Sci and Just 388.

[46] See *ENFSI Guideline for Evaluative Reporting in Forensic Science*, v.3.0 (8 March 2015) <http://enfsi.eu/documents/forensic-guidelines> accessed 23 January 2020; PCAST, *Report to the President: Forensic Science in Criminal Courts—Ensuring Scientific Validity of Feature-Comparison Methods* (Washington DC, Executive Office of the President, 2016) <https://obamawhitehouse.archives.gov/sites/default/files/microsites/ostp/PCAST/pcast_forensic_science_report_final.pdf> (accessed 1 March 2019); M Lynch, S A Cole, R McNally, and K Jordan, *Truth Machine: The Contentious History of DNA*

probability, and his unqualified insistence that criminal adjudication ultimately subordinates fact-finding and conceptual formalisms such as the theoretical fact-law distinction to individualized justice on the merits, remain forceful and highly salient counterweights to the juggernaut of contemporary scientific logic. Besides, the significance for British jurisprudence of Zuckerman's engagement and participation in the New Evidence Scholarship extends beyond discrete contributions to particular debates.

Zuckerman is not the most influential UK-based contributor to the New Evidence Scholarship. That accolade undoubtedly belongs to William Twining, whose historical excavations of Evidence theory, decades long campaign to promote 'taking facts seriously' in legal pedagogy, and central involvement in disinterring and reinventing the Wigmorean graphical method of evidence analysis and argumentation rank as peerless, trans-jurisdictional contributions to Evidence and Proof scholarship.[47] Zuckerman probably wasn't even the most influential New Evidence scholar on Oxford's High Street[48] (if we follow orthodox conceptions of New Evidence Scholarship as being primarily focused on epistemology, probability, information science, argumentation, and forensic logic).[49] Embroidering on his highly original, widely read and hotly debated book *The Probable and the Provable*,[50] Jonathan Cohen produced a clutch of important

Fingerprinting (Chicago UP 2008). For more broadly contextualizing discussion, see G Edmond, 'Reassessing Reliability' in P Roberts and M Stockdale (eds), *Forensic Science Evidence and Expert Witness Testimony* (Edward Elgar 2018); GS Morrison and WC Thompson, 'Assessing the Admissibility of a New Generation of Forensic Voice Comparison Testimony' (2017) 18 Col Sci & Tech L Rev 326; P Roberts, 'Paradigms of Forensic Science and Legal Process' (2015) 370 Phil Trans Royal Soc B Article 20140256; SA Cole, 'Forensics without Uniqueness, Conclusions without Individualization: The New Epistemology of Forensic Identification' (2009) 8 Law Prob Risk 233; MJ Saks, 'Forensic Identification: From a Faith-based "Science" to a Scientific Science' (2010) 201 Forensic Sci Int 14; MJ Saks and JJ Koehler, 'The Individualization Fallacy in Forensic Science Evidence' (2008) 61 Vand L Rev 199.

[47] See in particular T Anderson, D Schum, and W Twining, *Analysis of Evidence* (2nd edn, CUP 2005); W Twining, 'Hot Air in the Redwoods, A Sequel to the Wind in the Willows' (1988) 86 Mich L Rev 1523; W Twining, 'Taking Facts Seriously', in N Gold (ed), *Essays on Legal Education* (Toronto, Butterworths, 1982); W Twining, 'Taking Facts Seriously – Again', in P Roberts and M Redmayne (eds), *Innovations in Evidence and Proof* (Hart 2007); W Twining, 'The Boston Symposium: A Comment' (1986) 66 BU L Rev 391. Also see P Roberts, 'Rethinking the Law of Evidence: A Twenty-first Century Agenda for Teaching and Research' (2002) 55 Curr Legal Prob 297.

[48] L Jonathan Cohen was a fellow of the Queen's College, Oxford, which is right across the High Street from Zuckerman's academic home, University College, and can be seen from the window of Zuckerman's old college rooms.

[49] Vacuous as they are, any such ranking would be influenced by whether one regards attention to procedural context (undoubtedly a great strength of Zuckerman's approach, discussed below) as a trademark methodology of New Evidence Scholarship. I am doubtful: but cf B Robertson, 'Principles of Criminal Evidence' (1990) 106 LQR 510 (praising Zuckerman for 'breaking down the traditional distinction between evidence and procedure drawn by Cross', and linking his general approach to 'the "New Evidence" thinking').

[50] (OUP 1977). Cohen's Preface acknowledges 'details I discussed again and again with Dr A Zuckerman, and I owe very much to the patience and generosity with which he let me use his time'.

papers on cognition, belief and forensic process, including his Boston symposium essay.[51] It is telling, however, that neither Twining nor Cohen could be described as Law of Evidence specialists in the sense of being intimately acquainted with doctrinal sources and institutional materials and practices. This is precisely where Zuckerman led the way. Being knowledgeable in evidence law *and* theory, Zuckerman was able to combine both together to their mutual enrichment. This methodological premium can be seen, for example, in Zuckerman's distinctive approach to the right of silence, which combines attention to the logic of factual inference (gleaned, one might speculate, from Bentham[52] and Cross[53]) with an astute eye to the institutional dynamics of criminal investigations and the pragmatic requirements of effective procedural regulation.[54] Whilst his reformist strategy, dubbed 'exchange abolitionism' by critics,[55] may have perturbed criminal justice scholars with strong pro-defendant sympathies,[56] Zuckerman's general jurisprudential method clearly influenced the next generation of theoretically-inclined Evidence scholars including Andrew Choo,[57] Mike Redmayne,[58] Hock Lai Ho,[59] and David Hamer,[60] amongst many others.

The value of sustained attention to institutional context, exhibited in Zuckerman's Boston symposium paper and in several subsequent articles, leads directly to the second conceptual innovation that I want to highlight in this essay. As evidentiary discussion increasingly centres on jury verdicts, the right of silence, police interrogation and confessions,[61] unlawfully obtained evidence,[62] and

[51] Cohen, above n 32. Also see LJ Cohen, 'Should A Jury Say What it Believes or What it Accepts?' (1991) 13 Cardozo L Rev 465; LJ Cohen, 'Freedom of Proof' in W Twining (ed), *Facts in Law* (Franz Steiner 1983).

[52] See MA Menlowe, 'Bentham, Self-incrimination and the Law of Evidence' (1988) 104 LQR 286.

[53] R Cross, 'A Very Wicked Animal Defends the 11th Report of the Criminal Law Revision Committee' [1973] Crim L Rev 329; R Cross, 'The Right to Silence and the Presumption of Innocence – Sacred Cows or Safeguards of Liberty?' (1970) 11 JSPTL 66.

[54] AAS Zuckerman, 'Trial by Unfair Means' [1989] Crim L Rev 855; AAS Zuckerman, 'The Right Against Self-Incrimination: An Obstacle to the Supervision of Interrogation' (1986) 102 LQR 43.

[55] S Greer, 'The Right to Silence: A Review of the Current Debate' (1990) 53 MLR 709; S Greer and R Morgan (eds), *The Right to Silence Debate* (Bristol and Bath Centre for Criminal Justice 1990). Generally, see R Leng, 'Silence Pre-trial, Reasonable Expectations, and the Normative Distortion of Fact-finding' (2001) 5 IJEP 240; JD Jackson, 'Silence and Proof: Extending the Boundaries of Criminal Proceedings in the United Kingdom' (2001) 5 IJEP 145; D Morgan and G Stephenson, *Suspicion and Silence: The Right to Silence in Criminal Investigations* (Blackstone 1994).

[56] More recently, see H Quirk, 'Twenty Years On, The Right of Silence and Legal Advice: The Spiralling Costs of Unfair Exchange' (2013) 64 NILQ 465.

[57] Andrew Choo's Oxford DPhil thesis, supervised by Zuckerman, was published as A L-T Choo, *Abuse of Process and Judicial Stays of Criminal Proceedings* (1st edn 1993; 2nd edn OUP 2008).

[58] See in particular, M Redmayne, 'English Warnings' (2008) 30 Cardozo Law Rev 1047; M Redmayne, 'Rethinking the Privilege Against Self-Incrimination' (2007) 27 OJLS 209.

[59] HL Ho, *A Philosophy of Evidence Law: Justice in the Search for Truth* (OUP 2008).

[60] D Hamer, 'The Structure and Strength of the Propensity Inference: Singularity, Linkage and the Other Evidence' (2003) 29 Monash U Law Rev 137; D Hamer, 'Probabilistic Standards of Proof, Their Complements and the Errors that are Expected to Flow from Them' (2004) 1 UNELJ 71.

[61] AAS Zuckerman, 'Procedural Fairness During Police Interrogation and the Right of Silence' (1990) 54 J Crim Law 499.

[62] See above, n 54; AAS Zuckerman 'Illegally-Obtained Evidence – Discretion as a Guardian of Legitimacy' (1987) 40 Curr Leg Probl 55.

miscarriages of justice,[63] it becomes hard to ignore the indisputable fact that we are now chiefly concerned with evidence in *criminal* proceedings. Curiosity, if nothing else, should prompt reconsideration of what this topical refocusing might imply for the adequacy of a generic common law model of the Law of Evidence.

Institutional context: From transubstantivity to procedural differentiation

According to the standard common law model, the Law of Evidence is generic and unified or, as some US scholars put it, 'trans-substantive'.[64] That is to say, a single Law of Evidence regulates proof taking and fact-finding across all types of litigation, including criminal prosecutions, private law civil actions, family matters, and public law judicial review of administrative action. It is recognized that adaptations may be required to accommodate particular aspects of special procedural regimes, but these are regarded as exceptions to the common shared core of legal doctrines and principles. For example, criminal and civil cases have traditionally operated with different standards of proof, but this is not regarded as a serious threat to the transubstantive model. Marginal exceptions excepted, a generic and unified Law of Evidence is embraced as the default setting for evidentiary regulation in all types of legal proceeding.

The publication in 1989 of *The Principles of Criminal Evidence*, Adrian Zuckerman's landmark contribution to the well-regarded Clarendon Law Series published by Oxford University Press, issued a direct challenge to orthodox transubstantivity in the Law of Evidence. Having acknowledged a convergent epistemological investment in accurate fact-finding and a common adversarial heritage, Zuckerman nonetheless insisted on procedural differentiation:

> The law of evidence, as it is traditionally conceived, does not deal with every single legal procedure; it is confined to criminal and civil proceedings in the superior courts of the law and in magistrates' courts. However, even those procedures that the traditional law of evidence encompasses are so diverse as to make it impossible to observe any general underlying principles that might give coherence to this body of law. There are at least two distinct procedures, the criminal and the

[63] AAS Zuckerman, 'The Protection of the Accused from Miscarriages of Justice' (1997) 31 Israel Law Rev 590; AAS Zuckerman, 'Miscarriage of Justice – A Root Treatment' [1992] Crim L Rev 323; AAS Zuckerman, 'Miscarriage of Justice and Judicial Responsibility' [1991] Crim L Rev 492.

[64] See eg D Marcus, 'Trans-substantivity and the Processes of American Law' [2013] BYU L Rev 1191; S Landsman, 'Are the Federal Rules of Evidence Dynamite?' (2015) 33 BU Int LJ 343, 351–52. Zuckerman employed the term to describe nineteenth century unification of civil procedure under the Judicature Acts: see A Zuckerman, 'The Jackson Final Report on Costs: Plastering the Cracks to Shore Up a Dysfunctional System' (2010) 29 CJQ 263, 276.

civil, which are not only governed by different rules but also reflect entirely different concerns.[65]

Procedural differentiation is logical and pragmatic, Zuckerman insisted, because different rules of evidence apply to criminal and civil proceedings, respectively, and even when generic rules nominally apply they 'often undergo special modification when employed in criminal cases'.[66] Civil litigation is increasingly preoccupied with contested discovery, merging rules of evidence and procedure in a manner foreign to criminal process; and what is more, 'the parties' to criminal litigation are in reality the state and the accused, not the disputants of 'symmetrically competing claims'[67] as is typical of civil litigation. Recognizing the special role of the state in criminal prosecutions calls to mind a range of additional considerations reinforcing procedural differentiation. State officials involved in criminal investigations and prosecutions are entrusted with intrusive and coercive powers of surveillance, search, evidence-gathering (today including swabbing for DNA profiling),[68] detention, and interrogation, necessitating the provision of countervailing safeguards, such as the privilege against self-incrimination, to insulate the accused against abuse or oppression. Coupled with the primary objective of criminal adjudication, which is to censure and sanction criminal wrongdoers,[69] it becomes apparent that '[a] legal system which respects the rights of the individual has to devise a criminal procedure that affords due protection from punishment to the innocent citizen and the law of criminal evidence includes several measures for achieving this end'.[70]

Viewed in broader social and political context, criminal adjudication and the censure and punishment of offenders would not even be viable, at least in a democracy, without being able to generate some measure of normative legitimacy and social acceptance. 'Verdicts', in short, 'have to command public approval'.[71] There are many strands to this endeavour. For example, trial by lay jury is clearly an important factor in securing the public acceptability of verdicts, inasmuch as 'the people' themselves are called upon to decide whether the accused should be found guilty (a judgment with normative as well as epistemological credentials, as we have said). The form of trial process is also significant in ensuring the credibility of verdicts. As a general proposition, one may have greater confidence in the rectitude of outcomes if the process producing them is demonstrably fair, rational, and rigorous in its assessment of evidence, arguments, and claims. This is all the

[65] AAS Zuckerman, *The Principles of Criminal Evidence* (OUP 1989) 2–3.
[66] ibid 4.
[67] ibid.
[68] PACE 1984, ss 63–63U (as amended).
[69] See A von Hirsch, *Deserved Criminal Sentences* (Hart 2017); A von Hirsch, *Censure and Sanctions* (OUP 1993); A von Hirsch and A Ashworth, *Proportionate Sentencing* (OUP 2005).
[70] Zuckerman (n 65) 5.
[71] ibid 5.

more significant in criminal adjudication, given the absence of any systematic or socially credible external metric by which to assess the correctness of verdicts.[72] The upshot of these reflections (mostly rehearsing what everybody already knows), is that the more one contemplates the special public character, penal objectives, and social significance of criminal adjudication, the more sharply pronounced the contrast with routine civil litigation is drawn, not merely in incidental features, but also and especially in core values and basic procedural architecture. When systematically reviewed and squarely confronted, '[s]uch extensive differences between the law governing criminal and civil cases could hardly be accidental'.[73]

After a crisp three or four pages of argument throwing down the gauntlet to orthodox common law thinking, Zuckerman drew the logical conclusion:

> [A]s a result of numerous reforms, starting in the middle of the nineteenth century, criminal proceedings have been set on a separate course. This divergence reflects the special functions of our system of criminal justice. Consequently, whatever might have been the case half a century ago, it would be idle to pretend that today there is only one law of evidence subject merely to variations in criminal and civil proceedings. The law of criminal evidence has an independence of purpose and a cohesion of principle such that it requires a discrete treatment.[74]

The significance of this fundamental disciplinary re-conceptualization cannot be overstated, in my estimation, although the elegance, concision, and apparent simplicity of Zuckerman's original exposition may have contributed to its widespread under-appreciation and muted short-term impact. Disciplinary rethinking has immediately tangible and transparent pay-offs. Switching to an exclusive focus on Criminal Evidence makes room to accommodate new evidentiary topics and facilitates the rearrangement of old material now seen in new light. The orthodox Law of Evidence, as crystallized in—one might almost say *defined by*—Rupert Cross's authoritative textbook, does not devote entire chapters, as *The Principles of Criminal Evidence* did, to 'Proof Beyond Reasonable Doubt: The Law's Commitment to the Innocent', 'The Privilege Against Self-Incrimination', or 'Improperly Obtained Evidence', partly because these topical foci elude, and implicitly refute, transubstantivity. On the normative plane, procedural differentiation points the way towards systematic reconceptualization of criminal evidence as an applied branch of political morality, characterized by principled asymmetry (rather than presumptive equality in the application of procedural norms) and

[72] 'There is ... no external test for judging whether a criminal verdict reflects the truth. The past cannot, as it were, be revived for the purpose of checking conformity between the facts as they really happened and as they have been reflected in the verdict of the court': ibid.

[73] ibid 4.

[74] ibid 6.

animated by normative (rather than epistemic) coherence.[75] Subsequent developments in the law of criminal evidence and procedure, briefly summarized below, have amply confirmed the merits—arguably, the *necessity*—of this intellectual shift. To appreciate its radical creativity, however, we should first pause to consider how deeply transubstantivity is embedded within the common law evidentiary tradition.

There have been other texts, published before and after *The Principles of Criminal Evidence*, which have taken a procedurally differentiated approach to criminal evidence and procedure.[76] But the overwhelming weight of common law jurisprudential tradition, reflected in the array of contemporary textbooks on English evidence law,[77] lends immense ballast to the trans-substantive model. The conventional notion of a unified and generic Law of Evidence has been an article of faith for common lawyers since at least the mid-nineteenth century. Already by 1820 Best J was able to declare in *R v Burdett*:[78]

> It has been solemnly decided that there is no difference between the rules of evidence in civil and criminal cases. If the rules of evidence prescribe the best course to get at truth, they must be and are the same in all cases, and in all civilised countries. There is scarcely a criminal case, from the highest down to the lowest, in which courts of evidence do not act upon this principle.

Wigmore was emphatic in propagating this orthodoxy, insisting that '[t]here are . . . by no means two systems of rules, distinct in history and in method . . . There is but one system of rules for criminal and for civil trials'.[79] On the Wigmorean account (which subsequently dominated American common law jurisprudence, in particular), transsubstantivity was both theoretically and pragmatically sound: '[n]ot only in practice, but in principle and in spirit, there is no occasion for a distinction'.[80] In fact, Wigmore regarded any attempt to disaggregate the Law of

[75] See further, P Roberts, 'Five Foundational Fallacies of Common Law Evidence', published in Spanish (translated by Orión Vargas and Carlos Ivan Ruiz as *Cinco falacias fundacionales de la preuba en el common law*, in Grupo de Investigaciones en Derecho Procesal (ed), *La prueba: teoría y práctica* (Universidad de Medellin Press, 2019) and Chinese (translated by Ping Yang and Baosheng Zhang) (2018) 26 *Evidence Science* 93.

[76] See eg JA Andrews and M Hirst, *Andrews and Hirst on Criminal Evidence* (4th edn, Jordans 2001; 1st edn, Waterlow Publishers 1987); R May, *Criminal Evidence* (4th edn, Sweet & Maxwell 1999; 1st edn 1986); JC Smith, *Criminal Evidence* (Sweet & Maxwell 1995).

[77] Leading works include R Munday, *Cross & Tapper on Evidence* (13th edn, OUP 2018); I Dennis, *The Law of Evidence* (6th edn, Sweet & Maxwell 2017); A Choo, *Evidence* (5th edn, OUP 2018); R Glover, *Murphy on Evidence* (15th edn, OUP 2017); A Kean and P McKeown, *The Modern Law of Evidence* (12th edn, OUP 2018); HM Malek (ed), *Phipson on Evidence* (19th edn, Sweet & Maxwell 2017). At least one book has travelled in reverse: J Doak, C McGourlay, and M Thomas, *Evidence: Law and Context* (5th edn, Routledge 2018) was originally titled *Criminal Evidence in Context* (Sage 2005).

[78] (1820) 4 B & Ald 95, 122.

[79] JH Wigmore, *Wigmore on Evidence*, vol 1 (1st edn, Little, Brown & Co 1904) § 4.

[80] ibid.

Evidence into discrete institutional variants as itself an impertinent and wrong-headed fallacy ripe for refutation:

> [T]he occasional appearance, in works on the law, of the title 'Criminal Evidence' has tended to foster the fallacy that there is some separate group of rules or some large number of modifications. On the contrary, much is lost in utility in attempting a separate treatment; for most of the large principles of evidence are equally illustrated in both kinds of trials, and cannot be adequately followed, either in theory or in authority, if the precedents in either class of cases are ignored. The fallacy, however, is an inveterate one, and has had repeatedly to be repudiated . . .[81]

Wigmore's zealotry on the question of disciplinary unity may be compared, I think unfavourably, with the more nuanced position expressed twenty years earlier by Stephen, who noted that 'some of the more detailed rules of evidence . . . apply exclusively, and others most frequently to criminal cases, and . . . give much of its special character to an English criminal trial'.[82]

In this, as in so many other matters of jurisprudential controversy, comparative law affords welcome perspective. Conceptualizing the Law of Evidence as a unified field of legal scholarship and practice is a peculiarity of the common law imagination. Thayer marvelled, 'no other country has it; we alone have generated and evolved this large, elaborate, and difficult doctrine'.[83] Discovering that other major legal traditions lack any equivalent disciplinary taxonomy has even led some commentators to the preposterous conclusion that *rules of evidence* exist only in the common law world.[84] This is akin to saying that because the French don't drive on the left they don't have any cars. The orthodox common law conception of the Law of Evidence, in my view, suffers from multiple intellectual and practical deficiencies. These serious shortcomings ought to prompt scholars and practitioners alike to reconsider its continuing fitness for purpose and give serious consideration to differentiating criminal evidence and procedure from civil procedure—as Zuckerman contended, and as civilian jurists have always done.

The institutional reality of procedural differentiation is perforce more marked today than it was in 1989 when Zuckerman's *Principles* impertinently demanded foundational conceptual rethinking. At that time, PACE 1984 had only recently

[81] ibid.

[82] Sir JF Stephen, *A History of the Criminal Law of England* (Routledge 1996 [1883]) vol 1, 437.

[83] JB Thayer, *A Preliminary Treatise on Evidence at the Common Law* (Little, Brown & Co 1898) 7.

[84] See eg JW Jeans Sr, 'A Modest Proposal: Scrap the Rules of Evidence' (2007) 2 Liberty U L Rev 1, 8 ('When the fact-finder is a jurist or a tribunal of jurists, as in most European countries, there are no rules of evidence'). As WT Pizzi, 'Soccer, Football and Trial Systems' (1995) 1 Colum J Eur L 369, 370, wisely cautions, '[m]any of the generalizations that are frequently offered to describe continental trial systems—that they have no rules of evidence, that they are not adversarial, that they have no presumption of innocence, etc—are either inaccurate or misleading'.

entered into force and its evidentiary implications, which have since proven extensive and voluminous,[85] were barely being explored. Since that time, major legislative reform and an avalanche of new case-law have accumulated relentlessly. Even if generic transubstantive rules of evidence were commonplace in the century approximately bookended by Stephen's Indian Evidence Act and the last edition of *Cross on Evidence* written by Cross himself,[86] the traditional common law model is no longer even proximately faithful to the reality of contemporary procedural law and practice in England and Wales.

During the classical Stephen/Cross era there was an intuitive plausibility to treating significant chapters of evidentiary doctrine as common to all types of litigation. The rule against hearsay (and its common law exceptions), the law of presumptions and burdens[87] of proof, witness competency and credibility, privilege, collateral finality and the rule against narrative, the rules regulating expert opinion testimony, and so forth constituted a solid and substantial core of generic evidentiary law. But this convergence represented a phase in the historical evolution of common law evidence doctrine which has now passed. One way of understanding this transition is to say that a subject which was fashioned, historically, by common law judges responding on a more or less ad hoc basis to the practical challenges of litigation, has since been radically restructured through legislation. Parliament has relaxed or abolished evidentiary doctrines on the civil side,[88] whilst energetically introducing successive waves of new procedural and evidentiary rules applicable only to criminal proceedings. There has been statutory reform of police investigative procedures,[89] radical innovation in the area of 'special measures' for vulnerable and intimidated witnesses,[90] and systematic overhaul of hearsay and bad character evidence.[91] Case-law remains important, to be sure; and thanks to the indefatigable industry of the Court of Appeal (Criminal Division) and other appellate tribunals it is never in short supply. However, this burgeoning corpus of precedents and judicial guidelines is increasingly preoccupied with points of statutory interpretation confined to criminal litigation, rather than elucidating generic common law evidentiary doctrines.

[85] By my reckoning, there are over 1,000 cases invoking (or at least mentioning) a single provision, PACE 1984, s 78 (judicial discretion to exclude prosecution evidence obtained unfairly).

[86] R Cross, *Evidence* (5th edn, Butterworths 1979).

[87] As opposed to *standards* of proof, which are deviantly pluralistic on the orthodox view, as we have noted.

[88] Notably abrogating the common law hearsay prohibition: Civil Evidence Act 1995, s 1; facilitating the admissibility of expert (opinion) evidence: Civil Evidence Act 1972; and limiting the privilege against self-incrimination: Civil Evidence Act 1968.

[89] See eg Investigatory Powers Act 2016; Protection of Freedoms Act 2012; Regulation of Investigatory Powers Act 2000; Criminal Procedure and Investigations Act 1996; Police and Criminal Evidence Act 1984; and their related, ever-expanding Codes of Practice.

[90] Youth Justice and Criminal Evidence Act 1999; Coroners and Justice Act 2009.

[91] Criminal Justice Act 2003, ss 98–139.

De facto disaggregation of Evidence law has been in full swing for thirty years or more. Zuckerman was the first UK-based scholar to really grasp its implications. Two further institutional developments, which have significantly affected the law of England and Wales only since the turn of the twenty-first century, have made the divergence of criminal procedure and evidence from civil procedure more decisive and, to all intents and purposes, irrevocable. The first development is the 'human rights revolution' in English criminal procedure law precipitated by the entry into force of the Human Rights Act 1998 in October 2000.[92] From that decisive moment, traditional evidentiary doctrines and new statutory provisions have come under the scrutiny of the European Court of Human Rights (ECtHR) and have been obliged to comply with the Strasbourg Court's extensive 'fair trial' jurisprudence. Although Article 6(1) of the ECHR stipulates criteria of fairness applicable to all types of adjudication (including the threshold requirements of an 'independent and impartial tribunal constituted by law'), Article 6(2) and—especially—Article 6(3) specify detailed additional procedural requirements for fair *criminal* trials. The institutional wedge between criminal and civil proceedings is thus hammered home at the supra-national level. A second significant development of relatively recent vintage is the introduction of a set of Criminal Procedure Rules (CrimPR) in 2005. Subsequently updated at regular intervals, the CrimPR are an exemplar of what I call 'hard-working soft law': their enormous impact on the day-to-day conduct of criminal litigation is belied by their lowly formal status as delegated legislation or mere rules of court.[93] Revealingly, for our purposes, the Civil Procedure Rules (CPR) were introduced separately seven years earlier, following Lord Woolf's extensive review of civil proceedings,[94] as a discrete legislative exercise divorced from criminal procedure. In content, the two sets of rules are overlapping but substantially divergent, and even prescribe different 'overriding objectives'.[95]

The advent of the CrimPR might be regarded, in retrospect, as supplying the missing half of the procedural equation. At the operational level of real trials,

[92] P Roberts and J Hunter, 'Introduction—The Human Rights Revolution in Criminal Evidence and Procedure' in P Roberts and J Hunter (eds), *Criminal Evidence and Human Rights: Reimagining Common Law Procedural Traditions* (Hart 2012).

[93] The desirability and detailed implications of this impact are hotly contested, but its scale is beyond dispute. For contrasting evaluations, see M McConville and L Marsh, 'Adversarialism Goes West: Case Management in Criminal Courts' (2015) 19 IJEP 172; Lord Thomas of Cwmgiedd, 'The Criminal Procedure Rules: 10 Years On' [2015] Crim L Rev 395; J McEwan, 'From Adversarialism to Managerialism: Criminal Justice in Transition' (2011) 31 Legal Stud 519.

[94] Lord Woolf, *Access to Justice: Final Report to the Lord Chancellor on the Civil Justice System in England and Wales* (HMSO 1996). Now see <www.justice.gov.uk/courts/procedure-rules/civil/rules> accessed 23 January 2020.

[95] For criminal procedure, the prescribed 'overriding objective' is 'that criminal cases be dealt with justly': CrimPR, r 1. The corresponding provision in the CPR specifies 'enabling the court to deal with cases justly and at proportionate cost' as the 'overriding objective' of civil procedure. For further discussions, see P Roberts and A Zuckerman, *Criminal Evidence* (2nd edn, OUP 2010) 18–22, 35–37; A Zuckerman, *Zuckerman on Civil Procedure: Principles of Practice* (3rd edn, Sweet & Maxwell 2013) ch 1.

Criminal Procedure and Civil Procedure are now formalistically, as well as institutionally, disaggregated. Meanwhile, Law of Evidence textbooks continue to propound a mythical conception of evidentiary law that exists only in commentators' imaginations; or else, they trip over themselves repeating the solecism that criminal evidence represents an 'exception' to supposedly generic evidentiary doctrines. The fact is that the doctrinal law of criminal evidence has lately evolved into an almost entirely separate branch of procedural law, with precious little in common with its civil counterpart below the level of macroscopic normative and epistemic generalities. In England and Wales at least,[96] the traditional common law model has been transformed by events into a spectral anachronism. The argument was, to my mind, quite persuasive when Zuckerman first advanced it. Subsequent events make it compelling.

Normative sources: From evidentiary rules to principled discretion

A third major conceptual innovation in Zuckerman's thinking about evidence law in general, and criminal evidence in particular, concerns the sources and nature of evidentiary norms and their role in legal and judicial reasoning. It is important to stress that these ideas come as a package and need careful unpacking. There is nothing particularly distinctive about wanting to rid evidence law of excessive technicality, spurious distinctions, make-weight arguments, or doctrinally embedded irrationality. Cross, the author of the leading textbook on the English Law of Evidence, was barely less enthusiastic about modernist reform, rationalization, and simplification of procedural law than Bentham.[97] In fact, these rationalist objectives might plausibly be ascribed to just about any orthodox Evidence scholar or legal commentator in the analytical common law tradition. What is distinctive about Zuckerman's argument lies in the combination of what he wanted to subtract *and* add to the existing disciplinary corpus. His general preference for judicial discretion over inflexible evidentiary rules should not be equated with Benthamite

[96] For a rare concurring US voice, see MA Berger, 'Does the Search for Truth in Our Scholarship Continue in Our Classrooms?' (1998) 49 Hastings LJ 1179: '[A]n enormous split exists between our scholarship and pedagogy … In our classrooms, evidence is treated as a set of trans-substantive rules that apply across the board to all cases, except for a few carefully noted instances. The trial at which these rules apply is viewed as an isolated, disconnected moment in time. The consequence is the cutting-edge issues that most intrigue us as scholars often cannot be handled meaningfully in our classrooms'.

[97] According to W Twining, *Rethinking Evidence* (2nd edn, CUP 2006), 1, Cross once interjected into 'a heated debate about proposed reforms of Criminal Evidence' that he was working for the day when his subject would be abolished. The reforms in question were contained in the—to posterity, notorious—Eleventh Report of the Criminal Law Revision Committee on *Evidence: General*: see C Tapper, 'Evidence (General): Eleventh Report of the Criminal Law Revision Committee' (1972) 35 MLR 621.

antinomianism,[98] because Zuckerman insisted that exercises of judicial discretion should be rooted in a foundation of evidentiary *principle*. Inasmuch as criminal adjudication implements distinctively *penal* values and objectives (as opposed to the corrective, restitutory, or social justice normative frameworks structuring other types of adjudicative process), a principled approach to evidentiary regulation will necessarily reinforce procedural differentiation. In short, '[a] critical exposition of the law of criminal evidence has to be conducted by reference to *its* general principles'.[99]

Zuckerman originally proposed three core principles of the law of criminal evidence: truth discovery, protecting the innocent from conviction, and the maintenance of standards of propriety in criminal process. In *Principles'* successor, we subsequently worked this trio up into a revised 'five foundational principles of criminal evidence', adding in considerations of minimum state intervention and humane treatment and clarifying that all five principles serve the more basic objective of penal justice, ie censure and punishment of criminal wrongdoing.[100] Zuckerman advanced two main objections to the orthodox conception of evidentiary regulation as a set of exclusionary rules: firstly, he said, it presents a misleading picture of the institutional realities of law and legal practice; secondly, it is counterproductive in safeguarding foundational principles. The conventional picture is distorted because the rules, when examined more closely, are often subject to exceptions or overriding judicial discretions falsifying any expectation of their rigid and predictable application in the instant case. The rules might *appear* fixed and determinate when rehearsed in Evidence textbooks, but such appearances are deceptive:

> What is the difference between a fixed rule that may be side-stepped by the exercise of discretion when justice so requires and a declaration that the matter is governed by discretion to see that justice is done?... [I]n many contexts an explanation of the existing law in terms of such discretion is much more accurate than an exposition based on strict definitions of permissible and impermissible practices.[101]

The model of rules ill-serves institutional values in two conceptually divergent but, in their result, mutually aggravating ways. Strict application of evidentiary rules is problematic when the doctrinal law has, through judicial over-interpretation and embedded institutional wrong-turnings, become detached from

[98] On Bentham's 'anti-nomian thesis ... an attack on the idea that adjudicative decisions on questions of fact are susceptible to regulation by binding rules', see W Twining, *Theories of Evidence: Bentham and Wigmore* (Weidenfeld & Nicolson 1985), 66–75.
[99] Zuckerman (n 65) 6 (emphasis supplied).
[100] P Roberts and A Zuckerman, *Criminal Evidence* (1st edn, OUP 2004) § 1.3.
[101] Zuckerman (n 65) 11.

its underlying rationales. This occurs, for example, when perfectly reliable evidence is rejected simply because it falls into the technical definition of 'hearsay'.[102] Conversely, preoccupation with exclusionary rules crowds out other salient considerations. Foundational principles, in particular, do not figure as prominently in judicial thinking or feature as explicitly in courts' decision-making as they should do. More open and honest engagement with the discretionary reality of evidentiary practices, Zuckerman contended, would contribute to the continuous refinement of principled standards, 'bring into the open the full range of the considerations that affect judicial decisions',[103] and promote 'the development of the judicial instinct'[104] in their application. In this way, '[t]he development of guidelines for the exercise of discretion, far from weakening the protection of the innocent or undermining standards of propriety ... will promote better awareness of these important principles'.[105]

Zuckerman's conceptual innovation lay not in his *discovery* of judicial discretion in the application of evidentiary standards, but in his insistence that principled discretion should feature centrally in expository accounts of legal doctrine and in judicial reasoning. It has always been patently obvious that pockets of evidentiary doctrine involve a fair amount of judicial creativity and fact-specific determinations. Perhaps the most extreme illustration is the *res gestae* exception to the hearsay prohibition, a doctrine so amorphous and nubile that it is not even clear what the (conveniently Latin) words mean.[106] Having laboured to invest it with some sort of conceptual continence, Cross candidly wrote of *res gestae* that, 'owing to the fact that the cases in which it is employed are often ones in which the judge has a wide discretion, it is not a subject on which extreme precision is either possible or desirable'.[107] By the time that *The Principles of Criminal Evidence* appeared it was already widely appreciated that judicial discretion is an important dimension of criminal litigation,[108] Hart's general model of law as a system of rules had been challenged by Dworkin's advocacy of jurisprudential principle,[109] and the idea of 'discretion' had benefitted from extended critical exegesis.[110] Nonetheless, the tendency amongst Law of Evidence specialists to marginalize discretionary

[102] Also see AAS Zuckerman, 'The Futility of Hearsay' [1996] Crim L Rev 4.

[103] Zuckerman (n 65) 12.

[104] ibid 13.

[105] ibid.

[106] Or as Lord Wilberforce once more decorously put it, '[t]he expression "res gestae", like many Latin phrases, is often used to cover situations insufficiently analysed in clear English terms': *Ratten v R* [1972] AC 378 (PC) 388. For discussion, see D Ormerod, 'Redundant Res Gestae?' [1998] Crim L Rev 301; AL-T Choo, *Hearsay and Confrontation in Criminal Trials* (OUP 1996) ch 5.

[107] Cross, *Evidence* (2nd edn, Butterworths 1963), 480.

[108] R Pattenden, *The Judge, Discretion and the Criminal Law* (OUP 1982); *Judicial Discretion and Criminal Litigation* (2nd edn, OUP 1990).

[109] R Dworkin, *Taking Rights Seriously* (Duckworth 1977); R Dworkin, *A Matter of Principle* (OUP 1985).

[110] DJ Galligan, *Discretionary Powers: A Legal Study of Official Discretion* (OUP 1986).

decision-making as a mere afterthought or largely inconsequential supplement to the main business of stating and applying rules was obdurate. Early editions of *Cross on Evidence* flagged 'an increasing recognition of a wide field of judicial discretion with regard both to the inclusion and exclusion of evidence', but the topic merited only a half-page discussion, and concluded abruptly with the underwhelming observation that '[i]t remains to be seen whether the existence of a wide sphere of judicial discretion will be recognised in yet other branches of the English law of evidence'.[111] It is an ingrained habit in the common law tradition to think and talk of rules, not only in characterizing major doctrinal subdivisions ('the rule against hearsay', 'the opinion evidence rule', 'the similar fact evidence rule', 'the rule against narrative', 'the rule against third party admissions', etc.), but even in describing quite technical, fine-grained procedural practices and standards ('the rule in *Turnbull*',[112] 'the rule in *Browne v Dunn*',[113] 'the rule in *Hollington v Hewthorn*',[114] etc.) Zuckerman turned the tables on the traditional disciplinary model, insisting that faithful exposition should *begin with* evidentiary principles and keep them firmly in mind in the discretionary application and flexible development of the law of criminal evidence.

Three decades on, Zuckerman's argument has largely been vindicated by subsequent institutional developments, though there are some caveats and qualifications that need to be applied to the original—compactly stated—thesis, in my opinion. Five major jurisprudential innovations, none of them very predictable in the mid-1980s, are particularly pertinent in the context of criminal adjudication in England and Wales. First, the previously-mentioned Human Rights Act 1998 and ensuing 'human rights revolution' in English criminal procedure and evidence law[115] supplied English courts with new normative resources for principled argumentation,[116] and also contributed more generally to an intellectual climate in which direct appeals to principle are more commonplace, and potentially gain

[111] Cross, *Evidence* (n 107) 22–23. By the fifth edition (1979), Cross was (still) acknowledging 'increasing recognition of a wide field of judicial discretion in relation to the admissibility of evidence': above n 86, 29. Coverage had expanded to eight pages and, notably, was divided up into 'Improperly Obtained Evidence in Criminal Cases' (seven pages) and 'Civil Cases' (half a page).

[112] See eg *R v Yates* [2003] EWCA Crim 629 [25] (holding that the judicial direction challenged on appeal 'was adequate to cover the rule in *Turnbull*').

[113] *Browne v Dunn* (1894) 6 R 67 (HL); *R v M & N* [2011] EWCA Crim 1458 [48].

[114] *Hollington v F Hewthorn & Co Ltd* [1943] KB 587, CA; abolished in English civil proceedings by the Civil Evidence 1968, s 11; and superseded in criminal proceedings by PACE 1984, s 74. But cf *R v Hayter* [2005] UKHL 6, [2005] 1 WLR 605 (for a fleeting recent cameo).

[115] Roberts and Hunter (n 92).

[116] See eg P Roberts, 'Normative Evolution in Evidentiary Exclusion: Coercion, Deception and the Right to a Fair Trial' in Roberts and Hunter (eds), *Criminal Evidence and Human Rights* (Hart 2012); P Roberts, 'Criminal Procedure, the Presumption of Innocence and Judicial Reasoning under the Human Rights Act' in H Fenwick, G Phillipson, and R Masterman (eds), *Judicial Reasoning under the UK Human Rights Act* (CUP 2007). Generally, see J Jackson and S Summers, *The Internationalisation of Criminal Evidence* (CUP 2012); I Dennis, 'The Human Rights Act and the Law of Criminal Evidence: Ten Years On' (2011) 33 Syd Law Rev 333; A L-T Choo and S Nash, 'Evidence Law in England and Wales: The Impact of the Human Rights Act 1998' (2003) 7 IJEP 31.

more judicial traction, than was evident in the pre-HRA era. Secondly, numerous statutory provisions have been enacted conferring 'structured discretions' on judicial decision-makers.[117] These legislative provisions typically specify a general admissibility standard and then identify a set of potentially relevant criteria to be applied contextually to the demands of the instant case. These structured statutory discretions are, in effect, Parliament's implementation of Zuckerman's preferred technique of evidentiary regulation. Thirdly, the Court of Appeal (Criminal Division) has become a lot less rule-focussed or hidebound by precedent than it used to be in matters of procedural law. This is partly in pragmatic recognition of the truism (which courts ignore at their peril) that the application of evidentiary standards often involves inherently vague and open-ended conceptual classifications that necessarily turn on the facts of the instant case.[118] The Court of Appeal could never provide definitive rulings on the meaning of terms such as 'misconduct', 'unreliable', 'probative value', 'unfairly prejudicial', or 'adverse effect on the fairness of the proceedings' (or for that matter, 'relevant', 'evidence', or 'contrary to the interests of justice') even if it did not already have a massive caseload and stretched capacity. Fourthly, the proliferation of hard-working soft law as a bourgeoning source of evidentiary practice has up-graded the *de facto* jurisprudential status of a large miscellany of norms that are often framed in terms of general principles, competing criteria, and non-binding exhortations. The 'overriding objective' specified by the CrimPR is emblematic in this respect.[119] Finally, fifth, it bears repeating that since *Principles* was published the jurisprudence of section 78 of PACE 1984, latterly supercharged by Article 6 of the ECHR, has mushroomed beyond all anticipation into its own major chapter of evidentiary scholarship and practice.[120] Zuckerman wrote that, 'so far there has been little inclination to elucidate the principles which should govern the exercise of this discretion'.[121] We now

[117] See eg Criminal Justice Act 2003, ss 114(2), 116(2), and 117(7); Coroners and Justice Act 2009, s 89.

[118] See especially *R v Renda* [2005] EWCA Crim 2826, [2006] 1 WLR 2948 [3], where Lord Judge admonished counsel that 'the trial judge's "feel" for the case is usually the critical ingredient of the decision at first instance which this court lacks. Context therefore is vital. The creation and subsequent citation from a vast body of so-called "authority", in reality representing no more than observations on a fact-specific decision of the judge in the Crown Court, is unnecessary and may well be counter-productive'.

[119] Rule 1.1 of the CrimPR provides that '[t]he overriding objective of this procedural code is that criminal cases be dealt with justly', and then further specifies that: 'Dealing with a criminal case justly includes—(a) acquitting the innocent and convicting the guilty; (b) dealing with the prosecution and the defence fairly; (c) recognising the rights of a defendant, particularly those under Article 6 of the European Convention on Human Rights; (d) respecting the interests of witnesses, victims and jurors and keeping them informed of the progress of the case; (e) dealing with the case efficiently and expeditiously; (f) ensuring that appropriate information is available to the court when bail and sentence are considered; and (g) dealing with the case in ways that take into account (i) the gravity of the offence alleged, (ii) the complexity of what is in issue, (iii) the severity of the consequences for the defendant and others affected, and (iv) the needs of other cases'.

[120] See Roberts and Zuckerman, *Criminal Evidence* (n 95) ch 5. On the—initially unpromising—legislative history, see S Sharpe, *Judicial Discretion and Criminal Investigation* (Sweet & Maxwell 1998), 81–85; D Ormerod and D Birch, 'The Evolution of the Discretionary Exclusion of Evidence' [2004] Crim L Rev 767.

[121] Zuckerman (n 65) 352.

have over a thousand cases, scores of which make a decent stab at elucidating a principled approach to issues such as police 'entrapment',[122] deceptive custodial interrogation,[123] fair disclosure,[124] and the moral integrity of criminal procedure.[125]

Marching in step with the trajectory of recent institutional history does not necessarily put one on the right side of procedural law's *longue durée*. To the extent that excessive conceptual rigidity, doctrinal obsolescence, and bad faith rationalizations of the normatively indefensible[126] have been consigned to history's trashcan by a more principled approach to evidentiary regulation, nobody will mourn their passing. Yet that is not quite the whole of the story. Zuckerman anticipated the sceptical response that principled discretion could not achieve predictability and stability in the law or adequately safeguard procedural rights. His rejoinder denied the premise: the *existing*, ostensibly rule-based law was far from certain or predictable, since '[m]ost of the rules of evidence do not in fact provide fixed definitions of acceptable or unacceptable practices but rather lay down guidelines for decisions'[127] and what is more, 'the courts refuse to observe strict definitions when they consider the results of observance unsatisfactory'.[128] This is not entirely convincing; and Zuckerman was surely over-reaching in arguing that when admissibility decisions 'have to be justified on a case-by-case basis ... [this] will ensure that, instead of finding a convenient and often spurious exception for the purpose of admitting evidence, the trial judge has to consider the interest of the individual accused in a more open and reviewable manner'.[129] Really? The simplicity of this depiction of judicial psychology, innocent of the administrative pressures of criminal litigation and the malleability of doctrinal rationalizations, appears almost *faux naïf*; though we are now admittedly opening up complex and methodologically fraught issues, that can receive only superficial treatment in the balance of this essay.

[122] *R v Looseley; Attorney-General's Reference (No 3 of 2000)* [2001] UKHL 53, [2001] 1 WLR 2060; *R v Palmer* [2014] EWCA Crim 1681; *R v Redmond* [2006] EWCA Crim 1744, [2009] 1 Cr App R 25; *R v Jones (Ian)* [2007] EWCA Crim 1118, [2008] QB 460.

[123] *R v Mason* [1988] 1 WLR 139, CA: cf. *R v Plunkett and Plunkett* [2013] EWCA Crim 261, [2013] 2 Cr App R 2; *R v Bailey and Smith* (1993) 97 Cr App R 365, CA.

[124] *R v Boardman* [2015] EWCA Crim 175, [2015] 1 Cr App R 33; *R v Bard (and 28 others)* [2014] EWCA Crim 463.

[125] *R v S(D) and S(T)* [2015] EWCA Crim 662, [2015] 2 Cr App R 27; *R v Newell* [2012] EWCA Crim 650, [2012] 2 Cr App R 10.

[126] Zuckerman contemplated that 'the existence of strict definitions can be said to have undermined the protection of the innocent from conviction and the maintenance of standards of propriety in the criminal process. Definitions often provide the courts with an excuse for concealing the real reasons for their decisions by enabling them to take refuge in refined technical distinctions': Zuckerman (n 65) 11–12. Judicial resistance to a more principled approach could be attributed to 'a legal methodology, fast becoming the exclusive preserve of the English profession, according to which major problems of principle receive the kind of treatment that is more appropriate to the interpretation of technical tax provisions': ibid 352–53.

[127] ibid 10.

[128] ibid 11.

[129] ibid 12.

To begin with the transparency claim, one may doubt that a principled approach to evidentiary regulation will necessarily enhance public scrutiny of judicial reasoning or render its exercise more tractable to appellate supervision. Although express articulation of pertinent criteria is certainly a valuable feature of judicial deliberation, merely listing factors to be taken into account does not provide much insight into the actual processes of arriving at a decision or really explain the trade-offs made in ubiquitous judicial 'balancing'. In many ways, the more factors that are fastidiously enumerated, the more opaque the motivating or decisive considerations may become. Complexity is exacerbated by the realisation, not widely reflected in 1980s evidence law scholarship, that the interests of complainants and witnesses should also be taken into account in assessing procedural fairness[130] alongside 'the interest of the individual accused'. When the range of cognisable interests and considerations expands in this manner trial judges are often left with a variety of plausible options and a correspondingly capacious normative repertoire for rationalizing their ultimate choices, however the chips may fall in individual cases. So it is difficult to see how a methodological shift from rule to principle *in itself* makes judicial decision-making more transparent or less susceptible to bad faith rationalizations. This does not, however, contradict the plausible contention that more self-consciously principled decision-making is superior on its own intrinsic merits to formalistic rule-following (irrespective of transparency or reviewability).

The role that 'principles' do, or should, play in theoretical explanation or practical reasoning is controversial in modern normative philosophy.[131] Steadfast adherence to principles can be derided as priggishness or moral fanaticism, as where the Kantian categorical imperative against lying is 'logically' extrapolated to demand truthful betrayal of Jewish refugees' hiding place to the murderous Nazi Stormtrooper.[132] Principles, it might be said, are no less capable of misuse and normative perversity than rigid rules with 'strict definitions'. Sensibly[133] restricting ourselves to the specific institutional context of criminal adjudication in England and Wales, it is clear that contemporary procedural law routinely employs both general principles and well-specified, formalistic rules as regulative mechanisms.

[130] The standard position in English law now holds that 'fairness to the defence is of prime importance but fairness to the prosecution must also be taken into account': *R v Hayward* [2001] EWCA Crim 168, [2001] QB 862 [22]. As a basic conceptual matter, '[t]he concept of a fair trial involves fairness to the prosecution and to the public, as well as fairness to the defendant': *DPP v Meakin* [2006] EWHC 1067 (Admin) [23]. In assessing procedural fairness in the round, English courts have regard to 'the familiar triangulation of interests of the accused, the victim and society': *R v A (No 2)* [2001] UKHL 25, [2002] 1 AC 45 [38] (Lord Steyn).

[131] See J Dancy, *Ethics Without Principles* (OUP 2004); J Gardner, 'Ashworth on Principles' in L Zedner and JV Roberts (eds), *Principles and Values in Criminal Law and Criminal Justice* (OUP 2012).

[132] Cf. M Cholbi, 'The Murderer at the Door: What Kant Should Have Said' (2009) 79 Phil & Phenomenol Res 17.

[133] Because normative ethics is a vast sprawling field, and normative propositions are bedevilled by over-generalization and extrapolation to new contexts they have no business colonizing.

Many of the bright line rules, moreover, are widely endorsed, and some of them—such as the rule that the accused is never compellable in his or her own trial, even by a co-accused[134]—are about as specific, determinable, and uncontested as any legal rule could be. Other norms are agreed in principle—trials must be fair; the accused enjoys the presumption of innocence; coerced confessions are inadmissible; witnesses must not be exposed to gratuitous vilification or anguish—but controversial in their more detailed elucidation and applications. It then becomes an interesting question of institutional design to explore when the law does, and should, adopt one kind of regulative mechanism or another. Why, for example, is procedural integrity a question of general principle whereas legal professional privilege is an absolute rule?[135] This design vector is bisected by another dimension of procedural architecture, which was not very evident when *Principles* was published but has since become a major question in evidence law reform: to what extent can evidentiary rules of exclusion adequately be replaced by judicial warnings against misuses of information presented to the jury? Zuckerman presciently argued that the policies underlying some of the traditional exclusionary categories might be more effectively implemented by allowing the jury access to more (presumptively relevant) information with a careful judicial explanation of why 'the principles of criminal justice, which require resisting prejudice, reflect their own perceptions of justice'.[136] This revised approach, propounding renewed efforts to develop *effective* judicial directions[137] (under the rubric of what we later called 'forensic reasoning rules'),[138] would—Zuckerman anticipated—facilitate a shift in regulatory policy, which subsequent events have in large measure enacted:

> The availability of more effective means of persuading a jury to abide by the principles of criminal justice will make the question of admissibility less important because the tools will be in place for counteracting prejudice.[139]

[134] Youth Justice and Criminal Evidence Act 1999, s 53(4); PACE 1984, s 80(4); Criminal Evidence Act 1898, s 1(1).

[135] *R v Derby Magistrates' Court ex p B* [1996] 1 AC 487, HL; reversing, or possibly correcting, the position asserted in *R v Ataou* [1988] QB 798, CA, and reported in Zuckerman (n 65) 300, according to which 'the privilege is overridden where the information is required by an accused person to prove his innocence'. Zuckerman doubted the wisdom of the 'absolutist' stance adopted in *Derby Magistrates*, since '[i]n reality... there is no escaping the need for balancing interests', and speculated that 'the absolutist approach to legal professional privilege may well turn out to be short-lived': AAS Zuckerman, 'Legal Professional Privilege: The Cost of Absolutism' (1996) 112 LQR 535, 538, 539. In the event, English courts have steadfastly held the line (at least as regards the *admissibility* of privileged communications): *Three Rivers District Council v Bank of England (No 6)* [2004] UKHL 48, [2005] 1 AC 610; *McE v Prison Service of Northern Ireland* [2009] UKHL 15, [2009] 1 AC 908.

[136] Zuckerman (n 65) 245.

[137] Linking this point with the first conceptual innovation discussed earlier, Zuckerman complained that 'the effectiveness of judicial directions has been somewhat undermined by insufficient appreciation of the overall function of the jury... [W]ithin the law of evidence there is a dogged reluctance to accept the role of the jury as more than fact-finder': ibid 42–43.

[138] Roberts and Zuckerman, *Criminal Evidence* (n 95) ch 15.

[139] Zuckerman (n 65) 246.

For all its bold reinvention of common law tradition and impressive prognostication of future landscapes, there remains a missing dimension to this discussion, and in this respect Zuckerman might be regarded as channelling a general methodological limitation of orthodox evidentiary scholarship. Bluntly, there is too much focus on appellate decisions and not enough sociological realism about the conduct of criminal trial proceedings. Even in Crown Court practice,[140] it seems likely (as the fragmentary empirical record tends to confirm)[141] that counsel and trial judges operate according to general precepts of fair process and reasonable litigation practice, local courtroom conventions, and a shared institutional ethos expecting, and rewarding, 'adversarial' behaviour only in certain contexts and within defined limits, rather than by the strict letter of procedural law. This is not to deny any real-world significance to legal doctrine as appellate courts and law professors know and state it: rather, it is to call attention to the sociological fact that formal law, whether styled 'rules' or 'principles' (or something else), is always mediated by a set of more informal institutional understandings and behaviours, and we also need to think about *that relationship* between juridical and informal norms when we consider the propriety and effectiveness of evidentiary regulation. Whether discretionary standards of admissibility will sustain enough predictability and stability in litigation practice, for example, is not itself primarily a doctrinal question, but rather turns on how, if at all, reconceptualizing the theoretical basis of admissibility determinations will impact on subsisting courtroom routines and legal professionals' habitual working practices and expectations. Likewise, traditional common law approaches to, say, hearsay exceptions only really threaten the rule of law[142] as a practical achievement if institutional routines are incapable of making up for the absence of conceptual clarity and determinative normative guidance by improvising a reasonably stable and consistent judicial practice in borderline hearsay 'hard cases'.[143] From the perspective of institutional

[140] It is barely controversial to say that magistrates' court trials present a rather different picture of (non)compliance with formal evidentiary doctrine. Not for nothing are these characterized as 'summary' proceedings.

[141] Consider, for example, Quirk's empirical findings describing the mediated (non)impact on litigation practice of sections 34–38 of the Criminal Justice and Public Order Act 1994, regulating judicial directions on drawing inferences from silence: H Quirk, *The Rise and Fall of the Right of Silence* (Routledge 2017), 145–54.

[142] Cf. C Tapper, 'The Law of Evidence and the Rule of Law' (2009) 68 CLJ 67.

[143] The perennial question of 'implied assertions' provides the best demonstration of this diagnosis. If the logic of the majority's reasoning in *R v Kearley* [1992] AC 228, HL, had been taken seriously it should have created havoc in criminal litigation, but it did not do so because, as a practical matter, the ruling was treated as being confined to particular factual scenarios, chiefly those involving anonymous telephone calls. Conversely, section 115 of the CJA 2003, as masterfully elucidated in *R v Twist* [2011] EWCA Crim 1143, [2011] 2 Cr App R 17 should have solved the implied assertion problem in English law, but has not done so because (some) criminal practitioners and judges are still operating primarily on instinct: see eg *R v Midmore* [2017] EWCA Crim 533, [2017] 2 Cr App R 8; *R v KN* [2006] EWCA Crim 3309. For conceptually astute discussion, see D Birch and M Hirst, 'Interpreting the New Concept of Hearsay' (2010) 69 CLJ 72; C Callen, 'Interdisciplinary and Comparative Perspectives on Hearsay and Confrontation' in P Roberts and M Redmayne (eds), *Innovations in Evidence and Proof* (Hart 2007); CB Mueller, 'Incoming Drug Calls and Performative Words: They're Not Just Talking About It, Baron

sociology, then, repackaging rules as principled discretion *might* just be rearranging the disciplinary deckchairs. Only through other types of inquiry, including empirical studies of first instance proceedings, can it be discerned with any confidence whether we are sailing to our salvation in Noah's Ark or going under with the RMS *Titanic*.

The recent prominence of informal 'hard-working soft law' norms in English criminal evidence and procedure becomes salient again at this point in the discussion. Some of these provisions are formulated in sweeping terms, such that their application could easily be overextended if read out of context. This is not merely an hypothetical speculation: in one notable appeal, for example, the High Court had to remind a first instance judge that the CrimPR are not competent to erode settled common law rules of legal professional privilege.[144] Other norms are formulated as judicial 'guidance',[145] and in a perfectly laudable effort to maximize their helpfulness to practitioners, they tend to be presented in relatively loose, discursive treatments. Still other secondary norms overlap with statutory and common law evidentiary standards,[146] posing questions of selectivity, authenticity, and fidelity to the primary doctrinal corpus. It goes without saying that secondary sources have inferior constitutional pedigree, and in some instances no formal legal pedigree at all.[147] Much of their institutional value resides in the comparative ease and speed with which delegated legislation and soft law guidance can be improvised, developed, and adapted to meet unfolding contingencies, but their prosaic implementation—leveraging the *de facto* professional authority of judicial training delivered by the Judicial College[148]—occurs largely under the radar of routine democratic scrutiny.

English law is experiencing unprecedented fluidity and uncertainty in the jurisprudential constitution of modern criminal procedure. Some commentators worry that traditional principles of adversarial criminal litigation are being eroded piecemeal and almost by default, as individual judges and courts grapple with the practical exigencies of austerity policies, and in the absence of any wider public debate.[149] Zuckerman's argument for articulating and developing fundamental

Parke!' (1995) 16 Miss C L Rev 117; R Pattenden, 'Conceptual versus Pragmatic Approaches to Hearsay' (1993) 56 MLR 138.

144 *R (Kelly) v Warley Magistrates' Court* [2007] EWHC 1836 (Admin), [2008] 1 WLR 2001.

145 See especially the *Crown Court Compendium Part 1: Jury and Trial Management and Summing Up* (Judicial College, December 2018) <www.judiciary.uk/publications/crown-court-compendium-published-december-2018/> accessed 1 March 2019.

146 Notably, the Consolidated *Criminal Practice Directions 2015* [2015] EWCA Crim 1567.

147 See eg the guidance and materials provided to criminal advocates through The Advocate's Gateway, <www.theadvocatesgateway.org/> accessed 1 March 2019, which have judicial backing and are 'mandated as best practice by Criminal Practice Direction 3D.7': *R v Grant-Murray* [2017] EWCA Crim 1228 [113].

148 <www.judiciary.uk/publications/review-of-activities/> accessed 1 March 2019.

149 M McConville and L Marsh, 'Adversarialism Goes West: Case Management in Criminal Courts' (2015) 19 IJEP 172; J McEwan, 'From Adversarialism to Managerialism: Criminal Justice in Transition' (2011) 31 Legal Stud 519.

principles to structure and guide the exercise of judicial discretion in evidentiary regulation has lost none of its original currency, cogency, and vigour in this new institutional environment. In a world of fewer hard-and-fast rules, however, the project of formulating and propagating the right set of principles for criminal procedure and evidence acquires heightened, possibly existential, significance for the legitimacy of criminal adjudication.

Conclusion: Renewal in procedural jurisprudence

This essay celebrates Adrian Zuckerman's profound and lasting influence on the procedural law and scholarship of England and Wales. Having acknowledged the importance of Zuckerman's 'second career' as an expert on English civil procedure, I then ignored it to concentrate on earlier, 'phase one' work addressing more foundational jurisprudential themes (or at any rate, themes more important and interesting to me). Specifically, I identified and elaborated on three conceptual innovations concerning the (1) disciplinary domain; (2) institutional context(s); and (3) normative sources of evidence law, which I take to be especially important contributions to disciplinary thinking in evidentiary scholarship and practice. These conceptual advances may be encapsulated in terms of three correlative dynamic transitions: (1) from 'Law of Evidence' to 'Evidence and Proof'; (2) from transubstantivity to procedural differentiation; and (3) from evidentiary rules to principled discretion.

In relation to (1), I suggested that Zuckerman played a supporting but still pivotal role in the transmission of the New Evidence Scholarship to British shores, through his distinctively *jurisprudential* combination of new interdisciplinary studies of evidence and proof with more traditional doctrinal questions and materials. This first conceptual contribution, however, is something in the nature of a prelude to two further, more consequential innovations. Emphatic rejection of common law Evidence's orthodox transubstantivity in favour of procedural differentiation, focussing exclusively on the law of *criminal* evidence (2), and an inversion of the standard jurisprudential hierarchy to downgrade evidentiary rules to the servants of principled discretion (3), are unmistakably proprietary Zuckermanism. Subsequent developments in English criminal procedure law reform and practice over the last three decades have followed the trajectory of Zuckerman's disciplinary blueprint with almost uncanny resemblance. Is there any scholar better qualified as modern Evidence law's Nostradamus? Regardless, Zuckerman's reputation and esteem in our field rest on nothing so precarious or transient as fairground futurology.

In his 'first career' work on the principles of criminal evidence Zuckerman challenged us to rethink the disciplinary contours, normative foundations, and jurisprudential methodologies of common law evidence. Against the prevailing common law orthodoxy of a Thayerite model of generic exclusionary rules, Zuckerman insisted that criminal evidence should be reconceptualized as the practical wisdom of principled discretion rooted in the normative values and objectives of penal justice. That general argument, to my mind, remains entirely persuasive, eclipsing any incidental objections that some of the finer details of its original exposition have, almost inevitably, better withstood the test of time than others. If criminal adjudication and evidentiary scholarship both face new environmental stresses and agitations and an uncertain future in the coming decades (as I have intimated), litigation and legal theory are alike better equipped to cope, adapt, and survive as beneficiaries of Zuckerman's extraordinarily productive conceptual innovation.

PART II
THE FUTURE OF JUDGING

5
How Judges Decide

*Robert J Sharpe**

Introduction

In this chapter, I discuss some of factors that constrain and control judicial decision-making. The law is not always clear and while judges are sworn to follow the law, the law often does not provide them with clear guidance. I think that it is important for judges to admit that they have to make choices, to confront what influences them to decide this way or that, and to advert to the constraints on their decision-making authority. My topic gives rise to theoretic issues about the nature of law and the role of judges, but I write from the perspective of a sitting judge, not a legal philosopher. As seems appropriate for a volume dedicated to a great scholar of procedural justice, my focus will be on procedural values that constrain judges when they make decisions, the most important of which is the right of every litigant to a reasoned decision.

I begin by discussing the phenomenon of legal uncertainty and the challenge that feature of the law poses for judges, particularly in an era when most judges have lost faith in the narrowly legalistic version of formalism that formerly prevailed. I turn to the problem posed by 'hard cases' for which the law does not appear to provide a clear answer and consider the approach a judge should take to such a case. After examining formal constraints, such as the obligation to base decisions on accepted legal sources, I turn to procedural values that limit the capacity of judges to decide cases on the basis of their own personal views. The adversarial values of party definition and party presentation significantly constrain judicial choice. The enforcement of the boundaries of decision-making authority, limiting the capacity of appellate judges to interfere with the factual and discretionary decisions of trial judges, represents a significant constraint on the choices appellate judges make, while the control appellate judges exercise over the law constrains trial judges. Finally, and most importantly, I turn to the right of every litigant to a reasoned decision. I argue that the obligation to give reasons and thereby

* An earlier version of this chapter was delivered in April 2016 at a conference on judicial decision-making at The Foundation for Law, Justice, and Society, Wolfson College, Oxford. The chapter is drawn from my book, *Good Judgment: Making Judicial Decisions* (University of Toronto Press 2018) with the permission of Toronto University Press.

Robert J Sharpe, *How Judges Decide* In: *Principles, Procedure, and Justice*. Edited by: Rabeea Assy and Andrew Higgins, Oxford University Press (2020). © The editors and several contributors. DOI: 10.1093/oso/9780198850410.003.0005

expose judicial thinking to public scrutiny represents the most important constraint on judicial choice and one that operates to ensure the integrity of judicial decision-making.

Legal uncertainty

The very idea of law suggests the need for clear rules capable of producing just and predictable results to govern society and social relations. Yet one of the greatest judges of the twentieth century, Benjamin Cardozo, wrote: 'I was much troubled in spirit, in my first years on the bench, to find how trackless was the ocean on which I had embarked. I sought for certainty. I was oppressed and disheartened when I found the quest for it was futile.'[1] The ideal system, said Cardozo, would be 'a code at once so flexible and so minute, as to supply in advance for every conceivable situation the just and fitting rule'.[2] But that level of perfection, Cardozo realized, is unattainable. The judge is often confronted with the task of deciding cases for which the law seems to provide no clear answer. A different but related problem arises where the law does provide a clear answer but the result appears to the judge to be unjust.

The twin phenomena of legal uncertainty and laws that sometimes produce unjust results arise from what I believe to be an essential characteristic of law itself. Laws must be framed in terms of norms or standards that have general application. Aristotle observed that 'all law is universal'.[3] Generality gives the law its objective, rational, and systematic quality. It is what distinguishes the law, on the one hand, from judicial decisions in specific cases, on the other.

Laws set standards but they do not decide specific cases. To determine whether or how the law applies to a particular case requires the exercise of judgment. Someone must decide what the facts are, identify the relevant legal norm or standard, and then determine whether and to what extent the legal norm or standard governs. That is the role of the judge: to interpret the standard and decide whether or not it applies to the facts of the case. The need for judicial fact-finding and judicial interpretation injects a significant element of uncertainty into the law.

Aristotle also recognized that although universality is an identifying feature of law, it can also be the source of injustice. 'The law', he wrote, 'takes account of the majority of cases, although not unaware that in this way errors are made'. Despite the errors, 'the law is none the less right; because the error lies not in the law nor in the legislator, but in the nature of the case; for the raw material of human behaviour

[1] BN Cardozo, *The Nature of the Judicial Process* (Yale University Press 1921) 166.
[2] ibid 143.
[3] JAK Thomson (trs), *Nichomachean Ethics* (Penguin 1977) 1137 a-b, quoted in F Schauer, *Thinking Like a Lawyer* (Harvard University Press 2009) 28.

is essentially of this kind'.[4] In this passage, Aristotle identified a central dilemma in achieving justice under law. Universality of application is a necessary attribute of law and ensures that most cases will be justly decided. But because of the variability of the 'raw material of human behaviour', the universal legal norm will not yield just results in all cases. Needless to say, judges have a strong inclination to decide cases justly. One of the central conundrums of judging is knowing when it is best to accept a result that seems unjust in order to uphold the integrity of the universal standard, and when the standard leaves sufficient room for the judge to avoid the apparent injustice.

Law in context and legal formalism

Law is uncertain because its application is contextual. As a judge, I do not see the law as an abstraction but rather as a tool I work with to decide disputes in a practical way that achieves social peace and harmony in the real world. The proper interpretation and application of legal rules depend upon the context. To take a familiar example, the precise meaning of the law's promise of equality changes as social conditions and attitudes evolve. Same-sex relationships, not long ago criminalized, now enjoy legal protection. How did that happen? Equality has long been a cornerstone of the rule of law but its meaning takes on a changing hue as social attitudes and practices evolve.

But if the answer to the question 'what does the law say about this?' is always 'that depends upon the context', is the law rendered unstable and uncertain, and is there too much that is left subject to the perceptions, beliefs, biases, and prejudices of the judge deciding the case?

The narrow legalistic version of formalism that prevailed well into the twentieth century and that, to some extent, survives to this day, resists the idea that the meaning of the law is shaped by context. Legal formalism conceives the law to be an objective and internally coherent body of rules and principles that can be objectively derived from the text of statutes and precedents and applied deductively to decide disputes without reference to the social or political context.

While I accept that legal reasoning has a formal structure to which judges must adhere, my experience of hearing and deciding cases tells me that the law does not operate in a vacuum and that rigid adherence to the narrow legalistic formalist model misses or, even worse, conceals things that are very real and present in my work as a judge. The legal disputes I decide arise from the realities of daily life and from a wide range of changing social, economic, and political contexts. The legal texts and doctrines that I am sworn to follow and to apply, be they common law

[4] ibid.

or statutory in origin, are imbued with moral, philosophical, and social values. To pretend that the law can be mechanically applied in a purely objective, morally neutral manner would be to ignore the important question of what values actually drive and determine decisions. Judges do not decide cases entirely based on neutral, objective principles and to pretend that they do so conceals a significant component of judicial reasoning and discourages judges from reflecting upon and questioning the values they do apply.

The attack on legal formalism

For the past century, there have been waves of legal thinkers who have challenged the narrow legalistic version of the formalist ideal. The American legal realist movement of the 1920s to the 1940s undermined confidence in formalism. Realists argued that judicial decision-making essentially turns on the facts and on the personal or political biases of judges. The realists adopted an instrumentalist view that regarded law as a tool to serve broader social purposes, perhaps reflecting American legal culture's tendency to see litigation as a means of achieving legal and social reform. The realists urged greater reliance on the use of social science insights to enhance the quality of judicial decisions and to advance social, economic, and political goals.[5]

The legal realists were the forerunners of critical legal studies, critical race theory, and feminist legal theory. These diverse schools of thought are premised on progressive political attitudes and claim that conventional formal legal reasoning is incoherent, indeterminate, and based upon raw political choice. The critical legal studies movement took flight in the 1970s. Critical legal studies scholars vigorously rejected the formalist vision of law and asserted that law is radically indeterminate. They argued that as rights can be manipulated, the legal process is not a neutral tool to resolve differences on a principled basis but rather a political device to ensure the protection of vested interests.[6] Critical feminist and critical race theorists borrow, to some extent, the rhetoric of critical legal studies, but focus specifically on the evils of sexism and racism, and on the need to transform social and legal attitudes in order to achieve genuine equality.[7]

[5] See eg, K Llewellyn, *The Bramble Bush* (Oceana 1930); J Frank, 'Are Judges Human?: Parts I & II' (1931) 80 U Penn L Rev 17, 233; U Moore and T Hope, 'An Institutional Approach to the Law of Commercial Banking' (1929) 38 Yale LJ 703.

[6] See eg, D Kennedy, 'Form and Substance in Private Law Adjudication' (1976) 89 Harv L Rev 1685; R Mangabeira Unger, *The Critical Legal Studies Movement* (Harvard University Press 1983).

[7] See eg, C MacKinnon, *Sexual Harassment of Working Women* (Yale University Press 1979); J Nedelsky, 'Reconceiving Autonomy' (1989) 1 Yale JL & Feminism 7; ML Minow, *Making All the Difference: Inclusion, Exclusion & American Law* (Cornell University Press 1990); R Delgado, *Critical Race Theory: An Introduction* (New York University Press 2011).

From the other end of the political spectrum emerged the law and economics movement which shares the realist perception of law as lacking coherence or credibility as an autonomous discipline. Law and economics proponents view legal disputes as being nothing more than a point at which disparate forces and ideas compete for acceptance. Building on the utilitarian philosophy of Bentham and Mill, law and economics scholars argue that legal rules could best be explained, understood, and developed in terms of their attainment of economic efficiency.[8]

While these schools of thought have achieved less traction in Canada and the United Kingdom than in the United States, I think it would be a serious error to discount their influence. Many aspects of the once-radical realist attack have been more or less absorbed into conventional legal thinking. Most lawyers and judges now accept the notion that the law is imbued with moral, political, and social values. We accept as well that law and legal rules should be viewed and shaped in terms of the broader social, political, and economic context in which they operate. We no longer see law as a self-contained end in itself but rather as a tool that can be used to achieve social harmony, peace, and justice. We recognize that this renders the law less than certain and that there are hard cases in which the legal outcome is difficult to predict.

But if the law is uncertain in its application and its meaning depends upon the context, where does that leave the judge? Does it mean that unless I retreat to narrow legalism, a theory I reject, I have to go about my work on the basis that law is inherently indeterminate and that I can do as I please? HLA Hart aptly described these two extremes as, on the one hand, the realist 'nightmare' that judges never decide according to the law and, on the other hand, the idealist 'noble dream' that judges always decide according to the letter of the law.[9]

Some judges embrace as liberating the idea that the law is indeterminate. But others find the idea of indeterminacy unsettling and threatening. Probably most judges, including me, fit somewhere in between these two extremes. They reject the unthinking, narrow, and rigid formalism that prevailed during the early years of the twentieth century. At the same time, they realize that the abandonment of narrow legal formalism leaves them and the law they administer adrift and in constant search for an anchor to legitimate their task. As Michael Kirby, formerly a member of the High Court of Australia, put it, we search for a point 'somewhere

[8] See eg, R Coase, 'The Problem of Social Cost' (1960) 3 JL & Econ 1; G Calabresi, *The Costs of Accidents: A Legal and Economic Analysis* (Yale University Press 1970); RA Posner, *Economic Analysis of Law* (Little, Brown & Company 1973); RH Mnookin and L Kornhauser, 'Bargaining in the Shadow of the Law: The Case of Divorce' (1979) 88 Yale LJ 950.

[9] HLA Hart, 'American Jurisprudence through English Eyes: The Nightmare and the Noble Dream' in *Essays in Jurisprudence and Philosophy* (OUP 1983) 128.

between the spectacle of a judge pursuing political ideas of his or her own ... irrespective of the letter of the law, and the unrealistic mechanic deified by the strict formalists'.[10]

The practical certainty of law

Now it is important to put the question of judicial decision-making into proper perspective. We should not exaggerate the significance of the law's uncertainty by focusing exclusively on the most difficult and contentious cases that come before apex courts. As a practical matter, for most disputes, the law does provide a discernible rule by which the parties can govern their affairs. Virtually all social and economic interactions and transactions proceed without litigation on the basis of legal rules that the parties can identify, accept, and follow.[11] When disputes do arise, most settle before legal proceedings are initiated and, even when the parties do find themselves in litigation, most cases settle before trial. Of those that go to trial, most involve contested issues of fact, not law. Few trial decisions are appealed. So by focusing on difficult appellate decisions, we are looking at the very tip of the pyramid of disputes, and ignoring the vast bulk of readily resolved disputes that lie at the base.

I sit in an intermediate appellate court and a very high percentage of the cases we decide, I would say 80 to 85 per cent, fall into the category of 'error-correction'. These are cases where the issue is whether or not the trial judge erred in the application of a settled legal principle. In these cases, the law, combined with the trial judge's findings of fact and credibility, channels the debate and our decisions have little or no jurisprudential significance.

We should not become too obsessed with hard cases, the difficult, cutting-edge cases where uncertainly reigns. Our encounters with trees—the hard cases—may have caused us to lose sight of the forest—the law.[12]

Hard cases—Is there a right answer?

It must be admitted, however, that there are cases where the correct legal result is anything but clear. These are the cases that catch the headlines and that perplex

[10] MD Kirby, '"Judicial Activism"? A Riposte to the Counter Reformation' (2005) 11 Otago L Rev 1, 27.

[11] There are, however, undoubtedly some cases that settle because the law *is* uncertain and the parties decide to avoid the risk of litigation.

[12] See G Priest and W Klein, 'The Selection of Disputes for Litigation' (1984) 13 J Legal Stud 1, pointing out that as only contentious cases get litigated, they represent a biased sample of all legal events. See also, Schauer (n 3) 22.

legal theorists in search of a sound and coherent explanation for judicial decision-making. The prime example is decisions on fundamental rights and freedoms. What do we mean by equality? Liberty? Freedom of expression? The precise meaning of these rights and freedoms has been a matter of debate among politicians, lawyers, and moral philosophers for centuries and it is doubtful that we will ever arrive at a complete or settled meaning.

We realize that the direction the law takes in such cases is contingent on many factors: when the case comes before the court, who argues it, who decides it,[13] and the political climate of the day.

It is here that the once-radical but now accepted critique of the formalist model comes to the fore. I think it is important for judges to confront this difficult issue rather than hide behind the myth of strict legalism. The role of the judge is not, as Chief Justice John Roberts infamously claimed, simply that of the baseball umpire who simply calls balls and strikes.[14] Myths and fictions of that kind are dangerous, not only because they are wrong, but also because they discourage judges from being honest and reflective about the values they bring to judging.

If judges really believe that their personal views cannot influence their decisions, they will fail to make the necessary effort to put those personal biases and prejudices aside. The conscientious judge will not hide behind a façade of judicial neutrality but will engage in self-reflection, consciously striving to confront the influence of personal views and attitudes when making decisions. The judge should not pretend to be an amoral and apolitical automaton.

HLA Hart argued that in hard cases, when the law does not dictate an answer, the judge has the discretion to decide the cases 'according to his own beliefs and values' and 'to follow standards or reasons for decision which are not dictated by the law'.[15]

I accept that when the law does not dictate a clear answer, I do have a choice. But I am unable to infer that my decision-making responsibility can be accurately described as choosing from a range of equally acceptable results on the basis of my personal views and values. Indeed, Hart himself conceived of the judge's discretion as being circumscribed. He insisted that the choice the judge makes must not be arbitrary and that it should 'display characteristic judicial virtues' including 'a concern to deploy some acceptable general principle as a reasoned basis for decision'.[16]

I accept that any claim that we can confidently predict or know 'the right answer' to every case that comes before the courts is doomed to fail. Different judges see

[13] See *White v Chief Constable* [1998] 2 WWR 1509 at 1549 (Lord Hoffmann), describing an earlier decision as 'one of those cases in which one feels that a slight change in the composition of the Appellate Committee would have set the law on a different course'.

[14] J Roberts, *Confirmation Hearing on the Nomination of John G. Roberts Jr. to be Chief Justice of the United States*, 12 September 2005 (Serial No J-109-37), Washington: US Government Printing Office, 2005.

[15] HLA Hart, *The Concept of Law* (3rd edn, OUP 2012) 273.

[16] ibid 201–05.

legal issues in different ways and different judges, acting in perfect good faith and sharing an eager desire to do justice, will disagree. But when I sit down to write my reasons, I find it difficult to describe my approach as being other than to do my best to come to the legally correct decision. It seems to me that correct results are what the legal system aspires to achieve and that my working hypothesis has to be that I am in pursuit of the right answer, even though I know that I may not be able to claim with confidence that I have found it.

Many find this answer unsatisfactory. Even Ronald Dworkin, who argued that there were right answers, was driven to rely on the Hercules construct, 'a lawyer of superhuman skill, learning, patience and acumen'[17] to decide the 'hard cases' that cannot be decided 'under a clear rule of law, laid down by some institution in advance'.[18] I am no Hercules and my skill, learning, patience, and acumen are far from superhuman, yet I still must decide the hard cases.

I think that it is important for judges to focus on the noble dream, the ideals and aspirations of law, not on our shortcomings and human failings. That I am no Hercules does not relieve me from thoroughly performing my Herculean task. To carry it out in a manner acceptable in a democratic society, I must strive to identify and remain faithful to a vision of law as a coherent set of norms and standards. As a judge I work within an institutional framework that aims to achieve that aspiration: a framework that guides and disciplines the process of judicial decision-making and that seeks to limit the influence of the personal views of the judge. I have to be honest and admit that sometimes the framework only takes me so far, and that I could credibly decide the case either way. I concede that the law does not dictate one right answer, but I aspire to attain a result that displays what Dworkin calls integrity, the idea that 'the law is structured by a coherent set of principles about justice and fairness and procedural due process' and that judges must enforce those principles in every case 'so that each person's situation is fair and just according to the same standard'.[19]

I see the decision-maker's task as being constrained by the need to find a result that best comports with the fabric and texture of the legal rules and principles pertinent to the dispute. The integrity of the legal process compels me to define my responsibility in terms of providing a reasoned justification for my decision that aims to persuade the litigants, the legal community, and the public that I have reached the right result, the result that achieves justice under law, not justice according to my personal beliefs.

In hard cases, my decision will make new law. That is an awesome responsibility. To carry it out in a manner acceptable in a democratic society, I must strive to identify and remain faithful to a vision of law as a coherent set of norms and standards.

[17] R Dworkin, *Taking Rights Seriously* (Duckworth 1977) 105.
[18] ibid 81.
[19] R Dworkin, *Law's Empire* (Harvard University Press 1986) 243.

As a judge, I work within an institutional framework and a process that aims to achieve that aspiration, a framework that guides and disciplines the process of judicial decision-making.

Let me describe some of the constraints that guide me in this difficult task.

The 'artificial reason' of the law

Legal reasoning has much in common with forms of argument used outside the law.[20] Lawyers and judges use the methods of philosophy, reasoning by analogy, and logical progression from moral and ethical principles. To discern the meaning of legal doctrines, they look to history and the way the law has evolved over time. And like social scientists, they examine legal doctrine from the perspective of social values, mores, and welfare.

But while lawyers and judges draw on other disciplines to do their work, legal reasoning has distinctive features.[21]

Philosophy and the social sciences have much to teach about general principles of justice. But lawyers and judges have the special skills required to craft workable legal standards by which specific disputes may be decided in a fair and just manner. The distinctive task of the law is to move from the general to the particular and to deal with the crucially important details about the fair resolution of disputes, the precise contours of legal rights and their enforcement at the level of particular cases. So, for example, the law's commitment to the over-arching principle that promises should be kept derives from moral philosophy and social sciences such as economics. However, the important details of contract law are derived from on the ground experience of lawyers and judges resolving issues on a case by case basis.

Legal reasoning operates within a defined framework that requires arguments to have a pedigree that qualifies them as legitimate. This limits the bite of arguments lacking that pedigree and based on factors external to it. Fundamental to the very idea of law and to the nature of legal argument is that a judge's choice when deciding a case is constrained. Simply put, a judge is not free to decide cases on the basis of what seems to the judge, all things considered, to be the best possible outcome. The judge is not allowed to consider all things. The judge is charged with finding the result that best fits with the relevant legal rules and principles, not the result that comports with the judge's personal view of right and wrong.

Scientists, philosophers, and social scientists are engaged in a search for the truth unconstrained by authority. Legal reasoning is different. Sir Edward Coke, the great legal scholar and judge who fought to establish the common law constitution and

[20] The classic discussion is B Cardozo, *The Nature of the Judicial Process* (Yale University Press 1921).

[21] For an excellent discussion that has helped me shape my thinking on these issues, see Schauer (n 3).

the independence of the judiciary in the early seventeenth century, spoke of the 'artificial reason' of the law, which he distinguished from 'natural reason'. Refuting James I's claim to be the font of all justice, Coke argued that even if the King was endowed with 'excellent science', the rights of the King's subjects had to be decided not by the King using natural reason but by the judges using the 'artificial reason and judgment of law'.[22]

The 'artificial reason' of the law does not put judges and lawyers in an impossible straightjacket of strict legalism. Legal standards, I have suggested, are by nature general and open-ended. They afford judges considerable latitude to reach just results in individual cases and there is certainly scope for judges to develop the law to make it more just. The wise judge will take account of the moral, historical, and philosophical roots of the legal standards the judge is interpreting and applying. The wise judge will also probe and prod to see if there are not holes to be poked in a formal legal argument that leads to an unjust result.[23]

But wise judges must also recognize that the artificial reason of the law imposes limits on their capacity to make the world a better place. The 'pervasive formality of law'—and the 'tendency to take its rules and their words seriously even though in some cases they might work and injustice—is what distinguishes law from many other decision-making contexts'.[24]

So while I reject narrow legalism, I accept that there is a necessary element of formalism in judicial decision-making. Legal doctrine does matter and the law limits my choices even when I am trying to achieve justice in the individual case. I have to apply constitutionally valid statutes as they are written. To take a familiar example, I may not like statutory mandatory minimum sentences that require me to impose a sentence I consider to be unduly harsh, but if the statute passes constitutional muster, I have no choice.

The doctrine of *stare decisis* requires me to follow binding precedents even if I do not like the result. For example, there is a common law rule requiring 'consideration', a term indicating the exchange of something of value, to support the enforcement of a contract. Suppose that I think the need for consideration is outmoded and that all promises should be enforced. I hear a case where enforcement of a promise is resisted on the ground that there was no consideration for the promise. If I cannot fit the facts of the case into a recognized exception to the

[22] *Prohibitions del Roy* (1607) 12 Co Rep 63, quoted by J Bickenbach, 'The "Artificial Reason" of the Law' (1990) 12 Inf Log 23. See also C Fried, 'The Artificial Reason of the Law or: What Lawyers Should Know' (1981) 60 Texas L Rev 35.

[23] See A Barak, *The Judge in a Democracy* (Princeton University Press 2006) 59, 67: 'judges must not impose their own personal, subjective perceptions' but 'must aspire to reach just solutions.' And if the law seems to point to a result that contradicts the judge's sense of justice, 'the judge must retrace his footsteps' to see 'whether he has strayed from the path, for law's aspiration is to be just, and the judge's aspiration is to do justice'.

[24] Schauer (n 3) 33.

traditional consideration rule, I have no choice. Much as it may pain me to render what I consider to be an unjust result, I cannot enforce the contract.[25]

Even when deciding a hard case for which the precedents provide no clear answer, the doctrine of precedent constrains. If I make a decision in a 'hard case', my decision stands as a precedent that I, and all the other judges at or below my level in the judicial hierarchy, must follow in the future. The fact that my pronouncement will bind me, my colleagues, and the lower courts, makes me cautious. It significantly constrains my power to decide the case on the basis of my personal views and it reinforces my obligation to decide in a principled legal fashion, one that best fits with the established law and the prevailing norms and standards of our legal system.

Collegial decision-making

Another constraint is that as a judge of an appellate court, virtually every decision I make is reached through a collegial process. The process of collegial decision-making is a strong counter-weight to any tendency to be influenced by values extraneous to the law. It requires me to engage not only with the arguments presented by the litigants and the lawyers but also with any opposing views from my colleagues when we debate the case in the conference room and as we prepare our reasons for judgment. The collegial process ensures that the extraneous personal views of each individual judge are diluted; in my court, by two and sometimes four other judges and at the Supreme Court of Canada by eight others. Related to this is a kind of 'team spirit' that prevails in most collegial courts. We share a common interest in maintaining and enhancing the reputation of the institution as stable, reliable, independent, and committed to the legal integrity of its work.

Respecting the boundaries of decision-making authority

Another important constraint on judicial authority is imposed by the allocation of decision-making authority to other decision-makers. Judges operate within a legal and constitutional order that defines the decision-making powers of the various actors.

Judges must respect the decision-making authority conferred on other adjudicators. Administrative agencies and tribunals are empowered to decide myriad

[25] *Southern Pacific Company v Jensen* (1917) 244 US 205 at 221 (Holmes J): 'A common-law judge could not say, "I think the doctrine of consideration a bit of historical nonsense and shall not enforce it in my court".'

issues and disputes. Provided those agencies and tribunals are acting reasonably and within the limits of the powers they enjoy, judges must accept their decisions, even in cases where they would have decided otherwise. Trial judges are charged with the duty to find the facts and appellate judges must resist the temptation to retry the case on appeal. Here we encounter the competing principles of deference and legality.

Deference defines the measure of respect the reviewing or appellate court must accord the decision under review. Deference reminds the reviewing or appellate court that first-instance decision-makers have certain institutional advantages with respect to questions of fact, policy, and certain questions of law that are central to their mandate. Deference instructs reviewing or appellate courts to refrain from approaching the case as if they were the first-instance decision-maker. First-instance decision-makers are given a margin of appreciation, protecting their decisions from unduly strict scrutiny. This means that even if the reviewing or appellate court would have decided the case differently, ordinarily, it may not interfere with the decision unless it can say that the decision was unreasonable or infected by certain kinds of legal error.

Deference also reflects legislative supremacy and the right of Parliament and the legislatures to assign decision-making powers to administrative agencies, for example, human rights commissions, labour boards, and immigration and refugee tribunals. Provided the legislation that assigns decision-making authority does not infringe upon the constitutionally protected authority of the courts,[26] the legislator's choice must be respected.

But deference has its limits and at a certain point, confronts the competing principle of legality and the ideal of a uniform standard of justice. A reviewing or appellate court must reconcile the need to defer to first-instance decisions with the duty to ensure the overall legal integrity of the decision-making process. Reviewing and appellate courts are instructed by the principle of deference to refrain from unduly meddling with specific decisions but, at the same time, are encouraged by the principle of legality to intervene when first instance decisions do not respect the law's general standards.

Drawing the line between the principles of deference and legality has proven to be a notoriously difficult task. While this may sound like a purely technical question, it is probably the question that gnaws at my judicial conscience more than any other. The reason for that is very simple. As a judge, I am committed to the idea that every case should be decided justly. Yet the standard of review and the principle of deference instruct me on a daily basis to keep my appellate judicial hands off decisions that I would have made differently, decisions that I think are wrong but not so wrong that I can call them unreasonable.

[26] Constitution Act, 1867, ss 96–100; *Crevier v Quebec (AG)* [1981] 2 SCR 220.

My primary role as an appellate judge is to define, explain, and elucidate the law and to ensure its uniform application. When filtered through the screen of deference, this means that as an appellate judge, I apply a standard of correctness to a trial judge's conclusions in law. If I identify a legal error in the trial judge's decision, I can correct it.

On the other hand, I must accept and respect the trial judge's primary role of deciding specific disputes on their facts. I must defer to a trial judge's findings of fact and I may only reverse factual findings that exhibit a demonstrable error at the heart of the case, or to use the technical label, a 'palpable and overriding error'.[27] A palpable error is one that is obvious. For example, if there is no evidence to support a factual finding, it is obviously wrong. If one finding conflicts with another finding there is an obvious error. Speculative findings and findings based on a misapprehension of the evidence are further examples of obvious or palpable errors.[28] An 'overriding' error is one that is of sufficient gravity to 'vitiate the challenged finding of fact', in other words, an error that 'goes to the root of the challenged finding of fact such that the fact cannot safely stand in the face of that error'.[29] Errors of this nature implicate the integrity of the legal process and accordingly are not protected from appellate review. So if the finding is 'contrary, not merely to what the appellate court would have done, but contrary to what any trier of fact could reasonably have done',[30] the appellate court must intervene.

There are good reasons for the division of labour between trial and appellate courts. Let me first consider questions of law. It is basic to a sound system of justice that the law be applied uniformly to all. This is sometimes referred to as 'the principle of universality' that ensures 'that the same legal rules are applied in similar situations'.[31] Appellate courts have the duty to monitor and supervise the legal integrity of decision-making. They have an overview of the legal system and are ordinarily better placed to decide points of law than a single trial judge who is necessarily immersed in the facts and details of the specific case. Appellate decisions have precedential effect and will be binding in the future. This means that appellate judges have to focus not only on the specifics of the case but on the broader implications of the decision. This gives rise to a certain expertise in assessing how a specific ruling in one case may affect other cases in the future. Appellate courts also sit in panels of three or more judges. This ensures that points of law are decided on a collegial basis and it tends, thereby, to insulate decisions from the personal or idiosyncratic views of one judge.

[27] *Housen v Nikolaisen* 2002 SCC 33, [2002] 2 SCR 235.

[28] *Waxman v Waxman* 2004 OJ No 1765 (CA) at para 296.

[29] ibid at para 297.

[30] RJ Traynor, 'Some Open Questions on the Work of State Appellate Courts' (1957) 24 UCLR 211, 222.

[31] *Housen* (n 27) para 9.

When we turn to questions of fact, it is widely accepted that trial judges have the advantage. Trial judges are 'in the trenches' and on the front-lines of justice. They see and hear the parties and the witnesses. They watch the narrative of the case unfold and they guide the case from its start to its completion. The trial judge lives with the case for the duration of the trial, often days or weeks. This puts the trial judge in 'a privileged position'[32] to deal with issues of fact. By dealing with the dispute hands-on, trial judges gain an intimate understanding of the case. This first-hand perspective is impossible to replicate on appeal. In the words of an author cited with approval by the Supreme Court of Canada, the trial judge is 'exposed to the entire case' and gains a 'total familiarity with the evidence' which facilitates a 'far deeper' insight than is possible on appeal.[33] An appellate judge can only read the paper record. Oral argument on appeal will be time-limited. The view of the case is 'telescopic'[34] or 'myopic'[35] rather than at large.

Appeal courts are required to give deference to the trial judge's findings of fact for three reasons.[36]

First, it is unlikely that the quality of decisions on questions of fact would be improved by allowing open-ended appellate review. There is a significant risk that without the first-hand familiarity with the case that can only be gained by hearing and seeing the witnesses, appellate decisions on factual questions will be of a lower quality than those made by trial judges. So, however paradoxical it might seem, the curtailment of appeal rights and the restraint imposed on appellate judges from interfering with factual findings is motivated by a desire to get to the right result.

Second is the interest in efficiency and minimizing the cost of litigation. As there is nothing to be gained in quality, the interests of efficiency strongly favour limiting appeals on questions of fact. It would be costly and time-consuming to give appellate judges the time and resources they would require to be in the position where they could safely second-guess trial judges on questions of fact. And even then, it is unlikely that a full-blown appeal on factual issues would yield better or even equally sound results. Saddling the parties, especially litigants with limited resources, with the cost of such an appeal would be both inefficient and unfair.

I am generally wary of allowing systemic efficiency to trump individual justice. However, I accept that if the justice system is too costly, access to justice is lost and with lost access goes the protection of individual rights. Appeals are expensive and can be used by wealthy litigants to wear down their opponents. Modern civil procedure emphasizes the principle of proportionality, the idea that the nature and cost of the process should be proportionate to the value, complexity, and

[32] *Schwartz v Canada* [1996] 1 SCR 254 at para 32.

[33] RD Gibbens, 'Appellate Review of Findings of Fact' (1991–92) 13 Adv Q 445, 446, cited in *Housen* (n 27) para 14.

[34] Gibbens (n 33).

[35] Traynor (n 30) 221.

[36] *Housen* (n 27) paras 16–18, where these reasons are identified but listed in a different order.

importance of the case so that civil justice is more timely, efficient, and affordable. This curtails the unbridled pursuit of 'justice at all costs' that can put justice out of reach. Open-ended appeals could undermine the principle of proportionality and the encouragement of cost-effective justice.

The third reason for limiting appeals on questions of fact is promoting the integrity of the trial process. Allowing appeal courts to review all trial decisions on a correctness standard could undermine public confidence in the trial process. Trials would become nothing more than the first crack and if one party did not like the result they could have a second crack at the Court of Appeal. As the Supreme Court of Canada put it, an appeal should be 'the exception rather than the rule'.[37]

Trial judges have primary responsibility to find the facts. Appellate judges must respect that authority, unless the finding was unreasonable, even when they think the trial judge got the facts wrong. Many decisions by first instance decision-makers are discretionary. A judge who sits higher in the legal hierarchy may disagree with the first instance decision-maker's exercise of discretion, but if it falls within the margin of appreciation allowed by the law, the reviewing judge must swallow any personal misgivings and uphold the decision.

The obligation imposed on appellate courts to defer to the factual findings and discretionary decisions of trial judges represents a very significant discipline on appellate decision-making. Equally, the obligation of trial judges to base their decisions on the law as laid down by appellate courts disciplines the choices they make.

The evidence, the record, and the parameters of the dispute

Judges are also constrained by the way the parties have defined the dispute and by the evidence the parties have led. Party definition of the issues and presentation of the facts are fundamental features of the adversarial system. Judges do not define or shape the scope of the dispute they are to decide. That is left to the parties who have the right to plead their case as they see fit. The parties also control the evidence that is put before the court. It is only in rare and exceptional cases that a trial judge is permitted to insist that a witness be called. If a litigant decides not to advance an issue or an argument, judges almost always respect the litigant's choice, even if the judge would have presented the case differently. While modern procedural rules involve more and more judicial case-management, the parties still retain essential control over the definition of the issues and decide what evidence and arguments to present.

On appeal, the trial record is all-important and significantly constrains the appellate court. Appeal judges are reluctant to consider arguments or facts not

[37] ibid para 17.

introduced before the trial court. Allowing a losing litigant to shift ground and to advance a new argument on appeal would be unfair to the opposing party. It would also undermine the integrity of the trial process if a party was free to retry the case on a different theory or on different facts on appeal.

The discipline of reasons

There are certainly legal scholars and many lawyers and judges who doubt the efficacy of the constraints I am describing.[38] Critics acknowledge that the *form* of legal argument and judicial reasoning reflects those constraints, but argue that the form is little more than a convenient mask for what really drives judicial decision-making, namely, the judge's personal moral and political views.

That brings me to what I will describe as the discipline of reasons. The obligation to give reasons is more than a legal formality. Popular opinion is increasingly sceptical of those who have and exercise authority. The culture of transparency demands justification from all who wield power in modern democratic societies. The judiciary cannot escape the kind of scrutiny to which other public officials are exposed. The public wants to know what values, opinions, and attitudes judges bring to bear on the task of deciding cases.

This is closely related to the erosion of confidence in the legalistic ideal of the objectivity of law. One does not have to be a legal realist or part of the critical legal studies movement to be sceptical of Chief Justice Robert's claim that as a judge, he simply 'calls balls and strikes'. Because of our scepticism, we do not allow the Chief Justice to simply say 'strike'. We require him to provide a reasoned opinion based upon recognized and accepted legal sources to explain why.

The parties and the right to reasons

When the judge gives reasons, the first and, for most judges, probably the most important audience is the parties to the case and, in particular, the losing party. The parties have a right to reasons and the judge is speaking directly to them. Judges try to demonstrate as best they can that they have heard and understood the evidence, the arguments, and the relevant law, and that they have explained why one party lost and the other party won.

Litigants are entitled to reasons as a simple matter of justice and fairness. The right to a reasoned decision may be seen as an aspect of the right to be heard. As a reputed English judge observed in this regard, the most important person in the

[38] For a recent judicial perspective, see RA Posner, *Divergent Paths: The Academy and the Judiciary* (Harvard University Press 2016).

courtroom 'is the litigant who is going to lose'.[39] Without a reasoned decision to explain why the litigant lost the case, the litigant can have no confidence that the judge actually understood and grappled with the issues. As the English Court of Appeal stated: '[J]ustice will not be done if it is not apparent to the parties why one has won and the other has lost.'[40] Lord Denning explained that reasons give 'proof' that the judge 'has heard and considered the evidence and arguments' and 'has not taken extraneous considerations into account'.[41]

The Supreme Court of Canada has located the right to reasons in 'the dignity interest … an interest at the heart of post-World War II jurisprudence'.[42] An academic commentator puts it this way: '[R]easons may be regarded as an integral part of treating a disappointed litigant with the respect which his dignity as a citizen demands.'[43] In a like vein, another author states, that reasons have a 'humanizing' effect, demonstrating respect on the part of the judge towards the losing party.[44] And as Sir Robert Megarry put it years earlier: '[T]o be condemned without being understood is as bad as to be condemned unheard.'[45] We will never make the losing parties happy but a reasoned decision will be more acceptable because it demonstrates to losing parties that they were heard and that their arguments were understood and grappled with.

The appellate court and the facilitation of appellate review

For all but the judges of apex courts, the second audience when writing reasons is the Court of Appeal or the Supreme Court. Judges know that their reasons are subject to scrutiny by a higher court and that their decisions may be reversed if they reveal legal error. Judges must do their best to explain their decisions in a way that shows the higher court precisely why they decided as they did so that the higher court can exercise its oversight role and ensure that the decision comports with the law.

The requirement for reasons is formally cast by appeal courts as a means to facilitate appellate review.[46] From that perspective, reasons have an informational effect. They let the parties know why the decision was made so that they can decide whether to take the next step and appeal to a higher court. Reasons also provide

[39] RE Megarry, 'Temptations of the Bench' (1978) 16 Alta L Rev 406.
[40] *English v Emery Reimbold & Strick Ltd* [2002] EWCA Civ 605, [16].
[41] A Denning, *The Road to Justice* (Stevens and Sons 1955) 29.
[42] *R v M (RE)* [2008] 3 SCR 3, para 11.
[43] T Allan, 'Procedural Fairness and the Duty of Respect' (1998) 18 OJLS 497, 499; M Elliot, 'Has the Common Law Duty to Give Reasons Come of Age Yet?' [2011] PL 56, 62–63.
[44] M Cohen, 'Reason-Giving in Court Practice: Decision-Makers' (2007–2008) 14 Colum J Eur L 257, 258, 265.
[45] R Megarry, *Lawyer and Litigant in England* (Stevens and Sons 1962).
[46] *R v Sheppard* [2002] 1 SCR 869, 2002 SCC 26.

appellate courts with the tools they need to review trial decisions. An appellate court needs to be able to see the basis for the trial judge's factual findings and the train of legal reasoning that led to the decision. As the Supreme Court of Canada has explained, adequate reasons are essential to maintaining the boundary between the trial and appellate functions. The trial judge's 'clear articulation of the factual findings' allows the appellate court to correct errors while at the same time 'inhibiting appeal courts from making factual determinations "from the lifeless transcript of evidence, with the increased risk of factual error"'.[47]

The public and the integrity of the legal process

The third audience, especially important for apex courts, is the public, not just the wider legal community but also the public at large. Judges have to realize that their decision-making authority is an exercise of public power and that the integrity and authority of the court on which the judge sits will suffer if its decisions are not based on legally accepted standards.

Reasons make judges publicly accountable for their decisions. The public, as well as the litigants, is entitled to an explanation. The requirement of reasons may be seen as an element of the open court principle, the idea that the public has a right to attend court to see justice openly administered. Justice must not only be done, but also seen to be done.[48] As a Canadian scholar has observed, 'reasons provide a basis for ... public and political debate about the justice of the particular decision and of the underlying law that authorized it'.[49]

Reasons foster public confidence in the judicial process. The obligation to provide reasoned decisions forces judges to be transparent. The 'legal culture of justification'[50] comports with the more general culture of justification that pervades modern democratic life.[51] Reasons open the window to why a decision was made and that, in turn, assures the public that the decision was not arbitrary. The Supreme Court of Canada sees the need to provide reasoned judgments as being 'central to the legitimacy of judicial institutions in the eyes of the public'.[52] Reasons for judicial decisions are necessary to bridge the gap between judicial power and democratic legitimacy: reasons allow unelected judges to demonstrate to the public that the judicial process is legitimate and based on sound principle and

[47] *R v REM* [2008] 3 SCR 3, 2008 SCC 51 [11] quoting M Taggart, 'Should Canadian Judges be Legally Required to Give Reasoned Decisions in Civil Cases' (1983) 33 UTLJ 1, 7.

[48] *R v Sussex Justices, Ex parte McCarthy* [1924] 1 KB 256.

[49] H Stewart, 'The Trial Judge's Duty to Give Reasons for Judgment in Criminal Cases' (2009) 14 Can Crim Law Rev 19, 23.

[50] D Dyzenhaus, 'The Politics of Deference: Judicial Review and Democracy' in M Taggart (ed), *The Province of Administrative Law* (Hart Publishing 1997).

[51] J Rawls, *A Theory of Justice* (Harvard University Press 1971) 133.

[52] *R v Sheppard* (n 46) para 5.

rationality. By providing reasons and exposing to public view the basis for judicial decisions, judges provide the means for public scrutiny, accountability, and, where appropriate, criticism.

I believe that the obligation to expose one's reasons for decision to the legal community and the public at large represents a significant constraint on the exercise of judicial power. Judges are members of the legal community and the legal culture that publicly proclaims its sense of integrity, propriety, and commitment to the rule of law. Reasons cement the judge's adherence to those values and the obligation to abide by the limits they impose. By providing reasoned decisions, judges demonstrate that they are not, as the realists and judicial cynics claim, simply deciding on the basis of their own personal views but rather operating within the limits imposed by the legal regime and the judicial function. American Judge Patricia Wald explains that any temptation to reason backwards from desired result to rationale is inhibited on an appellate court: 'there are judges of other persuasions to brake the momentum; there are precedents galore that must be acknowledged and accommodated; there is always the judge's own sense of integrity toward the development of coherent law'.[53] And as EW Thomas puts it, judges 'are constrained by their adherence to the rule of law . . . [and] they will consciously strive to reach a decision which is acceptable within the bounds of that concept rather than self-indulgently impose their own will or ideal'.[54]

Reasons demonstrate that the decision was not arbitrary or based on personal whim. Reasons reflect our obligation to expose our thinking to the parties, the appeal process, the academics, the media, the public, and the politicians. If our reasons are not based upon sources and arguments accepted by the legal community or fail to abide by the relevant accepted legal norms, they will not withstand scrutiny, whether in the Court of Appeal or in the court of public opinion. Reasons thereby constrain judicial power. They limit and legitimate judicial creativity by demonstrating that judges are not simply deciding the case on the basis of their own personal views or predilections, but rather operating within the circumscribed boundaries implicit in the judicial function and imposed by the law.

Ronald Dworkin links the obligation to provide reasons with the virtue of integrity that requires all who exercise power 'to act in a principled and coherent manner toward all citizens'.[55] Reasons encourage judges 'to conceive of the body of law they administer as a whole rather than as a set of discrete decisions that they are free to make or amend one by one',[56] to avoid arbitrary distinctions between similar cases and to base the decision on a principle that forms part of 'a single, coherent scheme of justice and fairness'.

[53] P Wald 'The Rhetoric of Results and the Results of Rhetoric' (1995) 62 UCLR 1371, 1419.

[54] EW Thomas, *The Judicial Process: Realism, Pragmatism, Practical Reasoning and Principles* (CUP 2005) 248.

[55] *Law's Empire* (n 19) 165.

[56] ibid 167.

So as a judge, I see my task as being constrained by the need to find a result that best comports with the fabric and texture of the legal rules and principles pertinent to the dispute. I have to accept that there are too many gaps and holes in the fabric to provide me with a ready answer. But I do my best to complete the weave in a proper and coherent manner. While I make no philosophical claim that I have found the truth, the integrity of the legal process compels me to define my responsibility in terms of providing a reasoned justification for my decision that aims to persuade the litigants, the legal community, and the public that I did my best to reach the right result.

The logic of discovery and the logic of justification

Retired South African Constitutional Court judge Albie Sachs, by no means an unduly formalistic judge, provides a compelling explanation of the discipline of reasons. Sachs once stated: 'Every judgment I write is a lie'.[57] Why a lie? Because, according to Sachs, contrary to their appearance, '[l]egal judgments … [do] not emerge from the dispassionate placing of logical propositions in rationally ordained sequence' but rather from 'an inchoate—even chaotic—mental firmament'[58] with 'an enormous amount of random intuitive searching and a surging element of unruly, free-flowing sensibility'.[59] The final form of the judgment fails to reveal the complex mental process that the judge follows to come to a decision.

If Sachs stopped there judicial decision-making would be reduced to nothing more than a shallow charade and subterfuge for judges to decide cases on the basis of their own private and personal predilections.

But Sachs goes on to provide a valuable insight that significantly qualifies his claim that every judgment is a lie. Sachs identifies two phases of the judicial decision-making process. The first phase, the one that corresponds with intuition or the 'judicial hunch' account of decision-making, he describes as the 'logic of discovery'. The logic of discovery describes how a judge starts the mental process of sifting through the evidence and the legal arguments to come to an initial or tentative conclusion. The second phase, the 'logic of justification' reveals that the product of the initial journey of discovery will not suffice—'a discovery that cannot be justified simply cannot stand'.[60]

The sound and conscientious judge will not decide a case solely on the basis of an initial hunch or initial discovery of what seems to be the right result. The sound and conscientious judge must justify the result on the basis of what Sachs describes

[57] A Sachs, *The Strange Alchemy of Life and Law* (OUP 2009) 47.
[58] ibid.
[59] ibid 60.
[60] ibid 53.

as 'accepted principles, rules, and standards to arrive at a conclusion that is consistent with those rules, principles and standards'.[61]

Every judge has had a 'it just won't write' moment. After hearing the argument, at the 'discovery' stage, the decision seems clear. But after sitting down and trying to write reasons for a decision it becomes clear that the discovery cannot be justified. A discovery that 'won't write' cannot survive as a judgment. The judicial reasoning process that starts with intuition and flashes of inspiration must end with a reasoned judgment capable of justifying the result, even if that means, in Sachs words, 'causing [the judge] to abandon even the strongest initial intuitions . . . .'[62] Justice Ruth Bader Ginsberg of the United States Supreme Court makes a similar observation: 'A court charged with defining the law may not rely on unarticulated intuition ... the court is obliged conscientiously to reason why'.[63] Even Jerome Frank, who adhered to the 'hunch' school of jurisprudence, accepted that the discipline of reasons had to prevail: 'Often a strong impression that, on the basis of the evidence, the facts are thus-and-so gives way when it comes to expressing that impression on paper.'[64]

Conclusion

So, at the end of the day, after I have rendered my judgment in a hard case and I ask myself 'did I reach the right answer?' I am never quite sure. But I do want to be absolutely certain that my reasons demonstrate to the litigants, to the Supreme Court, and to the public at large that the parties were fairly heard; that I grappled with the arguments they made; and that I assessed those arguments and analysed them in a manner that respects the need for legal coherence and integrity, and that comports with the accepted principles and norms of our legal culture.

[61] ibid.
[62] ibid.
[63] RB Ginsburg, 'The Obligation to Reason Why' (1985) 37 U Fla L Rev 205, 207.
[64] *United States v Forness* (1942) 125 F 2d 928 (2nd Cir) at 942.

6

The Bright but Modest Potential of Algorithms in the Courtroom

Andrew Higgins, Inbar Levy, and Thibaut Lienart

Introduction

This chapter investigates the use of *algorithms and ML* as a mechanism of mitigating against inconsistency, legal error, and judicial bias in procedural and substantive decisions made by human judges. The chapter looks at the best roles for algorithms considering the types of decisions, areas of law, and the nature of legal decision-making and legal reasoning. Throughout this chapter we frequently use the common phrase AI or artificial intelligence, but it should be noted that this is a convenient, if technically inaccurate, shorthand for ML and algorithmic decision-making.

Machine learning systems play an increasing role in our everyday reality from recommendation systems to face-recognition technology. These systems are employed both by the private and the public sector worldwide, but the fairness and transparency of these systems has been questioned.[1] Recent proposals to use algorithms in the legal system still face significant challenges.[2]

This chapter considers some theoretical and practical challenges of developing and deploying ML and algorithms in the civil justice system, and where it might be necessary or desirable to maintain elements of human judgment. There are important human skills in judging, but algorithms might be able to perform some tasks as well as or better than human judges, by reducing error, the influence of bias, and achieving greater consistency.

The term 'error' in ML has a specific meaning that will not always correspond to the definition of legal error. In ML error implies that there is a metric for what

[1] DK Citron and F Pasquale, 'The Scored Society: Due Process for Automated Predictions' (2014) 89 Wash L Rev 1.

[2] See, for example, J Beatson, 'AI-Supported Adjudicators: Should Artificial Intelligence Have a Role in Tribunal Adjudication' (2018) 31(3) Can J Admin L & Prac 307–38, about the use of AI to support and enhance judicial decision-making; Australian Law Reform Commission, *Technology: What It Means for Federal Dispute Resolution* (Issues Paper No 23, 1998), for an example of an early discussion on the topic; L Al-Abdulkarim, K Atkinson, and T Bench-Capon, 'A Methodology for Designing Systems to Reason with Legal Cases using Abstract Dialectical Frameworks' (2016) 24(1) AI and Law 1–49, presenting one methodology to design and implement programs intended to decide cases, using Abstract Dialectical Frameworks (ADFs), a recent development in AI knowledge representation.

Andrew Higgins, Inbar Levy, and Thibaut Lienart, *The Bright but Modest Potential of Algorithms in the Courtroom* In: *Principles, Procedure, and Justice.* Edited by: Rabeea Assy and Andrew Higgins, Oxford University Press (2020). © The editors and several contributors. DOI: 10.1093/oso/9780198850410.003.0006

is 'good' or 'bad', 'correct' or 'wrong'. Once there is an agreed metric, it is possible to algorithmically optimise it and try to do 'better' according to that metric. This makes machine learning more suitable for certain real world tasks than others. In the world of medicine for example, the metric is often clear: medical diagnoses can be verified. The challenge is to improve the accuracy of diagnosis, its speed, and in some cases to identify high risk patients that would benefit from early medical intervention. Because humans have struggled to deal with the breadth and variety of information involved in the typical diagnostic process, substantial effort has been made to develop ML systems that can better process this information.[3] However even the case for widespread usage of AI systems in healthcare is not yet compelling. Often the human in the loop is not sure how to enter the right input into the algorithm (ie human communication and judgment cannot be bypassed altogether) and apart from rare situations where the relevant inputs are extremely clear, the algorithm does not fare much better than a human would.

In other fields, there are greater obstacles to the successful deployment of AI. In some fields there is no agreed metric, or more than one metric, which makes it difficult to identify 'errors' and difficult to 'fix' them even when identified. The complexity of the real world is not merely a product of sophisticated technologies, but also diversity in human behaviour and values. While machines use fixed rules, humans use many rules which are often contested and subject to change. Whether machine learning is capable of improving this form of 'non-scientific' decision-making is debatable, because what constitutes an improvement is itself debatable. Moreover, in inherently imperfect fields like law, even where certain metrics are agreed upon, there is no reliable technique for verifying whether they have been achieved. While it is widely accepted that the purpose of the common law trial is rectitude of decision, ie to correctly apply the law to the true facts, we have no meta-test to determine whether a trial has reached the correct result.[4]

Future options and current uses of AI in the civil justice system

At the outset of any discussion of the potential benefits and risks of AI, it is important to be clear about the potential functions that are, and are not, being proposed for technology and machine learning in the justice system. According to Margaret Boden, there are five major types of AI: (1) classical or symbolic AI;

[3] R Challen and others, 'Artificial Intelligence, Bias and Clinical Safety' (2019) 28 BMJ Quality & Safety 231–37, 231. See also (for the case of IBM's AI-powered medical technology, Watson): <https://www.wsj.com/articles/ibm-bet-billions-that-watson-could-improve-cancer-treatment-it-hasnt-worked-1533961147>; <https://spectrum.ieee.org/biomedical/diagnostics/how-ibm-watson-overpromised-and-underdelivered-on-ai-health-care>.

[4] This is why the legal trial is the quintessential form of imperfect procedural justice as Rawls described it: J Rawls, *A Theory of Justice* (rev edn, Harvard University Press 1999) 74–75.

(2) artificial neural networks; (3) evolutionary programming; (4) cellular automata; and (5) dynamical systems.[5] However, it is worth noting that this distinction between the major types of AI is controversial.

Initially, machine learning and neuroscience walked hand in hand and Boden goes as far as saying that ML originated from psychological concepts of learning and reinforcement, even though today ML no longer depends on psychology, but rather on mathematical techniques.[6]

ML is a major constituent part of what is now understood as 'AI'. ML can be considered to be a bundle of statistical algorithms; and, a neural network is only a specific case of such an algorithm. Also, ML is essentially concerned with the idea of systematically extracting exploitable information from data, and in that sense it is very much data analytics.

There are three types of machine learning: supervised, unsupervised, and reinforcement learning. For the reader's convenience, following is a description of each ML category, drawn principally from the work of Boden.[7]

In *supervised* learning, the programmer 'trains' the system by defining a set of desired outcomes for a range of inputs (labelled examples and non-examples), and providing continual feedback about whether it has achieved them. The learning system generates parameters about the relevant features. Whenever it makes an incorrect prediction, it amends its parameters accordingly. Software used to conduct discovery reviews uses this form of supervised learning.[8]

In *unsupervised* learning, the user provides no desired outcomes or error messages. Learning is driven by the principle that co-occurring features engender expectations that they will co-occur in future.[9] Unsupervised learning can be used to discover knowledge. The programmers need not know what patterns/clusters exist in the data: the system finds them for itself based on a notion of similarity.

Thirdly, *reinforcement* learning is driven by analogues of reward and punishment: feedback messages telling the system that what it just did was good or bad. Often, reinforcement isn't simply binary, but represented by numbers—like the scores in a video game. 'What it just did' may be a single decision (such as a move in a game), or a series of decisions (eg chess moves culminating in checkmate). In some video games, the numerical score is updated at every move. In highly complex situations, such as chess, success (or failure) is signalled only after many decisions, and some procedure for credit assignment identifies the decisions most likely to lead to success.

[5] MA Boden, *Artificial Intelligence: A Very Short Introduction* (OUP 2018) 5.
[6] ibid 39–40.
[7] ibid 40–41.
[8] See text to (n 11).
[9] Unsupervised learning should be understood as 'summarizing data' and 'comparing the similarity of data' which allows aggregation of data (effectively, summarizing it). Indeed there is no direct notion of whether this task is done 'well' or not. The algorithm attempts to find similarity (either given or learned) in the data and then uses that similarity to group data points.

Finally, it is important to note that reinforcement learning and supervised learning are not directed towards the same type of problems. Reinforcement learning is dynamic in the sense that it is designed to develop strategies to achieve an objective in response to changing inputs; trying to win a game against an opponent is a classic example. By contrast, supervised learning is static in the sense that it is designed to achieve an outcome with a given set of inputs; classifying scans or images or producing a diagnosis based on a range of data would be an example of this kind of ML. It follows that reinforcement learning is irrelevant to judicial decision-making; what we are really interested in is the potential for supervised learning in the court room.

Before discussing the future possibilities for AI in the court room it is also worth briefly noting the present widespread use of technology in civil justice systems. For example, there is an increasing use of discovery software which uses predictive coding to search often millions of documents and identify those documents relevant to the issues in dispute, and hence subject to disclosure.[10] Courts have sanctioned the use of these programs and in some cases even ordered their use over the objection of some parties on the grounds that there is no evidence that these software programs are any less accurate than disclosure by human reviewers and they are far cheaper and quicker.[11] Even more common is the use of legal databases as a means of storing, reviewing, and retrieving statutes, cases, and legal commentaries potentially relevant to a dispute. These un-contentious uses of technology are not within the scope of this chapter. Similarly, the 'Online solutions Court' in England that was proposed by Lord Briggs,[12] and currently being developed and rolled out incrementally by the HMCTS,[13] is a system of symbolic AI. It will operate in the form of decision trees so that litigants choose their options by box clicking, with a pre-determined result of a given input. Such a system does not involve ML or an algorithm and it therefore does not raise many of the issues discussed in this chapter.

The undoubted efficiency gains that AI could bring to civil justice are also not a focus of this chapter. Nonetheless, in tribute to Adrian Zuckerman, we feel obliged to make the quintessential Zuckerman point that whatever the limitations of AI, litigants might justifiably opt for quick and affordable algorithms, even if that involves compromising accuracy and/or transparency, as an alternative to the unaffordable, disproportionate, and often slow civil justice system that is presently available.[14]

[10] CT Nasuti, 'Shaping the Technology of the Future: Predictive Coding in Discovery Case Law and Regulatory Disclosure Requirements' (2014) 93 NC L Rev 222.

[11] See eg *Pyrrho Investments v MWB Property* [2016] EWHC 256 (Ch); *Triumph Controls UK Ltd v Primus International Holding Co* [2018] EWHC 176 (TCC); *Brown v BCA Trading Ltd* [2016] EWHC 1464 (Ch).

[12] Lord Justice Briggs, *Civil Court Structure Review: Final Report* (July 2016) Chapter 6.

[13] For current updates see <https://www.gov.uk/guidance/hmcts-reform-programme-reform-update> accessed 18 March 2020.

[14] AAS Zuckerman, 'Quality and Economy in Civil Procedure: The Case for Commuting Correct Judgments for Timely Judgments' (1994) 14 OJLS 353.

The really interesting question is whether AI would be better at *deciding* cases—not just achieving efficiency gains in processing cases, but also improving the accuracy or consistency of judicial outcomes. While there are common references to the spectre of 'robot judges', it is unlikely in the foreseeable future that there would be any serious proposals for the use of algorithms to conclusively determine cases without any human intervention. The main difficulty with such a proposal is the technical difficulties of designing algorithms that possess all the legal skills needed by a judge.

The use of 'robot judges' would also create problems of legal accountability. For example, what would be the appeal rights and processes from the decisions of a robot judge? In theory an appeal could take three forms: an appeal to another AI, which would not make much sense, because if the legal system were to have access to a superior AI then it would have been used in the lower court to begin with; an appeal to a human judge, which would also be problematic due to the different reasoning process of AI and human judges (for instance, human judges would not be able to process the same amount of information as an AI); lastly, there could be an appeal that would contest the algorithm itself (eg, arguing that there is a factor that was neglected in the model). If such appeal were to be allowed, then that would mean that future cases will be decided according to a different algorithm. In other words, the appeal decision would generate an AI precedent.

Other due process and accountability concerns about AI that have been raised in general discussion include its alleged opaque nature. It is submitted that the validity of this complaint varies depending on the type of algorithms employed. The Australian Human Rights Commission on Human Rights and Technology has criticized the lack of transparency behind the use of many algorithms:

> It is common for an algorithm to be opaque, in the sense that its operation is not usually apparent to anyone beyond the person or organisation responsible for deploying it . . . As a result, it can be difficult or even impossible to ensure accountability for anyone who is affected by an AI-informed decision.[15]

This criticism is misplaced if applied to the use of AI in legal systems. It would boil down to a complaint by one community (lawyers) that they do not understand the decision-making processes of another (in this case, the IT community using AI). The irony of such a complaint would not be lost on many lay people who find legal procedures and the law mysterious and confusing.[16] The better question is whether legal decisions rendered through HI and AI are capable of explanation, at least in

[15] Australian Human Rights Commission, *Human Rights and Technology Issues Paper* (July 2018), 31.

[16] For discussion of the challenges making law and legal process intelligible to the public see R Assy, 'Can the Law Speak Directly to Its Subjects? The Limitation of Plain Language' (2011) 38 J Law & Soc 376–404.

summary form, to the ordinary citizen, even if the technical principles and processes used to reach the decision involve such inherent complexity that they are incapable of being easily understood except by those who are fully trained within the relevant fields. In short, the legitimacy of judicial decision-making (be it HI or AI and HI in combination) requires the essence of the decision to be intelligible to the average citizen, and the exact process by which the decision was reached to be intelligible to the relevant experts.

There is, however, one form of ML algorithms where it is hard and often impossible to explain in a concise way, which is understandable to any expert or lay person, how the recommendation/decision generated by the algorithm was chosen. These are known as black box algorithms. At the technological level black box algorithms can be very successful. To see their potential value, we can consider the simple example of an assembly of experts. Let us imagine that we have a single doctor with a patient, the doctor may take a decision based on the patient's symptoms and then explain her reasoning in a concise way. Now imagine we have a room of five doctors, and we aggregate their opinion to take a decision, we might ask every single doctor how they came to their decision but it is more difficult to explain how the final decision came about. To bring the analogy back to ML, it may not be five doctors that are being used, but hundreds. Intuitively, it is not hard to see that we may be better off asking many experts and aggregating their opinion, however it also becomes increasingly difficult to explain how the ultimate decision was made. In practice, such algorithms are called 'ensemble methods' and are among the most successful supervised learning algorithms.

The lack of transparency in black box algorithms make them unsuitable for use in legal systems, although we should not forget that human judicial decision-making cannot be completely transparent either. Although the process of giving reasons for judgment promote accountability, and is a useful mechanism for the judge to test the soundness of their own intuitions,[17] practically no judgment can provide a complete account of the reasons behind a particular judgment.[18] Moreover, such a task would be impossible for any judge even if time and resources were no object given the potential influence of a judge's subconscious mind on their decisions. In other words, humans are also a 'black box', and unlike the ensemble methods used in black box algorithms—where at least all the inputs are known even if how the outcome they generate cannot be easily explained—in the case of human judgments we can never be sure whether unidentified factors influenced the outcome.

[17] RJ Sharpe, *Good Judgment: Making Judicial Decisions* (University of Toronto Press 2018) 54.

[18] In *Biogen Inc v Medeva plc* [1997] RPC 1, 45 Hoffmann LJ stated: '[S]pecific findings of fact, even by the most meticulous judge, are inherently an incomplete statement of the impression which was made on him by the primary evidence. His expressed findings are always surrounded by a penumbra of imprecision as to emphasis, relative weight, minor qualification and nuance ... of which time and language do not permit exact expression, but which may play an important part in the judge's overall evaluation.'

Fortunately, there are other AI models available where the relationship between the inputs to an AI and the outcome reached are capable of explanation. Yet AI models that use transparent reasoning processes creates another risk, namely users seeking to game the system. This phenomenon is sometimes referred to as 'adversarial learning' in machine learning, where people employ tactics designed to trick the model into producing a favourable outcome. But here too, the risk of adversarial learning is not unique to AI, nor alien to justice systems. Humans 'tricking' other humans into making decisions favourable to them is part of humanity itself. A primary function of advocacy is to find ways of persuading a decision maker to reach a favourable decision even if prima facie the relevant case law and evidence suggests a different conclusion. This is also a form of adversarial learning and one cannot reasonably deny that it sometimes works ie a decision maker reaches one decision when an objective assessment of the evidence and arguments would suggest a contrary conclusion. For the same reason while the use of AI can also raise equality and access to justice concerns where some litigants can afford better access to AI to predict the likely outcomes of the algorithms being used by the courts, one cannot ignore the fact that the playing field in many civil disputes is already grossly unequal. This is partly due to the phenomenon of repeat player litigants, typically large corporations, who are able to retain more and better lawyers than their opponents, have the capacity to choose which (problematic) cases to settle and which (helpful) cases to litigate, and shape the law in ways that favour their own interests.[19] By contrast, judicially assisted AI might actually help level the playing field provided that the technology used by courts is made readily available to all. In such a scenario, everyone would be capable of obtaining an 'opinion' as to the likely outcome that a court operated algorithm would produce in their dispute.

Given the multiple technical challenges and rule of law concerns raised by the use of 'robot judges', in the short to medium term the more realistic possibility is to use algorithms as a form of judicial assistant by designing algorithms which would suggest an outcome for a case, taking into account predetermined variables. A judge could then have regard to the algorithm's recommendation when giving their judgment—adopting the recommendation, varying it, or rejecting it outright. Even using algorithms as a 'non-binding' assistant could exert significant pressure on judges to accept the AI generated recommendation and provide an easy option for the lazy or overworked judge who has no interest or time to examine the case more closely. On the other hand, the use of algorithms to make recommendations as to the outcome could have a positive, disciplining effect on the judicial process, forcing a judge to clearly articulate the reasons why the recommendations of an algorithm should not be accepted. In turn this would lead to a body of case law identifying relevant factors in deciding whether to depart from the algorithm's

[19] For a famous description of the phenomenon see M Galanter, 'Why the Haves Come Out Ahead: Speculations on the Limits of Legal Change' (1974) 9 Law &Soc Rev 1.

recommendation, taking into account the strengths and weaknesses of both HI and AI. In the next section we consider some of those relative strengths and weaknesses.

Ability of AI to perform and improve specific legal tasks

Considering whether AI assisted judging could produce better legal decisions than judges alone requires us to have a proper understanding of legal expertise. But what constitutes legal expertise is far from straightforward. Even trained lawyers have different 'favourite' judges suggesting that there is no consensus as to the mix of skills that make the perfect judge. In psychological terms, expertise is defined as the ability to develop skilled intuition, acquired when people store experience-based information, to be accessed quickly, when relevant.[20] While using expertise, human experts often access their intuitive, fast cognitive system to make judgments, rather than their slow, deliberative, calculative system.[21] This is already different from algorithmic expertise that is based, in principle, on logic and calculation. Two conditions for acquiring human intuitive judgment skills that reflect true expertise are: (1) an environment that is sufficiently regular to be predictable; and (2) an opportunity to learn these regularities through prolonged practice.[22] A good example of expertise is chess players. It is estimated that chess masters and grandmasters store about 50,000 chess positions in their memory, to be applied when relevant. It takes about ten years to develop this kind of expertise.[23] Chess, however, is an extreme example of regularity—a set board, players, and clear rules. The legal environment does not have such regularity. In the legal sense, expertise may include not only practice in reading legal documents, for example, but also experience in the real world, due to the social nature of the law and the people subject to it. This is reflected in applying legal standards meant to be grounded in community standards and in judging the credibility and motivations of parties and witnesses.

The social nature of law is also inherently linked to the process of legal reasoning. Not only is legal reasoning necessary to explain the outcome of legal decisions (an issue further discussed below), but legal reasoning is also a skill that is a necessary condition for the development of legal systems, especially in the common law world. As explained by Levi:[24]

[20] See RP Larrick and DC Feiler, 'Expertise in Decision-Making' in G Keren and G Wu (eds), *Wiley Blackwell Handbook of Judgement and Decision-Making* (John Wiley & Sons Ltd 2015) 696, 697.

[21] D Kahneman, *Thinking, Fast and Slow* (Allen Lane 2011).

[22] D Kahneman and G Klein, 'Conditions for Intuitive Expertise: A Failure to Disagree' (2009) 64(6) Am Psychol 515, 519.

[23] N Charness and others, 'The Role of Deliberate Practice in Chess Expertise' (2005) 19 Appl Cogn Psychol 151; F Gobet and H A Simon, 'Recall of Random and Distorted Chess Positions: Implications for the Theory of Expertise' (1996) 24 Mem & Cogn 493.

[24] EH Levi, 'An Introduction to Legal Reasoning' (1948) 15(3) UCLR 501.

> In an important sense legal rules are never clear, and, if a rule had to be clear before it could be imposed, society would be impossible. The mechanism accepts the differences of view and ambiguities of words. It provides for the participation of the community in resolving the ambiguity by providing a forum for the discussion of policy in the gap of ambiguity.

This quote underlines the need for the community to be involved in the resolution of legal ambiguity, as that resolution often requires a debate on controversial social questions. These social issues cannot simply be decided based on existing data (judgments) fed into a model since the process must allow for legal developments and social change.

Interpretation

One legal skill arguably beyond the realm of artificial intelligence is that of interpretation. Language skills are integral to legal expertise. The law is expressed in language, and the meaning and interpretation of language is frequently the focus of legal debates. This is a part of the judicial function. Different words could mean different things in different contexts and the judge must use her discretion in any given set of circumstances in order to give the legal norm its practical meaning.[25] Algorithms face a formidable challenge when 'interpreting' laws or evidence since AI cannot understand language. The use of natural language processing (NLP), for example, poses real difficulties. This is because under a system of supervised learning, humans have to label vast amounts of data to enable the machine to 'understand' language; and, under unsupervised learning the results of a machine scanning raw data might be unstructured and useless for human need.[26] Nonetheless, others are more optimistic about the ability of AI to develop NLP skills using semi-supervised training and even through artificial neural networks.[27] For example, a novel study that used Natural Language Processing tools, managed to predict the outcome of cases tried by the European Court of Human Rights based only on textual content.[28] The study was set to predict whether a particular Article of the European Convention on Human Rights (ECHR) has been violated, given textual evidence extracted from a case. The researchers used textual features to train Support Vector Machine (SVM) classifiers (a form of supervised

[25] Sharpe (n 17) 54.

[26] B Sheppard, *Incomplete Innovation and the Premature Disruption of Legal Services* (2015) MICH. ST. L. REV. 1797.

[27] Adrian Zuckerman can be considered one of the optimists on this point : see A Zuckerman, 'Artificial Intelligence—Implications for the Legal Profession, Adversarial Process and the Rule of Law' (2020) LQR (forthcoming).

[28] N Aletras and others, 'Predicting Judicial Decisions of the European Court of Human Rights: A Natural Language Processing Perspective' (2016) 2 PeerJ Comput Sci 93.

learning), with high accuracy of 79 per cent on average. Even though this study was successful in predicting legal outcomes, it is limited to a specific context in which the text extracted from the legal documents bore a sufficient number of similarities. As explained in the paper:[29]

> The judgments of the Court have a distinctive structure, which makes them particularly suitable for a text-based analysis. According to Rule 74 of the Rules of the Court a judgment contains (among other things) an account of the procedure followed on the national level, the facts of the case, a summary of the submissions of the parties, which comprise their main legal arguments, the reasons in point of law articulated by the Court and the operative provisions. Judgments are clearly divided into different sections covering these contents, which allows straightforward standardisation of the text and consequently renders possible text-based analysis.

Since this is a form of supervised learning, the algorithm is able to learn which phrases are common in this type of decisions, but the algorithm still cannot understand their meaning. Not only that, but it would be difficult to apply this technique to all legal fields, considering that judges have different writing styles and that they are normally not limited to a specific format. Perhaps, in future, in certain cases, a standardized format of judgments would be mandated in order to allow its analysis by an algorithm.

Applying legal standards

The illusive nature of legal expertise also flows from the nature of law, and particularly the nature of legal rules. Even though the idea of law suggests the need for clear rules, that produce just and predictable results in order to govern society, in reality many legal rules are uncertain in scope, and in some areas no rules have yet been developed. As noted by Justice Robert Sharpe, 'Judges are confronted with the task of deciding cases for which the law seems to provide no clear answer'.[30] This uncertainty is often a result of the need to maintain flexibility, since there are circumstances that cannot be predicted in advance. For this reason, clear rules could lead to unjust results: precise rules would inevitably be over-inclusive and under-inclusive in different situations.[31] This possibility informs the rules versus standards debate, and in particular whether legal norms should be formulated as ex ante rules or as ex post standards. While rules are more certain, standards (eg,

[29] ibid.
[30] Sharpe (n 17) 53.
[31] ibid 53, 55.

'reasonable', 'proportionate', 'just') allow for more flexibility in their application. It is doubtful whether AI would be better at applying standards than a human judge because in deciding whether a standard has been met or breached, judges must draw on ill-defined principles and complex social and political ideas.

Experience and empathy

Life experience and the ability to empathize are qualities often looked for in judicial appointments. When running for President, then Senator Obama identified empathy as a key criterion for future appointments that he would make:

> [W]e need somebody who's got the heart, the empathy, to recognize what it's like to be a young teenage mom. The empathy to understand what it's like to be poor, or African-American, or gay, or disabled, or old. And that's the criteria by which I'm going to be selecting my judges.[32]

In the Canadian Supreme Court case *R v S (RD)*, Cory J stated that:

> The requirement for neutrality does not require judges to discount the very life experiences that may so well qualify them to preside over disputes ... Indeed, even if it were possible, a judge free of [their] past experience would probably lack the very qualities of humanity required of a judge.[33]

On its face, however, there are tensions between the ideal of the wise, experienced judge and the notion that justice is blind. Indeed, formal statements of the role of the judge suggest judges should have an automaton like ability to exclude *all* their own prior knowledge and experience when deciding the case before them based solely on the evidence and legal arguments presented to them. In the leading English case of *Locabail v Bayfield Properties Ltd* the English Court of Appeal defined the role of the judge as follows:[34]

> All legal arbiters are bound to apply the law as they understand it to the facts of individual cases as they find them. They must do so without fear or favour, affection or ill will, that is without partiality or prejudice. Justice is portrayed as blind not because she ignores the facts and circumstances of individual cases but because she shuts her eyes to all considerations extraneous to the particular case.

[32] In a speech to the Planned Parenthood Conference in Washington, DC: C Dann, 'Obama on Judges, Supreme Court', *NBC News* (17 July 2007) <http://firstread.nbcnews.com/_news/2007/07/17/4439758-obama-on-judges-supreme-court> accessed 6 July 2017.

[33] *R v S (RD)* [1997] 3 SCR 484 [119] (Cory J).

[34] *Locabail (UK) Ltd v Bayfield Properties Ltd* [2000] QB 451 [2].

For the same reason, there is an obvious tension between the claim that a judge should decide cases solely based on the evidence presented to them, and the claim that humans will always be better judges than algorithms. This issue is further examined below when considering the potential of algorithms to reduce the influence of bias. The notion that judges are blind is rarely taken literally even by those who maintain that judges should never decide cases based on their experiences and views that have been shaped by them. An interesting middle ground position between the idea that judges bringing their own experience to the role represents good judging, and that a judge's experience is always irrelevant to the case before them, is the concept of 'vicarious experience' (ie observing and understanding the experiences of others) and the idea that observing the experience of others, typically through representing a wide variety of clients in practice, is a valuable judicial skill. This concept was suggested by Lord Sumption in a controversial speech in 2012, in which he proclaimed that 'Racial identity or gender are not relevant to a candidate's ability to do the job.'[35] Lord Sumption went on to argue that through intelligent social observation, judges were capable of showing empathy to those who find themselves in situations that the judge is unlikely to have experienced themselves:

> No judge, from whatever background he or she may come, can ever claim personal experience of more than a tiny proportion of the situations which he or she is called upon to consider. Most judicial experience is necessarily vicarious and always will be ... We quite rightly expect judges to understand the position of, for example, asylum seekers, immigrants, and other socially disadvantaged categories, without personal experience of being in their position.[36]

Recognizing that human experience is always limited, but the ability to empathize with others is considered an important judicial skill, is it possible that algorithms could perform the quintessentially human trait of 'understanding the position' of others, as Lord Sumption puts it, even better than a human judge could? Notwithstanding ML's inability to experience anything directly, ML is capable of amassing levels of vicarious experience beyond that of any human, and to take it into account in *all* decision-making in a way that humans sometimes fail to do. In this regard, it is well known that humans can suffer 'empathy fatigue' or 'compassion fatigue', and the phenomenon extends to professionals, such as those working in health care fields.[37] This is one example

[35] Lord Sumption, 'Home Truths about Judicial Diversity' (Bar Council Law Reform Lecture, 15 November 2012) 4.

[36] ibid 19.

[37] CR Figley, 'Compassion Fatigue: Toward a New Understanding of the Costs of Caring' in BH Stamm (ed), *Secondary Traumatic Stress: Self-care Issues for Clinicians, Researchers, and Educators* (The Sidran Press 1995) 3–28.

where the assumed strengths and weaknesses of HI and AI are not always neatly separated.[38]

Probability and standard of proof

Courts frequently need to resolve disputed questions of fact when deciding cases before them. In the absence of admissions, such factual findings are invariably derived from probability estimates: what are the chances that X happened, X will happen, or that X would have happened but for Y? There is no obvious reason to believe that algorithms would be *less* accurate than a human judge when answering these questions, although that is partly because in many instances neither the assessment of a human judge or an algorithm can be verified. Some disputed questions of fact relate to issues for which there is very limited evidence and limited means of testing it: the archetypal example being he said/she said disputes. An algorithm may not be well suited to determining credibility of a witness, which is widely accepted to be more art than science.[39] Equally, there is not much concrete evidence that humans can reliably detect when a witness is lying or telling the truth.[40]

Whether algorithms could be more accurate in determining disputed questions of fact than the human judge depends in large part on the sources of data available, and the probative value of data that algorithms could synthesize more effectively (at least quantitatively) than a human judge.[41]

Accurate fact finding in complex and large scale litigation usually requires a fact finder to 'digest' very large amounts of information, sometimes hundreds of thousands and millions of pages. One of the more obvious advantages of an algorithm over a human judge is its ability to process vast amounts of information. Humans often suffer from 'cognitive overload' due to their limited cognitive capacities. This is relevant in many legal cases, where there is often a high volume of materials which not only requires long hours of human labour to review, but it also makes it more likely that a human error would occur during the processing of information, due to cognitive fatigue.[42] Many lawyers will have heard of the litigation tactic

[38] As observed by Margaret Boden, AI is not only an attempt to imitate the human brain, but it also taught us a lot about it: 'AI has enabled psychologists and neuroscientists to develop powerful theories about the human brain.' (n 5) 2.

[39] *R v S (RD)* [1997] 3 SCR 484 [128] (Cory J).

[40] People are only slightly better than chance at detecting lies. See: CF Bond Jr and BM DePaulo, 'Accuracy of Deception Judgments' (2006) 10(3) Pers Soc Psychol Rev 214–34. Not only that but sometimes witnesses are not even aware they are 'lying', as human memory is fallible and can be easily distorted. See, for example: EF Loftus, 'When a Lie Becomes Memory's Truth: Memory Distortion after Exposure to Misinformation' (1992) 1(4) Curr Dir Psychol Sci 121–23.

[41] This is because human could suffer from information overload: I Levy, 'Simplifying Legal Decisions: Factor Overload in Civil Procedure Rules' (2017) 41 Melb UL Rev 727. See discussion below.

[42] For more on information overload see: R Marois and J Ivanoff, 'Capacity Limits of Information Processing in the Brain' (2005) 9(6) Trends Cogn Sci 296–305; NK Malhotra, 'Information and Sensory

of trying to 'drown' an opponent in a paper storm. This is simply not an obstacle for AI.

A more speculative benefit of AI is whether it can be used to process information that is traditionally not taken into account by a court but may still be relevant to the issues in dispute. In most cases the additional data that an algorithm might be able to utilize is population wide data involving the same variables and similar fact patterns from which inferences can be drawn as to the likely outcome in a specific case. In many instances population wide data can be highly probative of the facts of an individual case: there is a high probability that a smoker's lung cancer is caused by their smoking,[43] and there is a high probability that if a person contracted mesothelioma it is caused by asbestos even if a person is not even aware of any asbestos exposure.[44] Use of probability estimates in biological or other scientific processes is one thing. But probability assessments also raise philosophical questions about the autonomy of individuals. Is it fair to judge the likely actions of individuals based on what others typically do in similar situations even if it is a reliable predictor?[45] In this regard, algorithms would have to address exactly the same kinds of dilemmas that lawyers confront when considering the relative probative and prejudicial value of certain propensity evidence, or just the plain fairness of taking into account certain categories of evidence. This includes the fairness of taking into account population wide data as well as the far older[46] problem as to whether it is fair to have regard to one's past actions in determining what they have done or are likely to do in the future?[47] It is doubtful that AI can meaningfully contribute to this fairness debate, for the reasons set out above. Similarly, while an algorithm may be able to produce probability estimates as to the likelihood of a certain state of affairs, turning these estimates into a binary legal decision (proven or not proven) would

Overload. Information and Sensory Overload in Psychology and Marketing' (1984) 1(3–4) Psychol Mark 9–21; MJ Eppler and J Mengis, 'The Concept of Information Overload: A Review of Literature from Organization Science, Accounting, Marketing, MIS, and Related Disciplines' (2004) 20(5) Inf Soc 325–44; D Bawden and L Robinson, 'The Dark Side of Information: Overload, Anxiety and Other Paradoxes and Pathologies' (2009) 35(2) J Inf Sci 180–91.

43 *Surgeon General's Report: The Health Consequences of Smoking* (Centers for Disease Control and Prevention 2004) <https://www.cdc.gov/tobacco/data_statistics/sgr/2004/index.htm> accessed 18 March 2020.

44 See eg IJ Selikoff, J Churg, and EC Hammond, 'Relation between Exposure to Asbestos and Mesothelioma' (1965) 272 N Engl J Med 560–65.

45 The potential to be damned by association—and hence by geography, class, race, gender, etc—is substantial. To use an example relevant to the criminal sphere, were an algorithm takes into account a defendant's postcode for crime statistics, it would become evidence that they were more likely to have committed the crime, but also that they were more likely to be the victim of a crime. Even if the data were to produce more reliable probability estimates, the potential for injustice is obvious. The risk of algorithms exacerbating inequalities through 'nasty feedback loops' has been highlighted by others, especially in the field of public policy: C O'Neil, *Weapons of Math Destruction: How Big Data Increases Inequality and Threatens Democracy* (Broadway Books 2016).

46 Given the limited availability of population wide data historically.

47 For a controversial example of what English criminal law does with 'bad character' evidence see: Criminal Justice Act 2003, s 101.

be an altogether different and much more complex task. This problem is familiar territory for lawyers. The challenge of converting probability estimates into legal judgments should not present lawyers with too many difficulties given we are used to dealing with evidential uncertainty. Indeed, in the civil sphere lawyers often express the relevant standard of proof in mathematical terms: 'more likely than not'. The key point is that AI cannot replace the rules on standards and burdens of proof used to allocate the *risk* of error as between the parties.

Reducing inconsistency and bias

Although fairness may remain an alien concept to AI for the foreseeable future, there are two distinct contributions that AI could make to the fairness of the judicial process quite apart from AI's ability to improve the accuracy of judicial decisions. Both contributions centre on the reliability of machine learning that no human judge can hope to match. In particular AI has the ability to consistently replicate outcomes using the same or similar inputs, no matter their number or complexity. Put simply, machine learning is really good at achieving consistency, even with a vast amount of complicated data.

A fundamental objective of law is equal treatment before the law, which in turn requires treating like cases alike and different cases differently. Achieving this goal requires a metric of similarity and this requires human guidance. However, once a metric of similarity is established, machine learning is capable of handling and synthesizing non-identical inputs. Given much of the business of first instance courts involves handling routine matters involving similar fact patterns an algorithm could work well in these contexts. Moreover, the effect of the trend towards mass living in the modern world ought not be overlooked. The rise of mass production, mass marketing, mass consumption, and even mass law means courts are increasingly determining the same questions in multiple proceedings.[48] In such cases the rule of law requires consistent outcomes, and machine learning could help courts achieve this goal.

We should be clear that consistent outcomes, however, do not necessarily mean correct outcomes. It is here that the trade-off in machine learning is arguably most obvious and controversial. If the inputs used by machine learning include cases decided by human judges in an imperfect justice system, some of which are correct and some of which are wrong, an algorithm is going to aggregate and average out these results so that all decisions are mostly right (or a little wrong). By contrast, an imperfect human justice system, where there are no reliable meta tests for

[48] For further discussion of the implications of multiplicity for civil justice systems see A Higgins 'The Rule of Law Case Against Inconsistency and in Favour of Mandatory Legal Process' (2019) OJLS <https://doi.org/10.1093/ojls/gqz015>.

determining decision, is very likely to deliver a mixture of both correct and incorrect decisions. Because it is impossible to verify which decisions are correct and which decisions are wrong—certainly where judgments are based on questions of fact—using machine learning to achieve consistency in an imperfect justice system inevitably involves sacrificing the correctness of some decisions to mitigate the extent of error in others. Of course, this trade-off is an unappealing option when AI is compared against an idealized Judge Hercules,[49] but when AI is compared with the outcomes produced by real justice systems compromising many different judges with different levels of experience, ability, and temperament the AI consistency/accuracy trade-off looks more attractive. The case for AI generated consistency is arguably even stronger in the context of judgments based on discretion, where it is accepted that there are no right or wrong answers except in extreme cases where a judge's discretion might be said to have miscarried.

The other related area where AI may contribute to the fairness of judicial decisions is in mitigating against the effects of bias. The reason does not lie so much in the effectiveness of machine learning, but in the limitations of human decision-making which renders all judgments, even by those trained to make judgments, subject to the influence of implicit bias. What constitutes relevant evidence and what constitutes irrelevant biases, even judged from an exclusively legal standpoint, is a subject that is more complex than one might at first imagine. This issue is beyond the scope of this chapter,[50] but one key point is worth emphasizing as it is highly relevant to the question of whether AI could improve judicial decision-making. While the formal role of the judge in English law implicitly assumes judges are capable of acting as automatons,[51] the literature on cognitive biases demonstrate, and even the courts accept,[52] that this ideal is unattainable in practice for no judge is a blank canvas and a judge's experiences and knowledge do influence their decision-making even if they are trained to ignore them. There are more than a few examples in the cognitive psychology literature that show that judges can be influenced by extraneous factors when judging cases. Psychological studies, including studies of judges, suggest that the influence of life experiences, and the values, intuitions, and implicit biases that those experiences create, is an inevitable part of judging. Judges are trained professionals, but their decisions are inevitably affected by human nature.[53] While many judges now undertake potentially useful implicit

[49] R Dworkin, *Law's Empire* (Harvard University Press 1986).

[50] A Higgins and I Levy, 'Judicial Policy, Public Perception, and the Science of Decision Making: A New Framework for the Law of Apprehended Bias' (2019) 38(3) CJQ 376–99.

[51] *Locabail* (n 34).

[52] One famous example comes from Judge Frank in 1943 in which he observed that if bias and partiality were defined to mean the total absence of pre-conceptions in the mind of the judge, then no one has ever had a fair trial, and no one ever will: *Re JP Linahan*, (1943) 138 F 2d 650 (2d Cir). See also BN Cardozo, *The Nature of the Judicial Process* (Yale University Press 1921) 12–13, 167

[53] See, for example, J Rachlinski and others, 'Does Unconscious Racial Bias Affect Trial Judges?' (2009) 84 Notre Dame Law Rev 1195.

bias training,[54] it is impossible to completely eliminate the human element from judicial decision-making given that the decision-makers are, after all, human beings. For example, a study in the United States suggests that judges with daughters are more likely to vote in favour of women's rights than judges who only have sons.[55] According to the study the 'daughter effect' is most pronounced among male judges appointed by Republican Presidents. Importantly there is evidence to suggest that the life experiences of other judges can also affect court decisions, at least where those other judges are on the same bench. Another US study found that the presence of one woman on three-judge appeals panel increased the success rate for female complainants in sexual discrimination cases compared to all male panels.[56,57]

These studies demonstrate that variables external to the legal case, such as gender, can have an effect on legal decisions. This is where AI models might be useful, by helping to distil relevant legal considerations while leaving other, irrelevant factors out of the equation. On the other hand, an algorithm risks building in the biases of its creator and even amplifying these biases.[58] The fact that algorithms and ML only have the 'experiences' and 'intuitions' that their programmers provide them with creates two tantalizing possibilities. First, could we neutralize the effect of human biases in judgments by designing an algorithm that effectively incorporates the effects of *all the biases* as reflected in all of the judgments? This would not be an achievable goal in current circumstances because it depends on their being a diverse judiciary producing judgments influenced by a diverse range of experiences—which at present we do not have.[59] Even were the judiciary to be more diverse, and thus the pool of judgments would be subject to a broader range of implicit biases, there is also the disturbing possibility that rather than neutralizing the effect of these biases, aggregating the data could have an additive effect on the biases in them, producing an algorithm that is prejudiced against everyone for some reason or another. While such an algorithm may be technically even handed as between the parties, whether it would render fairer judgments is a different

[54] See, for example: American Bar Association, 'Judges: 6 Strategies to Combat Implicit Bias on the Bench' (September 2016) <https://www.americanbar.org/publications/youraba/2016/september-2016/strategies-on-implicit-bias-and-de-biasing -for-judges-and-lawyer.html> accessed 23 May 2019.

[55] A Glynn and M Sen, 'Identifying Judicial Empathy: Does Having Daughters Cause Judges to Rule for Women's Issues?' (2015) 59 AJPS 37–54.

[56] J Perisie, 'Female Judges Matter: Gender and Collegial Decision Making in the Federal Appellate Courts' (2005) 114 Yale Law J 1759–90; B McLachlin, '*Why We Need Women Judges*' (International Association of Women Judges, Sydney, Australia, 3–7 May 2006).

[57] Higgins and Levy (n 51).

[58] The risk of discrimination in AI-informed decisions was recently raised in an AHRC report on Human Rights and Technology: Australian Human Rights Commission, *Human Rights and Technology Issues Paper* (July 2018).

[59] For current statistics on the limited diversity within the English judiciary see: <https://www.judiciary.uk/wp-content/uploads/2019/07/Judicial-Diversity-Statistics-2019.pdf> accessed 18 March 2020. The number of women judges varies depending upon judicial role but is well below 50 per cent for all judicial roles. The level of minority ethnic representation on the judiciary varies between 5 and 15 per cent depending on judicial role. Diversity levels are better within Tribunals.

matter. The other possibility that has attracted some attention is whether an algorithm could be 'de-biased' to make it, for example, gender blind and colour blind by removing all references to race and gender from the relevant data. This exercise could, however, fail if there is other data available to the algorithm that is strongly predictive of the very same characteristics (eg postcode, salary, employment history, level of deprivation might also correlate closely with race). A more realistic possibility is to use an algorithm to emulate decision-making by past judges and then test the extent to which those judgments might be dependent on certain characteristics such as race. For instance, a judge could ask for an estimated ruling from an algorithm based on all available earlier judgments. The judge could then ask for the same estimated ruling if keeping all else equal, the race of the claimant or defendant is changed. Such an exercise (variations of which are already being used to assess the relative treatment of ethnic minorities in the justice system[60]) could confirm whether there is an institutional discrimination and the potential extent of it, but it would fall to human judges, and lawyers, to decide how to respond to those results—whether it be in the instant case or implementing wider reforms more generally. In other words, while AI can highlight discrimination, it cannot solve the problem of what to do about it.

Ossification and innovation—Correcting the data

It is a common saying, even amongst those with limited understanding of AI, that an algorithm is only as good as the data available to it. One of the downsides of AI's ability to perform consistently is that it necessarily involves a lack of innovation, and similarly leads to the entrenchment of wrong decisions. One of the strengths of judge made common law is that wrong decisions can effectively be expunged from the body of case law that constitutes 'good law'. Similarly, the courts can update the law to take account of changes in values, social practices, and technology. AI cannot do any of this yet without human intervention.

Here too, however, the limitations of AI should not be overstated. Of course, where human judges decide to change the law, the data sets used in an algorithm will need to be revised to take account of the new decisions and remove previous decisions no longer considered good law. And like human judge's departing from the recommendations of AI in individual cases, humans revisiting and revising the inputs of an algorithm would need to do so as part of a careful deliberative process supported by clear reasons. Certainly, it is safe to assume that algorithms that use commands and data (specifically judgments) generated by humans subject to

[60] See for example: 'Statistics on Race and the Criminal Justice System 2016', A Ministry of Justice publication under Section 95 of the Criminal Justice Act 1991 <https://www.gov.uk/government/statistics/race-and-the-criminal-justice-system-2016> accessed 23 May 2019.

explicit and implicit biases, would require regular review and modification to remove, or at least minimize, the influence of these biases. Once legal change or error is established, however, it would not be a problem for ML to implement the new approach by invalidating past data and to train the ML on the new rule.

Conclusion

The use of algorithms and ML in the legal world is still underdeveloped. While the use of digital tools is becoming more and more common, it is difficult to imagine an algorithm that would completely replace the judicial function, for a number of reasons, including the significance of language comprehension in the legal profession. AI cannot presently replicate the full panoply of legal skills required for judicial decision-making, quite part from the legitimacy and accountability concerns raised by robot judges. Nonetheless as a tool in the judiciary's toolkit for determining disputes, algorithms offer several substantial advantages. Given a proper algorithm design and enough data, algorithms and ML could improve the consistency of legal decision-making, reduce cognitive overload in cases with vast amounts of information and documents, and streamline the judicial work. We therefore believe that an addition of an algorithmic judge to judicial panels might not be a bad idea, provided that an AI recommendation could always be varied or rejected by a human judge, and that the resulting judgment, and the influence that AI played in it, would also be subject to appeal. In a sense, HI combined with AI could be a new form of judicial diversity.

PART III

CULTURE, TECHNOLOGY, AND A NEW PARADIGM FOR PROPORTIONALITY

7

The Civil Online Court in England

Michael Briggs

This chapter provides only a snapshot in a fast-moving story. It will be out of date even before it is published. In ten years' time it will read either as a timid groping towards the greater thing that has come to pass, or as a wistful attempt to foretell what might have been. This is because the online court, though much trumpeted, has yet truly to be born. It is a concept which, if fully realized, will revolutionize civil procedure and transform access to justice. But it is at the time of writing still just around the corner. There is already a story to tell, about its origins, the void which it may fill, the hopes of its progenitors, and the fears of its detractors. I was lucky to have been given a small walk-on part at a pivotal moment in its gestation, since it was the centre-piece in the reforms of the English civil jurisdiction being considered at the time of my Civil Courts Structure Review (CCSR), in 2015–16.[1] I did what I then could to encourage it. But I claim no credit at all for its invention or design.

The phrase online court has yet to acquire a settled meaning. It is certainly not confined in its ambition to civil courts. There is already Online Divorce, Online Probate, at least two largely online tribunals, and the criminal courts are moving online from paper at a spectacular rate. Aspects of the work of the UK Supreme Court are now online. Nor is the concept of an online court or tribunal one confined to England. Indeed there is at least one overseas jurisdiction well ahead of us, from which we are gratefully learning. But my experience (and lack of time to do proper research) confines me to focus mainly upon the English (and Welsh) civil online court, recently, if less than snappily, named Online Civil Money Claims (OCMC).

It is necessary to start with a perception of what the OCMC is not. It is not merely a digitized version of the existing civil court, still operating under the same procedural rules, but merely replacing that part of the process currently carried out on paper with a means of communication online, although that will be an important and beneficial part of it. Nor is it to be a completely online process of dispute resolution, entirely replacing oral communication, courtrooms and hearings, as may be found for example in the dispute resolution facility offered by eBay to its customers. Nonetheless many, even the majority, of claims are likely to be resolved

[1] See, as Lord Justice Briggs, 'Civil Courts Structure Review: Interim Report' (December 2015) and 'Civil Courts Structure Review: Final Report' (July 2016). Both available at: www.judiciary.uk.

Michael Briggs, *The Civil Online Court in England* In: *Principles, Procedure, and Justice*. Edited by: Rabeea Assy and Andrew Higgins, Oxford University Press (2020). © The editors and several contributors.
DOI: 10.1093/oso/9780198850410.003.0007

without any need for those kinds of oral process, as indeed they are at present. It is certainly not (at least in the minds of its current designers) intended that decisions by judges should be replaced by any form of Artificial Intelligence (AI).

Rather the online court may best be seen as a new digital platform, upon which the resolution of (initially small) civil claims may be achieved, by choice from a variety of routes (including ADR) of the one best suited to each claim, in which the improved facilities for efficient communication and triage which digital offers over paper will be available to enable court users, court officers, and judges to participate with greater efficiency, better speed, and at reduced cost.

Origins

The fact that a civil online court is now in the process of design, testing, and roll-out to court users may be seen as the result of the coming together of a number of separate strands. The first is the inexorable march of technology. An ever-increasing range of ordinary tasks are now, optionally or even compulsorily, carried out online as part of daily life in the UK. These range from retail banking, consumer purchases, ordering groceries, booking cinema tickets, and renewing insurance at the mundane end, to buying and selling homes, completing tax returns, credit checks, and mortgage applications as well as securities and commodities trading at the more sophisticated end. Many people, and most young people, treat social media and email as their primary means of remote (ie non face to face) communication, and regard the post box just as the repository for unwanted advertisements and bills. Communication with a court, and with opponents in civil litigation, may fairly be regarded as lying at the more complicated and occasional end of remote communication. Nonetheless, but for the current reforms of the civil courts, the procedure for the conduct of civil litigation would have come to be regarded as increasingly out of touch and even anachronistic by continuing to use paper and the occasional telephone call as the only means of remote communication, and by requiring a face to face encounter in situations where most comparable transactions are carried out remotely.

The importance of the technology strand is not limited to the mere replacement of paper and oral address by digital substitutes. Key to the unlocking of an online court is the capacity for digital technology to provide facilities which paper and voice simply cannot manage, or at least not without prohibitive expense and delay. They include triage, asynchronous ('chat line') conversation, instant payment, and the proof of identity. Of these triage may, at least at present, be the most important.

Those who now complete tax returns online will know how greatly the complexity of the old paper form has been simplified by triage. That is the ability of the online form to respond to the answering of questions by automatically presenting relevant pages (in the form of screens) for completion, while omitting all those pages which the answer to the question makes irrelevant. In the context of civil claims, triage enables the court to probe the court user's case by presenting successive questions in successive screens automatically selected by the user's answers, so as to convert what may start out as an incoherent grievance into something which the court, the opposing party and the judge may understand, respond to, and eventually resolve. The underlying design of the triage process resembles a decision tree.

This process of triage has revolutionary potential in at least three respects. The first is that it reduces the need for the court to return incorrectly completed forms from a flood to a trickle. The early statistics gathered from the first public testing of Online Divorce are said to have reduced the rate of returned forms from over 40% to about 0.4%. This is because the triage process is programmed to refuse to permit a form to be sent (and particular pages to be treated as completed) where there are outstanding questions which have not been answered in an intelligible way.

The second is that online triage can enable lay court users to communicate directly with the court about simple claims without the constant need for the intervention of a lawyer. It is a tool which will enable court users to articulate their case in a way which the court can understand. This facility, more than any other, is what is likely to transform access to justice in small civil cases, where the current need for professional assistance makes small claims prohibitively expensive both to make and to defend.

The third is that triage (in its widest sense) can replace the complicated procedural rule book, which a lay litigant is currently expected, wholly unrealistically, to know and abide by. In short, a triage based online procedure need have only one rule: do what it tells you on the screen.

The second important strand is the growing awareness that the modernization of civil procedure thus far, coupled with the withdrawal of the state from a universalist approach to the provision of Legal Aid, has not addressed a comprehensive shortfall in access to justice for small to moderate sized civil claims. This means that, for most people, the prosecution or defence of those types of claim just cannot sensibly be afforded, so that the court is only theoretically available for the delivery of just resolution. That is not to decry the Woolf and Jackson reforms. They have made large strides in the improvement of civil procedure and have gone a long way to bringing costs expenditure and exposure to costs risk under control, both in larger civil cases generally, and in specific types of smaller cases such as RTA claims (there incidentally by an online process). But as Professor Zuckerman presciently observed when the Woolf reforms were in draft, no system which places the decision-making about the intensity of the conduct of civil litigation in the hands of the professional service providers will ever conquer the disproportion between cost and value at risk.[2]

[2] See AAS Zuckerman, 'Lord Woolf's Access to Justice: Plus ça Change' (1996) 59 MLR 773, 786–87, 795.

The essential problem is that the typical civil claim of an ordinary individual gives rise to a value at risk (ie amount at stake, or value of the disputed issue, such as an injunction) which simply does not justify the cost of legal representation, coupled with the risk as to the costs of a represented opponent, as a remotely sensible investment of hard-earned money. For as long as the Civil Procedure Rules (CPR) are written by lawyers for use by lawyers, and a standard legal services retainer runs for the whole of the dispute and covers every communication with the court and the opponent, actual cost will often be as much or more that the value at risk, and the risk of an adverse costs order will roughly double it. Feedback from numerous public meetings and other contributions during the CCSR revealed almost no-one who would put the level of value at risk at which a civil claim made legal representation a sensible investment below £25,000, and most put the break-even point much higher than that.

Nor did the modest amendment of the CPR to make express provision for litigants in person (LIPs) make any significant inroads into the problem. They did nothing to equip the typical LIPs with a sufficient understanding of the rules of the game to place them on anything approaching a level playing field with represented parties. Their ever-increasing complexity made it a full-time professional task to understand them at the level necessary to be able to conduct litigation, and the disapplication of some of them to proceedings in the small claims track, coupled with the generally sympathetic approach of the District Judges hearing and managing small claims was never going to be more than a palliative. Thus this second strand created a yawning gap in the ability of the courts, the professions, and current civil procedure to provide access to justice for small to moderate civil claims, just waiting to be filled by something much more modern, and a readiness to contemplate radical solutions after others had failed.

The third strand consisted of a series of mainly small-scale attempts to create something like an online court or tribunal, aimed specifically at providing access to justice to litigants in contexts where recourse to a lawyer would be prohibitively expensive. With the benefit of hindsight (and apologies to others not mentioned) those which stand out are the Traffic Penalty Tribunal (TPT), Money Claims Online (MCOL), and Possession Cases Online (PCOL) in England, Rechtwijzer in the Netherlands and the Civil Resolution Tribunal (CRT) in British Columbia.

The TPT is an online route of appeal from parking penalties and toll penalties on the Dartford Crossing. Beginning in March 2016 it provides a simple triaged process whereby appeals are processed, referred to the respondent councils for comment, and then (if not settled) subjected to determination by a small team of adjudicators, either on the online materials, with clarification by online messaging, or by short telephone hearing, as appropriate. It was an ideal test bed for triage, due to the very limited number of grounds of appeal specified in the relevant legislation. The online programme was developed by an imaginative partnership between the long serving Chief Adjudicator, Caroline Sheppard (for which she received an OBE) and a small software firm, Resolver.co.uk.

MCOL and PCOL are first generation methods of civil claim initiation, available as options within the CPR, whereby (as their names suggest) small civil money claims and possession claims may be initiated. MCOL began in 2002 and PCOL in 2006. MCOL in particular was quite widely used by unrepresented claimants, although it contained no triage at all, just a blank screen on which users could type in their particulars of claim online, but with no assistance in the ordering of what they might say. It operated only as an online method of claim initiation, being converted to a paper process upon receipt by the court, for service by post on the defendant, and case management, if disputed, in the time-honoured way for small claims. MCOL suffered from an input capacity limit of only 1,080 characters.

PCOL has the advantage of being more recent, and is designed in a limited way to enable landlords to navigate the shark-infested water of the statutory code for claiming possession of residential premises, by something resembling triage. It also permits a defendant to respond online, and certain applications (such as for a warrant of possession in an undefended case) to be made online. It also permits an element of online e-messaging between parties and the court. It is governed by a bespoke Practice Direction 55B but, if defended, then proceeds in accordance with the standard rules for such claims in the CPR found in Part 55.

Rechtwijzer was the brainchild of the Hague Institute for Innovation of Law (HiiL), working in partnership with the international online platform Modria and the Dutch Legal Aid Board. Starting in 2014, its second version was developed as a very attractive online dispute resolution tool for family separation and divorce, with triage and e-messaging guiding the parties towards a settlement agreement suitable for court approval. It differed from the Online Court as currently envisaged not only by operating entirely outside the auspices of the court, but also in providing no system for the adjudication of disputes which could not be settled. To use an increasingly inappropriate acronym, it was pure ADR. Although its style and sophistication inspired many involved in the development of the Online Court, it sadly died in 2017, for reasons which remain in dispute.

The CRT has always been seen, at least by those promoting and designing the online court in England and Wales, as the trailblazer which sets the standard to beat. Canada, and British Columbia in particular, is another essentially common law jurisdiction which experienced insuperable difficulties in moulding a paper and face to face based system of civil litigation into something capable of providing access to justice for small civil claims. British Columbia is a large, sparsely populated state, well suited as a test bed for remote (ie digital) solutions to problems of communication. Their solution was, again, not to digitize their court process, but to set up an online tribunal outside it, providing built-in ADR and then non-binding adjudication, with an option for the dissatisfied party to challenge the outcome in the traditional court process. Key features of the development of the CRT included governmental support from day one, backed by primary enabling legislation in 2012, sufficient time for development and testing, and a graduated roll-out starting with strata claims (disputes between flat owners and management within condominium structures) aimed at the areas of dispute worst-suited to traditional civil procedure. It pioneered the design process of using a small team including IT experts, lawyers, and communicators, with iterative destruction testing of early models on invited participants before any public launch. Its online offering builds forms of ADR into the process, with adjudication to follow if unsuccessful. The CRT went live for strata claims in July 2016. It has since expanded to admit cases about debt, construction, employment insurance, and property. Such has been its success that it is shortly to become the mandatory first port of call for small personal injury claims. Application to court after adjudication has been very limited.[3]

The next strand in the originating process was (and continues to be) the HMCTS Reform Programme. This project, launched jointly by the judiciary and government, is designed radically to reform the whole of the justice system in England and Wales, with objectives which include a reduction and modernization of physical court buildings, thoroughgoing digitization of communications, the replacement of many (but certainly not all) face to face hearings with processes using forms of remote electronic communication (online, email, telephone, and video), and improvements to access to justice, but all at reduced running cost to the taxpayer, after a capital injection of over £1bn. Reform of the Civil Courts is only a modest part of the programme overall, but it is intended to be much more closely integrated, at least in terms of digitization, with the Family Courts and the Tribunal Service, under the acronym 'CF&T'.

The creation of a civil online court was not an original element in the Reform Programme, and the student of the published information about the programme will, even now, look in vain for the use of the phrase 'Online Civil Court' as a heading for anything. But the commitment of government money and resources on a scale much greater than anything available for example in British Columbia or the Netherlands for the furtherance of objectives which will clearly be served by an online civil court turned out to be a major plank in the emergence of such an animal, not just as a concept but as a practical and achievable reality.

HMCTS is (perhaps uniquely among court services) the vehicle for a unique roughly equal partnership between government (in the person of the Secretary of State for Justice and Lord Chancellor) and the Judiciary (in the person of the Lord Chief Justice and Senior President of Tribunals) dedicated to the running of the courts of England and Wales (but not the Supreme Court, which is entirely

[3] For the latest statistics, see <https://civilresolutionbc.ca/crt-statistics-snapshot-september-2018/> accessed 25 March 2020.

independent as a UK court). Although of course the government side holds the purse strings, the structure of HMCTS depends upon full and close co-operation between the MoJ and the judiciary at every level, from the main board down to the most humble committees and management bodies. This has been instrumental in bringing about one feature of the development of the English and Welsh Online Court which sets it apart from its predecessors, eg in British Columbia, namely the detailed engagement of judges in every aspect of the consultation, design, and implementation of the concept. This has been manifested in particular in the regular meetings of the Civil Judicial Engagement Group, which scrutinizes and advises on every aspect of the civil part of the reform programme.

The final strand in the gestation of the Online Court in England consisted of a series of ground-breaking reports, recommending its introduction here and developing the model now being followed by its designers within the HMCTS Reform Programme. The first and most important was the report for the Civil Justice Council (CJC) in February 2015 entitled 'Online Dispute Resolution for Low Value Civil Claims' by an advisory group led by Professor Richard Susskind OBE, then and now the IT Adviser to the Lord Chief Justice.[4] Building on the precedents set by the TPT, Rechtwijzer, and the CRT, this report recommended something called HM Online Court (HMOC), with the following features: First it was to combine ADR with legally binding judicial determination, all as part of a civil court offering, and almost completely online. Secondly, it was to operate in three stages or tiers. The first was to involve online evaluation, by forms of triage. The second was to provide online facilitation, by the intervention of court-based facilitators, seeking to bring the parties to a settlement through mediation and negotiation either online or, where appropriate, on the telephone. The third tier was to consist of online judges (full or part time) resolving disputes still outstanding after tier two, mainly on the online files, but with teleconferences where necessary. The terms of reference for this report confined the concept to dealing with small claims up to £25,000, and sought alternatives to the traditional face to face encounters in a courtroom, which therefore formed no part in its recommendations.

Hot on the heels of the CJC Report, in April 2015, came 'Delivering Justice in an Age of Austerity', a report commissioned by JUSTICE from a working party led by Sir Stanley Burnton.[5] This was not required by its terms of reference to focus either on small claims or online processes. It began with a clear view that the then current structures of the civil courts were failing to provide access to justice, and recommended a new two-tier model for civil litigation generally. The first was to be built around a Registrar, trained to specialize in particular types of dispute, whose

[4] Available at: <https://www.judiciary.uk/wp-content/uploads/2015/02/Online-Dispute-Resolution-Final-Web-Version1.pdf> accessed 25 March 2020.

[5] Available at: <http://2bquk8cdew6192tsu41lay8t.wpengine.netdna-cdn.com/wp-content/uploads/2015/04/JUSTICE-working-party-report-Delivering-Justice-in-an-Age-of-Austerity.pdf> accessed 25 March 2020.

function was to investigate defended cases and steer them proactively to a resolution using ADR. The second was to be determination by judges of the residue of disputed cases not resolved at tier one. Both tiers were to use an integrated system of online and telephonic means of communication. This concluding paragraph sums it up concisely:

> Our recommended integrated online and telephone portal enlists the power of technology in the endeavour to ensure access to justice for all. The service will have an important dispute avoidance and diversionary role, or, when court proceedings are necessary, will guide litigants through the reformed justice system. The portal will provide legal advice and assistance to the majority of those for whom such assistance would otherwise be out of reach, while freeing up scarce personally delivered services for those who need them most.

JUSTICE followed up this report by the further paper 'What is a Court' by a committee chaired by Alexandra Marks and published in May 2016.[6] It was mainly concerned with taking a completely fresh approach to the optimal use of physical court space, under the conceptual heading: 'a court is what a court does', but it warmly commended the TPT as a model for the digitization of the court system, funded by the resources of the HMCTS Reform Programme.

Meanwhile, in July 2015, I had been commissioned by the Lord Chief Justice, Lord Thomas and the Master of the Rolls, Lord Dyson to undertake the CCSR. My terms of reference extended to all levels of the civil courts (other than the Supreme Court) and made no express reference to anything online. But the review was required:

> to make recommendations for structural change including, in particular, the structures by which the fruits of the Reform Programme may best be integrated into the present structure of the Civil Courts.

My Interim Report was delivered in December 2015, and the Final Report in July 2016. Both placed the development of an Online Court as part of the Reform Programme at the forefront of my recommendations. It was intentionally and unashamedly a judicial contribution to the debate, although my small 'hard working group' of three civil judges of different seniority was greatly assisted by including Richard Goodman, then and now a very senior HMCTS member of the Reform Programme. I was greatly educated by a three stage written and oral process of public and stakeholder consultation, which included an invaluable visit to the CRT

6 Available at: <https://2bquk8cdew6192tsu41lay8t-wpengine.netdna-ssl.com/wp-content/uploads/2016/05/JUSTICE-What-is-a-Court-Report-2016.pdf> accessed 25 March 2020.

design team in Vancouver, and a live demonstration of Rechtwijzer by its principal designer.

In bare outline (detail would replicate the description of the thing itself which follows) the review recommended the creation of an Online Solutions Court for small civil claims up to £25,000 in value, but with a first step up to £10,000, as the (eventually) mandatory forum for cases within its jurisdiction, formed of three stages broadly along the CJC model, but with stage one (triage) being wholly online, stage two (dispute resolution managed by Case Officers) being online and by telephone, and stage three (judicial determination) being such combination of online, telephone, video and face to face hearing as each case merited. I followed both the CJC and Justice reports in concluding that an Online Court was the best solution to the crippling lack of access to justice for small to moderate civil claims, and that it should be configured so as to make use of advances in digital technology, and online triage in particular, to reduce recourse to lawyers by court users bringing and defending such claims from the current cradle to grave structure of entire retainer to those contributions such as early bespoke advice on the merits and skilled advocacy and cross examination at those few trials which turned out to be necessary where their added value made the cost proportionate. I need only refer to the first paragraph in the Online Court chapter of the Interim report:

> The development of the Online Court is the single most radical and important structural change with which this report is concerned. It provides the opportunity to use modern IT to create for the first time a court which will enable civil disputes of modest value and complexity to be justly resolved without the incurring of the disproportionate cost of legal representation. In my view it offers the best available prospect of providing access to justice for people and small businesses of ordinary financial resources. It will therefore go a long way towards providing a remedy for what I have described in Chapter 5 as the most serious and long-standing weakness of the civil courts.

What happened?

Rules and jurisdiction

The main recommendations in the CCSR for a civil Online Court were quickly accepted in principle both by the MoJ and by the Judiciary, so that they became, in a loose sense, the guiding principles for the development of the thing itself. In order to explain what is meant by 'loose' in the last sentence, and to be able to discover the development of an online Civil Court within published materials that hardly ever refer to the concept expressly, it is necessary to explain a little of the processes by which the Reform Programme is driven. Mention has already been made of the aspiration to develop IT and other processes on a harmonized basis across the whole field of the civil, family, and tribunal jurisdiction (CF&T). Within that whole, particular projects are identified and given both a budget and a time-line. In Family, there is a divorce project devoted to the design and roll-out of Online Divorce, for non-contested divorce petitions. Also within Family (although it is only there for historical reasons) is the probate project, dedicated to the design and roll-out of Online Probate for non-contentious probate applications. Within Civil there are projects to digitize the High Court and (one day) the Court of Appeal, and to digitize and streamline both possession cases and the enforcement of judgments. But the sole repository (or laboratory) for the development of the online Civil Court is known as the 'civil money claims project'. This is because civil money claims below £25,000 were identified at the outset as in urgent need of at least reform and digitization, even before the recommendations in the three reports for an Online Court became known, let alone firm HMCTS policy.

The reader may be wondering how harmonization across CF&T is likely to be able to be achieved by a programme that carves up reform into separate projects along essentially traditional boundaries. The answer is that it was recognized that many of the digital components of each project were likely to serve very similar needs, such as party identification, payment of fees, service of process, and delivery of judgment. This is because all the projects proceed in stages and at different speeds, and IT solutions developed in and for one project can easily then be re-used, if necessary with small modifications, in one or more others. And so it has proved.

It was also recognized, at least dimly, that going fully online would be likely to require radical changes in procedure rules, and that there was likely to be just as much value in harmonizing those rules across CF&T as there was proving to be in harmonizing the IT itself. To that end primary legislation for the creation of a single Online Rule Committee for the whole of CF&T was included in the Prisons and Courts Bill, and well into its committee stages when it unfortunately fell in April 2017 because of the last general election. This new committee would have been constituted on very different lines from the Civil Procedure Rules Committee (CPRC), which is dominated by legal professionals, with a very small lay element. It would have included among its members technical IT experts and persons experienced in assisting litigants in person, as would befit the rule-maker of an Online Court dedicated to making justice accessible to those unable to afford full retainer legal representation.

Even more unfortunately, although not by design, legislation to create an Online Rule Committee was not speedily resurrected in the last parliament, and like its predecessor again fell victim to a General Election, in late 2019. The result is that the development of a civil Online Court is, currently at least, being undertaken within the procedural jacket of the CPR. A large amount of work is being undertaken by a sub-committee of the CPRC to fashion pilot scheme Practice Directions, so as to clothe the public testing (on real cases) of what will become the civil Online Court with the procedural legitimacy required by the Civil Procedure Act 1997.

It was necessary at the outset also to address the fundamental question: what was to be the source of the new court's jurisdiction? A deliberate decision was taken (to the regret of many) not to create a new jurisdiction, but to rely upon the jurisdiction of the existing courts for all versions of the Online Court across the CF&T. Thus the civil Online Court will (at least for the foreseeable future) be exercising the jurisdiction of the now unified single County Court. Some would say that this means that it will not be a new or separate court at all, but the English system frequently creates courts within courts to good effect. For example the Companies Court, the Technology and Construction Court, the Patent Court, and even the Commercial Court and Admiralty Court (which are parts of the Business and Property Courts) all exercise the jurisdiction of the High Court. They are all regarded to a greater or lesser extent by their users as having many of the characteristics of separate courts, in terms of dedicated expertise, special procedures, and indeed a distinctive brand recognized worldwide.

Nonetheless the combined effect of preserving separate sources of jurisdiction along traditional lines together with separate procedure rules and rule-making bodies means that, at least at present, the concept of an Online Court unified over the whole CF&T field remains something yet to be achieved. This is not by itself necessarily a bad thing. There is much to be said for avoiding a 'one cap fits all' approach to the creation of Online Courts, and nothing about their separate development to date has prevented the ready transfer and adaption of new IT developed in one of them to the service of the others.

The ongoing delay in the creation of an Online Rule Committee has a number of important consequences for the development of a civil Online Court. The first is that the vital blue sky thinking about the nature and function of procedure rules in an online context is currently still-born. Procedural rules for a traditional civil court have a well-recognized role, in a context where it is assumed that court users will generally be represented by lawyers. They regulate every aspect of the litigation process at a level of detail which can, in reality, only be grasped by full-time legal professionals. They are rules written by lawyers for use by lawyers, and their inaccessibility to the lay court-user is a principal reason why the civil courts provided limited access to justice for small value civil cases.

There are by contrast conflicting theories about the role of procedural rules in an online context. Many say that the detailed procedure needs to be hard-wired into the online screens, so that the only rule which the court user need follow is to comply with the on-screen instructions, and with time prompts delivered (like NHS appointment reminders) to their smart phones. Of course the instructions in the software behind the screens need to be properly authorized. Although that might in theory be achieved by framing the rules as instructions to programmers, they will need to be capable of being understood by some members of the public, if only to ensure public scrutiny of the process.

Others say that there will still need to be a procedural rule book, but something of the utmost brevity and simplicity that can be read and understood by every reasonably literate intending court user, in stark contrast with the CPR. Yet others advocate some compromise between the two. But none of the necessary discussion of these procedural fundamentals has yet really got off the ground. Meanwhile the civil Online Court is, thus far, being built, brick by electronic brick, and brought into public use, under the auspices of the culture and content of the CPR, which were designed for a completely different purpose, and for professional rather than lay guidance.

The second, more beneficial, consequence of delay in providing for online procedure rules is that the inevitable chicken and egg question: do we design the rule book and then the thing itself, or vice versa, is being resolved in favour of the thing itself, effectively by default. As in British Columbia, the process of what is called 'agile' design produces new bits of IT and associated process to add to the project, tests it until ready for trial on real cases, and the CPRC sub-committee then designs a pilot rule framework simply to authorize it. The beneficial result is that the structure is being built up by the designers on the basis of trial and error, rather than having to accommodate a pre-conceived notion of what the complete structure should be and do, already laid down in mandatory rules. That is why at present the procedural authority of CPR pilot rules might turn out to be a jacket rather than a straitjacket.

Nonetheless there must come a time when the loving embrace of pilot rules will generate something more like claustrophobia. It is to be hoped that the necessary primary legislation will quickly come before Parliament, that the current impasse in the creation of this vital body will be resolved, just in time.

Minimum viable product

The chosen design method for the civil online court (within the civil money claims project) involves an essentially protean stage by stage process towards an ultimate goal identifiable only in outline. The early emphasis has been on getting a minimum viable project into public use as quickly as possible, and then adding elements to it until a fully finished product has been created. While the whole project underwent a high-level discovery stage, each element once designed undergoes first 'private beta' and then 'public beta' stages of testing. This step by step process is not merely, or even primarily, designed to accelerate the time at which the project may begin to contribute to the cost-saving objectives of the Reform Programme. Rather, its primary motivation is a perception that developing and adding to something already in public use is likely in the end to produce a much better product, than something fully designed and built before launch.

The minimum viable product arrived in the public domain (for public beta testing on real cases) in mid-2018, in the form of an entirely new online platform for initiating a small money claim by a lay litigant, with scope for online response by a defendant, and the ability for an undefended case to go to an early judgment. As such it may best be viewed as a form of MCOL mark 2, since it largely replicated what MCOL already delivered, but with critical differences. It resembled MCOL in that it contained no triage to assist the lay litigant, and no provision to take the case forward online once it became defended. The main improvement over MCOL (apart from transformed user-friendliness much appreciated in public feedback) was that it was built upon an IT platform easily capable of almost unlimited further development, whereas MCOL was built upon a first-generation IT platform which was ruinously difficult and expensive to modify or extend. The new platform has also escaped from the constriction of the very small input data capacity which hamstrung MCOL.

This new (optional) process of online initiation and response to a claim delivers undefended claims to early judgment, and otherwise delivers defended claims into the ordinary County Court process for case management and trial on paper, just as did MCOL. It is not yet in any sense an online court, but an important part in the building bricks from which it will eventually be constructed.

Since launch, this embryonic structure has been augmented with a parallel system for professional issue and response, provision for the creation of a chronology or 'time-line', and for a summary of each party's evidence. The existing free telephone mediation service is being added to the process on an opt-out basis for very small claims. Meanwhile development of the other elements necessary to turn this structure into a true online court continues. At the time of writing there have been over 115,000 users of this new structure, with a reported 89 per cent satisfaction rate. Early statistical analysis suggests that the bulk of the users of the new system are not just migrants from MCOL or the paper-based process. In other words, it is already beginning to deliver improved access to justice by attracting court users who might not have gone to court before. It also generates a higher proportion of active defendants.

The design objective

The ultimate goal, a civil Online Court which really can empower ordinary people to enforce low value civil rights and resolve relatively simple civil disputes without the disproportional expense of full-retainer professional representation, currently has the following features. First, it is to be available initially as an optional route for the pursuit and defence of money claims up to £25,000 in value, with an initial ceiling during development of £10,000. Money claims will include both debt and damages, but will not extend to personal injury claims, at least while the attempted refashioning of the RTA Portal consequent upon raising the Small Claims costs regime from £1,000 to £5,000 is being pursued so as to admit lay litigants.

Secondly, the Online Court will involve three stages, first online triage, second resolution and case management by Case Officers, and third determination by judges, online, on documents, by telephone, video, or face to face hearing as appropriate for each case. It will not therefore be a pure online court in the sense that no other type of communication takes place between the parties and the court. Rather it will, in accordance with a founding principle of the Reform Programme, normally be done digitally, while allowing for other means of communication and types of hearing where necessary.

Thirdly, it is intended that the stage one process, by which claims and defences are communicated between the parties and to the court, will include triage in the form of decision tree like structures designed to guide lay litigants to articulating their cases in a way which the court and their opponents can understand. This is going to be the most complex part of the structure to design, and is likely to need constant maintenance, as the relevant law changes over time. But it is also likely to be the part of the structure which will most assist lay litigants, and thereby deliver the hoped-for improvements in access to justice. That has been the experience in British Columbia, and there is no reason to think that it will not eventually be replicated in England.

Fourthly, stage one already includes an online process for the early creation of a chronology of agreed and disputed facts, and will enable the uploading of documents upon which the parties wish to rely, thereby creating an online case file, accessible to the parties, the case officer and the judge.

At the centre of stage two will sit the Case Officers (so named in the CCSR, but it remains to be seen what they will eventually be called). Their function will be to guide and manage each case to its most appropriate resolution, either by negotiation or ADR, or by judicial determination. The Case Officer will not be a judge, but will be legally qualified, judicially trained and supervised, will operate on independent Bangalore principles, and be answerable to the Lord Chief Justice, although employed by HMCTS. The Case Officer will be the first human being on the court side to review the electronic file generated by stage one, and will have recourse to a range of state and private dispute resolution options to which to direct the parties. They may include online dispute resolution options, such as blind bidding online, judicial early neutral evaluation, and mediation (either online, by telephone, or face to face). The expectation is that, as indeed at present, the large majority of cases which are disputed up to the beginning of stage two will be resolved by one of those methods. The objective has been described as taking the 'A' out of ADR, by making it the normative form of dispute resolution even within the court's own offering.

The residue of cases which the Case Officer cannot resolve by one of those stage two methods will be case managed for determination by a judge, at stage three. But there will be no default assumption that the default mode is a face to face trial. On the contrary, subject to one point, the default mode will, at least for the smallest cases, be determination online, save to the extent that the nature of the issues or the intensity or complexity of the dispute requires something else, such as a telephone, video, or face to face hearing. The responsibility for making that choice will, in the first instance, be a case management matter for the Case Officer, but subject to review by a judge, either on the application of a dissatisfied party or on his own initiative. Mode of hearing will therefore remain a matter of judicial discretion.

The 'one point' referred to above is the Article 6 right to a fair and public hearing, and the English (or common law) notion that this involves something communicated to the ears rather than just the eyes of the judge.[7] The oral tradition is rightly regarded as a (if not the) jewel in the crown of English legal procedure, and it is not the ambition of the designers of the civil online court to do away with it, where its potential for inconvenience, delay, and expense is not disproportionate to the value or importance of the issue to be resolved, or where it continues to offer the best guarantee of a public and just outcome. Very short oral hearings remain the key element in the court's participation in the resolution of quantum disputes in low value RTA cases, and their conduct by experienced professional lawyers and specialist District Judges makes them a formidable vehicle for efficient and cost-effective resolution of very large numbers of low value money claims. Short trials remain an efficient and fair means of resolution of that small proportion of the other small claims which cannot otherwise be resolved. But a reduction in the current extent of the use of the face to face trial is a major plank in the cost savings sought to be achieved by the Reform Programme, so that the point at which over time this balance will come to be struck once the civil Online Court is fully operational remains to be worked out by experience.

Naming of parts

A curiosity of the history of the promotion, design, and development of the concept of a civil online court in England has been the difficulties encountered from time to time in agreeing upon names for things. 'Triage' as a name for the online decision tree process designed to enable lay litigants to articulate their case without

[7] On procedural fairness requirements under article 6(1) ECHR, see generally *Jussila v Finland* (2007) 45 EHRR 39 (Grand Chamber) [41]–[42] and *Miller v Sweden* (2006) 42 EHRR 51 [29]. For the common law position, see *R (Osborn) v Parole Board* [2013] UKSC 61, [2014] AC 1115 [2], [81] and *R (Heather Moor & Edgecomb Ltd) v Financial Ombudsman Service* [2008] EWCA Civ 642, [2008] Bus LR 1486 [61].

lawyers was initially frowned upon, perhaps by those with unhappy experiences of A&E, and it is in the process of being replaced with the rather better phrase 'Case Builder'. 'Case Officer' recommended in the CCSR was the replacement for the awful 'Delegated Judicial Officer' originally proposed, and the perhaps old-fashioned 'Registrar' proposed by the JUSTICE report. There seems now to be some support for calling that person 'Legal Adviser', which reflects the requirement that they be legally qualified, even if strictly forbidden from giving court users any legal advice. But the primary legislation which makes provision for them calls them authorized officers.[8]

Above all, the name for the civil online court has thus far eluded any real consensus. The CJC report called it 'HM Online Court'. The CCSR proposed 'Online Solutions Court' and this has since been endorsed by the Master of the Rolls. The thinking was that just calling it 'Online Court' might give the impression that it operated purely online, and the reference to 'Solutions' was designed to emphasize the bringing together of all methods of dispute resolution under one roof, taking the A out of ADR, just as the same concept inspired the naming of the CRT in British Columbia. But it has yet to catch on. For its part HMCTS has continued to avoid the choice or use of any catchy name, having just decided to call it Online Civil Money Claims (OCMC).

The underlying difficulty appears to be an inability to decide whether to name things or people by reference to existing or historical types, to use phrases of perfect accuracy to an expert lawyer, or to use a name or acronym which will become the logo for an attractive item in the minds of the public.

Public justice

A real challenge to the development of a civil Online Court has been, and will continue to be, the non-negotiable requirement to maintain at least as much openness and transparency in a digitized system as is presently available from the current paper-based and heavily oral process which it is being planned to replace. Modern IT is by no means the enemy of transparency, as the current live streaming of all Supreme Court and Privy Council hearings all round the world demonstrates. Nor does the replacement of paper files with electronic equivalents of itself reduce the scope for their inspection by the public. In many respects it is likely to make it easier. Video hearings can easily be observed by the public (at one end or the other of the transmission process, or both), and even telephone hearings can be observed, albeit only heard in a one-sided way, by the judge being required to conduct them in a court room open to the public.

[8] Courts and Tribunals (Judiciary and Functions of Staff) Act 2018.

The real problem in maintaining transparency lies in the likely reduction in face to face hearings coupled with an increase in the number of cases determined purely on the (electronic) documents. Solutions to this real problem are being mulled over, but have yet to emerge into the public domain. There is undoubtedly a consensus in all quarters about the need to maintain openness and transparency at current levels, at least.

The challenges

The biggest challenge to the full development of the civil Online Court, and to the realization of the ambition that it will transform access to justice, is the design and ongoing maintenance of the stage one triage process now called Case Builder, currently only at an early stage of design. The central problem with civil litigation (compared with family, tribunals, or even crime) is its almost limitless variety. You can have a small civil dispute, or money claim, about almost anything. The essence of triage is that it elucidates from the court user the precise legal category into which the claim falls, and then asks expertly focused questions about it. Unless like the TPT or, in its initial stages, the CRT, the jurisdiction of the new court is limited to a small number of frequently encountered types of claim, for each of which triage can be designed and then maintained, the designers are faced with the difficult choice between triage which is so generalized as to offer no real help to litigants, or with the daunting task of designing a multitude of case-type specific avenues, each of which will require specialized input, both at the design stage, and thereafter.

The solution is likely to lie in some compromise, at least in the early stages, between the breadth of the new court's subject matter competence, the number of case types for which Case Builder can be rolled out, and the depth of the online questioning, at this relatively early stage in the development of the concept. There will be a need for HMCTS to make a long-term commitment to the constant maintenance of the triage which is made available, unless of course politicians can be persuaded to exercise restraint in constantly changing the law, which recent history suggests is most unlikely.

The next challenge is for lawyers. Currently for historical, procedural, and insurance-related reasons, the typical legal litigation retainer is a whole or entire contract, under which all aspects of the representation of the client to (and in) the court is undertaken by the professional lawyer, either alone, or in part by delegation between solicitor and counsel. Much of the expense to the client comes from the lawyer undertaking routine tasks, like correspondence, photocopying, collation, and service of documents, and acting as an intermediary in every encounter between the client, the court, and their opponent. It is the ambition that the civil Online Court should replace much of the routine aspects of this, leaving the lawyer to provide that which their skill contributes the greatest added value, such as early bespoke advice on the merits and skilled forensic advocacy and cross examination at a trial.

The solutions consist of the unbundling of their services by solicitors, and improved direct access services by barristers. These may be shortly stated but their achievement will not be easy. They require a fundamental change of litigation culture by lawyers wishing to provide services to litigants in small civil cases.

The third challenge is the provision of help for those who are digitally challenged. Although the preservation of a parallel paper path for those unable or unwilling to use IT (usually tablets or smartphones rather than laptops or desktops) may be a necessary palliative, it is simply not a solution. This is because the critical respect in which an online court can improve access to justice lies in the provision of triage and other facilities to lay litigants which paper cannot provide. Thus to leave the digitally challenged merely with a parallel paper path will be to discriminate against them, quite apart from the hindrance thereby imposed at the court end in the way of cheaper, more streamlined services. The solution surely lies, in the middle to longer term, in providing assistance to the diminishing class of those who find IT hard to navigate, online (by help boxes), by telephone, and, crucially, by face to face encounter. There is a project being trialled within the reform programme to do just that. It is recognized that it cannot just be left to the providers of pro bono help, invaluable though their assistance is bound to be. It will be an added cost to the court service, but one which ought to produce improvements in case handling at the court end which will eventually make that cost worth incurring.

8

Compliance Problems and Digitizing Case Management in England and Wales

John Sorabji

Introduction

Adrian Zuckerman's most significant contribution to English civil procedure is, arguably, his development of the idea that, as a public service it must be managed effectively.[1] There were a number of aspects to this idea, which he summarized in a discussion of the operation of the Civil Procedure Rules in 2007. First, it required a clearly articulated objective to govern procedure's operation. Secondly, it required the courts to be given the necessary powers to enable them to implement the objective. Finally, it required the judiciary, who were to use the powers, to both properly understand 'the nature of the objective and [to] have the will to use their powers in order to achieve it'.[2]

The first aspect of Zuckerman's approach is well-known. It is the idea that the civil courts should replace a commitment to a one-dimensional theory of justice, one that understood the judicial role as 'predominantly to deliver judgments that are well founded in fact and law'[3] ie, a just decision or justice on the merits, with a multi-dimensional one. That latter theory was one that required the court to act consistently with three imperatives, each of which had to be balanced with the others. The imperatives were: securing a justice decision; securing procedural economy; and securing procedural efficiency. No longer were the civil courts to seek solely to secure a just decision. They were to seek to secure a just process for litigants, which would include but go beyond securing a just decision.[4] Broadly speaking, this approach was adopted by the CPR through the introduction of its overriding objective (CPR r 1.1), albeit it was not explicitly acknowledged as doing

[1] See, for instance, A Zuckerman, 'Quality and Economy in Civil Procedure—A Case for Commuting Correct Judgments for Timely Judgments' (1994) 14 OJLS 353.

[2] A Zuckerman, *Weakness of Will—The Exercise of Case Management Discretion under the CPR* (unpublished paper presented at Atlantic Chambers, 24 May 2007, copy on file with the author) at [24].

[3] A Zuckerman, *Zuckerman on Civil Procedure—Principles of Practice* (Sweet & Maxwell 2013) 4.

[4] H Woolf, *Access to Justice: Interim Report to the Lord Chancellor on the Civil Justice System in England and Wales* (HMSO) (1995) 216; *Adoko v Jemal* (CA 22 June 1999, unreported) 8, 'The proper and proportionate use of court resources is now to be considered part of substantive justice itself.'

John Sorabji, *Compliance Problems and Digitizing Case Management in England and Wales* In: *Principles, Procedure, and Justice.* Edited by: Rabeea Assy and Andrew Higgins, Oxford University Press (2020). © The editors and several contributors.
DOI: 10.1093/oso/9780198850410.003.0008

so until 2013.[5] Nor was it acknowledged as having done so as a consequence of Zuckerman's work.

The second aspect is equally well-known. It was the idea, first advanced by Zuckerman in 1994 and then in 1995, that party-control of litigation, a fundamental aspect of the articulation of the principle of party autonomy in litigation in English procedure and one that was understood to be a significant contributor to excess litigation cost and time,[6] be replaced by court-control of litigation ie the introduction of active court case management. This was understood to be necessary to enable the judiciary to have an effective means of ensuring that parties conducted litigation consistently with the new multi-dimensional theory.[7] Active court-based case management was not, of itself, novel to English procedure. A first step in that direction was taken at the same time as Zuckerman was developing his approach in 1995 through the introduction of *Practice Direction (Case Management)* [1995] 1 WLR 262. It had previously been recommended by the Heilbron-Hodge Report in 1994, and prior to that the Civil Justice Review in 1988.[8] It was an idea adopted by the Woolf Reforms[9] and incorporated in the CPR.[10]

It is the third aspect of Zuckerman's contribution that has formed the most significant aspect of his work since the CPR was introduced in 1999. The central issue that he has focused on is, as he has argued, that the judiciary has failed to use their case management powers effectively so as to further the new theory of justice set out in the CPR's overriding objective.[11] His focus here has been on what he has suggested is a 'weakness of will' on the part of the judiciary to give proper weight to the imperatives of economy and efficiency.[12] The judiciary, as he has put it, have

[5] A point noted by Zuckerman in Zuckerman (n 3) 8.

[6] See J Jacob, *The Fabric of English Civil Justice* (Stevens & Sons 1987) 9ff; N Andrews, 'A New Civil Procedural Code for England: Party-Control Going, Going, Gone' (2000) 19 CJQ 19.

[7] A Zuckerman, 'A Reform of Civil Procedure—Rationing Procedure rather than Access to Justice' (1995) 22 J L & Soc'y 155, 171.

[8] H Heilbron and H Hodge, *Civil Justice on Trial—A Case for Change* (1993) (Joint report of The Bar Council and Law Society) 5 and Appendix 1 [25]; Civil Justice Review Body, *Civil Justice Review 1988* (Cmd 394, 1988) 154–62. There were, however, earlier attempts to introduce court-based case management. The earliest explicit attempt was arguably that contained in the procedure applicable to the Commercial Court from its inception, see, *The Queen's Bench Division Judges' Notice as to Commercial Causes* (February 1895) and Rules of the Supreme Court (1965) Ord 72, r 2(3), 'The judge shall have control of the actions in the Commercial List . . .' reprinted in A Colman, *The Practice and Procedure of the Commercial Court* (Lloyd's of London Press 1983) 7–8 and 47.

[9] Woolf (n 4) s II; H Woolf, *Access to Justice: Final Report to the Lord Chancellor on the Civil Justice System in England and Wales* (HMSO) (1996) Section II.

[10] CPR Pt 3.

[11] See R Jackson, *Review of Civil Litigation Costs: Final Report* (TSO) (December 2009) 386 and 397ff. As noted at 386, the position Zuckerman argued for as a necessary underpinning of a change in approach to non-compliance was, as he had been arguing consistently since 1994, 'The management task that the court is expected to discharge is relatively uncomplicated: to ensure that case management directions are implemented as laid down, unless a change of circumstances demands otherwise. But this simple task requires the court to abandon its almost religious attachment to the one dimensional understanding of justice and accept that doing justice means more than delivering a judgment on the merits; that time and the use of resources are just as significant imperatives of justice.'

[12] Zuckerman (n 2).

continued to place too great a weight on securing accurate decisions. They have not, for instance, had the strength of will to impose effective sanctions for procedural non-compliance. His argument has thus been that if the civil justice system is to be properly managed, the judiciary must change their approach to procedural non-compliance. To adapt his terminology the civil courts must show greater strength of will in taking a less lenient, just decision-weighted, approach to non-compliance and the applications for relief from sanctions that follow upon it.

Zuckerman's focus, in respect of the third aspect of the idea that the civil justice system requires effective management, has accordingly been non-compliance with case management decisions (the non-compliance problem).[13] His particular concern was that, unless the courts took a properly robust approach to ensuring rules, practice directions, and court orders were complied with, they would lose their normative force. Too lenient an approach to non-compliance would, as it had under the pre-CPR approach to litigation, result in 'a culture of optional compliance',[14] which would in turn lead to time-consuming and expensive satellite litigation. The ultimate consequence of that would then be that litigation would continue to be conducted at disproportionate cost and time to the parties, and to the court. Thus, the aim of marshalling the civil justice system's resources effectively would be frustrated, just as the aim of increasing access to justice through reducing litigation costs would be frustrated. Much has been written on the non-compliance problem,[15] and since the CPR was introduced there have been repeated attempts, of varying degrees of success, to remedy it by the Court of Appeal.[16]

While the non-compliance problem should not be underestimated, Zuckerman identified a number of other weaknesses in the implementation of effective case management. Taken together they could be described as a 'compliance problem', although he does not use that term.

These weaknesses are, first, the absence of any real oversight of the use of judicial resources, and secondly, the absence of any mechanism through which to evaluate the operation of the civil justice system to determine where and why management

[13] See Zuckerman (n 2); A Zuckerman, 'Litigation Management under the CPR: A Poorly-used Management Infrastructure', in D Dwyer (ed), *The Civil Procedure Rules Ten Years On* (OUP 2009) 89; A Zuckerman, 'The Continuing Management Deficit in the Administration of Civil Justice' (2015) 34 CJQ 1.

[14] Zuckerman (n 2) [7].

[15] In addition to Zuckerman, it has been considered by, amongst others, D Piggot, 'Relief from Sanctions and the Overriding Objective' (2005) 24 CJQ 103; A Higgins, 'The Costs of Case Management: What Should Be Done Post-Jackson' (2010) 29 CJQ 317; C Crifo, 'Enforcement of Process Requirements: A Search for Solid Grounds' (2014) 34(2) OJLS 325; J Sorabji, *English Civil Justice after Woolf and Jackson* (CUP 2014); M Ahmed, 'Procedural Non-compliance and Relief from Sanctions after the Jackson Reforms: Striking the Balance' (2015) (No 5.1) IJPL-RIDP 71; D de Saulles, *Reforming Civil Procedure—The Hardest Path* (Hart 2019).

[16] *Mitchell v News Group Newspapers Ltd* [2013] EWCA Civ 1537, [2014] 1 WLR 795; *Denton v White* [2014] EWCA Civ 906, [2014] 1 WLR 3926; *British Gas Trading Ltd v Oak Cash and Carry Ltd* [2016] EWCA Civ 153, [2016] 1 WLR 4530. It remains an open question whether this attempt will, over the long term, succeed where previous ones have failed.

problems arose in specific cases and through which reform recommendations can be made.[17] It is readily apparent when case management problems arise where applications are made for relief from the consequences of non-compliance, and where appeals from decisions on such applications reach the Court of Appeal. In such cases, disproportionate use of court and party resources is patent.[18] Non-compliance with case management obligations and thereafter with 'unless' orders seeking to enforce compliance expend significant amounts of court, and party, time and financial resources due to the multiple applications and appeals that were the result. It is not, however, as apparent when compliance problems arise. They are issues that are largely hidden from scrutiny, and have not been explored by Zuckerman, although he has critically commented upon the adverse consequences of compliance with court orders in other contexts.[19] The purpose of this chapter is, first, to outline the nature of the hidden compliance problem of case management, and then to suggest ways in which it could be overcome by both the current courts and tribunals modernization programme (the HCMTS reforms)[20] and by the potential use of artificial intelligence as an aid to the delivery of civil justice.

Compliance problems

The non-compliance problem rests on an assumption: that the initial case management order was consistent with the CPR's overriding objective. Compliance with such an order, whether it is the extent to which disclosure is required, whether to appoint a single joint expert, party experts, or multiple party experts, or whether it is compliance with the date by which compliance is required, would, if the assumption were correct, secure the overriding objective. By definition, non-compliance would thus carry with it, at the least, the potential to frustrate its achievement. Should parties fail to limit disclosure to the amount provided for or fail to disclosure material by the due date, the overriding objective's achievement would be put at risk.

The consequences of such non-compliance can readily come to light in arguments concerning the effect of the non-compliant party's behaviour on their

[17] The various criticisms are made throughout Zuckerman (2015).

[18] See, for instance, *Prince Abdulaziz v Apex Global Management Ltd (Rev 2)* [2014] UKSC 64, [2014] WLR 4495.

[19] He commented critically, for instance, on the development of a closed, secret system of justice where so-called super-injunctions were concerned. Compliance with such orders not only kept them out of the public eye, ie public scrutiny, but equally gave rise to a jurisdiction that was not subject to appellate scrutiny or control; see A Zuckerman, 'Super Injunctions—Curiosity-Suppressant Orders Undermine the Rule of Law' (2010) 29 CJQ 131.

[20] *Transforming our Justice System*, Joint Statement of the Lord Chancellor, the Lord Chief Justice, and the Senior President of Tribunals, Reforming HM Courts and Tribunals Service (September 2016) <https://assets.publishing.service.gov.uk/government/uploads/system/uploads/attachment_data/file/553261/joint-vision-statement.pdf>.

entitlement to costs or to the imposition of indemnity costs upon the conclusion of proceedings. Such arguments would concern the question whether disclosure beyond the scope of the order, which would have engendered work being carried out on the disclosed documents by the receiving party beyond that which would have been necessary if the order had been complied with, amounted to unreasonable conduct. The adverse consequences of non-compliance would equally come to light through the imposition of sanctions for non-compliance, applications for relief from sanctions under CPR r 3.9. In both situations, steps could be taken by the court to secure future compliance by individual parties and litigants in general through, for instance, the imposition of cost sanctions and a robust approach to the imposition of other sanctions for non-compliance. Those steps do not call into question the assumption noted above; whether or not the original case management decision was consistent with the overriding objective. The relevant question at the costs assessment stage at the conclusion of proceedings does not concern the reasonableness of case management orders, or whether they furthered the overriding objective. Such considerations would amount to a collateral attack on the case management order. They concern the parties' conduct in complying with the terms of court orders.[21] Where relief from sanctions for non-compliance is concerned, questions as to the appropriateness of the original order, or of 'unless orders' to secure compliance, cannot be raised at further hearings. The question focuses on the party's non-compliance with the order, not the order itself.[22]

The implicit assumption underpinning Zuckerman's focus on the non-compliance problem then is this: if the courts eliminate, or at the least significantly reduce, non-compliance, the civil justice system will operate more effectively and efficiently than prior to the CPR's introduction. A culture of compliance will produce proportionate use of party and court resources consistently with the overriding objective and its multi-dimensional theory of justice. That assumption in turn rests on the belief that the case management orders which are to be complied with are themselves consistent with the overriding objective. It is not however clear that that assumption is necessarily correct. A number of issues arise.

First, if case management orders are not consistent with the overriding objective, compliance with them will result in both parties and the court using disproportionate resources to reach trial and judgment. In turn this will have an adverse effect on the court's ability to distribute its resources appropriately across all litigants, as required by CPR r 1.1(2)(e). Compliance with disproportionate orders will embed disproportionality. Secondly, if parties challenge orders which they view as

[21] CPR r 44.2(4)(a).

[22] eg, *Oak Cash & Carry Ltd v British Gas Trading Ltd* [2016] EWCA Civ 153, [2016] 1 WLR 4530 [40] where the Court of Appeal emphasized how, in assessing the question of relief from sanctions, the nature of the non-compliance was to be looked at both in terms of non-compliance with an 'unless order', while also taking account of the broader non-compliance with the original case management order. And see *Denton v TH White Ltd* [2014] EWCA Civ 906, [2014] 1 WLR 3926 [27].

disproportionate in nature, those orders are unlikely to be subject to appellate scrutiny. It is well-established that permission to appeal from case management orders requires a putative appellant to satisfy a high threshold for the grant of permission; a threshold intended to ensure that such decisions are not 'lightly interfered with' by appellate courts.[23] There is thus little prospect that disproportionality in such orders will come to light, be subject to scrutiny, and where necessary be corrected. Absent appellate scrutiny, there will either be compliance or non-compliance with the order. Compliance raises the previous problem ie, it embeds disproportionality. Non-compliance, as it will not give rise to scrutiny of the original order, will equally embed disproportionality whether it is ultimately complied with or not.

In both situations, the disproportionate nature of case management orders is hidden from view. Compliance embeds poor management practice. It embeds a culture of disproportionality just as readily as non-compliance does. A clear example of this can be seen in the approach taken to disclosure since the CPR was introduced. Disclosure, discovery as it was then known, was identified by Woolf as one of the main aspects of civil litigation that contributed to disproportionate cost and time. As he concluded in his Interim Report from 1995,

> The scale of discovery, at least in the larger cases, is completely out of control. The principle of full, candid disclosure in the interests of justice has been devalued because discovery is pursued without sufficient regard to economy and efficiency in terms of the usefulness of the information which is likely to be obtained from the documents disclosed.[24]

The reason for this was said to be the nature of the test governing the scope of the discovery obligation established by the Court of Appeal in *Compagnie Financiere du Pacifique v Peruvian Guano Company* (1882) 11 QBD 55. That decision was said to render the obligation one that was 'virtually unlimited' in application.[25] It was neither constrained by party or court resource considerations ie, cost, nor any other procedural imperatives. The CPR was intended to restrict its scope and ensure that what was to be known as disclosure was to be carried out proportionality. The cost and time expended on it was no longer to be unbound, but rather was to be limited by reference to the overriding objective. This was to be achieved by introducing a tailored approach to disclosure. In the first instance, this limited disclosure to 'standard disclosure'; to those documents a party intended to rely upon and those which were adverse to their case or supported their opponent's case.[26] Where that was unnecessary, standard disclosure could be limited or dispensed

[23] G Vos (ed), *Civil Procedure 2019* vol 1 (Sweet & Maxwell 2019) para 52.3.11; *Abdulle v Commissioner of Police for the Metropolis (Practice Note)* [2015] EWCA Civ 1260, [2016] 1 WLR 898.
[24] Woolf (n 4) 8.
[25] ibid 166–67.
[26] CPR r 31.5(1)(a) and r 31.6.

with in its entirety.[27] Disclosure going wider than standard disclosure required the grant of an application for specific disclosure.[28] As Zuckerman has pointed out, this differential approach was intended to ensure that the disclosure obligation was carried out so as to properly balance the three elements of multi-dimensional justice.[29] It did not, however, achieve its objective, as Jackson concluded in 2009, as part of his Costs Review,[30] and as the Disclosure Working Party concluded in 2017,[31] following its review of the failure of the reforms that followed from the Costs Review.

The problem was that parties did not actively consider whether standard disclosure was the proportionate order ie, they did not seek to displace it entirely or limit disclosure. Nor did the courts challenge parties sufficiently on the question of what an appropriate, proportionate disclosure order ought to be. Post-1999, as noted by Jackson in 2013, the approach taken was that the power to restrict disclosure was 'not often given serious consideration'.[32] An approach was taken to such orders, and to determining which type of order was appropriate, which was 'formulaic and ineffectual'.[33] Moreover, in complex, high value cases where specific disclosure was often required, both standard and specific disclosure were often not carried out in a way to render the process proportionate.[34] Orders were made and complied with, where they were not proportionate. This continued to be the case after the disclosure obligation was revised following the Jackson reforms in 2013,[35] which specifically removed standard disclosure as the default option. As Sir Rupert Jackson put it in 2016,

> In large commercial actions and other substantial cases too often people are treating standard disclosure as the default option. Parties frequently agree standard disclosure, seemingly without considering whether other options may be preferable, and the courts accept their agreements. It would be to the public benefit if all involved in the disclosure process gave more attention to the full range of options before simply proposing or agreeing to 'standard disclosure'.[36]

[27] CPR r 31.5(1)(b).
[28] CPR r 31.12.
[29] Zuckerman (n 3) 721, 'The CPR arrangements are better designed to achieve a satisfactory accommodation between the need to secure access to all the relevant evidence in the interest of the determination of truth, on the one hand, and on the other hand the need to avoid wasteful, costly and oppressive processes. however, the tensions between these different needs cannot be completely resolved by rules.'
[30] R Jackson, *Review of Civil Litigation Costs: Preliminary Report* (May 2009) Vol II, 388ff.
[31] Disclosure Working Party, *Proposed Disclosure Pilot Briefing Note* (Judicial Office) (2 November 2017) <https://www.judiciary.uk/wp-content/uploads/2017/11/dwg-guidance-note-2-nov-2017.pdf>.
[32] Jackson (n 30) 389.
[33] R Jackson, *Confronting Costs Management* (15 May 2015) [2.10] <https://www.judiciary.gov.uk/wp-content/uploads/2015/05/speech-jackson-lj-confronting-costs-management-1.pdf>.
[34] Jackson (n 30) 393ff.
[35] J Baxter, 'Litigation Trends—Over Disclosure? Why Costs Aren't Working', New Law Journal (15 June 2016) <https://www.russell-cooke.co.uk/media/1039159/litigation-trends-over-disclosure-why-aren-t-costs-working-russell-cooke-in-new-law-journal.pdf>.
[36] R Jackson, *Disclosure* (Law Society, Commercial Litigation Conference lecture, 10 October 2016).

The point would be reiterated in 2016, by the GC 100 Group of in-house counsel[37] and again by the Disclosure Working Party in 2017,[38] the latter concluding that disclosure orders were not sufficiently focused on those issues for which disclosure was necessary and that too often standard disclosure was ordered when it was unnecessary. From 1999 and despite attempts to rectify the problem, parties failed to ensure that the disclosure order made was proportionate to the case at hand. Orders made were disproportionate. Compliance with a disproportionate order or orders, just as much as non-compliance,[39] embedded disproportionate case management. In such circumstances, the more effective compliance was, the worse the mismanagement of court and party resources would be, as the complaints noted by Jackson about the disproportionate cost and time spent on disclosure suggests.

The established answer to the problem of disproportionate disclosure is for the rules to be amended, as happened in 1999, 2013, and as now proposed through a pilot scheme[40] applicable to commercial cases, which resulted from the Disclosure Working Party's review. Such rule changes are then to be given proper effect through a change in litigation culture, one which sees the rules used as intended.[41] The culture change was to be one where the only orders made where those which required proportionate disclosure, and which were to be complied with by the parties. There is, however, a fundamental difficulty in securing a culture change in litigation. Historically, such changes have been effected where the need and nature of such a change is understood by lawyers and the courts, and consistent and clear guidance of a sustained period of time by appellate courts is provided. This was the case, for instance, in the 1870s to 1880s,[42] where a liberal approach to relief from sanctions and to amendment of process was embedded in the Rules of the Supreme Court and it is currently being attempted now by the Court of Appeal through the *Mitchell* and *Denton* line of authority,[43] which seeks to replace the past liberal approach to relief from sanctions with a narrower one. A consistent line of Court of Appeal authority depends upon appeals being brought from case management decisions. As noted above, given the approach to appeals from such decisions, such a

[37] ibid, where it was noted that, 'There was a general recognition that the tools for controlling disclosure have been in place since April 2013, but the parties and the courts are not making sufficient use of them.' <https://www.judiciary.uk/wp-content/uploads/2016/10/lj-jackson-speech-disclosure-10102016.pdf>.

[38] Disclosure Working Party (n 31) [3(ii)] and [3(iv)].

[39] Non-compliance was equally a problem. As Jackson noted at R Jackson, *Review of Civil Litigation Costs: Preliminary Report* (May 2009) (Vol I) 368, there was also a tendency for parties to disclose more than was required by standard disclosure. Hence the compliance problem ie, over-disclosure because standard disclosure was disproportionate, was compounded by over-disclosure on top of that.

[40] CPR PD51U.

[41] Disclosure Working Party (n 31) [5], 'The unanimous view of the Working Group was that a wholesale cultural change is required and that this can only be achieved by the widespread promulgation of a completely new rule and guidelines.' In this it echoed the Woolf Reforms, see Woolf (n 4) 172, 'Discovery is an area where the culture has to change.'

[42] See Sorabji (n 15) 201ff.

[43] See Vos (n 23) para 3.9.1ff for a discussion of the case law in this area.

line of authority is unlikely to be secured absent a change in approach to the grant of permission to appeal in such cases. There is no apparent indication that such a change will be effected. The question then becomes how to secure the necessary cultural change to give effect to the latest attempt to render disclosure proportionate without recourse to guidance from the Court of Appeal. This question is a particular application of the broader one Zuckerman raised, which was noted earlier: how to secure effective oversight of case management orders and hence the use of judicial as well as party resources and, in the absence of appellate review, how to determine where and why management problems were arising in specific cases. In the absence of appellate review, or repeated complaints by litigants as is the case with disclosure's cost, how can the courts know that the case management orders made and complied with further the overriding objective?

Before considering how that question can potentially be answered by the digitization of the courts, a further compliance problem arises: inconsistency in judicial decision-making. This potentially arises in two different ways: decision-making that is inconsistent with the overriding objective due to lack of information; and decision-making that is internally inconsistent by the judiciary.

First, lack of information. The second feature of effective case management that Zuckerman identified in 2007, as noted above, was that the judiciary be given sufficient powers to achieve the overriding objective.[44] That requires them to have sufficient knowledge of the individual case before them. In that way they have sufficient information to be able to determine directions that enable that claim to progress 'justly and at proportionate cost' in respect of the immediate parties.[45] Such information is a matter for the parties to provide the court in advance of the case management conference where directions are given. Effective management goes beyond the management of the individual claim. It is equally a matter of ensuring that each claim is allotted such court time and resources as are proportionate vis-à-vis the needs of other litigants, as provided for by CPR r 1.(2)(e) and acknowledged by the Court of Appeal in *Re L (a child)*[46] and *Mitchell*.[47] Such information cannot, however, be provided by the parties who will have no access to data concerning the overall demands on the civil courts' resources. If those demands are to be taken account of properly, such data needs to be available at case management conferences so that the parties can make submissions concerning it, as it will have an impact on the directions given in their case, and so that the judge can take account of it.

At the present time such information is not, however, available. Case management directions are taken in the absence of what could properly be thought to be a key set of information required to inform their decision-making. The courts have

44 Zuckerman (n 2) [24].
45 CPR r 1.1.
46 [2013] EWCA Civ 1778 [12].
47 [2013] EWCA Civ 1537, [2014] 1 WLR 795 [38]–[39].

not yet been given sufficient powers to properly achieve the overriding objective. In the absence of such information, case management decisions may take account of some, but no more than some, system-wide information available to the judge. As Master McCloud noted in *Mitchell*, the effect of the claimant's non-compliance had a negative impact on the needs of other claims that she was due to hear, but which had to be adjourned to accommodate the relief application.[48] They could therefore take account of information they know about their own listings. Such information will, however, only be partial. It is likely to be limited to the judge's understanding of the own scheduled listings. Different judges, some of whom will be part-time, may have a greater or lesser understanding of those listings than others. Furthermore, it is unlikely that they will know or be able to ascertain the wider systemic context of any particular decision. A combination of partial knowledge of their own availability to hear and list proceedings, of different judges having differential levels of knowledge, and an absence of systemic knowledge, would at the least suggest that different judges are unlikely to be able to take a consistent approach to case management decisions. Either such information will be disregarded entirely, in which case decisions will be made solely be reference to the parties' submissions, they will thus focus on managing the individual claim, rather than managing the claim in the context of the overall efficiency of the system, or they will, as in *Mitchell*, take account of potentially partial, anecdotal information concerning the effect upon the system as a whole of individual case management decisions. In either case, it is difficult to see how the courts would be able to manage numerous individual claims consistently with the overriding objective. Having introduced the requirement to manage cases consistently with what Ryder LJ in *Re L* has referred to as collective proportionality,[49] there is a need to provide the courts with the necessary information to do so. That is currently lacking.

Secondly, internal inconsistency. If we assume that the courts are provided with sufficient information by the parties and by HMCTS, a further problem arises. A number of studies have shown that there is a real risk that different judges do not decide similar cases in a consistent way. More problematically, some have also shown that individual judges can and do decide the same case in different ways at different times ie, they may not be internally consistent.[50] This can manifest itself in a number of ways.

First, it has been shown that given a common factual and legal scenario, individual judges can demonstrate markedly differences in approach. A study by Austin and Williams, which examined judicial approaches to sentencing decisions in criminal proceedings, found that judges took different approaches on

[48] [2013] EWHC 2355 (QB) [28].
[49] [2013] EWCA Civ 1778 [12].
[50] For an overview see H Fry, *Hello World—How to be Human in the Age of the Machine* (Penguin 2019) 51ff.

three different metrics: conviction; sentencing; and magnitude of punishment.[51] There was a lack of consistency in approach to the same factual and legal scenarios. Secondly, a study of bail decisions by magistrates carried out by Dhami and Ayton demonstrated that individual judges are not internally consistent.[52] Eighty-one magistrates completed a questionnaire which asked them to consider forty-one hypothetical bail applications. A number of the scenarios were repeated randomly. The study again demonstrated inconsistency across magistrates. It also demonstrated that faced with the same factual and legal scenario in multiple instances the same magistrate would reach different decisions. These studies concerned criminal procedure. Comparable studies on case management decisions in civil proceedings have not been carried out. As such it may be the case that these results would not be replicated.

Given, however, that the two studies were based on the application of law to agreed facts, the individual judges would have been expected to use the same skills as those used in civil proceedings; a point underscored by the approach taken by the Judicial College which now focuses on the provision of generic judicial skills ie, case and trial management and judgment writing that is applicable across all forms of proceeding.[53] Given this, the two studies should, at the least, suggest that were judges to be given full information to determine case management decisions consistently with the overriding objective, they may well reach different decisions on similar facts. As such the risk would be, were parties to comply with those decisions, that some of them would provide parties with a proportionate process, while others would not. Not only would this undermine equal treatment, it would also tend to undermine effective management of the courts' resources, whilst also potentially having an adverse effect on other litigants' right to receive a just process.

The two studies cited do not seek to provide an explanation why there is a disparity in approach across judges and internally by judges. They consider whether there is consistency and if not the extent to which there is inconsistency. Other studies have sought to explain why inconsistency arises. Danziger et al, in a study of judicial decision-making in Israel, concluded that a parole application is more likely to be granted if heard at the start of the judicial day or immediately after lunch.[54] The rate at which applications were granted declined as lunch approached,

[51] W Austin and T Williams III, 'A Survey of Judges' Responses to Simulated Legal Cases: Research Note on Sentencing Disparity' (1977) 68(2) JCLC 366.

[52] M Dhami and P Ayton, 'Bailing and Jailing the Fast and Frugal Way' (2001) 14 J Behav Decis Mak 141–68.

[53] See the Judicial Skills Framework 2014, <https://www.judiciary.uk/about-the-judiciary/training-support/judicial-skills-framework-resources/resources/judicial-skills/>. Additionally, the courses provided by the Judicial College to judiciary encompass the following: 'Assessing evidence, Litigants in person, Victims and other vulnerable witnesses in court, Case Management, Making a structured decision, Decision and judgment writing, Giving an oral decision, Judicial ethics, Business of judging, The Adversarial system of trial.' <https://www.judiciary.uk/about-the-judiciary/international/training-for-overseas-judges/>.

[54] S Danziger and others, 'Extraneous Factors in Judicial Decisions' (2011) 108 PNAS 42, 6889.

and then again from lunch to the end of the judicial day. The explanation for this was, relying on previous studies, said to be various external factors on the judiciary eg, reduction in blood sugar levels as they day went on, the absence of rest breaks, or the judge's mood.[55] Other studies have shown, for instance, that where an individual takes a number of similar decisions over a period of time, those past decisions can have an impact on a later decision ie, the latter is not determined on its merits but unconsciously due to the decisions taken in previous cases. While not a study of judicial decision-making, this was borne out by a study by Simonsohn and Gino.[56] They examined decision-making in respect of college applications in the United States. Their study of 9,000 such applications demonstrated that where an individual had assessed three applications positively, they were less likely to assess a fourth positively. If this holds for judicial decision-making it would suggest that were a judge has granted, for instance, four contested applications for expert evidence to be by way of a single joint expert, they would be less likely to grant the fourth. That decision would, according to Simonsohn and Gino's study, arguably be a result not of the merits of the application, but of the judge's past decisions. If correct, such a decision would not only be unjust, it could equally be one that failed to properly secure the overriding objective, ie, by resulting in party experts being appointed.

The various studies are suggestive of a problem. They are no more than that as they have not been replicated in respect of case management decision-making and, as such, point to a potential compliance problem. If they are correct, and case management decisions can and perhaps are in certain circumstances influenced by factors other than those relating to the legal and factual merits, which would include data concerning the overall operation of the civil courts assuming that was available, then it points to such orders potentially failing to secure the overriding objective. By being based on extraneous factors, they may result in orders being made that grant too much or too little process to particular cases. Compliance with such orders would then undermine effective case management. The question then becomes how to determine whether or not this potential problem is a real one, if so, the extent to which it is a problem and then how to cure it.

[55] ibid 6892. There conclusions have, however, been criticized by K Weinshall-Margela and J Shapard, 'Overlooked Factors in the Analysis of Parole Decisions' (2011) 108 PNAS 42, E833. They explain the inconsistency as arising from the way cases are scheduled. Represented parties were scheduled at the start of the day, unrepresented parties were scheduled to be heard at the end of the day. That raises the question whether increased failure rate arose from the fact of or absence of representation, or again from the time of day when the hearings were scheduled, a combination of both or other factors. See, however, B Dietrich and others, 'Emotional Arousal Predicts Voting on the US Supreme Court' (2019) 27(2) Polit Anal 237, for a consideration of the effect of mood or emotional arousal on judicial-decision making and reference to further studies on the issue.

[56] U Simonsohn and F Gino, 'Daily Horizons: Evidence of Narrow Bracketing in Judgments from 9,000 MBA Admission Interviews' (2013) 24(2) Psychol Sci 219–24.

Digitizing consistency in order to improve compliance

If compliance is to result in a properly and effectively managed civil justice system, the orders complied with need to be consistent with the overriding objective. If not, and absent appellate review, curing the non-compliance problem may cause more harm than good by embedding a culture of compliance with orders that fail to secure the overriding objective. With this in mind the compliance problem can be seen as having a number of facets. First, it can arise through a failure to provide judges who make case management decisions with sufficient information to enable them to take proper account of collective proportionality. Their orders may be based on partial information or no information concerning their effect on the effective management of the courts' resources and their effect on other litigants' access to those resources. If access to justice is to be a form of rationed access in order to facilitate its achievement for the broadest spectrum of litigants,[57] and if it is to be, as Zuckerman has it, a properly managed public service,[58] then case management decisions need to be made in the light of relevant evidence concerning the operation of the civil justice system. Secondly, it can also arise through the potential risk that judges can and, the evidence suggests may well, make some case management decisions on factors extraneous to the merits of applications before them ie, the time of day when the application is heard, previous decisions they have made that day, or even unconscious biases[59] or heuristics.[60] Consequently again, such decisions may fail to secure collective proportionality.

Looking to Zuckerman's criteria for effective management, the question is how are judges to be given the tools to overcome the twin aspects of the compliance problem? How are the judiciary to be given the means, as he put it, to overcome the absence of real oversight of the use of judicial resources, and the absence of a mechanism to determine where and why management problems arose, which could then be used to help formulate reform recommendations.[61] Effective oversight mechanisms, if the information they contained were made available to the judiciary, could help to solve the first aspect of the compliance problem. Such information could inform case management decisions so that they took proper account of collective proportionality. It should be noted that such information would have to be made

[57] *Mitchell v News Group Newspapers Ltd* [2013] EWCA Civ 1537, [2014] 1 WLR 795 [38]–[39].

[58] Zuckerman (n 3) 2–5.

[59] While not considered here, studies have shown the effect of unconscious bias on decision-making, D Nugent, 'Judicial Bias' (1994) 42(1) Clev St L Rev 1. For instance, A Glynn and M Sen, 'Identifying Judicial Empathy: Does Having Daughters Cause Judges to Rule for Women's Issues?' (2015) 59(1) Am J Pol Sci 37, have suggested that judicial decision-making may be effected in certain circumstances depending on the gender of a judge's children. For a discussion of the different types of bias see, G Persad, 'When, and How, Should Cognitive Bias Matter to Law' (2014) 32 Law & Ineq 31.

[60] E Peer and E Gamliel, 'Heuristics and Biases in Judicial Decision-Making' (2013) 49 Court Rev 114.

[61] See n 17, above.

available to parties to litigation in order for them to be able to make submissions on matters that were to be taken account of in decisions affecting the management of their claims. Such mechanisms could also help provide a basis to improve judicial training, and to act as a check against judicial decision-making to help reduce the potential scope for extraneous factors to influence case management orders. What then are the mechanisms that could be developed to achieve these ends? One potential set of mechanisms, to help overcome the first aspect of the compliance problem, could arise via the digitization of the civil courts and their processes. The second aspect of the problem could be cured through the potential use of artificial intelligence as a means to assist judicial decision-making.

Digitization

First, digitization. Since the turn of the twenty-first century, there has been a trend towards the transformation of court processes through the increasing use of digital technology. This has ranged from the unsuccessful attempt to create a wholly digital, online, court in Michigan in 2002, the *Cyber Court*,[62] to the creation of the Hanghzou internet court in China,[63] the Civil Resolution Tribunal in British Columbia, Canada.[64] It has also encompassed the introduction of online dispute resolution systems eg, e-negotiation or e-mediation, as part of the civil court process, for small claims, such as the approach taken in Utah in the United States.[65] Less ambitious reforms, by comparison, have seen the introduction of digital or e-filing, video-conferencing, and digital case management systems in a number of jurisdictions, such as Australia.[66] In England and Wales, basic online claim filing for debt and possession claims were also introduced in 2001 and 2006, respectively.[67] At the present time, digitization is being further developed in England and

[62] L Ponte, 'The Michigan Cyber Court: A Bold Experiment in the development of the first public virtual courthouse' (2002–2003) 4 NC J L & Tech 51; N Vermeys and K Benyekhlef, 'ODR and the Courts' in M Abdel and others, *Online Dispute Resolution: Theory and Practice* (Eleven Publishing 2012) 298.

[63] For details see, The National Center for Technology and Dispute Resolution <http://odr.info/hangzhou-internet-court/>; and see, the court's website at <https://netcourt.yuncourt.com/portal/main/en/index.htm>.

[64] S Salter and D Thompson, 'Public-Centred Civil Justice Redesign: A Case Study of the British Columbia Civil Resolution Tribunal' (2016) 3 McGill J Disp Resol 113.

[65] D Himonas, 'Utah's Online Dispute Resolution Program' (2018) 122 Dick L Rev 875.

[66] The Federal Court of Australia's eCourtroom; see Vermeys and Benyekhlef (n 62) 300. E-filing and video-conferencing in the Federal Court was first introduced in 1995, see M Black, 'The Federal Court of Australia: The First 30 Years—A Survey on the Occasion of Two Anniversaries' [2007] Melb U L Rev 38 at XIII. Also see, for instance, comparable developments in New South Wales, M Evers and P Ryan, 'Exploring eCourt Innovations in New South Wales Civil Courts' (2016) 5(1) JCivLP 65.

[67] See CPR PD 7E and PD 55B respectively. For a discussion, see G Lupo, *The case of money claim online and possession claim online in England and Wales*, Research case study in Building Interoperability for European Civil Proceedings Online <http://www.irsig.cnr.it/BIEPCO/documents/case_studies/MCOL_Lupo_FINAL%20REVISION.pdf>.

Wales through the HMCTS reform programme,[68] which commenced in 2013 and is (as of 2019) expected to be completed in 2023.

There are two main parts to the reform programme, each of which fits with the general trend of digitization as well as provides a basis to overcome the first aspect of the compliance problems. The first, and perhaps more prosaic, part of the reform programme is focused on both the replacement of traditional paper-based court processes, such as filing and serving written claim forms, defences, and evidence, with e-filing ie, online filing of electronic forms and the eventual ability to upload evidence online, and the creation of a fully digital case filing and management system.[69] The former is currently being implemented through, for instance, the progressive roll-out of what is known as CE-File across the civil justice system.[70] It is also being implemented through a number of procedural pilot schemes running under the CPR, which are testing online claim and defence filing and serving both by litigants-in-person and legal professionals, online settlement processes, and video hearings.[71] The latter, digital case management system is, for civil claims,[72] still in the process of development,[73] albeit a comparable system is operational in the criminal justice system.[74] The second part of the reform programme goes wider than moving the present approach to filing and managing claims to a digital process. Building on recommendations made initially by the Civil Justice Council,[75]

[68] HMCTS is Her Majesty's Courts and Tribunals Service, which administers, amongst others, the civil courts. For a discussion of the programme see, J Rozenberg, *The Online Court: Will IT Work?* (2016) <https://long-reads.thelegaleducationfoundation.org/will-it-work/>.

[69] The necessity of such has not been lost on previous procedural reformers. Woolf understood that for his case management reforms to work effectively it would be necessary to implement effective court IT, see M Briggs, *Chancery Modernisation Review: Provisional Report* (July 2013) 14. That was not done: see H Brooke, 'Technology and the Judicial Process', in *Essays in Honour of Sir Brian Neill: The Quintessential Judge* (LexisNexis UK 2003).

[70] See the use of CE-File: CPR PD510 and <https://www.gov.uk/guidance/ce-file-system-information-and-support-advice> accessed 9 March 2019.

[71] See, CPR PD51R, PD51S, and PD 51V. The pilots have not, as yet, progressed to online filing of evidence.

[72] The HMCTS Reform Programme notes, as of June 2019, that this system is to be completed by July 2020, where it notes that this is 'Tranche 2' of the reforms, which focuses on 'Delivering a digital case management system for the civil jurisdictions of the High Court and Court of Appeal, Upper Tribunal, the Employment Appeal Tribunal, Regional Business and Property Courts and District Registries' <https://www.gov.uk/guidance/hmcts-reform-programme-projects-explained>.

[73] It is variously referred to as 'core case data' or 'core case management', see HMCTS Reform—Delivery of professional application User Interfaces, Point 20, 'The HMCTS Reform programme is highly complex and is dependent on a multitude of new and legacy systems, such as; Core Case Data, Identity Access Management, Reference Data, Fees & Payments, Workflow/Rules, Common Component Services to name a few.' (18 March 2019) < https://www.digitalmarketplace.service.gov.uk/digital-outcomes-and-specialists/opportunities/8487>; S Acland-Hood (26 October 2017), 'The system will also start to support cases as they go to and through court, providing a new 'core case management' system for the civil courts which will move us away from the current very paper-heavy operation and start to allow fully digital working (so that, for example, advocates can access case information and work on it from anywhere).' https://insidehmcts.blog.gov.uk/2017/10/26/susan-acland-hood-sets-out-our-priorities-for-the-next-phase-of-courts-and-tribunals-reform/.

[74] The Crown Court Digital Case System <https://crowncourtdcs.caselines.co.uk>.

[75] Civil Justice Council, *Online Dispute Resolution for Low Value Claims* (2015).

and then Justice[76] and the Civil Courts Structure Review,[77] it is intended to introduce, initially for low value claims ie, those below £10,000, an online procedure that is akin to that developed in the British Columbia's Civil Resolution Tribunal.[78] It thus intends to introduce a form on digital or online procedure for County Court claims that has three stages: stage 1, e-evaluation, which would ultimately require the court, via its website, to help parties to evaluate whether they had a valid claim or defence and, if so, whether and how it might best be resolved.[79] This process would primarily be automated ie, it would rely on the use of automated decision trees; stage 2, e-facilitation, which assuming the claim was not resolved at stage 1, would involve a member of the court staff to help bring about a consensual settlement of the dispute via an e-negotiation or e-mediation process, or via a telephonic version of these approaches; and, finally, stage 3, e-adjudication, which if the claim had not settled, result in adjudication by a judge on the papers, or in rare cases at a hearing.[80] At the present time, this three-stage model's implementation remains an aspiration, with the reform programme's focus being to introduce digital filing and case management and the incorporation of the pre-existing small claims mediation scheme into the online pilot schemes. In other words, it has opted to implement stage 3 first.[81] Assuming all parts of the reform programme are implemented a number of potential means would exist to help cure the first aspect of the compliance problem.

At its most basic level the reform programme is intended to render the civil litigation process more cost-effective and efficient for both parties and the court.[82] It thus seeks to promote a more proportionate means of resolving disputes. The elimination of the need to file paper forms with the court, to have them processed, stored, retrieved, and transported to the correct judge to and between court buildings is expected to reduce both the capital and running costs of the courts.[83] It is also expected to reduce the cost of litigating by, for instance, reducing the costs to litigants-in-person or lawyers of travelling to court to file documents. Equally, through the use of e-alerts to parties or their lawyers, or as Cabral and Clarke refer to it, 'proactive messaging from the Court',[84] either from a judge or court officer

[76] JUSTICE, *Delivering Justice in an Age of Austerity* (2015).

[77] See *Terms of Reference—Civil Courts Structure Review* (19 August 2015); M Briggs, *Civil Courts Structure Review—Interim Report* (December 2015); M Briggs, *Civil Courts Structure Review—Final Report* (July 2016). For a detailed discussion of these proposals see the various papers published in the Civil Justice Quarterly's Briggs Special Edition (2017) 36(1) CJQ.

[78] Salter and Thompson (n 64).

[79] See the discussion by E Katsh and O Rabinovich-Einy, *Digital Justice* (OUP 2017) 160, on the operation of this type of approach in Canada.

[80] See Briggs (2015) (n 77) and the Civil Justice Council (n 75) for a discussion of the approach.

[81] Rozenberg (n 68), notes that the genesis of this implementation approach.

[82] See, L Leo, 'Case Management—Drawing from the Singapore Experience' (2011) 30 CJQ 143.

[83] See, for instance, M Santo, *Resourcing and Staffing of the Courts*, House of Lords' Library Note (11 July 2016); the same benefits are noted as underpinning similar reforms in Australia, see, for instance, Evers and Ryan (n 66).

[84] J Cabral and T Clarke, 'Access to Justice Integration with Emerging Court Technologies' (2012) 26(1) Harv J L & Tech 278, 289. The importance of such 'nudges' to secure compliance was noted, in

who have themselves been alerted to an impending procedural deadline in the claim or via an automated process akin to those bank account holders receive via text message to warn them that they are reaching their overdraft limit, the digitized case management system could be expected to reduce the potential for unintended non-compliance with case management orders. Such alerts would thus act as compliance prompts. As such they could thus reduce the need by both parties and the court to expend time and financial resources on applications for relief from sanctions. Moreover, if the second aspect of the reform programme is fully-realized, as its design is intended to be such as to enable a litigant-in-person to litigate effectively without legal advice or assistance, it might be expected to reduce the cost of litigation considerably by eliminating lawyers and their costs from the process.[85] Benefits such as these, assuming they are realized and do not produce unintended negative consequences, may reduce the cost of litigation but they are unlikely themselves to cure the compliance problem. The digitized case management system could, however, provide two distinct means to reduce the compliance problem.

First, it could have a systemic effect, which may lead to a more proportionate distribution of the court's resources across litigants. This could be achieved through implementation of stage 1 and 2 of the Briggs Review recommendations. Most obviously, it could promote proportionate case management through promoting what could be called 'dispute defusion' via the stage 1 facilitation.[86] By providing potential litigants with information that would enable them to ascertain whether their dispute is a legal dispute this initial online stage of the process, it could help parties gain a greater understanding of their dispute at an early stage. This essentially diagnostic tool, akin that available in British Columbia's CRT, could thus lead to a reduction in unmeritorious claims being brought, not least when in the context of the wider context of increasing numbers of litigants-in-person.[87] Assuming claims not defused, then both stage 1 and stage 2, through the provision of information to litigants, facilitating exchange of information and evidence between them, and in stage 2 particularly, e-negotiation or e-mediation, would help facilitate resolution via settlement. As these two stages, and particularly the first stage, are primarily automated and hence involve no real human intervention from court staff or the judiciary, it might then be anticipated the civil court's resources could

the context of the pre-digitized approach to case management in the Jackson Costs Review, see Jackson (n 11) 398.

[85] It is an explicit aim of the second, CCSR-inspired, part of the reform programme to achieve the creation of a civil process designed for litigants-in-person and not lawyers; see Sir Terence Etherton MR, *The Civil Court of the Future* (14 June 2017) at [28] 'The processes will be designed and, where necessary, operated so that individuals can access the system effectively without the need for legal advice or assistance.'

[86] See M Ahmed, 'A Critical View of Stage 1 of the Online Court' (2017) 36(1) CJQ 12.

[87] See Salter and Thompson (n 64) 129, on his this approach works in the CRT.

be targeted more effectively than at present. Essentially this would mean that for those claims that do not require active case management to trial, which would arise in stage 2, the court would expend minimal human resources, enabling it to target its resources on those claims that are not capable of settlement. At the present time, it is unable to do this as once a claim is issued active case management, involving court staff to administer the process and judicial time and decision-making, is the norm. At a systems-level then, full implementation of Briggs' three-staged model could be anticipated, as in British Columbia, to enable compliance by litigants with a case management system that targeted its resources on those claims that required active case management, rather than on all claims issued. Implementation of stages 1 and 2 could go further in its promotion of proportionate case management at a systems-level. Three future possibilities exist.

First, Hodges has argued that implementation could form part of a broader reform of the civil justice system, which could create a 'holistic', coherent dispute resolution system. The idea advanced, which in many ways is an updated variant of Sander's multi-door courthouse,[88] would see the digitized process not just, as Briggs recommended, providing links to Ombudsman schemes, consumer, or regulatory complaints bodies, or advice bodies, it would go beyond that. It could, for instance, through its online portal, once a claimant had input the details of the dispute, create a digital case file that could then be sent to those bodies, to see if they were able to resolve the dispute. If they were not, the digital file would then progress through the digital system to stage 2. In other words, the system could be configured digitally to create a single dispute case file, which would pass through a process that integrated advice and regulatory redress or Ombudsman schemes, before it progressed to the stage 2 and 3 dispute resolution process, which would involve the court. While Hodges noted in 2016 that the timeframe within which Briggs made his recommendations did not allow for this idea to be considered, given that the reform programme's implementation is not now expected to be before 2023 and that work on stages 1 and 2 has not yet commenced, such time for consideration now exists.[89] Given that the senior judiciary have both noted that when implemented the reform programme will enable the civil process to be updated on a continuing basis there seems to be no reason in principle why this could not be considered.[90] If it were, and were implemented, it could further the aim of targeting case management by the courts to those claims that could not be resolved more appropriately via other means.

[88] F Sander, 'Varieties of Dispute Processing' (1976) 70 FRD 111; C Hodges, 'Proposed Modernisation of Courts in England and Wales: IT and the Online Court' (2016) 6(1) IJPL-RIDP 149; and, see, J Sorabji, 'The Online Solutions Court—A Multi-door Courthouse for the 21st Century' (2017) 36(1) CJQ 86.

[89] C Hodges (n 88) 159.

[90] Lord Burnett CJ, *The Age of Reform* (7 June 2018) at [38] <https://www.judiciary.uk/wp-content/uploads/2018/06/speech-lcj-the-age-of-reform2.pdf>.

Secondly, if an integrated design approach were taken to stage 1, the creation of a structurally link between the courts and ombudsman schemes could help conserve court resources by increasing the potential for a reduction in future disputes ie, as Sir Terence Etherton MR has put it, there is scope to develop an effective means of 'preventive justice' or preventive dispute resolution.[91] Prevention could be increased through the provision of case data from civil claims commenced digitally to Ombudsman schemes, irrespective of whether the dispute was referred by stage 1 to an Ombudsman. Such data could then be used by the Ombudsman to determine whether the disputes arising suggested that there were systemic legal problems in any particular area eg, consumer protection, consumer credit law, etc. This could then provide a basis for the Ombudsman to take steps to reduce or eradicate the problem.[92] It could, for instance, publicize the issue, make recommendations to Parliament to reform the law, or assuming it had the power to do so, take remedial action in the market. Integrating the civil process and Ombudsman schemes in this way could thus result in a reduction in specific types of dispute through eliminating their causes. As such it would again, at a systems-level, enable case management to be targeted to disputes that were not otherwise preventable.[93]

Finally, digitization of process could be a means to introduce effective systems-evaluation into the civil justice system ie, the creation of what Zuckerman identified as an effective means to evaluate the operation of the system.[94] A digital case management system could enable the introduction of both quantitative and qualitative means to assess the civil justice system's operation. Quantitative data could be obtained from data extracted from the digital case management system concerning the timeliness through which cases progress through each of the stages, the number of case management orders that result in non-compliance, and so on. Such information could also be used to identify, for instance, the extent to which certain types of order were being made. If it had been in operation, for instance, from 1999 it could have identified at an earlier stage than the Jackson Costs Review, that standard disclosure orders had become the norm. As such it could have brought to light the failure to change the approach to such orders following the CPR's implementation and thus enable remedial action to be taken by rule change or guidance prior to 2009. It could also, following such remedial steps, have enabling scrutiny of any implementation effect ie, whether the reforms had resulted in a change in

[91] Sir Terence Etherton MR (n 85) [24]. It is notable that such an idea was hinted at in Sander's development of the multi-door courthouse when he refers to 'preventive law', albeit there the idea rested on legal assistance being made available more widely to the general population, see Sander (n 88) 112. Also see Katsh and Rabinovich-Einy (n 79) 165.

[92] See C Gill, 'The Evolving Role of the Ombudsman: A Conceptual and Constitutional Analysis of the "Scottish solution" to Administrative Justice' (2014) (Oct) Pub Law 662.

[93] Both Hodges' and Sir Terence Etherton MR's ideas here could be understood as a variant on Hough and Zorza's five stage triage approach outlined in B Hough and R Zorza, 'Tech-supported Triage: The Key to Maximizing Effectiveness and Access' (2012) 26(1) Harv J L & Tech 292.

[94] See n 17, above.

approach by individual judges. It could thus not only provide a basis to promote systems-level improvements to case management via self-evaluation, but it could also help to reduce one specific aspect of the compliance problem eg, case management orders that are not consistent with the overriding objective.

In addition to quantitative data, qualitative data could also be obtained from the introduction of so-called feedback loops into the system; an idea which has particularly been promoted by Sir Terence Etherton MR and Sir Ernest Ryder SPT.[95] Feedback loops operate as an essential part of the success of online forms of dispute resolution, such as that provided by eBay,[96] or more formally and annually by British Columbia's CRT. They are the means by which the particular system secures feedback on ie, user-evaluation of how it operates. Such user-feedback can, as is the case in the CRT, be used to evaluate how the system is operating and thus form the basis of informed continuing improvement. It could thus form the means by which to assess whether and if not where and how case management problems are arising, and thus provide the basis for reform to be effected more readily than it is at present.

It is an open question at the present whether the first two of these reforms will or could be implemented. They require reform to more than the civil justice system, as they would also require reforms to the provision of legal advice and to Ombudsman and regulatory schemes. That would require consideration of issues of principle, as it might be suggested that further diversion of disputes from the courts could undermine access to justice in the sense of access to judgment. Equally, it might be argued, as Genn has argued, that further increasing diversion of claims to settlement undermines the provision and proper status of the civil courts.[97] More practically, it would require digitized systems in the courts and in the various Ombudsman and regulators to be inter-operable, which may be difficult to achieve absent the implementation of new systems. Implementation may thus be difficult to achieve. Where the third potential reform is concerned, it is likely to be carried into effect. As Byrom notes, HMCTS has committed to implementing such an approach as part of the reform programme.[98] The possibility then that this reform, one Zuckerman argued is essential to effective management of the civil justice

[95] Sir Terence Etherton MR (n 85) [39]; Sir Ernest Ryder, 'Securing Open Justice' in B Hess and A Koprovica Harvey (eds), *Open Justice—The Role of Courts in a Democratic Society* (Nomos 2019) 139–40; Sir Ernest Ryder SPT, *What's happening in justice: the view from England and Wales* (UCL Future of Justice Conference, May 2018) [27]–[30] <https://www.judiciary.uk/wp-content/uploads/2018/05/speech-ryder-spt- ucl-may-2018.pdf>.

[96] Katsh and Rabinovich-Einy (n 79) 70ff; T Rosteck, *Happy First Birthday, Strata Solution Explorer!, and Solution Explorer Quarterly Update: 2017 Q4*, <https://civilresolutionbc.ca/happy-first-birthday-strata-solution-explorer/>.

[97] H Genn, *Judging Civil Justice* (CUP 2009).

[98] N Byrom, 'Developing the Detail: Evaluating the Impact of Court Reform in England and Wales on Access to Justice' (2019) <https://research.thelegaleducationfoundation.org/wp-content/uploads/2019/02/Developing-the-Detail-Evaluating-the-Impact-of-Court-Reform-in-England-and-Wales-on-Access-to-Justice-FINAL.pdf> accessed 9 March 2019.

system, may now be realized. If that is ultimately the case, much will then depend on the information it provides be acted on effectively.

The first three potential reforms focus the issue of how to improve the system's ability to distribute its resources in a targeted way ie, to enable proportionate resources to be expended on litigants consistently with CPR r 1.2(2)(e). Digitization also provides a potential basis to cure the compliance problem as it focuses on individual judicial decision-making. It could do this in two ways. In the first instance, as is already said to be the case in the criminal justice system through the use of its digital case management system, the availability of a variety of data concerning judicial availability and other proceedings moving through the system, it could enable case management orders to make case management orders that took better account of the system's resources. In the criminal courts, for instance, separate proceedings can now be listed before the same judge on the same day so as to maximize court utilization. They can be listed before the most appropriate judge, whether that is a salaried judge or a part-time judge, such as a Recorder.[99] As such case management can now be done in such a way as to promote the most efficient and proportionate use of the court's resources by providing all judges, and court listing officers, with comparable and detailed knowledge of the overall resources available throughout the system. Digitized case management could enable case management in civil proceedings to operate in the same way. It would thus increase the prospect that compliance with such orders would be compliance with an order that furthered the overriding objective.

The availability of data concerning other proceedings in the system could also act as a 'fact-checking' mechanism for case management judges. Assuming that digitization moves from the concept of uploading claim forms to the entry of details on digital claim forms and digital statements of case, there would seem to be no reason why such data could not be capable of being provided to a judge, and necessarily to parties at case management hearings to enable them to make submissions in respect of it. The information may need to be anonymized and it may need to be aggregated, but it could provide judges with information on what case management orders had been made by other judges in comparable situations. It could thus act as a means by which judges and parties could assess potential orders ie, to consider whether they are within a reasonable range of other orders in order to test the extent to which they may be consistent with the requirements of collective proportionality. This is not to suggest that a case management judge would be bound to follow the approach taken in such other decisions. There may be reasons why a different approach is necessary on the facts of the individual case. It would, however, provide them with an insight into the question of whether or

[99] See *The Better Case Management Handbook* (Judiciary of England and Wales, 8 January 2018) 6–7 <https://www.judiciary.uk/wp-content/uploads/2018/02/bcm-guide-for-practitioners-20180207.pdf>.

not the order they intend to make, and with which compliance is expected, is likely to further this aspect of the overriding objective. At the least it could provide them with greater information than they have at present to guide their decision-making, and to ensure that they do focus on this issue and not exclusively or predominately on the individual case before them, which, as Piggot observed, there is a noted tendency towards.[100] An increase in information on this issue may well, and this ought to be subject to digitally-enabled evaluation, help to reduce that tendency and thereby further help reduce the compliance problem.

The promise of artificial intelligence

The final area where digitization could help improve case management is through the use of artificial intelligence (AI) within the civil process. The development and utilization of AI in the justice system remains at a very early stage,[101] although notwithstanding that its involvement is already controversial.[102] In England its use in the civil justice system is, in 2019, no more than embryonic. While its utility in improving discrete aspects of the civil process, such as disclosure, have been accepted by the High Court, as yet there has been little consideration of its application more broadly.[103] It was not until March 2019 that the judiciary established an Advisory Panel to consider how AI could properly be used within the justice system.[104] Considerations here must of necessity therefore be tentative. With that caveat in mind, there are two potential ways in which the use of AI could help ameliorate the compliance problem:[105] judicial training; and as a judicial 'decision

[100] Piggot (n 15).

[101] Fry (n 50) 49ff.

[102] Use of AI in respect of the justice system via its potential ability to predict judicial decision-making is now, for instance, a criminal offence, see, art 33 Justice Reform Act 2019 (France) <https://www.legifrance.gouv.fr/eli/loi/2019/3/23/2019-222/jo/article_33>.

[103] In *Pyrrho Investments v MWB Property* [2016] EWHC 256 (Ch), the High Court followed the approach taken in New York and in Ireland (*Moore v Publicis Groupe* 11 Civ 1279 (ALC)(AJP) (SDNY 24 February 2012); *Irish Bank Resolution Corporation Ltd v Quinn* [2015] IEHC 175, [2015] 3 JIC 0306, Irish High Court (Comm)) and accepted that predictive analytics or coding where applied to disclosure could secure three benefits: (i) greater accuracy; (ii) greater speed; and (iii) lower cost than when carried out by lawyers. Also see M Grossman and G Cormack, 'Technology-Assisted Review in E-Discovery Can Be More Effective and More Efficient Than Exhaustive Manual Review' (2011) 17(3) Richmond JOLT 1.

[104] The Lord Chief Justice's AI Advisory Panel <https://www.judiciary.uk/announcements/lord-chief-justice-sets-up-advisory-group-on-artificial-intelligence/>.

[105] These are in addition to the potential use AI could be put to in order to automate the dispute diagnosis aspect of stage 1 of the Briggs' model, and e-negotiation and e-mediation within its second stage. For an insight into the potential roles it may play in this respect see, A Lodder and J Zeleznikov, 'Artificial Intelligence and Online Dispute Resolution' in M Wahab, E Katsh, and D Rainey (eds), *Online Dispute Resolution: Theory and Practice* (Eleven Publishing 2012) 61. There is also the potential to move to algorithmic adjudication, potentially, for low value claims if and to the extent the speed and lower cost of such an approach is accepted as a viable trade-off for traditional forms of participation and accountability through a reasoned judgment, see Katsh and Rabinovich-Einy (n 79) 48 for an outline of how such an approach operates in private ODR systems. Such decision support systems could equally

support system'.[106] Both mechanisms could potentially be used to improve judicial decision-making by reducing the problems identified earlier of judicial bias and judicial inconsistency in decision-making.

The benefit that could be gained for judicial training stems ironically from one of the main concerns about the use of AI at the present time; that it encodes human bias in its decision-making processes. The problem is, essentially, that were AI systems are developed to predict human decision-making they do so on the basis of past human decisions or, more broadly, previous human behaviour. Whether it is using AI to predict which potential employee is the best to hire, or whether it is using data on past recidivism rates in individuals convicted of specific offences, two things have become apparent. First, that bias, as Raub puts it, is encoded into the AI process, into the prediction.[107] A biased input in terms of data, or for that matter bias in the way that the system is programmed,[108] leads to a biased output. For this reason its use in the criminal justice system in the United States to assist parole decisions has been subject to criticism.[109]

There is a potential benefit that can be drawn from this, as has been noted by Koulu.[110] Where an AI programme is developed to predict judicial decision-making, as can be done at the present with high levels of accuracy,[111] they have the potential to bring to light bias in individual judicial decision-making. Given a sufficient data base, or a sufficiently powerful AI programme, or both, the possibility arises that previously subconscious bias in individual judges or previously unidentified institutional bias in the justice system could be identified. This

be developed for use in stage 2 of the Briggs' model, if implemented, as an aid to e-negotiation or e-mediation, see A Lodder and J Zeleznikov, *Enhanced Dispute Resolution through the use of Information Technology* (CUP 2010) 58ff.

[106] For background see Lodder and Zeleznikov (n 105) 62ff.

[107] M Raub, 'Bots, Bias and Big Data: Artificial Intelligence, Algorithmic Bias and Disparate Impact Liability in Hiring Practices' (2018) 71(2) Ark L Rev 529, 570, 'Bias is a challenge that is rooted in human nature, and it is passed in code to predictive hiring algorithm.'

[108] Katsh and Rabinovich-Einy (n 79) 49.

[109] ProPublica, *Machine bias—risk assessments in criminal sentencing*, <https://www.propublica.org/article/machine-bias-risk-assessments-in-criminal-sentencing>; '*State v. Loomis* Wisconsin Supreme Court Requires Warning Before Use of Algorithmic Risk Assessments in Sentencing' (2017) 130 Harv L Rev 1530 <https://harvardlawreview.org/2017/03/state-v-loomis/>. Its use in predictive policing has also been subject to criticism as a consequence of predictive bias, see for instance, P Brantingham, M Valasik, and GO Mohler, 'Does Predictive Policing Lead to Biased Arrests? Results From a Randomized Controlled Trial' (2018) 5(1) Stat and Pub Pol 1;

[110] As she put it in 2019, '... there is some potential here [from AI predictive bias], as it is useful to recognise the fact that biases exist and then reveal the existence of biases in human action', see R Kolou, reported at <https://www.law.ox.ac.uk/sites/files/oxlaw/post-conference_report_0.pdf>

[111] T Ruger and others, 'The Supreme Court Forecasting Project: Legal and Political Science Approaches to Predicting Supreme Court Decision-making' (2004) 104 Colum L Rev 1150; N Aletras and others, 'Predicting Judicial Decisions of the European Court of Human Rights: A Natural Language Processing Perspective' (2016) Peer J Comput Sci, doi: 10.7717/peerj-cs.93 <https://peerj.com/articles/cs-93.pdf>; N Katz and others, 'A General Approach for Predicting the Behavior of the Supreme Court of the United States' (2017) 12(4) PLoS ONE <http://journals.plos.org/plosone/article/file?id=10.1371/journal.pone.0174698&type=printable>.

information could then be used in England by the Judicial College, the judiciary's training body, to form the basis of unconscious bias training programmes to help reduce or eliminate it from decision-making. Equally, it could be used by the Lord Chief Justice, who is under a statutory responsibility to provide guidance to the judiciary of England and Wales,[112] where and if necessary to take steps to eliminate institutional bias. Such steps would focus on seeking to improve the quality of judicial decision-making and procedural fairness generally. In terms of the compliance problem, they could help to reduce the possibility of case management orders being subject to unconscious bias. As such training and guidance based on such information as derived from predictive AI could help to expose where, and reduce the prospect of, some case management decisions failing to take proper account of the need to consider collective proportionality either because the judge may be more or less favourably included to the party in the case before them.

In addition to training, AI has the potential to improve the quality of case management decisions by aiding decision-making. As such it could support judicial decision-making. Here, it must be assumed that the AI programme has reached the stage where its predictions are free of bias. Assuming this, a case management judge could use an AI prediction of the case management order to check against the order they intended to make. Again, such a prediction would need to be made available to the parties so that they may make submissions in respect of it. In this way AI could be used as an aid to judicial decision-making in the same way that 'driver-assistance technology'[113] in so-called self-driving cars, or auto-pilot programmes in commercial aircraft, can improve consistency and accuracy in human decision-making.[114] Hence it could improve the quality of the case management order, which is to be complied with by the parties. In both cases an AI programme drawing on a wide-range of data, in the present case all those cases and decisions that will shortly be managed digitally via the newly digitized civil court process, could be used to provide predictions concerning how the case management decision could best be made. Just as with driver-assistance or a plane's autopilot, the AI programme could draw on the available data to provide a base line decision based on an evaluation of the data available for that case and from other cases, and from its knowledge of the resources available to the court. By providing such a baseline, drawing on information not available to the judge, it could then enable both the parties—to whom the AI prediction would have to be made available, and the court to focus their attention on the individual context of the case.

Equally it could enable general consistency to be balanced more effectively than at present with the need to secure individualized case management decisions, where individual differences in cases justify that. The prediction could in

[112] Constitutional Reform Act 2005, s 7(2).
[113] Fry (n 50) 131ff.
[114] Fry (n 50).

this way, as Katsh and Rabinovich-Einy have argued, lead to more consistent judicial decision-making,[115] and ones that are thus better able to lead to orders that match court resources to cases and are thereby consistent with the overriding objective. At the very least, it could provide judges with the material to, again, act as a reality check on their own inconsistency by providing them with an arguably neutral and objective assessment of the approach to be taken in the case before them. Where judicial decisions can be swayed by the time of day, by their decision-making in previous cases, by whether or not their favourite sports team won the night before,[116] a neutral guideline acting as a check on judicial decision-making could potentially improve it and in so doing secure a more consistent and effective allocation of case management resources across all actual and future claims, as Zuckerman and Woolf both argued was fundamental to a modern, properly managed civil justice system.[117]

In approaching such a development care would, however, need to be taken. The provision of an AI prediction to case management judges as a means to check against their proposed decision could, subtly, lead to the judge relying to too great an extent on the AI prediction. If, for instance, it was assumed that the AI prediction was more objective, a judge may feel a subtle pressure to accept or adopt the AI prediction. Rather than being a reality check on judicial decision-making, the prediction would thus become the de facto decision. Equally, use of predictive AI in judicial decision-making could, as in other industries lead to what is known as the 'auto-pilot' problem. That is to say that reliance on auto-pilot in commercial aircraft lead to a reduction in pilots' skills, and as a consequence an increase in the risk in flying. That risk had to be overcome by mandating a set minimum number of flying hours for pilots, where they flew without the aid of auto-pilot.[118] The comparator for judges might be that such a de-skilling through reliance on or use of AI predictions could lead to a reduction in the skills necessary for judicial decision-making generally. Without the practice given by case management, judges may not develop the necessary skills to handle increasingly complex trials, to make proper findings of fact, or to develop the skills that enable them to arrive at clearly reasoned judgments. In a common law jurisdiction particularly, that may

[115] Katsh and Rabinovich-Einy (n 79) 48, where they stress the benefit to be derived from the use of algorithms in decision-making to increase consistency, albeit with limited discretion available. The question for case management would be the extent to which AI-guided decision-making was built into a model that was still committed to a 'fair' amount of judicial discretion. That question will need careful consideration by future policy-makers.

[116] Fry (n 50) 73ff provides an overview of each of these examples.

[117] For this use of AI to develop a number of problems will, however, need to be overcome; hence this is only a potential area of benefit. Those problems are: the potential that AI-assistance may reduce the ability of judges to make decisions themselves; the possibility that judges may simply rely on and endorse the AI-prediction: see Fry (n 50) 141ff; and, '*State v. Loomis* Wisconsin Supreme Court Requires Warning Before Use of Algorithmic Risk Assessments in Sentencing' (2017) 130 Harv L Rev 1530. For AI to develop to benefit case management, these amongst other problems will need to be overcome.

[118] See Fry (n 50) 131ff for one re-telling of this problem.

well pose a significant problem for the future.[119] If the potential benefit of reduced inconsistency in judicial decision-making is to be realized, this issue will need to be grappled with so that judicial skills-development is not denuded at the cost of curing the inconsistency through unconscious factors on decision-making aspect of the compliance problem.

Conclusion

The focus of Zuckerman's critique of the English civil justice system since the implementation of the Woolf reforms by the CPR has quite properly been the adverse effect that non-compliance with case management orders has had on the system's operation. The civil court's inability to develop a consistent approach to non-compliance, and applications to relief from the adverse consequences that flow from it, has rightly been noted as posing a significant problem for the achievement of the CPR's aims and the effective operation of a multi-dimensional theory of justice. This paper has suggested that in addition to this well-known and considered issue, there is a further one that flows from Zuckerman's critique: the compliance problem ie, the problem that arises from flawed case management decisions that are complied with by the parties. Compliance with decisions that are not themselves compliant with the CPR's overriding objective, and do not therefore take proper account of the requirement under CPR r 1.1(2)(e), pose a potentially more significant problem for effective case management. They do as they embed into case management disproportionality.

Consideration has been given to how digitization of the civil courts process via the HMCTS reform programme and implementation of the Briggs' review recommendations could help reduce the compliance problem. It has also, to a lesser extent, considered how the potential use of AI as an aid to judicial training, guidance, and decision-making could also reduce the scope for inconsistency in, and the effect of unconscious influences or bias on, judicial decision-making. This discussion can only properly be seen as the start of an examination of this issue, one which digitization and AI can perhaps bring to the fore for the first time. Digitization, through providing a basis for making available quantitative data on case management orders, and through making available the possibility of qualitative data, may for the first time provide an effective evidence-base to scrutinize case management in England and Wales. If it does, it is to be hoped that steps can and will be taken to enable consideration of the compliance to be as detailed in the future as it has been for the problem of non-compliance.

[119] Evers and Ryan (n 66), not a comparable problem where the use of technology may result in the de-skilling of junior lawyers.

9

Taking Seriously Affordability, Expedition, and Integrity in Adjudication

Rabeea Assy

Introduction

Jeremy Bentham observed that the function of procedural law is to apply the correct substantive law to the true facts of the case.[1] This, he insisted, is the *only* defensible function of procedural law,[2] and should be achieved while avoiding 'delay, vexation, and expense'.[3]

Adrian Zuckerman has spent the last twenty years systematically exposing an important flaw in the design and philosophy of the English legal system. It is the belief (far from being unique to that system) that the duty to arrive at correct outcomes is the ultimate duty of court, to which considerations of time and cost are secondary. Zuckerman's primary concern with this system has been its failure to appreciate fully the importance of resources to achieve justice in adjudication. Justice, he has regularly insisted, is three dimensional: cost and time are intrinsic components of the definition of justice, just as accuracy of outcome is. Generally speaking, Zuckerman's influential work has been an extensive exercise in illuminating the appropriate point of balance between the three, often conflicting imperatives of justice in the legal process: a correct judgment, within a reasonable time, and at a reasonable cost. As the need to strike a satisfactory point of balance

[1] *The Works of Jeremy Bentham* (ed J Bowring, William Tait 1838–43) vol 2 at 5: 'By procedure, is meant the course taken for the execution of the laws.'

[2] *The Works of Jeremy Bentham* (n 1) vol 2 at 5–6: 'For in jurisprudence, the laws termed adjective, can no more exist without the laws termed substantive, than in grammar a noun termed adjective, can present a distinct idea without the help of a noun of the substantive class, conjoined with it. As in fact every act by which a course of procedure is commenced has for its end or object, the bringing about the execution of some law of the substantive class, so, in point of utility, it may be said that the course of procedure ought to have in every instance, for its main and primary end at least, the accomplishment of the will manifested in the body of substantive laws. For this is not only a use of it, but the only use for it.... Of the adjective branch of the law, the only defensible object, or say end in view, is the maximization of the execution and effect given to the substantive branch of the law'; see also vol 6 at 7: 'The *adjective* branch of law, or *law of procedure,* and therein the *law of evidence,* has everywhere for its object, at least ought to have, the giving effect throughout to the several regulations and arrangements of which the *substantive branch* or *main body* of the law is composed' (emphasis in original).

[3] *The Works of Jeremy Bentham* (n 1) vol 6 at 11.

Rabeea Assy, *Taking Seriously Affordability, Expedition, and Integrity in Adjudication* In: *Principles, Procedure, and Justice.* Edited by: Rabeea Assy and Andrew Higgins, Oxford University Press (2020). © The editors and several contributors.
DOI: 10.1093/oso/9780198850410.003.0009

is not unique to the English system, Zuckerman's work has been greatly relevant worldwide.

This chapter offers a preliminary exposition of the potentially far-reaching consequences of treating cost and time as *dimensions* of justice. Furthermore, it briefly explores the multi-dimensional nature of justice beyond the trifecta of accuracy, cost, and time.

The basic objectives of adjudication

One of Zuckerman's main methodological contributions to the study of civil procedure is his insistence on first principles. One such principle, featuring in most of his work, is that the legal process ought to enforce legal rights. That is, litigants are entitled to expect a process that aims to identify the legally relevant facts and declare their legal consequences.

While disputants may be offered alternative methods for resolving their disputes, such methods derive their authority from the mutual consent of disputants. What make courts unique, therefore, are their monopoly over the delivery of binding resolutions and their formal commitment to determining legal rights and obligations. Unlike arbitration, mediation, or other methods of dispute resolution, court adjudication can be invoked unilaterally, without the consent or cooperation of the opponent. Once invoked, the legal process is duty bound to apply the law. In other words, courts do not merely resolve disputes peacefully; they declare legal rights and grant remedies that are enforceable through public agencies and, when needed, by using state force.

The importance of this function cannot be overstated. Law enforcement lies at the foundation of any legal system governed by the rule of law. The accessibility of the courts is, in turn, a critical requirement of the rule of law.[4] Rights have little value for their holders if they are not adequately enforced. Without a robust and accessible system of resolving disputes according to public, stable, and pre-established rules, communities will find it difficult to escape the state of nature, maintain social order,[5] and justify the state's monopoly over the use of force.[6] Such

[4] J Raz, 'The Rule of Law and its Virtue' (1977) 93 LQR 195, 217: 'The courts should be easily accessible. Given the central position of the courts in ensuring the rule of law ... it is obvious that their accessibility is of paramount importance. Long delays, excessive costs, etc, may effectively turn the most enlightened law to a dead letter and frustrate one's ability effectively to guide oneself by the law.'

[5] See, eg, FA Hayek, *The Road to Serfdom* (Chicago University Press 1944) 85–86: 'Stripped of all technicalities [the rule of law] means that government in all its actions is bound by rules fixed and announced beforehand—rules which make it possible to foresee with fair certainty how the authority will use its coercive powers in given circumstances, and to plan one's individual affairs on the basis of this knowledge.' See also L Fuller, *The Morality of Law* (2nd edn, Yale University Press 1969).

[6] See, eg, D Luban, *Lawyers and Justice: An Ethical Study* (Princeton University Press 1988); S Issacharoff, *Civil Procedure* (3rd edn, Foundation Press 2012); K Scott, 'Two Models of the Civil Process' (1975) 27 Stan L Rev 937.

a system is necessary also to maintain a social and legal environment sufficiently conducive to economic prosperity and welfare.[7] Moreover, individuals can lead autonomous lives, make short- and long-term plans, pursue their own desires and careers, or otherwise develop as autonomous agents, only if they can know with reasonable certainty what the legal consequences of their actions are.[8]

Here comes a crucial point that Zuckerman repeats consistently in his work: law enforcement is not a resource-free exercise. It is time consuming and requires financial resources from litigants and the legal system alike. Naturally, the more accurate we want court judgments to be, the more thorough the process has to be, and, consequently, more costly and lengthier. The main problem identified by Zuckerman has been that many legal systems have chosen to pursue high levels of accuracy even when this has rendered the process enormously expensive and lengthy. Such a process, however, is no less harmful to the rule of law than an erroneous judgment. It is likely to deter litigants from pursuing rights enforcement in the first place. Furthermore, the outcome of such a process will likely be highly susceptible to financial inequalities between disputants.

The tension between cost and length, on the one hand, and accuracy, on the other, has therefore been a corrupting force in the design of many legal systems, including the English system which Zuckerman has focused on. It inevitably calls for compromise, and requires balancing and prioritizing.[9] While everyone may agree on the general principle that the pursuit of accurate judgments must be restricted by considerations of resources, the real controversy concerns the degree to which we are prepared to forsake accuracy in favour of quick, inexpensive resolutions.

[7] See, eg, Lord Neuberger, 'Justice in an Age of Austerity', Tom Sargant Memorial Lecture, 15 October 2013, para 5: 'The defence of the realm from abroad and maintaining the rule of law at home are the two sole traditional duties of a government. More importantly, they are fundamental. If we are not free from invasion, or the rule of law breaks down, then social security, health, and education become valueless, or at any rate very severely devalued'. (Available at: https://2bquk8cdew6192tsu41lay8t-wpengine.netdna-ssl.com/wp-content/uploads/2015/02/Justice-in-an-age-of-austerity-Lord-Neuberger.pdf; accessed 20 January 2020).

[8] See, eg, F Michelman, 'Formal and Associational Aims in Procedural Due Process' in R Pennock and J Chapman (eds), *Nomos: Due Process* vol 18 (New York University Press 1977) 126, 129: 'According to [a positivistic and libertarian] model, all allowable impairments of our immediate freedom are clearly set out in general rules emanating from a legislative sovereign whose rule-enactments can be seen as somehow embodying our more fundamental and comprehensive consent. The rules thus have a double aspect. By their very effect of staking out zones of autonomy wherein each is protected from exposure to unpredictable, arbitrary or discretionary interferences by others. In this model, the only, but necessary, job of judges is to make sure that the rules are applied as enacted.' See also R Assy, *Injustice in Person: The Right to Self-Representation* (OUP 2015) ch 7.

[9] Bentham was fully aware of this tension: 'When the whole body of the Law has for its object the greatest happiness of the greatest number, the whole of the adjective branch taken together may be said to have two specific ends: the one *positive*, maximizing the execution and effect given to the substantive branch; the other *negative*, minimizing the evil, the hardship [ie, delay, vexation and expense—RA], in various shapes necessary to the accomplishment of the main specified end. Between these two-pursuits the conflict is all pervading and perpetual. Whatsoever arrangement is taken for the attainment of the one end, it can scarcely avoid being in a greater or less degree obstructive to the attainment of the other end' (emphasis in original); *The Works of Jeremy Bentham* (n 1) vol 2 at 8.

There can be several points of balance between the competing imperatives of justice (accurate judgments, reasonable costs, and reasonable duration). Every jurisdiction must decide for itself the degree of accuracy it delivers against time and cost. The optimal point of balance may depend on various cultural, social, or legal conditions; it may also vary within a single jurisdiction, depending on the type of case in question, its importance to the parties, the presence of a special public interest, and so on (a family case, for example, may entail different considerations than a case involving loan return).[10]

While implementation can take different forms, it is critical to have a clear vision of what our priorities are and what precise principle courts ought to follow. Zuckerman has correctly argued that the fundamental right of access to court must not be conflated with unregulated adjudication or with a judicial approach where 'anything goes' as long as the court is able to uncover the facts and apply the law. Zuckerman has persistently warned against a 'justice on the merits' approach that permits the pursuit of accurate judgments regardless of the cost or duration of litigation. Such a single-minded approach fails to ascribe due weight to time and cost as components of justice, and it cannot be justified merely by pointing to the old days of 'forms of action' where the slightest technical defect could have nullified the whole process, causing great injustice and immense waste.[11] The fear of rigid formalism must not lead to the adoption of rigid 'substantialism' (so to speak), that is, policies preferring substance over form at all time and at any cost.

Justice as proportionality

The current trends in common law countries, including in England and Wales, are to develop concise proceedings for relatively low value claims, to divert cases to ADR or otherwise encourage settlements, and to require judges to promote efficient litigation by taking over the management of cases (enforcing deadlines and time limits more strictly than before, and refusing to tolerate frequent procedural default).

[10] On the relationship between procedure, culture, and tradition, see H Patrick Glenn, *Legal Traditions of the World* (3rd edn, OUP 2007). It might be interesting to conduct an experiment to test actual preferences of potential users, when presented with a choice between an expensive and lengthy, but highly accurate process, and one that offers fast and cheap adjudication, but is potentially less accurate. Empirical data can inform policy makers in this respect. However, devising such an experiment will face several challenges because the nature of the specific choices presented are likely to impact the preferences expressed by the participants. Preferences may also depend on the type of dispute, emotional involvement, stakes, and other specific circumstances, which may be difficult to replicate in a laboratory.

[11] For a concise description of forms of action, see F Maitland, *Equity: Also the Forms of Action at Common Law* (CUP 1910). On the rigidness of this system, see WB Odgers, 'Changes in Procedure and in the Law of Evidence' in *A Century of Law Reform* (Macmillan and Co 1901) 203.

To guide these efforts, the Civil Procedure Rules 1998 (specifically, rule 1) employ a principle of proportionality as part of their definition of what a just process is. The Australian state Victoria has followed suit and incorporated a similar principle in its procedural code.[12] Under this principle, courts are required to allocate resources to cases in proportion to such considerations as the value of the case, its importance, its complexity, and the financial positions of the parties. However, these criteria are open-ended and potentially conflicting, rendering the proportionality test all but meaningless.[13] The absence of a clear and coherent principle leaves judges with no concrete guidance on how to determine proportionality, which is likely to produce inconsistency and unpredictability—in other words, a judge-dependent style of implementation. Moreover, the current definition of proportionality does not rule out a scenario in which the resources allocated are beyond the reach of either or both litigants, since the financial means of the parties constitutes just one consideration among many others.

In order for the conceptualization of cost and time as *dimensions* of justice to mean anything more than merely eliminating waste, the proportionality test should be replaced by tests for affordability and expedition. The conceptualization of time and cost as dimensions of justice requires treating affordability and expedition as separate objectives that can be pursued independently of accurate judgment. When affordability and expedition are given priority, courts will be expected to ensure that litigation remains within the financial reach of litigants and that it concludes within a short time. This means that the court must avoid unaffordable spending or lengthy litigation even when these might otherwise be justified by the features of the case in question, namely its value, complexity, importance, etc. In other words, rather than ask how much time or money a given case deserves based on the features of the case itself, the court should focus instead mainly on the financial and temporal resources available to the parties, and aspire to achieve the most accurate result within these constraints.

Taken seriously, therefore, the principles of affordability and expedition can have far-reaching implications not only for judicial discretion on case management, procedural default, or time limits, but also for procedural design as a whole. Take, for example, the aspect of lawyers' fees. A strong commitment to affordability may require us to challenge the toxic combination of unrestricted hourly fees and a cost-shifting rule, which have substantially increased cost liability, sometimes beyond the amount at stake, thus intimidating litigants from bringing their meritorious claims forward. Prioritizing affordability enables us to reconsider both the cost-shifting rule and lawyers' freedom to charge as they like—such as by

[12] Civil Procedure Act 2010 (Victoria, Australia) ss 7, 24, 25.

[13] For a useful analysis of the proportionality requirement, see A Higgins and A Zuckerman, 'Lord Justice Briggs' "SWOT" Analysis Underlines English Law's Troubled Relationship with Proportionate Costs' (2017) 36 CJQ 1.

regulating legal fees or limiting recoverable costs to fixed and relatively low tariffs, as in Germany.[14] Such modifications may become legitimate even if they might risk lowering the quality of legal representation, thus limiting the legal system's ability to achieve an accurate outcome.

Even more ambitiously, prioritizing affordability can trigger a discussion of restricting the right to legal representation in circumstances in which this could help achieve a cheaper (and quicker) outcome, or eliminate inequalities between parties (in some countries, for example, legal representation is prohibited in small claims court).[15] Another proposal may be to adopt a more liberal scheme of lay representation that can enhance competition in the market for legal services and potentially reduce the cost of legal services, including those provided by lawyers.[16]

These are merely initial thoughts that can be contemplated under a conceptual framework that treats affordability and expedition as imperatives of justice in adjudication. Such a framework paves the path for implementing bold and unorthodox measures that go beyond modest exercises of eliminating unnecessary waste through case management. Obviously, any such measure may be fraught with risks and disadvantages that require careful and detailed assessment of their own merits.

Measurability

One of the often overlooked aspects of adjudication is the fact that the correctness of judgments is neither measurable nor verifiable. The truthfulness of judgments delivered by courts is generally uncertain, especially in relation to factual findings, which can only be ascertained as a matter of probability.[17] Questions of law and interpretation, too, are often debatable, and disagreements about them can be prevalent and intense.[18]

This makes 'accuracy' an unnatural term in this context. We can measure neither the level of accuracy that current procedures achieve, nor the loss of accuracy that policies pursuing fast, cheap litigation enable (if at all). These variables are

[14] See, eg, P Murray and R Stürner, *German Civil Justice* (Carolina Academic Press 2004) 112–23, 239–45, 626–28; G Wagner, 'Litigation Costs and their Recovery: The German Experience' (2009) 28 CJQ 367; B Hess and R Heubner, 'Cost and Fee Allocation in German Civil Procedure' in M Reimann (ed), *Cost and Fee Allocation in Civil Procedure* (Springer Netherlands 2012) 151.

[15] See, eg, California Code of Civil Procedure s 116.530; Revised Code of Washington s 12.40.080; Nebraska Revised Statute 25-2803; Magistrates Court Act 1991 s 38(4) (South Australia); Victorian Civil and Administrative Tribunal Act 1998 s 78. In England and Wales, however, legal representation is permitted as a matter of right; see in general CPR Pt 27.

[16] This was the effect of reforms allowing non-lawyers to do conveyances; see S Domberger and A Sherr, 'The Impact of Competition on Pricing and Quality of Legal Services' (1989) 9 IRLE 41.

[17] See generally K Popper, *The Logic of Scientific Discovery* (Routledge edition 2002); LJ Cohen, *The Probable and the Provable* (OUP 1977).

[18] See discussion of Hart and Fuller's views on whether legal rules have a clear 'core', or whether uncertainties are typical only of the 'fringes' of rules, in F Schauer, *Thinking Like a Lawyer* (Harvard University Press 2009) 151–58.

uncertain and unquantifiable, and any attempt to devise a method of measurement would be subjective. This subjectivity is further complicated by the fact that, as we shall see in the following sections, the adjudication process is sometimes expected to serve additional objectives—beyond the mere application of substantive law—that are themselves imprecise and therefore immeasurable (eg integrity or good faith). This creates fertile ground for controversy regarding the extent to which a given process delivers, and on what promises.

Unlike outcome accuracy, the cost and duration of litigation are generally measurable. This renders the principles of affordability and expedition attractive and easy to use, and policies promoting them easier to assess and control. But there is more to this than meets the eye. Difficulties may arise if we adopt broad definitions of cost and time that incorporate such factors as the social and economic cost of erroneous judgments for the litigants and other relevant non-parties, or the detrimental impact of continuous uncertainty pending final resolution. For instance, a mistaken decision to shut down a factory or a decision that establishes a misguided rule of law may affect many more people than just the direct litigants. Litigation also creates additional, indirect costs for litigants who must delay certain decisions or purchases until a case has been decided (eg family members, investors who want to purchase a property whose ownership is disputed, children in a divorce case).

For affordability and expedition to be reasonably measurable, there must be a narrow interpretation of the cost and time factors. Such is the case if the cost factor is limited to the direct costs incurred by parties in carrying out the actual court proceedings (mainly court fees and fees for lawyers and experts), and if the time factor is limited to the length of the actual court proceedings. However, even under such narrow definitions, controversies may still arise regarding what counts as affordable or timely, and from whose perspective: the claimant's? the defendant's? the average person's (whoever they may be)?

More fundamentally, the fact that a factor is easier to measure does not necessarily make it a more desirable or appropriate factor for measuring the adequacy of a legal system. The ranking of scientific journals, for instance, has been criticized precisely on the ground that impact factor does not fully capture academic novelty and contribution.[19] The seduction of quantification has been resisted in several contexts; arguably, numbers cannot capture the intangible value of, say, human rights or intellectual development, and their seemingly objective nature is a fallacy used to disguise agendas and subjective beliefs.[20]

The answer to this criticism of measurability lies in Zuckerman's insistence on conceptualizing cost and time as dimension of justice. Whether or not the

[19] See, eg, R Perry, 'The Relative Value of American Law Reviews: A Critical Appraisal of Ranking Methods' (2006) 11 VJOLT 1.

[20] See, eg, S Merry, *The Seductions of Quantification: Measuring Human Rights, Gender Violence, and Sex Trafficking* (University of Chicago Press 2016).

frequency of citation serves as an adequate proxy for assessing academic contribution, the length of and the expenses incurred during litigation are not proxies or indicators for measuring other objectives. They are themselves objectives of the process, therefore measuring them is a valid measurement of the justice of the process. If cost and time are dimensions of justice, then the numbers do matter, and the costs and the time spent on any given proceeding become criteria for measuring the quality of such a process. For there can be no doubt that expensive and lengthy litigations are bad in and of themselves and should be avoided; no intangible value lies in them. The pressing question concerns the price—in terms of accuracy—that we are willing to pay to achieve that goal.

Nevertheless, the measurability feature of time and costs gives rise to two serious problems which are important to note. The first is how to strike a balance between an immeasurable parameter (accurate judgments) and measurable parameters (time and cost), which poses a potential problem of incommensurability.[21] The second problem is how to avoid the temptation and convenience of focusing on the measurable factors (cost and time) at the expense of the immeasurable (accuracy). Arguably, focusing only or mainly on what is measurable may blind us to the value of the immeasurable. In other words, measurability creates a practical bias and temptation for focusing disproportionately on convenient and easy to use numbers.[22]

Curiously, current legal systems have traditionally avoided the potential risk of preferring the measurable to the immeasurable, and tended to focus more on accuracy than on affordability and expedition. But this has been changing. Ongoing attempts to optimise the administration of courts require that judges be responsible for managing their own cases. Concerns have arisen, therefore, that during this process, judges have become less worried about resolving disputes correctly than they are about how their dockets look and how to speed through cases as quickly as possible.

The upshot of this discussion is that defining justice in a three-dimensional fashion raises several theoretical questions and practical challenges that require detailed assessment and exploration. It is striking that little scholarly effort has been put in trying to think outside the boxes of strict case management, ADR, and low value claims.

[21] For a general discussion of incommensurability and for possible techniques to address it, see R Chang (ed), *Incommensurability, Incomparability, and Practical Reason* (Harvard University Press 1977); D Luban, 'Incommensurable Values, Rational Choice, and Moral Absolutes' (1990) 38 Clev St L Rev 65; J Waldron, 'Fake Incommensurability: A Response to Professor Schauer' (1993) 45 Hastings LJ 813; F Urbina, 'Incommensurability and Balancing' (2015) 35 OJLS 575.

[22] On a potential bias in favour of measurable factors, see discussion in M Nussbaum, 'The Costs of Tragedy: Some Moral Limits of the Cost-Benefit Analysis' (2000) 29 J Legal Stud 1005; F Ackerman and L Heinzerling, 'Pricing the Priceless: Cost-benefit Analysis of Environmental Protection' (2002) 150 U Pa L Rev 1553; H Richardson, *Practical Reasoning about Final Ends* (CUP 1994); L Caviola and others, 'The Evaluability Bias in Charitable Giving: Saving Administration Costs or Saving Lives?' (2014) 9 Judgm Decis Mak 303.

Beyond the accuracy-cost-time trifecta: The pursuit of other ends

Considerations of cost, time, and accuracy are inherent to every process that seeks to resolve disputes according to the law. They are therefore the most visible dimensions of justice. Every legal system must address, balance, and manage the potentially competing needs for accuracy, expedition, and affordability. But the concept of justice is sufficiently broad and rich as to accommodate additional values that the legal process may serve or be influenced by. Indeed, most legal systems allow for additional values and devise their procedures to accommodate them, even in ways that may undermine the pursuit of optimal law enforcement.[23]

Values may affect the procedural design in two ways: negative and positive. In a negative way, promotion of a given value may require the procedural system to refrain from acting in ways that undermine the value in question, even if such actions would have contributed to optimal law enforcement. Consider, for example, procedural rules that privilege communication with priests or lawyers, or that exclude illegally obtained evidence, prohibit torture, prohibit the use of the criminal records of witnesses or litigants as evidence against them, or prohibit a lawyer from examining witnesses on their sexual history or posing offensive questions to them. Such rules create constraints on the pursuit of accurate and efficient litigation because they screen out information that could have helped obtain accurate outcomes; this, in turn, means that such information must be obtained in other, possibly more expensive ways. Nevertheless, such procedural rules exist in many legal systems and are justified independently of their impact on outcome or resources, with reference to such values as privacy, bodily integrity, good name, physical liberty, and human dignity.

While values can impose restrictions on the legal system's pursuit of optimal law enforcement, they may also operate as potential ends that place positive demands on the court system, requiring it to act to promote such values. The requirement that judges must provide reasons for their decisions, for instance, has been defended as an expression of respect for the litigants' efforts and contribution to the process, and thus as a recognition of their value as subjects, rather than objects.[24]

[23] See discussion in R Summers, 'Evaluating and Improving Legal Processes: A Plea For "Process Values"' (1974) 60 Cornell L Rev 1, 20–27; M Bayles, 'Principles for Legal Procedure' (1986) 5 Law Phil 33, 50–57. Compare A Stein, *Foundation of Evidence Law* (OUP 2005) 31–33; L Alexander, 'Are Procedural Rights Derivative Substantive Rights?' (1998) 17 Law Phil 19; J Mashaw, 'Administrative Due Process: The Quest for a Dignitary Theory' (1981) 61 Boston U L Rev 885; and M Redish and L Marshall, 'Adjudicatory Independence and the Values of Procedural Due Process' (1986) 95 Yale LJ 455, 481–91; Assy (n 8) ch 8.

[24] L Tribe, *American Constitutional Law* (2nd edn, Foundation Press 1988) 666–67: 'Both the right to be heard, and the right to be told why, are analytically distinct from the right to secure a different outcome; these rights to interchange express the elementary idea that to be a *person*, rather than a *thing*, is at least to be *consulted* about what is done with one ... For when the government acts in a way that singles out identifiable individuals ... it activates the special concern about being personally *talked to* about the decision rather than simply being *dealt with*.' (emphasis in original)

The negative and positive senses can help us see that the legal system can promote a given value in varying degrees.[25] Take the right to have a voice in proceedings that concern oneself or may affect one's interest. This right has been defended regardless of whether such a voice will actually impact the final decision, and despite the cost of such participation. It has been grounded in such considerations as human dignity and respect for litigants as subjects rather than objects, and in empirical data showing that participation increases the acceptability of adverse outcomes and perceptions of fairness of the legal process.[26] A legal system can promote these values more positively, for example by licensing legal experts who offer parties professional advice and representation, and by providing legal aid to enhance the participation of poor litigants and render their voices more effective.

The right to self-representation is another example of how the legal system can promote a value to varying degrees. Common law jurisdictions allow litigants to represent themselves out of respect for their personal autonomy and free choice, even though self-representation increases the risks for erroneous judgments and drains court resources.[27] Mandatory representation, a widely accepted practice in civil law countries, has never been applied in common law jurisdictions.[28] The legal system can further promote self-representation by adjusting its procedures and practices with a view to meeting the special needs of self-representing litigants, for example by instructing judges and court staff to help them navigate the legal process, and by providing them with explanatory material and 'standby counsel' who would help them make the most of their self-representation.[29]

The influence of such values is not limited to sporadic procedural aspects, but can affect the entire procedural ideology and the procedural structure as a whole. The adversarial system—in which litigants enjoy high levels of control over the conduct of litigation—is often justified by reference to the values of free choice and human dignity. Arguably, treating litigants as subjects rather than objects requires the system to allow them to decide for themselves how best to promote their ends.[30] Litigant control over the process has also been justified based on empirical

[25] It should be noted, however, that the validity of the negative–positive distinction may be disputed in this context. This is because procedural activities can exist only as part of an institution. To some extent, then, all procedural entitlements are positive, in the sense that they are given to litigants rather than merely permissible. Unlike, say, freedom of speech, whose negative sense requires that the state merely avoid interfering in people's speech, freedoms to self-represent in court or have a voice in the process need to be afforded by the legal system, and require that the system facilitates them, for example by accepting papers signed by the litigant in person, affording her rights of audience, and so on. In the light of this scepticism, the classification of the examples in the text as negative or positive is mainly suggestive, indicating the degree of effort put by the legal system to promote a given value.

[26] See Tribe (n 24); J Thibaut and L Walker, 'A Theory of Procedure' (1978) 66 Cal L Rev 541.

[27] *Faretta v California* (1975) 422 US 806. For an argument that mandatory legal representation is compatible with the commitment to personal autonomy, see Assy (n 8) ch 7.

[28] Except in the Star Chamber period. See review in Assy (n 8) ch 1; R Assy, 'Revisiting the Right to Self-Representation in Civil Proceedings' (2011) 30 CJQ 267.

[29] Assy (n 8) ch 6.

[30] A useful summary of the potential justifications of adversarial litigation can be found in: N Brooks, 'The Judge and the Adversary System' in A Linden (ed), *The Canadian Judiciary* (Osgood Hall Law

evidence suggesting that high levels of litigant control can enhance the legitimacy of the process and increase public confidence in it.[31]

It is therefore evidently clear that the justice of a legal process has been perceived as a multi-dimensional concept that is not limited to accuracy, cost, and time.

Three senses of integrity

The value of integrity occupies a significant place in the procedural law of common law jurisdictions. It is promoted most manifestly through the doctrine of abuse of process, whose basic idea is that the court may impose sanctions on parties who litigate in an improper or inappropriate manner. As Lord Diplock famously noted, the court has inherent jurisdiction

> to prevent misuse of its procedure in a way which, although not inconsistent with the literal application of its procedural rules, would nevertheless be manifestly unfair to a party to litigation before it, or would otherwise bring the administration of justice into disrepute among right-thinking people.[32]

This formulation encapsulates at least two senses of integrity: litigant integrity and court integrity. While related, it is important to note their different points of focus. The former is concerned with the litigant's standard of behaviour (eg good faith, honesty, fairness, etc), while the latter focuses on the court as an institution (eg its moral coherence, public legitimacy, public image, etc).

Integrity is important in civil and criminal proceedings alike. In the criminal context, abuse of state power may lead to staying criminal charges—whether in circumstances of double jeopardy, entrapment, or because of other impropriety by state agents—even at the possible risk of setting a guilty person free.[33] In making this point, English courts have relied on both senses of integrity, holding that a general power to stay proceedings seeks to 'prevent unfairness to the accused'[34]

School 1976) 90–116. See also D Luban, *Lawyers and Justice: An Ethical Study* (Princeton University Press 1988) ch 5; S Landsman, 'A Brief Survey of the Development of the Adversary System' (1983) 44 Ohio St LJ 713.

[31] Thibaut and Walker (n 26).

[32] *Hunter v Chief Constable of West Midlands* [1982] AC 529, [1981] All ER 727, 729 (HL). See, generally, A Choo, *Abuse of Process and Judicial Stays of Criminal Proceedings* (2nd edn, OUP 2008); IH Jacob, 'The Inherent Jurisdiction of the Court' (1970) 23 CLP 23.

[33] See, eg, *R v Derby Crown Court* (1985) 80 Cr App R 164, 168–69 (Divisional Court): 'It may be an abuse of process if … the prosecution have manipulated or misused the process of the court so as to deprive the defendant of a protection provided by the law or to take unfair advantage of a technicality …'; see also *R v Horseferry Rd Ct, Ex p Bennett (HL(E))* [1994] 1 AC 41, 62 (HL); *R v Looseley* [2001] UKHL 53 [19].

[34] *Connelly v DPP* [1964] AC 1254, 1347 (HL): '… a general power, taking various specific forms, to prevent unfairness to the accused has always been a part of the English criminal law …'. A similar power has been recognised also in the US, in circumstances where 'the police conduct … shocked the

(litigant integrity) and to prevent such 'an abuse of its own process' that 'offends the court's sense of justice and propriety' (court integrity).[35]

Likewise, illegally or improperly obtained evidence can be ruled inadmissible even when the evidence is probative and may help the court determine the facts of the case.[36] This has been defended on the grounds that admitting such evidence would encourage improper behaviour on the part of state officials (ie undermine litigant integrity), compromise 'the integrity of the judicial process', and 'dishonor the administration of justice' (ie undermine court integrity).[37]

Integrity assumes particular significance in criminal proceedings, both because the potential consequences for the defendant in such proceedings can be severe, and because state officials have immense power with the potential to be misused. Furthermore, as many scholars have argued, moral responsibility stands at the heart of a criminal trial and, consequently, courts must have sufficient moral authority to denounce wrong and to inflict punishment. In this view, defendants are entitled to expect all other participants in the criminal trial—decision makers, prosecutors, and witnesses—to abide by high ethical standards and to assume a high moral standing.[38] Andrew Ashworth has referred to a similar idea as 'moral coherence',[39] and Adrian Zuckerman and Paul Roberts have gone as far as defending 'moral integrity' as a foundational principle of criminal evidence law. Drawing on Kant, they write:

> To pursue justice through injustice is a contradiction in terms, since two wrongs do not make a right, in the administration of criminal justice any more than

conscience of the Court or reached that "demonstrable level of outrageousness" necessary to compel acquittal so as to protect the Constitution': *United States v Beverly* (1983) 723 F2d 11, 13 (US Court of Appeals, 3rd Circuit); see also *United States v Russel* (1973) 411 US 423, 431–32.

[35] *Regina v Horseferry Road Magistrates' Court, Ex parte Bennett* [1993] 3 WLR 90 [1994] 1 AC 42, 47 (HL): '... a court has a discretion to stay any criminal proceedings on the grounds that to try those proceedings will amount to an abuse of its own process ... because it offends the court's sense of justice and propriety to be asked to try the accused in the circumstances of a particular case.'

[36] Section 78 of the Police and Crime Evidence Act 1984 ('PACE') allows courts to exclude evidence that could affect the fairness of the proceedings, including evidence obtained in bad faith or illegality, and section 76 enables the court to exclude confessions obtained through oppression or in any circumstances likely to make is unreliable. See also *R v Alladice* (1988) 87 Cr App R 380, 386, CA. For Canada, see Canadian Charter of Rights s 24(2).

[37] *A and Others v Secretary of State for the Home Department* [2005] UKHL 81 [87]. There have been several accounts of the underlying rationale, such as a right-based idea that considers the exclusion of illegally obtained evidence as a remedy for violating individual rights, or based on the need to deter illegality by removing the incentive for engaging in it. See discussion at A Duff and others, *The Trial on Trial: Towards a Normative Theory of the Criminal Trial* vol 3 (Hart Publishing 2007) 229–34; A Zuckerman and P Roberts, *Criminal Evidence* (OUP 2004) 153; *Adams v New York* (1904) 192 US 585, 595.

[38] See, eg, Duff and others (n 37) mainly ch 8. On this account, a 'Not Guilty' verdict may either suggest that there is some doubt about whether the epistemic conditions of guilt have been met, or that there is doubt about the moral standing of the state to condemn the defendant. Procedural integrity, in this view, legitimates the process and justifies the condemnation of the defendant.

[39] A Ashworth, 'Testing Fidelity to Legal Values: Official Involvement and Criminal Justice' in S Schute and AP Simester (eds), *Criminal Law Theory: Doctrines of the General Part* (OUP 2002); A Ashworth, 'Exploring the Integrity Principle in Evidence and Procedure' in P Mirfield and R Smith (eds), *Essays for Collin Tapper* (LexisNexis 2003).

> in the school playground. Righting wrongs, in fulfilment of a requirement of justice, can be achieved only through action which is itself just and otherwise in conformity with relevant ethical standards. Maintaining such standards in service of the legitimacy of the verdict, and in accordance with the basic precepts of retributive justice, is a fifth foundational principle of the law of criminal evidence.[40]

While the criminal process contains features that reinforce the need for a principle of integrity, such a principle cannot be limited to the criminal context, to state actions, or to state-individual relationships.[41] Integrity—including other associated values such as good faith and fair play—can be defended more generally and be applied also to the actions of private litigants, if only because the procedural activity is performed in the public spheres of court and as part of the formal legal process. If illegality were permissible in civil proceedings, and if litigants could benefit from it, courts would risk being seen as both morally hypocritical and legally inconsistent. A law-enforcing agency cannot rely on illegality as a means of enforcing the law; courts should teach not only through speech, but also lead by example.[42]

Furthermore, civil trials involve the use of state force. Witnesses can be summoned and brought to court by force, and final judgments are enforceable with the aid of state power. As noted earlier, litigants turn to court seeking to invoke state protection, and courts both facilitate and supervise the use of state power through due process. Against this background, it is perfectly legitimate for the court to refuse to aid litigants who jeopardize its integrity and, accordingly, its public legitimacy.

[40] A Zuckerman and P Roberts, *Principles of Criminal Evidence* (2nd edn, OUP 2010) 22; see also 188–91. See also A Zuckerman 'Illegally-Obtained Evidence: Discretion as a Guardian of Legitimacy' [1987] CLP 55, 59.

[41] In England and Wales, the traditional position was that in civil matters courts have no power to exclude evidence on grounds of how it was obtained. However, CPR r 32.1(2) now allows the court to exclude evidence that 'would otherwise be admissible'. The Court of Appeal has interpreted this rule to allow courts to exclude evidence on account of the circumstances under which it was obtained; but the Court also mentioned that court disapproval can be expressed through other means, primarily costs orders. See, eg, *Jones v University of Warwick* [2003] EWCA Civ 151; *Tchenguiz v Imerman* [2010] EWCA Civ 908 [177]; compare *Ronald Olden v Serious Organised Crime Agency* [2010] EWCA Civ 143 [46]. In the US, too, the traditional approach has been against applying the exclusionary rule to civil matters where evidence is obtained through the illegal or improper actions of private agents rather than state officials. The exclusionary rule has been limited to criminal matters where evidence was obtained through violation of constitutional rights, primarily those in the Fourth, Fifth, and Sixth Amendments (eg, violation of privacy by means of illegal search, unduly obtained confession, or failure to notify a suspect of their rights); see, eg, JH Wigmore, *Evidence in Trials at Common Law* (McNaughton rev 1961) vol 8, para 2183 at 7. There have been exceptions, however; see, eg, *Lebel v Swincicki* (1958) 384 Mich 427, 93 NW2d 281; *One 1958 Plymouth Sedan v Pennsylvania* (1965) 380 US 693. In specific contexts, inadmissibility was promoted through federal or state legislation prohibiting the admission into evidence of unlawfully intercepted electronic communication or otherwise illegal eavesdropping (eg, (2000) 18 USC 2515; 720 Ill Comp Stat Ann 5/14-2(b)).

[42] As the US Supreme Court noted in *Olmstead v US* (1928) 277 US 438, 484–85: 'Our government is the potent, the omnipresent teacher. For good or for ill, it teaches … by its example … If the government becomes a law breaker, it breeds contempt for law; it invites every man to become a law unto himself; it invites anarchy.'

Indeed, civil courts have long defended the principle of integrity in various contexts. One is the so-called judicial estoppel rule.[43] This rule prohibits litigants from making a factual allegation that contradicts another factual allegation made in a previous case, regardless of which statement is the true one. Such a rule promotes procedural coherency, prevents inconsistent determinations of fact, and sets a high behavioural standard of good faith and diligence on the part of litigants. Courts in common law jurisdictions have made it clear that the rule is intended to ensure 'fair dealings among the parties'[44] and to protect 'the integrity of the judicial process'.[45] Once again, the same two senses of integrity come into play. One is concerned with how courts can encourage litigants to conduct proceedings in ways that are diligent, moral, and fair (ie litigant integrity); the other is concerned with how the court should behave to preserve its own morality and public confidence in it.

Another context in which civil courts have defended integrity was in the personal injury case *Fairclough Homes Limited v Summers*.[46] Although the claim in this case was essentially genuine, it was inflated through fraud and misrepresentation, and advanced through false evidence and perjury. The Supreme Court ruled that the court is entitled to refuse to disentangle truth from falsity and, consequently, to throw out the whole claim for abuse of process. The Supreme Court held that such power should be used scarcely and as a last resort, when the other means available for deterring dishonest litigants are unlikely to be adequate (eg cost orders, reduced compensation, proceedings for contempt of court, criminal charges, etc). Parliament followed up with a law that compels courts to dismiss such claims unless substantial injustice would follow.[47] Arguably, the Supreme Court's approach, being concerned primarily with deterrence and with encouraging litigants' good behaviour, focused on litigant integrity, while Parliament's approach, being firm and broad, focused more on the integrity of the court as a law-enforcing institution.

Although Zuckerman's run-of-the-mill scholarship focuses on the importance of rights enforcement within limited resources, his take on this matter

[43] While this rule has received more attention from US courts, it has also been discussed by English courts. See, eg, *Gandy v Gandy* (1885) 30 Ch D 57, 82; *Bradford & Bingley Building Society v Seddon* [1999] 4 All ER 217, [1999] 1 WLR 1482, CA; *First National Bank Plc v Walker* [2001] 1 FCR 21, [2001] 1 FLR 505, CA. Occasionally, discussion of this rule has also been conducted in relation to the equity doctrine of election, or of approbate and reprobate (*quod approbo non reprobo*); see, eg, *Representative Claimants v MGN Ltd* [2016] EWHC 855 (Ch); *Twinsectra Ltd v Lloyds Bank Plc* [2018] EWHC 672 (Ch).

[44] *Edwards v Aetna Life Ins Co* (1982) 690 F2d 595, 598.

[45] *New Hampshire v Maine* (2001) 532 US 742, 749–50. See also *Allen v Zurich Ins Co* (CA4 1982) 667 F2d 1162, 1166; *Konstantinidis v Chen* (CADC 1980) 626 F2d 933, 938; *Browning Mfg v Mims (In re Coastal Plains, Inc)* (5th Cir 1999) 179 F3d 197, 205.

[46] *Fairclough Homes Limited v Summers* [2012] UKSC 26.

[47] Criminal Justice and Courts Act 2015 s 57 provides that, in relation to personal injury cases where the claimant has been fundamentally dishonest, the court must dismiss the claim unless it is satisfied that this would cause substantial injustice. However, the amount of damages that would have been awarded is taken into account in determining the claimant's cost liability or in sentencing the claimant in subsequent criminal proceedings.

relies on considerations of integrity.[48] Categorically calling upon courts in these circumstances to refuse to grant remedies that are entailed by substantive law, Zuckerman argued that fraudulent claims discredit the legal process and 'court involvement with dishonest causes or dishonest litigants can bring it into disrepute'.[49] Invoking the principle of equity, encapsulated in the maxim *ex turpi causa non oritur actio* (an action does not arise from a dishonourable action), he went on to say:

> Striking out a case for abuse of process is primarily designed to protect the legitimacy of the court's own process. For a court that suffers its process to be used for the commission of a crime or a wrong will lose public confidence in its ability to maintain the rule of law.[50]

What prevents the concepts of legitimacy and public confidence from being reduced to populist versions of law or justice is their normative underpinning. In ordinary circumstances, court legitimacy and public confidence are promoted when courts fulfil their basic function to grant remedies entailed by substantive law. The position that public confidence is better served by refusing to grant substantive remedies when a case is advanced through dishonesty expresses the notion that honesty and integrity are triumphant values that may override entitlements under substantive law and thus override the law enforcement objective.

This brings up a third sense of integrity, an expressive one. It involves the expressive value of procedure and the message that the law and its agents send through procedure. Whether or not litigants will be deterred when courts strike out cases for abuse of process, and whether or not striking out such claims is required to preserve the morality of the legal system, there might be value in striking out such claims to make a statement on the values that the court stands for. As the saying goes, justice must not only be done, but also be seen to be done.

To sum up, then, it might be useful to differentiate between the following types of integrity-based justifications for striking out cases that rely on dishonesty and fraud. To be sure, public confidence and court legitimacy may be served by each

[48] A Zuckerman, 'Court Protection from Abuse of Process—the Means are there but not the Will: *Summers v Fairclough Homes Ltd* [2012] UKSC 26' (2012) 31 CJQ 377; A Zuckerman, 'Access to Justice for Litigants who Advance their Case by Forgery and Perjury' (2008) 27 CJQ 419. See also A Zuckerman, *Zuckerman on Civil Procedure: Principles of Practice* (3rd edn, Sweet & Maxwell 2013) [11.325]–[11.276].

[49] Zuckerman 'Court Protection from Abuse of Process' (n 48) 379; see also p 378: 'The rule of law can be maintained only if the court is seen as an instrument for the good, not evil, only if it promotes standards of probity and rectitude.'

[50] Zuckerman, 'Court Protection from Abuse of Process'(n 48) 378. See also p 379: '... it would affront public opinion if the court were seen to grant relief to claimants whose cause was seriously tainted by criminal activity. The refusal of relief, it merits stressing, was not founded on the need to deter others but on the need to maintain confidence in the administration of justice.'

of these different senses of integrity. One is concerned with the integrity of litigants, using legal sanctions to deter dishonest or otherwise abusive behaviour, and thus increasing the frequency of honesty and proper conduct. The success of such an approach would be measured through the consequences it brings about (namely the extent to which it reduces dishonesty or increases honesty on the part of litigants). The second focuses on the morality of the court, requiring it to keep its hands clean and refuse to engage with proceedings that have been promoted through fraud and falsity. Doing so preserves the court's own morality, regardless of how such a course of action affects litigants' incentives and behaviour. The third type of integrity-based justification focuses on the message a court sends by refusing to grant remedy in these circumstances, regardless of both the impact this refusal may have on the court's moral standing or the deterrent effect it may have on other litigants contemplating the use of dishonesty.

Conclusion

The classical definition of the function of procedural law as laid down by Bentham is that it should facilitate the enforcement of substantive law. This chapter has shown that this function should be interpreted in a broad manner that is not necessarily identical to a commitment to high degrees of accuracy in adjudication. An exaggerated pursuit of accurate judgments may undermine the effort to enforce the law, because it produces lengthy and expensive litigation that is likely to deter many from seeking enforcement in the first place. Furthermore, lengthy and expensive litigation can distort justice by subjecting the process to economic inequalities and by forcing the parties to make substantial sacrifices in terms of resources. Optimal law enforcement cannot therefore be achieved by a high commitment to accurate judgments. Affordable and expeditious resolution of disputes reduces the uncertainty concerning the legal rights of the litigants, which has value that is independent of outcome accuracy; it simply enables people to move on with their lives.

This chapter has also shown that the function of law enforcement is not exhausted by the formula that the court should apply the specifically relevant law to the true facts of the case. Applying the substantive law (broadly understood) may require the enforcement of a certain value or right, such as integrity, good faith, bodily integrity, privacy, human rights, etc, in ways that may run counter to the obligation of applying the relevant law to its relevant facts. In other words, when courts strike out a potentially genuine claim for abuse of process, or when they exclude potentially probative evidence because of the illegal means used to obtain it, they enforce the substantive law (broadly understood), notwithstanding the denial of remedy otherwise entailed by the relevant piece of legislation.

Finally, this chapter has offered a conceptual clarification regarding the value of integrity, often relied on by courts and scholars. It offers to distinguish between three different (albeit related) senses of integrity. One is concerned with the integrity of litigants, using procedural sanctions to deter abusive behaviour. The second focuses on the morality of the court, requiring it to keep its hands clean and refuse to rely on illegality or engage with proceedings advanced through fraud, falsity, and illegality. The third sense of integrity focuses on the message a court sends by imposing procedural sanctions on abuse of process.

PART IV
FUNDING JUSTICE

10
Funding Civil Litigation Through Legal Expenses Insurance in Germany

Peter Gottwald

Introduction

Adrian Zuckerman is widely acknowledged to be a master of the law of civil procedure. In his brilliant textbook, he showed that what was previously considered mere 'practice and procedure' is now better understood as 'principles of practice'.[1] While teaching at Oxford he attracted visits from scholars from all over the world. For many of them (including me) he was a wonderful interlocutor and a generous host. In thankful memory of these times I would like to address a topic he has been interested in for a long time. For many years Adrian has been concerned about the financial burdens preventing access to justice in the courts of Great Britain.[2] Looking around in the world to see whether there are states which solved the problem of costs more satisfactorily, he thought that the German system of fixed fees for lawyers when litigating and legal expenses insurance might be a solution which could be followed by English legislators. As the financial hurdle has not really been removed by the Jackson report and will survive any form of 'Brexit', I would like to present some information on German legal expenses insurance and its importance for financing civil proceedings in Germany.

Insurance against legal expenses

Legal expenses insurance is insurance against the risk of having to pay for legal advice out of court and/or the costs of court proceedings. Like accident insurance, liability insurance or health insurance, it insures against possible expenses within the scope of the policy,[3] and is financed by monthly or yearly contributions. By implementing Article 3 of the European Council Directive 87/344/EEC and later

[1] cf A Zuckerman, *On Civil Procedure Principles of Practice* (3rd edn, Sweet & Maxwell 2013).
[2] See A Zuckerman, 'Justice in Crisis', in *Civil Justice in Crisis* (OUP 1999) 3, 7 seqq.
[3] G Hillmer-Möbius, in H-P Schwintowski and C Brömmelmeyer, *Praxiskommentar zum Versicherungsvertragsrecht* (3rd edn ZAP 2017) Vorbem zu §§ 125–29 VVG n 8; C Armbrüster, in E Prölss/A Martin, *VVG* (30th edn, CH Beck 2018) Vorbem zu §§ 125–29 VVG n 2.

Peter Gottwald, *Funding Civil Litigation Through Legal Expenses Insurance in Germany* In: *Principles, Procedure, and Justice*. Edited by: Rabeea Assy and Andrew Higgins, Oxford University Press (2020). © The editors and several contributors.
DOI: 10.1093/oso/9780198850410.003.0010

the Solvency II Directive, German legislators opted for a model in which legal expenses insurance may be offered together with other kinds of insurance. However, in such cases an independent claims processing company has to handle the claims which are covered by the legal expenses insurance policy.[4] The reasons for this approach are to have transparency and clarity about who is responsible for dealing with an insured case and to avoid conflicts of interest. Whereas health insurance, automobile liability insurance, and fire insurance are mandatory, a person can freely decide whether they want to insure themselves against the risk of being involved in (certain kinds of) legal disputes.

About forty years ago, as part of the access to justice debate, making legal expenses insurance compulsory was discussed.[5] The idea was, however, not adopted. There was the fear that such insurance would be misused to fund frivolous proceedings in the absence of a financial obstacle to going to court. In addition, some models involved the welfare state paying insurance premiums for the poor. Funding a legal aid scheme for them instead seemed significantly cheaper.[6]

In Germany, legal expenses insurance started with insurance against legal expenses incurred in contesting the civil and penal consequences of traffic accidents. All other types of legal expenses insurance developed later on. For a long time, policies were only regulated by the insurer's standard terms and conditions. This changed after the European Community adopted the Council Directive 87/344/EEC of 22 June 1987, which required the Member States to regulate the basic elements of legal expenses insurance.[7] This directive was implemented in the German Law on Insurance Contracts (VVG). Since this law was revised in 2007, the relevant rules are now §§ 125 to 129 VVG.

Today, about fifty insurance companies offer legal expenses insurance in Germany, in a market which seems to be highly competitive but saturated and stagnating. It is reported that about 40 per cent of all German households have one or more legal expenses insurance policies[8] and that in the last years about 35 per cent of all people seeking legal advice out of court or being a party to court proceedings (itself a very small part of the population) paid their legal expenses by way of insurance.[9] In 2015, insurance companies received EUR 3.6 billion in premiums from this kind of insurance. The gross amounts the insurance companies paid out for insured risks amounted to EUR 2.8 billion (in 2016), EUR 1.9 billion of which was

[4] A Bruns, in E Bruck and H Möller, *VVG*, vol 5 *Rechtsschutzversicherung* (9th edn, de Gruyter 2019) § 126 VVG n 3; E Schmitt, in W Harbauer, *Rechtsschutzversicherung* (9th edn, CH Beck 2018) Einl n 34.

[5] cf F Baur, *Armenrecht und Rechtsschutzversicherung*, JZ 1972, 75.

[6] cf S Möbius, *Das Prinzip der Rechtsschutzgleichheit im Recht der Prozesskostenhilfe* (Mohr Siebeck 2014) 339 et seq. According to the legal aid scheme of 1980 the state pays a reduced tariff to an assigned lawyer (§§ 45, 48, 49 RVG—Law on the Remuneration of Lawyers).

[7] OJ 1987 L 185/77.

[8] E Schmitt, in W Harbauer, *Rechtsschutzversicherung* (9th edn, CH Beck 2018) Einl n 16; KSchneider, *Rechtsschutzversicherung für Anfänger* (CH Beck 2011) n 3.

[9] C Hommerich and M Kilian, *Rechtsschutzversicherung und Anwaltschaft* (Dt Anwaltverlag 2010) 153.

in lawyers' fees. It is reported that insurance payments made up about 20 per cent of the total revenue of all German law firms.[10]

Years ago, there was a feeling among the judiciary that legal expenses insurance was responsible for the increasing caseload of the courts.[11] Many judges thought that legal expenses insurers funded cases that were weak on the merits to attract more customers. However, a 1981 study came to the conclusion that holders of a legal expenses insurance do not take more process risks than other litigants.[12] The study compared the number of out of court settlements for cases with and without legal expenses insurance, the rate of court-facilitated settlement, and the rate of filing appeals. In any event, practicing lawyers report that, since the market is stagnating, in the last years legal expenses insurers have more closely examined whether applications have sufficient prospect of success and whether the resulting costs are seriously disproportionate to the desired result (§ 3a (1) lit.a, b ARB 2012).

Since there is no obligation to take out legal expenses insurance, the parties are in general free to agree on the terms of the insurance under the principle of freedom of contract. However, standard form contracts offered by insurers must be in line with the general law's limits on standard terms. Such terms may not be unfairly prejudicial to the insured (§ 307 BGB). However, permissible terms include that the insurer will only pay the costs of a civil action in court if a previous attempt to solve the dispute by mediation or other way of dispute resolution out of court has failed, and provisions granting the insurer the right to nominate the mediator.[13]

In many areas of insurance, the policyholder is not the only insured person. In traffic accident insurance for a family, the insurance policy may also cover the policyholder's spouse or partner and children (§ 21 (11) ARB 2012). A policy may also insure a car, whoever is driving it at the time of the accident (§ 22 ARB 2012). Similarly, a 'private' legal expenses insurance policy includes the policyholder's spouse or partner and the children (§ 23 (1), (2) ARB 2012). The same is true for a contract protecting private and occupational interests of a private household (§ 25 (1), (2) ARB 2012).

[10] U Eberhardt, *Rechtsschutzversicherung im Wandel*, VersR 2013, 802 (refering to 2006); R Obarowski, *Münchener Kommentar VVG* (2nd edn, CH Beck 2017) § 125 n 10 (refering to 2004); H Buschbell, in H Buschbell and M Hering, *Handbuch Rechtsschutzversicherung* (6th edn, Dt Anwaltverlag 2015) § 4 n 15.

[11] Since 2002 the number of filed cases has, however, declined by about 25 per cent (cf P Gottwald, *Ein fast perfektes System, Festschrift für Wolfgang Krüger* (CH Beck 2017) 375).

[12] E Schmitt in W Harbauer, *Rechtsschutzversicherung* (9th edn, Ch Beck 2018) Einl Rn 132. This result is confirmed by the study of Hommerich and Kilian (n 9) 65ff. However, a later study of 1993 initiated by the German Federal Ministry of Justice came to the result that insured parties pursue their rights more persistently than other parties in about 10 per cent of cases (cf E Schmitt, in W Harbauer above.).

[13] BGH VersR 2016, 1113; D Böhm and M Fries, *Streitbeilegungstarife in der Rechtsschutzversicherung*, VersR 2016, 1092.

The relationship between legal expenses insurers and lawyers

Insurance companies are not allowed to offer legal advice themselves. The German Legal Services Act 2007 (RDG) prohibits legal services by persons other than lawyers with few exceptions (listed in §§ 6 to 8 RDG). In addition, § 4 RDG prohibits a person from providing legal services which are incompatible with their other obligations (for example, because they may present a conflict of interest). Such a conflict of interest arises here: the insurer's interest is in keeping the legal expenses as low as possible, which conflicts with a lawyer's duty to pursue the best outcome for their client (which may involve incurring higher expenses).[14] Consequently, the insurer is not allowed to give legal advice through its own employees,[15] but has to co-operate with self-employed lawyers.

According to § 127 (1) VVG, the insured person can freely choose a lawyer to represent them. Insurers are not allowed to restrict this freedom to the disadvantage of the insured person (§ 129 VVG). In the majority of cases, where the insured person first contacts a lawyer of their choice and this lawyer then notifies the insurance company, the issue does not arise. However, if the insured person directly contacts the insurance company, the insurer has to recommend a lawyer, and will often recommend one who has a pre-existing relationship with the insurer.[16] It is then up to the insured to contact and instruct this lawyer, or else choose another lawyer. One would think that the insurer would not be concerned with whatever the insured decides, as the insurer has to pay the mandated lawyer for the same performance in any case.

In practice, however, so-called 'efficiency agreements' between the insurer and the recommended lawyer are fairly common.[17] Under such 'efficiency agreements', the insurer exclusively recommends the lawyer for cases within a certain area, and the lawyer agrees to accept a lower rate of fees. Such arrangements have no influence on the standard and quality of services, and are based on the lawyers' freedom to set their own fees for out of court services. In the end this arrangement has benefits for both sides: if the lawyer is frequently recommended by the insurance company they have more cases and earn more than without such referrals, and the insurer saves costs.[18]

If the insured contacts and chooses to instruct this lawyer, this is simple enough. However, if the insured is unhappy with this lawyer, they can instead choose another lawyer. This freedom is guaranteed by § 127 (1) VVG. The insurance company has to accept this choice, but may limit its coverage of the legal expenses. The

[14] H Buschbell, in Buschbell and Hering (n 10) § 1 n 6.

[15] ECJ, C-442/12, ECLI:EU:C:2013:717—*Jan Sneller v DAS Nederland* = NJW 2014, 373.

[16] As to the criteria to select those lawyers cf U Eberhardt (n 10), VersR 2013, 802, 806 ff.

[17] cf Hommerich and Kilian (n 9) 111 ff.

[18] Such an agreement is only valid for out-of-court services, as participation in court proceedings is regulated by fixed costs; see No 6 c.

German Federal Court of Justice has held that, in contracts with variable deductibles, the insurer may impose a higher deductible when the client instructs a different lawyer.[19]

As the market is highly competitive, some insurance companies now offer additional services to attract customers, such as online legal advice,[20] sometimes even in fields of law which are not covered by the insurance policy. Again, as the insurance company is not allowed to give legal advice, this advice is provided by self-employed lawyers working for the insurer.[21] For the same reason, some legal expenses insurers offer to pay for mediation in appropriate cases.[22] In addition, some insurers offer their customers a list of relevant court decisions. This is permissible as this list only contains general legal information, as opposed to advice for the customer's particular case.

Insurance for specific risks

Legal expenses insurance is not comprehensive,[23] but only covers particular types of claim. According to § 2 ARB 2012 (General conditions for legal expenses insurance), insurance is offered for policyholders who are (1) seeking damages, (2) defending employment contract claims, (3) defending interests in tenancies or real estate, (4) defending other rights in rem or private contractual rights,[24] (5) defending taxation claims, (6) defending social security claims, (7) defending traffic matters, (8) defending civil service disciplinary claims, (9) defending against criminal charges (i) for traffic offences, (ii) for other offences involving negligence,[25] (10) defending against administrative offences, (11) seeking out of court advice for family or succession matters,[26] or (12) victims of crimes seeking representation in criminal proceedings.

In practice, legal expenses insurance is mainly taken out by private parties such as consumers. However, some of the activities above could also cover commercial risks. According to § 24 ARB 2012 legal expenses insurance for self-employed persons, partnerships, corporations, other commercial enterprises, and registered associations is possible. However, because the legal risk is too high, since 1984 legal expenses insurance has no longer been offered for commercial enterprises.[27]

19 Federal Court of Justice (4.12.2013, IV ZR 215/12), VersR 2014, 98.

20 cf Eberhardt (n 10) VersR 2013, 802, 805.

21 H Buschbell, in Buschbell and Hering (n 10) § 1 n 9.

22 cf Eberhardt (n 10) VersR 2013, 802, 811 ff; D Wendt, *Leistungspflichten des Rechtsschutzversicherers nach § 125 VVG*, VersR 2014, 420, 424 ff.

23 cf H Plote, *Anwalt und Rechtsschutzversicherung* (Beck 2000) n 18.

24 cf OLG Nürnberg VersR 2016, 1371 (problem with private tenancy as to a financed flat).

25 There is no insurance for offences committed intentionally. If a person is first accused of an offence of negligence, but eventually convicted for an intentional crime, they have to repay the insurer.

26 § 3 (2) g ARB 2012 expressly excludes any further coverage in this field.

27 R Obarowski, in RM Beckmann and A Matusche-Beckmann, *Versicherungsrechts-Handbuch* (3rd edn, CH Beck 2015) § 37 Rechtsschutzversicherung n 133.

§ 3 ARB 2012 contains a very long and important list of matters which are excluded from legal expenses insurance policies. The list includes risks which are not susceptible to actuarial calculation, like the consequences of war, earthquakes, civil unrest, or nuclear accidents. Also excluded are the costs of defending claims in relation to planning or building houses (including related questions of tax law: §§ 3 (1) d, 3 (2) i) and claims under company law, business law, competition law, and law of industrial property (§ 3 (2) c, d, e ARB 2012). Defending such claims is too expensive and risky to be insured.

Standard form contracts offered to consumers are aimed at meeting the practical needs of an average citizen. Often, insurers offer four types of basic contracts, insuring (1) the risks of private life, (2) risks of occupation, (3) risks of traffic accidents, and (4) risks of accommodation and real estate.[28] This basic protection can often be expanded by paying for some optional extras. The end result may come close to an 'all round carefree package'.

The monthly rate for an insurance policy for the risks of private life for a single person varies from EUR 9.26 to about EUR 35. For a family the rate is generally about 20 per cent higher. Traffic accident insurance is offered at a yearly rate of about EUR 78.90 for one vehicle and EUR 109.30 for all vehicles operated by a family. These prices, the calculation behind them and the whole system of insurance are based on the existence of fixed fee arrangements when litigating.[29]

Prerequisites of insurance

Legal expenses insurance must be taken out before a risk has eventuated.[30] In most cases the insurance is valid from the payment of the first insurance premium (§ 7 ARB 2012). But many companies also impose an additional general waiting period of three to six months. For special risks, some insurers demand even longer waiting periods up to three years.[31]

If the risk eventuates after any waiting period is over, the insurer is obliged to pay the costs of legal advice and (if necessary) the costs of proceedings in court.[32] The insurer is, however, entitled to examine whether the intended claim actually results from an insured event. Insurers are now scrutinizing this connection more closely. Moreover, § 3a (1) ARB 2012 provides that the insurer may refuse to pay out if (1) in the cases of categories (1) to (7) identified above at 3.a, there are insufficient

[28] Schneider (n 8) n 40.

[29] cf B Hess and R Hübner, 'Germany', in C Hodges, S Vogenauer, and M Tulibacka, *The Costs and Funding of Civil Litigation* (Hart 2010) 349, 359.

[30] For details cf J Cornelius-Winkler, *Kausalität und Rechtsschutzfall*, VersR 2015, 1476.

[31] For example, the ARAG Company, which imposes longer waiting periods for legal protection in marital matters before the court and in cases regarding the allocation of study places.

[32] cf D Wendt (n 22) VersR 2014, 420.

prospects of success, or (2) if the claim is raised in bad faith,[33] a concept defined to include claims which involve costs grossly disproportionate to the amount claimed. Insurers have some discretion in determining whether these exceptions apply.

If the insurer decides not to cover the claim because it has insufficient prospects of success or is disproportionate, the policy holder may appeal the insurer's decision. The dispute will be determined by expert determination by an independent lawyer with at least five years of practice, appointed by the president of the local bar association. This attorney delivers an opinion about whether either exception applies. Such opinion is binding on the insurer and the policyholder (§ 3a (4) ARB 2012).[34]

'Precautionary' legal advice and the 'cover note' procedure

Legal expenses insurance only covers cases where a person has *in fact* breached a contract or committed a tort. Otherwise, there is no 'damage' to insure.[35] Costs for *precautionary* legal advice, where no wrong was in fact committed, are not covered.[36]

In the majority of cases, the lawyer whose advice is sought will notify the insurer and ask for a 'cover note', confirming the advice will be covered by the insurance policy, before taking instructions.[37] The insurer will examine the case and decide whether or not to issue a cover note. If it issues a cover note, it is bound by it and must cover the expenses, even if it issued the note without acknowledging any legal obligation to do so.[38]

Costs covered by legal expenses insurance

Once the insurer has sent a cover note, it is obliged to indemnify the policyholder from costs within the scope of the policy.

In the great majority of cases, the client is a consumer. In such cases, a preliminary oral advice by a lawyer costs up to EUR 190, and a written legal opinion costs up to EUR 250 (§ 34 I 3 RVG—Law on remuneration of lawyers 2004). If the client

[33] B Richter, in T Langheid and M Wandt, *Münchener Kommentar zum VVG* (2nd edn, CH Beck 2017) § 128 n 26 f; cf also LG Detmold, VersR 2016, 1493 (action for delivery a new 'clean'diesel car).
[34] E Schmitt, in W Harbauer, *Rechtsschutzversicherung* (9th edn, CH Beck 2018) § 3a ARB 2010 N36, but cf LG Detmold VersR 2016, 1493.
[35] cf M Schaltke, *BGH-Leitsätze zum Rechtsschutzfall und ihre Auswirkungen auf die Praxis*, VersR 2016, 373.
[36] cf Plote (n 23) n 136.
[37] cf G Terriucio, *Einholung der Deckungszusage durch den Rechtsanwalt*, AnwBl 2017, 44 (separate remuneration only after special information of client).
[38] OLG Düsseldorf, VersR 2016, 1051.

requires more detailed legal advice, or the lawyer has to contact the opponent, the lawyer should enter into a costs agreement with the client (§§ 3a (1), 34 (1) 1 RVG). Absent such an agreement, the lawyer can charge fixed fees according to the Civil Code (§ 34 (1) 2 RVG). In the absence of a particular amount set by law (§ 612 (2) BGB), this will be 1.3–1.5 fee units, depending on the amount in dispute according to the fee schedule annexed to § 13 RVG.[39] For example, assuming that the value in dispute is EUR 10,000, the usual fee would be between EUR 725.40 and EUR 837. In very complex and time-consuming cases, the lawyer may charge a higher fee. Whether the insurance company covers this remuneration completely or partially depends on the insurance contract and the content of the cover note issued by the insurer.

Insurance companies offer various rates for insurance with or without deductibles paid by the insured (of differing values). The most common form of deductible is a fixed sum (usually EUR 150 or 250) for each case. There are also policies where the amount of the deductible or premium varies depending on the number of cases the insured is involved in. Some insurers do not require the insured to pay any deductible if the case only requires preliminary oral advice.

If the insured case goes to court, the court and legal fees for both sides are fixed by law. The lawyer earns 1.3 fee units for accepting instructions and 1.2 fee units for participating in an oral court hearing or in negotiations out of court with the opponent. If the case is settled the lawyer earns an additional 1.0 fee unit depending on the value in dispute (VV RVG No. 3100, 3104, 1003).[40] To start court proceedings the claimant has to pay an advance payment of 3 fee units depending on the value in dispute (§ 6 (1) 1 with cost index No. 1210 GKG – Court Costs Act). Thus, for a dispute about EUR 10,000 the insurer has to pay EUR 723 in court fees[41] and EUR 3,367.70 in legal fees[42] if the case is lost.

Conclusion

In Germany, legal expenses insurance is an important instrument for ordinary citizens to protect themselves (and their families) against costs arising out of pursuing or defending private claims. The insurer provides the necessary upfront payment, and pays the total costs at the end of proceedings if the insured is unsuccessful.

[39] The former framework tariff for out-of-court advice (0, 5 to 2, 5 fee units) has been abolished, but survives for the calculation of the 'usual remuneration' for out-of-court advice.

[40] cf G Wagner, 'Litigation Costs Recovery—Tariffs and Hourly Fees in Germany', in P Gottwald, *Litigation in England and Germany* (Gieseking 2010) 149, 156 et seq.

[41] In addition, there may be substantial payments for expert witnesses and so on.

[42] Without taking into consideration the remuneration for out-of-court advice given by the claimant's lawyer.

The major advantage of insurance as opposed to legal aid is that it does not prevent the successful opponent from seeking costs against the losing party.[43]

Insurance companies offer specific policies, in particular covering traffic accidents or problems with occupation, but also policies covering all the ups and downs of private life. About 40 per cent of German households have taken out such insurance, indicating that they think such insurance is a useful protection against the financial burden of being involved in legal disputes. This precautionary instrument is not expensive, but is only available for the ordinary risks of private life (and not, for example, for construction and land cases). At present the whole area of commercial disputes is completely excluded. Thus, beyond traffic insurance for cars and drivers, even small or medium sized enterprises cannot insure against the risk of legal expenses.

[43] cf B Hess and R Hübner, 'Germany', in C Hodges, S Vogenauer, and M Tulibacka, *The Costs and Funding of Civil Litigation* (Hart 2010) 349, 358.

11
Controlling Recoverable Costs

Rupert Jackson

Introduction

The problem of controlling costs in civil litigation is one with which law reformers, judges, practitioners, and academics have grappled over the last two centuries. A universal regime of fixed recoverable costs (FRC) is in the eyes of many the ideal to which we must aspire.

Professor Zuckerman in his writings has consistently espoused the German system and has urged that we should adopt something like that in this jurisdiction. Let me turn, therefore, to the costs regime prevailing in Germany.

The German system

For litigation work, the German scheme of FRC prescribes a statutory fee for lawyers on the basis of the value of the claim. This gives the base fee to which a number of multipliers, changing according to the stage of proceedings reached and the nature of the instructions, can be applied to give the fixed costs figure. Section 13 of the Law on the Remuneration of Lawyers (RVG) provides that when the value of the claim is less than €500, the base fee shall be €45. For claims above €500, the base fee rises progressively in accordance with the value of the claim.

Annex 1 to the RVG provides a full and comprehensive list of legal fees. The schedules in annex 1 cover everything from initial appointment as the client's attorney through to an appeal to the Federal Court of Justice (*Bundesgerichtshof*).

In non-contentious business, the amounts in annex 1 can be either a specific payment range (for example, €50.00 to €640.00 for an attorney instructed in a social security law matter), a single multiplier (0.3 for an attorney instructed only to draft simple documents), or a multiplier range (0.5 to 2.5, depending on complexity, for an attorney instructed generally).

In litigation, an attorney's fee is in two parts. First, the *Verfahrensgebühr* covers out-of-court work, which attracts a multiplier of 1.3. Secondly, the *Terminsgebühr* covers the hearing and meetings with the opposing party's lawyer. This has a multiplier of 1.2. A lawyer who performs both roles can claim a multiplier of 2.5 (in addition to any other work done and disbursements).

Rupert Jackson, *Controlling Recoverable Costs* In: *Principles, Procedure, and Justice*. Edited by: Rabeea Assy and Andrew Higgins, Oxford University Press (2020). © The editors and several contributors.
DOI: 10.1093/oso/9780198850410.003.0011

The German costs regime brings undoubted benefits.[1] First, the fact that recoverable costs are limited has the effect of reducing what lawyers charge their own clients in everyday cases. Secondly, it is within the means of ordinary citizens to bring and defend modest claims. Thirdly, the costs of litigation are certain and predictable. Fourthly, and as a consequence of the foregoing, insurance against the costs of litigation (often referred to in England as 'Before the Event' or 'BTE' insurance) is widespread. That in turn promotes greater access to justice. Indeed, the efficiency and accessibility of Germany's civil justice system has probably been one of the factors contributing to that country's remarkable economic success over the last fifty years. The Mittelstand firms can afford to bring or defend claims when the need arises and the costs of doing so are not ruinous.

Before we get carried away with enthusiasm for adopting the German costs regime, there are two important points to bear in mind. They are first, the international aspect and secondly, the different context in which the German costs regime sits.

The international aspect

The courts of Germany are not a magnet for international litigation in the same way that the English courts are. Language may be part of the reason, although some German courts now offer an English language service. One important factor is the common law of England and Wales, which is widely regarded as a safe legal foundation for resolving business disputes. Another factor is the high quality of English judges—I am talking here about the High Court judges who sit in the Rolls Building. (No-one who choses England as their forum is much interested in the Court of Appeal or the Supreme Court.) For these and possibly other reasons many global businesses prefer to bring their disputes to London, despite the high litigation costs of this jurisdiction.

Different context

When examining the German costs regime, it is important to remember the different context. Under German civil procedure, disclosure of documents is strictly limited. The court establishes the facts using the 'Relationsmethode'. Under this procedure the judge does some of the work which in England is undertaken by the parties. The German courts make much greater use of court appointed experts than we do. There is far less oral evidence. Litigation is quicker and hearings are shorter than in England. There is also a cultural difference between the legal professions of

[1] See further The Review of Civil Litigation Costs Preliminary Report, chapter 55 'Germany'.

the two countries. The separation between practitioners and judges occurs 'at birth' in Germany, in that lawyers are divided into the practitioner stream and the judicial stream as soon as they qualify. In England, by contrast, most judges (certainly in the commercial sphere) have practised as barristers for twenty-five years before going onto the bench. Also, my impression (and it is only an impression, because I have not researched this) is that successful German lawyers may be content with more modest remuneration than their counterparts in England. The German costs rules are instructive, but they cannot be transplanted to England without appropriate modification.

What then can we learn from Germany?

The example of Germany teaches that certainty and predictability of litigation costs is a public benefit. We should be seeking to achieve that goal, so far as it is possible to do within the context of the English common law adversarial system.

That is the challenge which I faced during the first seven months of 2017.

The review of fixed recoverable costs in 2017

On 11 November 2016, the Lord Chief Justice and the Master of the Rolls commissioned me to carry out a review with the following terms of reference:

> (i) To develop proposals for extending the present civil fixed recoverable costs regime in England and Wales so as to make the costs of going to court more certain, transparent and proportionate for litigants. (ii) To consider the types and areas of litigation in which such costs should be extended, and the value of claims to which such a regime should apply. (iii) To report to the Lord Chief Justice and the Master of the Rolls by the 31st July 2017.

I appointed fourteen assessors drawn from a wide spectrum. They included the Senior Costs Judge, the Senior Master, the President of the Association of Costs Lawyers, judges, practitioners, and two economists. The assessors and I met once per month, usually on a Wednesday morning, to review the evidence and debate the issues. Although we all approached the task from different angles, a considerable degree of consensus emerged as time went on.

I invited stakeholders and court users to send in their views as well as any evidence of litigation costs which they were willing to disclose. There were 141 responses. Most were highly informative and helpful, although quite a few had an underlying tone of hostility.

Budget exercise

I asked all courts to send in copies of the budgets which were approved or agreed at costs and case management conferences between 5 December 2016 and 20 January 2017, together with the associated statements of case. Some courts were able to comply, others were not. As material came in, my team of five judicial assistants (two barristers, two solicitors, and an actuary) divided cases into the following categories:

A. Clinical negligence
B. Personal injury
C. Business disputes
D. Chancery
E. Technology and construction (TCC)
F. Defamation
G. Other

They eliminated those budgets which were unusable for one reason or another. They then extracted the available information and summarized it in extensive tables which are annexed to my July 2017 report.[2] By way of example, an abbreviated summary of the personal injury budgets is as follows.

Table 1 Personal injury: agreed/approved budgets for claimants and defendants, split by incurred and future costs

Personal Injury – Claimant – Average				
Value (£)	**Number of Budgets**	**Incurred (£)**	**Agreed or Approved Future (£)**	**Total (£)**
0–25k	13	16,723	34,589	51,312
25–50k	17	21,151	47,912	69,062
50–100k	10	30,074	52,592	82,667
100–250k	9	51,443	97,593	149,035
250k+	1	40,703	92,908	133,611
Value unknown	6	26,962	45,718	72,680

[2] Review of Civil Litigation Costs, Supplementary Report, July 2017.

Table 1 Continued

Personal Injury – Defendant – Average				
Value (£)	**Number of Budgets**	**Incurred (£)**	**Agreed or Approved Future (£)**	**Total (£)**
0–25k	14	3,954	26,542	30,496
25–50k	17	3,652	29,847	33,499
50–100k	11	4,062	36,726	40,787
100–250k	9	14,621	72,230	86,851
250k+	1	15,422	114,880	130,302
Value unknown	5	2,712	41,458	44,170

Seminars and meetings

During the review, I chaired five public seminars to hear people's views and oral argument. The seminars and the topics were as follows:

- 6 February 2017 at Leeds: chancery and property cases
- 7 February 2017 at Manchester: personal injury and clinical negligence
- 13 March 2017 at London: judicial review and general issues
- 16 March 2017 at Birmingham: mercantile and business litigation
- 5 April 2017 at Cardiff: judicial review and structural issues.

At each of the seminars there were two formal presentations, then a discussion session, then two more formal presentations, then a second discussion session. My experience during the 2009 Costs Review was that this was the most productive format for such seminars. There was lively debate at all the seminars and quite a few brickbats were thrown in my direction. I learnt a huge amount at these seminars and soon recovered from the bruises inflicted by hostile speakers.

I also held separate meetings with individuals or bodies who could contribute to the review. There was also a seminar at Oxford organized by Professor Zuckerman and Associate Professor Higgins (both of whom had made substantial contributions during my 2009 Costs Review). Chapter 4 of the July 2017 report contains a summary of all those events.

Recommendations made at the end of the fixed recoverable costs review

At the end of the fixed recoverable costs review I reached clear conclusions. Chapter 11 of my July 2017 report made eleven recommendations, namely:

(i) All recoverable costs in the fast track should be fixed and the figures should be reviewed every three years.
(ii) A new 'intermediate' track with a streamlined procedure should be created for monetary relief cases above the fast track, which are of modest complexity and up to a value of £100,000.
(iii) There should be a grid of FRC for intermediate track cases and the figures should be reviewed every three years.
(iv) There should be FRC for (a) applications to approve settlements for children and protected parties and (b) costs only proceedings, in respect of intermediate track cases.
(v) Save as set out in recommendation (iv) above, Part 8 claims should be excluded from the proposed FRC regime.
(vi) The Civil Justice Council should, in conjunction with the Department of Health, set up a working party, including both claimant and defendant representatives, to develop a bespoke process for clinical negligence claims up to £25,000, together with a grid of FRC for such cases.
(vii) There should be a pilot of capped recoverable costs, in conjunction with streamlined procedures, for business and property cases with a value up to £250,000. Draft rules for that pilot were approved by the Civil Procedure Rule Committee in May 2017, at my request.[3]
(viii) If the pilot is successful, such a regime should be made available at the judge's discretion for any suitable case in the Business and Property Courts or the Business and Property Lists of the County Court.
(ix) The Aarhus Rules should be adapted and extended to all judicial review claims.
(x) Costs management should be introduced, at the discretion of the judge, in 'heavy' judicial review claims.
(xi) When the reforms recommended in this report have bedded in, consideration should be given to:
   a. developing (1) a grid of FRC for incurred costs in different categories of case, and (2) a pre-action procedure for seeking leave to exceed the FRC in that grid; and
   b. extending the scope of the intermediate track and the range of FRC.

[3] The pilot could not start in June as hoped, because of the General Election and the period of Purdah in the run up to the Election. In the event it did not start until January 2019.

The fast track

This was really a 'no-brainer'. The fast track has a simplified procedure. Cases proceed from issue to trial under written directions, which are generally given on allocation. That track therefore lends itself to FRC. Indeed, many fast track cases already have FRC, in accordance with recommendations made in my January 2010 report. During the 2017 review there was widespread acceptance that the remainder of the fast track must also have FRC. The only real issue was what the figures should be. How should that issue be tackled?

The recent analysis of budgets provided no relevant evidence, because that related only to multi-track cases. We did, however, have a great deal of data on fast track cases settled since 1 April 2013 when rule 44.3(5), the new proportionality rule, came into force. That rule, which I had proposed in chapter 3 of my previous report at paragraph 5.15, provides:

> Costs incurred are proportionate if they bear a reasonable relationship to –
> (a) the sums in issue in the proceedings;
> (b) the value of any non-monetary relief in issue in the proceedings;
> (c) the complexity of the litigation;
> (d) any additional work generated by the conduct of the paying party; and
> (e) any wider factors involved in the proceedings, such as reputation or public importance.

My assessors and I took those data and made discounts for savings to be achieved through having no process of detailed recording, negotiation, or assessment of costs. We also had regard to the recent mediated 'industry' agreement concerning the costs of noise induced hearing loss claims. On that basis, I proposed that fast track cases should be divided into four complexity bands with the following grid of FRC:

Table 2 Matrix of FRC for fast track claims (applies to both claimant and defendant recoverable costs)

	Complexity Band			
Stage:	1	2	3	4
Pre-issue £1,001–£5,000		£104 + 20% of damages	£988 + 17.5% of damages	£2,250 + 15% of damages + £440 per extra defendant
Pre-issue £5,001–£10,000		£1,144 + 15% of damages over £5,000	£1,929 + 12.5% of damages over £5,000	
Pre-issue £10,001–£25,000	£500	£2,007 + 10% of damages over £10,000	£2,600 + 10% of damages over £10,000	

(continued)

Table 2 Continued

	Complexity Band			
Stage:	1	2	3	4
Post-issue, pre-allocation	£1,850	£1,206 + 20% of damages	£2,735 + 20% of damages	£2,575 + 40% of damages + £660 per extra defendant
Post-allocation, pre-listing	£2,200	£1,955 + 20% of damages	£3,484 + 25% of damages	£5,525 + 40% of damages + £660 per extra defendant
Post-listing, pre-trial	£3,250	£2,761 + 20% of damages	£4,451 + 30% of damages	£6,800 + 40% of damages + £660 per extra defendant
Trial advocacy fee[i]	a. £500 b. £710 c. £1,070 d. £1,705	a. £500 b. £710 c. £1,070 d. £1,705	a. £500 b. £710 c. £1,070 d. £1,705	a. £1,380 b. £1,380 c. £1,800 d. £2,500

"i a. claim value up to £3,000; b. claim value .... "

[i] a. claim value up to £3,000; b. claim value £3,001 to £10,000; c. claim value £10,001 to £15,000; d. claim value £15,001 to £25,000.

The figures in all boxes are cumulative, except for the trial advocacy fees shown in the bottom line. The word 'damages' is used as shorthand for debt, liquidated sum, or other monetary relief. There is obviously some difficulty in applying the above table to claims for, or including, non-monetary relief, but the court must assign a value to such relief (as the courts do in Germany). A claim for a declaration or injunction should be treated as the equivalent of a claim for £10,000, with the court having power to vary that figure upwards or downwards, if appropriate.

Cases above the fast track

Cases above the fast track present a more difficult problem. My ultimate conclusion, after examining the arguments and data, was that there should be FRC for cases of moderate complexity where no more than £100,000 is in issue. Such cases should go into a new 'intermediate track' with a streamlined procedure. I proposed that the cases should be divided into four complexity bands with the following grid of FRC:

Table 3 Proposed grid of FRC for intermediate track cases

Stage (S)	Band 1	Band 2	Band 3	Band 4
S1 Pre-issue or pre-defence investigations	£1,400 + 3% of damages	£4,350 + 6% of damages	£5,550 + 6% of damages	£8,000 + 8% of damages
S2 Counsel/ specialist lawyer drafting statements of case and/or advising (if instructed)	£1,750	£1,750	£2,000[a]	£2,000[b]
S3 Up to and including CMC	£3,500 + 10% of damages	£6,650 + 12% of damages	£7,850 + 12% of damages	£11,000 + 14% of damages
S4 Up to the end of disclosure and inspection	£4,000 + 12% of damages	£8,100 + 14% of damages	£9,300 + 14% of damages	£14,200 + 16% of damages
S5 Up to service of witness statements and expert reports	£4,500 + 12% of damages	£9,500 + 16% of damages	£10,700 + 16% of damages	£17,400 + 18% of damages
S6 Up to PTR, alternatively 14 days before trial	£5,100 + 15% of damages	£12,750 + 16% of damages	£13,950 + 16% of damages	£21,050 + 18% of damages
S7 Counsel/ specialist lawyer advising in writing or in conference (if instructed)	£1,250	£1,500	£2,000	£2,500
S8 Up to trial[c]	£5,700 + 15% of damages	£15,000 + 20% of damages	£16,200 + 20% of damages	£24,700 + 22% of damages
S9 Attendance of solicitor[d] at trial per day[e]	£500	£750	£1,000	£1,250
S10 Advocacy fee: day 1	£2,750	£3,000	£3,500	£5,000
S11 Advocacy fee: subsequent days[f]	£1,250	£1,500	£1,750	£2,500
S12 Hand down of judgment and consequential matters	£500	£500	£500	£500
S13 ADR: counsel/specialist lawyer at mediation or JSM (if instructed)	£1,200	£1,500	£1,750	£2,000
S14 ADR: solicitor at JSM or mediation	£1,000	£1,000	£1,000	£1,000

(continued)

Table 3 Continued

Stage (S)	Band 1	Band 2	Band 3	Band 4
S15 Approval of settlement for child or protected party	£1,000	£1,250	£1,500	£1,750
Total: (a) £30,000 (b) £50,000, (c) £100,000 damages[g]	(a) £19,150 (b) £22,150 (c) £29,650	(a) £33,250 (b) £37,250 (c) £47,250	(a) £39,450 (b) £43,450 (c) £53,450	(a) £53,050 (b) £57,450 (c) £68,450

[a] £3,000 if there is a counterclaim and defence to counterclaim. The rules may need to specify how costs are split between claim and counterclaim.
[b] £3,000 if there is a counterclaim and defence to counterclaim. The rules may need to specify how costs are split between claim and counterclaim.
[c] If the receiving party did not prepare the bundle, subtract: (a) £500 for a Band 1 case, (b) £750 for a Band 2 case, (c) £1,000 for a Band 3 case, and (d) £1,250 for a Band 4 case.
[d] In this table 'solicitor' includes a representative of the solicitor's firm.
[e] To be halved if attendance is for half a day or less.
[f] To be halved if attendance is for half a day or less.
[g] Assuming a one-day trial in Band 1, a two-day trial in Band 2, and a three-day trial in Bands 3 and 4. For all bands, it is assumed that there was no counterclaim, that the receiving party prepared the trial bundles, that there was unsuccessful ADR, and that there was no approval of settlement for a child or protected party.

The following rules apply to the grid:

(i) In the grid, the word 'damages' is used as shorthand for damages, debt, liquidated sum, or other monetary relief.
(ii) If the claimant succeeds, the specified percentage applies to the sum recovered. If the defendant succeeds, the specified percentage applies to the claim defeated, as valued in the particulars of claim.
(iii) The figures in each of stages S1, S3, S4, S5, S6, and S8 are the cumulative totals for costs incurred up to and including that stage. I have shaded these cumulative boxes for ease of use.
(iv) The figures in stages S2, S7, and S9–S15 are separate sums for those items, if carried out.
(v) The figures in stages S2, S7, and S13 are ring-fenced for counsel or a specialist lawyer. The sums in the other boxes are for division between the solicitors and counsel/specialist lawyer as appropriate in the individual case.
(vi) For non-personal injury cases which are settled before issue, the figures in stage S1 are capped costs, rather than FRC.

Any fixed costs regime must go hand in hand with a streamlined procedure limiting the work to be done. I therefore propose reduced disclosure and early case management directions which will focus the evidence on defined issues. There should be restrictions on the length of pleadings, witness statements, and expert reports.

Business and property litigation falls into a separate category. There are often hard-nosed businessmen on both sides. Quite often small and medium-sized enterprises need to limit their costs exposure and are willing to forego full costs recovery in order to achieve that. The Intellectual Property Enterprise Court has a capped stage costs regime, together with a streamlined process and tight control of evidence. That has been highly popular with court users. I have therefore recommended that a similar regime should be piloted on a voluntary basis in a small number of Business and Property Courts on a voluntary basis. If the pilot is a success, that regime should be rolled out to other courts, to be applied at the court's discretion in appropriate cases.

Judicial review

The Aarhus Rules apply only to environmental claims. They provide an optional regime under which claimants can greatly limit their adverse costs risk and forego any costs recovery above £35,000. Most of the feedback was positive and suggested that the Aarhus Rules promote access to justice. I have recommended that they should be extended to all judicial review claims. I have also recommended that costs management should be available, at the discretion of the court, in 'heavy' judicial review claims.

The future

At the time of writing, the Government is consulting stakeholders about most, but not all, of the proposals in the July 2017 report. The Government is proposing to extend the fast track to incorporate the intermediate cases, rather than to create a separate intermediate track. This approach could work, provided that a separate section is added on to CPR Part 28, to make appropriate provision for the management of intermediate cases. In relation to judicial review, the Government is proposing to introduce costs management for heavy cases, but it is not minded to extend the Aarhus Rules to other JR cases.

Can we eventually move to a totally fixed costs regime?

No. There is an inextricable link between the shape of any procedural regime and the costs shifting rules (assuming that there is costs shifting). It is feasible to have FRC in the fast track and in the proposed intermediate track, because those tracks have or will have streamlined procedures. That is about as close as we can get to something like the German costs regime. It is not possible to extend FRC across the whole of the multi-track, unless we subvert existing procedures for high value cases. That would be contrary to the public interest. It would also destroy many of the features which make the English courts attractive to overseas business litigants.

12
Just Costs

*Frederick Wilmot-Smith**

Introduction

An unsigned note in the 1940 *Yale Law Journal* said that 'remarkably little critical analysis' had been given to the puzzle of 'distributing court costs and attorneys' fees between litigants'.[1] Costs have long been of central practical importance and academic works have catered accordingly: Hullock's *Law of Costs*, published in 1793, contained over a thousand references. But it remains remarkable how little theoretical analysis has been given to the topic.[2] In this essay, I aim to redress the balance.

I begin with a brief overview of the law of costs, explaining the justificatory puzzle they raise. I turn then to the central theoretical distinction of the essay, between 'individualist' and 'holist' justificatory approaches to any domain of law. That discussion reveals that the anonymous author has a mistaken presupposition. It is wrong to assume that the distribution of costs is one *between litigants*. Instead, we should think of costs as one mechanism by which the law might secure distributive justice in the legal system. And it is only if certain contingent facts hold that the expenses are most sensibly to be distributed between litigants.

Costs

An overview

In his *Duties of a Proconsul*, Ulpian wrote that

> He who ... has without cause summoned the other party to court will be obliged to pay the other party's traveling expenses.[3]

* I am grateful to Adrian Zuckerman, an anonymous referee, and the editors for their comments on earlier drafts.

[1] 'Distribution of Legal Expense among Litigants' (1940) 49 Yale L Rev 699, 699.

[2] cf RK Wilson, 'Lawyers' Bills—Who Should Pay Them?' (1896) 12 LQR 368, a superb and unjustly neglected piece on the topic. Jeremy Bentham also wrote numerous pieces of importance.

[3] D.5.1.79 translated in A Watson (tr), *The Digest of Justinian: Books 1–15* (rev, vol 1) (CUP 1998) 174. For a collection of Roman texts on expenses, see H Erman, *La Restitution des Frais de Procès en Droit Romain* (C ViretGenton 1892) 109, fn 2–3.

Frederick Wilmot-Smith, *Just Costs* In: *Principles, Procedure, and Justice*. Edited by: Rabeea Assy and Andrew Higgins, Oxford University Press (2020). © The editors and several contributors. DOI: 10.1093/oso/9780198850410.003.0012

Something like this is our law today: the party who loses has to pay the other side's court, expert, and lawyers' fees. Yet, despite the ancient Civilian antecedents, English law had no costs rules until the Statute of Gloucester (1278), c.1. Over the centuries, statutes added to its rules. By the time of the Judicature Acts, Lord Blackburn explained, the general rule at common law was that

> the party who succeeded got his costs, whether he was Plaintiff or Defendant ... [T]he costs followed the event, and that the party who was successful had them as a matter of right.[4]

This rule was subject to various exceptions. For example, one statute excepted actions of slander where damages were less than forty shillings: the plaintiff could have no more than the sum of damages.[5]

The Judicature Acts unified the rules for law and equity; from 1875 there was a general rule that costs followed the event.[6] That remains the law today.[7] This basic position is subject to a plethora of complications, many of which we can set to one side. Some, such as the assessment procedure, are not fundamental to the rules on costs.[8] Others are best seen as attempts to work through the basic rule in the complications of litigation. For example, it is not easy to apply the basic rule to situations where a litigant is successful only in part.[9] Questions about how to implement a rule are logically secondary to questions about how the rule itself is justified.

Some complications to the basic rule do warrant our attention. The court is able to vary a costs order to sanction misconduct.[10] If a litigant fails to comply with a rule of the CPR, a practice direction, or a court order, or if the litigant's conduct is ruled unreasonable or improper, a *prima facie* claim to costs might be disallowed.[11] Costs orders can also vary quite drastically depending on when and in what form a losing party offered to settle the case.[12] Perhaps the most important of these in contemporary costs is Part 36 offers. A plaintiff who beats their own Part 36 offer

[4] *Garnett v Bradley* (1878) 3 App Cas 944 (HL) 962 (Lord Blackburn).

[5] 21 Jac 1, c 16, s 6. Given my argument in this chapter it is worth noting Lord Blackburn's analysis, that the statute was 'passed to discourage frivolous actions of slander' (*Garnett v Bradley* (n 4) 963).

[6] Chancery's practice before the Judicature Acts was said to be more discretionary than the common law's. As with all such claims to equity's discretionary exceptionalism, it is unclear that the practice was any different from the common law.

[7] CPR 44.2(2)(a) ('the general rule is that the unsuccessful party will be ordered to pay the costs of the successful party'), qualified by CPR 44.2(2)(b) ('the court may make a different order').

[8] Briefly, English law distinguishes between summary and detailed assessments. Summary assessments take place at the end of the hearing; detailed assessments take place at a separate hearing. This manner of assessment has, so far as I can see, no real philosophical significance; at any rate, we can consider the reason for costs shifting quite apart from technical matters like this.

[9] eg *Medway Oil and Storage Co Ltd v Continental Contractors Ltd* [1929] AC 88 (HL).

[10] A note on terminology. CPR r 3.9 grants the court power to relieve against sanctions. That jurisdiction is irrelevant to my claims: I am using the word 'sanction' in its ordinary sense, in the way we might describe punitive damages as a 'sanction for misconduct'.

[11] CPR, r 44.2(4)(a).

[12] CPR, r 44.2(4)(c).

can obtain, *inter alia*, an 'additional amount' beyond their basic award of costs: this is a sum (not exceeding £75,000) calculated as a percentage of the amount won in litigation.[13]

Two features of these complications are important for my claims. First, both the power to sanction for misconduct and the Part 36 regime display a concern for the integrity of the civil justice system overall. Courts apply sanctions for failure to comply with practice directions to incentivize compliance and compliance is required to ensure that the system functions as it should. We can understand Part 36 in the same way.[14] One justification of the regime is that it attempts to channel cases which ought to settle out of courts, freeing up scarce legal resources for other cases.[15]

The second feature, nascent in the sanctions regime and blatant in the Part 36 regime, is that certain costs rules seem entirely unconcerned with costs accrued. The rule to disallow costs, for example, can be seen as a stick to incentivize compliance with a broader procedural regime. The concern is with the integrity of the civil justice system; the rules on costs are used instrumentally.[16] This structure is clearest in the Part 36 regime when the additional sum is awarded: that sum, by hypothesis, exceeds the litigant's costs; the justification for it cannot be any costs incurred.

The question

Any legal rule must be justifiable if it is to be acceptable. Some legal rules unite two individuals in a liability nexus: a defendant is responsible to a plaintiff. The justificatory burden is to explain why the two individuals are united in this precise manner. There are philosophical controversies about what counts as a good justification. I will, for now, skate lightly over these complications; I return to them in section 4.

The law of costs unites two individuals in this way. The defendant might have to pay the plaintiff, or vice versa, depending on the outcome of the suit. For ease

[13] CPR, r 36.17(4)(d). Technically, the law distinguishes between the award for 'costs' (CPR, r 36.17(4)(b)) and this 'additional amount'. I take it that the additional amount is helpfully thought of as part of the costs regime, even if it does not have the object of indemnification.

[14] Andrew Higgins has pointed out to me that virtually all procedural processes can be understood in this way. I agree: I do not mean to suggest that costs are in any way special as a matter of procedural law.

[15] This is not the only justification of Part 36. It also allows parties to insure themselves against the risk of an adverse costs order which, given the grotesque expense of legal services, can be extremely important.

[16] An analogy. Peter Birks once argued that 'All awards of damages punish. The crucial way in which restitutionary damages do differ from punitive damages is that they are not arbitrary and indeterminate': P Birks, *Civil Wrongs: A New World* (Butterworths 1992) 86. On this reductive view, the concern of restitutionary damages is not with restitution but with punishment; the limit to restitutionary measures is justified by rule of law concerns, with the goal being punishment.

of exposition let us suppose that the plaintiff always wins. My principal question in the essay—what might justify the rule that costs follow the event?—can be put in this way: why should the plaintiff get costs from the defendant? The question is important for reasons of sheer intellectual interest. More practically, costs is a domain subject to perpetual reform; that reform will be rudderless without a sound theoretical framework. And, more concerning, the entire law might need to be abolished: on a prominent account of how legal rules stand to be justified, costs rules look unjustifiable. Although abolition might seem a radical proposal, costs-shifting rules are not universal.[17]

Before I turn to the question in earnest, I need to introduce a distinction from the literature on distributive justice, one that is vital to illustrate my claims.

Holism and individualism

Samuel Scheffler draws a distinction between holistic and individualistic theories of justice. A rough approximation of the distinction can be grasped by contrasting the way in which different theories approach token allocations (such as the payment of wages) and general states (such as the distribution of economic benefits in society). A holistic theory of justice makes a claim about a general state and derives justice in token allocations from that claim. An individualistic theory of justice makes a claim about token allocations and derives the justice of general states from that claim.

I will describe this distinction in more detail before mapping it onto more conventional categories of legal theory.

The distinction

Holism

A holistic theory, Scheffler writes, is one where 'the justice of any particular assignment of benefits … depends—directly or indirectly—on the justice of the larger distribution of benefits and burdens in society.'[18] For such theories, 'we cannot tell whether a particular person should receive a given benefit without knowing how such an allocation would fit into the broader distribution of benefits and burdens within the society.'[19]

[17] The black swans in the common law are the United States of America (minus Alaska) and Lithuania: C Hodges, S Vogenauer, and M Tulibacka, 'The Oxford Study on Costs and Funding of Civil Litigation' in C Hodges, S Vogenauer, and M Tulibacka (eds), *The Costs and Funding of Civil Litigation: A Comparative Perspective* (Hart Publishing 2010) 17.

[18] S Scheffler, 'Rawls and Utilitarianism' in *Boundaries and Allegiances* (OUP 2001) 166.

[19] ibid 167.

An illustrative example is utilitarianism. Jeremy Bentham claimed that we should aim, in all our decisions and actions, to achieve 'the greatest happiness of the greatest number'.[20] To know whether a particular assignment conforms with this principle we need to know whether that assignment furthers the project of maximizing happiness. It is not enough to know that the assignee is made happy by the transfer; we will have to investigate all others in society.

Another example is John Rawls's theory of justice. Unlike Bentham, Rawls did not propose an independent criterion—such as the sum of happiness—with which to assess a distributive arrangement of economic benefits. He thought that no one had an innate claim to particular economic benefits. It followed that justice in distribution was a matter of 'pure procedural justice', a situation where 'there is a correct or fair procedure such that the outcome is likewise correct or fair, whatever it is, provided that the procedure has been properly followed'.[21] Individuals were entitled to, and only to, those benefits allocated to them under a just distributive scheme, a scheme Rawls termed the 'basic structure'.[22] It follows, as Scheffler points out, that

> The justice or injustice of allocating a particular economic benefit to a given individual will always depend instead on whether that allocation is part of an overall distribution that is produced by a basic structure conforming to Rawls's principles of distributive justice.[23]

Individualism

An individualistic theory is one where the justice of some allocation depends on 'some characteristic of, or fact about, the deserving person'.[24] As Scheffler explains,

> No assessment of the overall distribution of benefits and burdens in society or of the institutions that produced that distribution is normally required in order to decide whether a particular individual deserves a certain benefit. Instead, it is a constraint on the justice of distributions and institutions that they should give each individual what that individual independently deserves in virtue of the relevant facts about him or her.[25]

[20] J Bentham, 'Preface to "A Fragment on Government"' in JH Burns and HLA Hart (eds), *A Comment on the Commentaries and A Fragment on Government* (first published 1776, The Collected Works of Jeremy Bentham, OUP 1977) 393 (emphasis removed).

[21] J Rawls, *A Theory of Justice* (rev edn, first published 1971, Harvard University Press 1999) 75.

[22] ibid 6: the basic structure is defined as 'the way in which the major social institutions distribute fundamental rights and duties and determine the division of advantages from social cooperation'.

[23] S Scheffler, 'Justice and Desert in Liberal Theory' in *Boundaries and Allegiances* (OUP 2001) 191.

[24] Scheffler (n 18) 168.

[25] ibid.

Perhaps the most iconic contemporary theory which fits this classification is Robert Nozick's. He proposes two principles of justice:

1. A person who acquires a holding in accordance with the principle of justice in acquisition is entitled to that holding.
2. A person who acquires a holding in accordance with the principle of justice in transfer, from someone else entitled to that holding, is entitled to the holding.[26]

Because 'not all actual situations are generated in accordance with the two principles of justice in holdings', those principles must be supplemented by a further principle for 'the rectification of injustice in holdings'.[27] But the core of the theory is contained in the two principles. The justice of a particular allocation depends on whether an individual acquired a benefit in accordance with a principle of just acquisition or just transfer. There is no reference to a wider distributive scheme.

For Nozick's theory to be individualist, his principles of just acquisition and just transfer must not refer 'directly or indirectly… [to] the larger distribution of benefits and burdens in society'. Such principles may do so, of course. But they need not. A principle of justice in transfer might, for example, depend on the quality of individuals' intentions; and that ground might be defended by reference to a broader view of human agency (rather than a claim about how such a rule will further a broader pattern of distribution). These principles and grounds do not seem distributive in nature. They are about characteristics of individuals.

Legal theory

This distinction is an illuminating lens through which to view two generic strategies used to justify legal norms. One strategy, most often seen in discussions of property and contract, supposes that certain legal rules are justified (when justified) by the benefits their existence instantiates in the population at large.[28] Various outcomes, including the distribution of benefits and burdens generated by the practice, will have to be weighed up to justify the legal rule. When that rule is justified, its application can (the theory supposes) explain individual claims under the rule.[29] The approach relates closely to holistic theories of justice: the justice of individual claims under a rule is ultimately to be assessed by reference to the justice

[26] R Nozick, *Anarchy, State and Utopia* (Basic Books 1974) 151. He adds that 'No one is entitled to a holding except by (repeated) applications of 1 and 2.'

[27] ibid 152.

[28] eg D Hume, *A Treatise of Human Nature* (DF Norton and MJ Norton eds, first published 1740, OUP 2008) 3.2.2 and 3.2.5.

[29] J Rawls, 'Two Concepts of Rules' (1955) 64 Philos Rev 3.

of the rule, and the rule is justified by considering the wider distribution of benefits the rule secures.

Other scholars claim that private law norms should be justified without regard to (for example) wider patterns of distribution.[30] A standard approach starts from the premiss that a legal system should aim to ensure each individual's equal freedom.[31] It takes from that premiss the idea that legal norms stand or fall by reference to that standard: the question is always and only whether the defendant's action inhibited the plaintiff's freedom. The salient considerations are those local to the bilateral nexus.[32] More narrowly construed, they are grounded in considerations about the plaintiff's position: the law's concern is securing the plaintiff's 'independence from the choice of others'.[33] There is an analogy, in this respect, with Scheffler's category of individualism.

The task ahead

I start with individualist accounts of the law of costs. Insofar as there is an orthodox position, individualism seems to be it. But, I argue, it is fatally flawed. So I turn, in the last main section, to holist approaches. These are more fruitful, but they also show that the task ahead is more complex than is commonly perceived.

Individualism in costs

The orthodox account

Any justification of a jurisdiction to award costs has to say why the plaintiff should be entitled to them. Despite the court's ultimate discretion over the order—Lloyd LJ once remarked that 'There is only one immutable rule in relation to costs, and that is that there are no immutable rules.'[34]—judges have talked of a plaintiff's *prima facie* 'right' to costs.[35] That right is encoded in the 'general rule' that costs

[30] Although the precise contours are unimportant, I mean here to characterize the 'corrective justice' school, derived primarily from the work of Ernest Weinrib, as well as the 'civil recourse' school. The latter account differs from the former chiefly in the centrality given to the power to bring a civil suit.

[31] I choose the label 'premiss' advisedly: there is, so far as I am aware, no argument for the postulate; it is taken to be morally basic. The sketchiest part of the theory is not the claim about equal freedom but the interpretation offered *of* freedom.

[32] eg EJ Weinrib, *The Idea of Private Law* (rev, OUP 2012) 122.

[33] I Kant, *The Metaphysics of Morals* (L Denis ed, M Gregor tr, 2nd edn, first published 1797, CUP 2017) 6:238.

[34] *Taylor v Pace Developments Ltd* [1991] BCC 406 (CA) 408.

[35] eg *Cooper v Whittingham* (1880) 15 Ch D 501 (CA) 504 (Sir George Jessel MR) ('the Court has no discretion, and cannot take away the plaintiff's right to costs'); *Civil Service Co-operative Society v General Steam Navigation Co* [1903] 2 KB 756 (CA) 765 (Earl of Halsbury LC) ('rights of which he is by law possessed'); *F King & Co v Gillard & Co* [1905] 2 Ch 7 (CA) 12 (Romer LJ) ('the costs to

follow the event.[36] But this merely pushes the inquiry back a stage. What is the ground of this right (or justification of the general rule)?

Baron Bramwell explained things in these terms:

> Costs as between party and party are given by the law as an indemnity to the person entitled to them; they are not imposed as a punishment on the party who pays them, nor given as a bonus to the party who receives them.[37]

Something like this is the orthodox account. It gives a compelling reason why the plaintiff should be indemnified. But it fails to explain why the defendant should be the one to bear the burden of indemnifying the plaintiff.

Some have thought this question very easy. Sir George Jessel was customarily pithy: 'some one must pay the costs, and I do not see who else but the defendants who do wrong are to pay them.'[38] This claim can be understood in one of two ways. Jessel might mean: there is no one else who might justly be called upon to pay the plaintiff's costs, therefore the defendant should pay. This is a very bad argument. Its antecedent is false: in principle costs could (as with a legal aid fund) be paid out of the public fisc.[39] And the inference is invalid: the fact that there is no one else against whom the claim can justifiably be brought does not entail or even suggest that it is justifiably brought against the defendant.

The second possible interpretation picks up on the reference to wrongdoing. If a defendant has infringed a right of the plaintiff causing them to incur costs in seeking reparation, the ground of the right to costs could be the underlying right. On that interpretation, there would be no freestanding right to costs; the 'right' to costs would emanate from the right to claim consequential damages.[40] This is

which … they were justly entitled'); *McDonald v Horn* [1995] ICR 685 (CA) 694D-E (Hoffmann LJ). See, too, *Ritter v Godfrey* [1920] 2 KB 47 (CA) 59–60 (Atkin LJ).

[36] CPR 44.2(2)(a).

[37] *Harold v Smith* (1860) 5 Hurl & N 381, 385; 157 ER 1229, 1231 (Exch). See, in the modern era, *R v Lord Chancellor Ex p Child Poverty Action Group* [1999] 1 WLR 347, 356 (Dyson J). *Quaere* A Zuckerman, *Zuckerman on Civil Procedure: Principles of Practice* (3rd edn, Sweet & Maxwell 2013) 27.48 ('a person should not be out of pocket as a result of having to seek court adjudication to vindicate his rights.')

[38] *Cooper v Whittingham* (n 35) 507.

[39] An anonymous referee points out that contemporary political reality is such that legal aid funds are unlikely to be replenished any time soon. Maybe so. But I take Jessel's claim to be one of justice; it is immutable to transient political facts. This raises complicated philosophical issues about feasibility constraints to principles of justice. I have set out my own views on that issue, so far as it pertains to this, in F Wilmot-Smith, 'Just Injustice' in *Equal Justice* (Harvard University Press 2019).

[40] In its most extreme form, this account lumps costs with claims for damages: see, for example, Belgian Supreme Court 2 Sept 2004, *Rechtskundig Weekblad* 2004–05, 535. This may have been the 'logical' view entertained by the only London solicitor to serve on the judicature commissions: Sir J Hollams, *Jottings of an Old Solicitor* (John Murray & Co 1906) 66. In those pages, Hollams objects to the rule, laid down in the memorandum of James LJ (1875–76) 1 Ch D 41, that costs would follow the event in appellate cases, because it created a 'gambling system': litigants were incentivized to appeal in the hope of recovering their costs.

plausible in some cases but it will do no work where the *defendant* is awarded her costs. Nor will it work where the plaintiff does not assert a wrong: where she seeks an account of a fund held on trust, brings an action for the agreed sum, for specific performance, for restitution of an unjust enrichment, and so on. What justifies requiring the defendant to pick up the tab in these cases?

A picture of the contemporary orthodoxy can be glimpsed through Millett LJ's analysis of third party costs orders. He said that

> where the third party has been responsible for bringing the proceedings and they have been brought in bad faith or for an ulterior purpose or there is some other conduct on his part which makes it just and reasonable to make the order against him.[41]

Consider, in similar fashion, Lord Phillips MR's influential claim, that

> if one party *causes* another unreasonably to incur legal costs he ought as a matter of justice to indemnify that party for the costs incurred.[42]

Phillips has moved from ideas of the defendant's underlying wrong grounding a claim to consequential damages to a free-standing right to costs 'unreasonably incurred'.[43] In that sense, we can read it as an extension of Jessel's analysis, one which would not cover not-wrongs cases. There is, though, no actual argument for the extension; we are left with a bald assertion that the rule is called for 'as a matter of justice'.

A kernel of an argument can be conjured from the invocation of causation: the defendant causes the plaintiff's loss, thus they ought to pay for it. The defendant causes this *unreasonably*; this reference to reasons invokes notions of responsibility. Thus the idea is that the defendant should pay the claimant's costs because she is responsible for their creation. Perhaps the most natural way of understanding

[41] *Mettalloy Supplies Ltd v MA (UK) Ltd* [1997] 1 WLR 1613, 1620. See also, in this context, discussions of the importance of causation to a non-party's costs liability: *Globe Equities Ltd v Globe Legal Services Ltd* [1999] BLR 232, 241 (Morritt LJ); *Dymocks Franchise Systems (NSW) Pty Ltd v Todd (Associated Industrial Finance Pty Ltd, Third Party)* [2004] UKPC 39, [2004] 1 WLR 2807 [20] (Lord Brown).

[42] *Arkin v Borchard Lines Ltd* [2005] EWCA Civ 655, [2005] 1 WLR 3055 [23] (Lord Phillips MR). Professor Zuckerman has objected that this has moved from 'restoration' to 'blame': A Zuckerman, 'The Costs Indemnity Principle—From Restoration to Blame' (2008) 27 CJQ 281; Zuckerman (n 37) 27.51. Zuckerman gives a range of objections to that move, not least that blameworthiness is a difficult standard to apply: it is 'inherently controversial'. But nowhere is it apparent what justification Zuckerman thinks there is for making the defendant 'restore' the plaintiff. I will offer a candidate below, where I endorse holism—and it is plausible that Zuckerman's account is consonant with my own, for his ultimate concern is to ensure that the costs rules do not lead to a 'denial of access to justice'.

[43] The adverb is infelicitous insofar as it suggests that it was unreasonable of the litigant to incur the costs. What is unreasonable, on Phillips's analysis, is the decision which caused the litigant to incur those costs.

this claim is as saying that the defendant is responsible for the costs order because she was blameworthy (= unreasonable) in causing the plaintiff to incur the costs.[44] This, for example, is how Zuckerman reads the passage.[45] A different interpretation is that the defendant is responsible for the creation of the costs notwithstanding the absence of blame. On this interpretation, the defendant can be responsible for the plaintiff's costs if some action of hers failed to conform with the demands of reason—even if that non-conformity was not blameworthy. We should consider both these possible explanations when trying to understand the orthodox account.

This completes a candidate explanation for the rule that costs follow the event. It purports to justify the rules on costs by reference to factors local to the two parties to the litigation. Once it is shown that the plaintiff has incurred costs, and that the defendant is responsible for those costs, no further inquiry is needed. It is an individualistic account.

Problems with orthodoxy

Orthodoxy's interpretation

To invoke a right is generally thought to invoke a peremptory consideration, a constraint on the pursuit of the good.[46] It would be good to save the life of the five individuals awaiting transplants, but the right of the man in the waiting room is such that his organs cannot be harvested. Such rights are also often associated with individualism: Immanuel Kant, for example, sourced an entire theory of law out of his equal freedom postulate. These points are non-coincidentally linked: rights grounded in individual concerns are least amenable to trumping by the good. This also shows why it is no accident that Robert Nozick, a trenchant critic of holist theories, begins *Anarchy, State and Utopia* with his question-begging pronouncement, that '[i]ndividuals have rights, and there are things no person or group may do to them (without violating their rights)'.[47] Nozick wanted to resist the idea that individuals could be sacrificed at the altar of the good and believed that Rawls's holistic theory was, in that respect, too concessive to utilitarian demands.

A number of judges have talked of a plaintiff's 'right' to their costs.[48] Hale LJ has said that this right is grounded in 'considerations of justice to the individuals concerned'.[49] All this might lend some plausibility to orthodoxy's individualism. But

[44] There is a disagreement in the literature about whether there is a conceptual connection between reasons and blame. Probably the orthodox view is that there is no such connection. Compare, however, S Darwall, *The Second-Person Standpoint: Morality, Respect, and Accountability* (Harvard University Press 2006) 27–28.

[45] Zuckerman (n 37) 27.51–27.53.

[46] Hence Dworkin's evocative metaphor: R Dworkin, 'Rights as Trumps' in J Waldron (ed), *Theories of Rights* (OUP 1984).

[47] Nozick (n 26) ix.

[48] See the references at n 35.

[49] *Hamilton v Al Fayed (No 2)* [2002] EWCA Civ 665, [2002] QB 1175 [73].

the so-called 'right' to costs does not behave in the manner of an individual's right to not have their organs harvested. For one thing, they are comparatively easily defeased. Consider Order LV of the 1875 Judicature Act. Costs were to follow the event in any trial before a jury unless, 'for good cause', the court ordered otherwise. In *Harnett v Vise*, James LJ accepted the submission of a young Fletcher Moulton that the grounds of 'good cause' were not limited to 'the conduct of the parties in the litigation itself'.[50] Two months before, Sir George Jessel had said that the right to costs was defeated by

> misconduct in commencing the proceedings, or some miscarriage in the procedure, or an oppressive or vexatious mode of conducting the proceedings, or other misconduct which will induce the Court to refuse costs[.][51]

The plaintiff's right to costs today is, in similar fashion, at the discretion of the judge.[52] This shows a flaw in orthodoxy's account: the right to costs is quite different in character than the right not to be enslaved or tortiously harmed; *those* rights do not admit of defeat for 'good cause'. On one view, this simply makes the law of costs a moral monstrosity. But it is unintuitive to regard the deprivation of costs for good cause as akin to the harvesting of organs for multiple transplants. Instead, a better interpretation of the 'right' holds that its grounds are non-individualistic; it is, therefore, unobjectionable to say that such grounds can operate to defeat the right.

Orthodoxy's argument

Orthodoxy's argument is: the plaintiff ought not to be out of pocket; the defendant is responsible for the plaintiff incurring these costs; therefore the plaintiff ought to be entitled to an indemnity from the defendant. The argument has two difficulties: it is unsound and invalid.

Consider soundness. The second premiss of the argument is that the defendant is to blame for the plaintiff's costs. This is a dubious claim.[53] Very many of the conditions which determine the value of those costs are not within the defendant's control. The fact that legal services are so expensive, for example, is a function of various choices made (rightly or wrongly) by system-designers, not the defendant.

[50] *Harnett v Vise* (1880) 5 Ex D 307 (CA) 310 (James LJ). The report suggests that Fletcher Moulton led his silk. See, too, *Bostock v Ramsey Urban District Council* [1900] 2 QB 616 (CA) 622 (AL Smith LJ).

[51] *Cooper v Whittingham* (n 35) 504. This is very similar to Moulton's submission: *Harnett v Vise* (n 50) 310, the only difference being Moulton included conduct *before* the issue of the writ. See, too, *Dicks v Yates* (1881) 18 Ch D 76 (CA) 85 (Sir George Jessel MR); *Willmott v Barber* (1881) 17 Ch D 772 (CA) 774 (Sir George Jessel MR); *Civil Service Co-operative Society* (n 35) (Earl of Halsbury's speech).

[52] See n 7, above.

[53] I discuss some of these points in more detail in F Wilmot-Smith, 'The Expense of Justice' in *Equal Justice* (Harvard University Press 2019), where I consider the 'responsibility' account, the idea that a litigant should pay the costs of litigation because they are responsible for those costs.

This fact cannot erase responsibility entirely, but it puts pressure on the idea that the concept can have the explanatory power claimed.

Further, when responsibility is invoked (as here) to justify some reallocation of resources, this usually supposes that the burden-bearer somehow failed to act for the right reasons in the past. If I am responsible for injuring you, this story goes, I can be made responsible for the costs of your treatment because my bearing those costs is the next-best thing to my not having injured you in the first place. The payment of compensation is a way of bringing my actions into closer conformity with my underlying reasons for action, reasons I have (by hypothesis) failed to act on in the past.[54] It is, though, difficult to say in the normal case of costs that the defendant ought not to have acted as they did.[55]

As Adrian Zuckerman has argued, the defendant

> has merely chosen to assert or defend his perceived entitlements by exercising his fundamental civic right of access to court. Although litigation, like any other activity, can be conducted in an improper manner (e.g. malicious prosecution or abuse of process), there is nothing inherently wrong in seeking court adjudication … There is plainly nothing unlawful, improper, or even undesirable in seeking court adjudication.[56]

Turn now to validity. The analysis of responsibility as blame-centric has a close analogy with one view of the law of tort. Tort law determines the rights a plaintiff has against a defendant (and, thus, provides remedies where the defendant violates those rights). Some accounts of tort law conceive of the subject as a method of compensating deserving plaintiffs for losses they ought not to have suffered. These accounts say that the reason for the plaintiff's claim is that she should be compensated; the reason the claim is against the defendant is (often said to be) to deter individuals from unreasonable or costly action. This purports to justify the position of plaintiff and defendant in almost the same fashion as the blame-centric costs rules: each account gives a different reason why the plaintiff has a claim from the reason why the defendant is subject to a liability.

But, as Ernest Weinrib has pointed out, the legal rule cannot be justified

> 'by reference to the need both to deter actors and to compensate sufferers'.[57]

[54] See, for example, J Gardner, 'What is Tort Law For? Part 1. The Place of Corrective Justice' (2011) 30 Law & Phil 1.

[55] My slippage from 'reason' to 'ought' is quite deliberate, to foreclose the possible argument that the defendant had a reason not to act as she did, viz. that she was in the legal wrong. Even so, I want to say, it does not follow that she ought not to avail herself of legal procedures.

[56] Zuckerman (n 42) 282.

[57] Weinrib (n 32) 122.

Such explanations fail because they offer only

> An accumulation of considerations that apply separately to the two parties but embrace them both only when taken together.[58]

And this, without more, could not justify the rule.[59] It is not enough to say why the plaintiff should have a claim (in the circumstances that she does) and why the defendant ought to incur a liability: that does not say why the defendant should pay the sum *to the plaintiff*. Why not have the defendant pay into a central insurance fund against which the plaintiff can bring a claim? There would be various advantages to such an approach. It might be more efficient. It also would allow the risk of exculpatory defences to be socialised: if the reason to compensate the plaintiff is unilateral, unconcerned with the defendant's blameworthiness, the defendant's exculpation does not reduce the weight of that reason.[60] If this argument is sound, the blame-centric argument for the law of costs is invalid: even if the plaintiff ought to be indemnified, and even if the defendant is to blame for the loss such that she should pay a sum (even the precise sum of the plaintiff's costs), the costs rule would not be justified. All we would have is an argument for the plaintiff being indemnified and the defendant paying a sum; that is not an argument for the bilateral nexus of the costs rule.

A defender of orthodoxy might respond with a rule-consequentialist explanation. The justification for the liability nexus, they might say, is that a rule uniting the doer and sufferer of the wrong leads to greater conformity with the underlying reasons (= compensation and deterrence) than any alternative rule. There is no reason to rule out such an explanation a priori, though it has the whiff of prestidigitation. But it would no longer be an individualist account. Notions of responsibility to one another have dropped out of the explanation; responsibility is merely a vehicle to secure some wider social policy.[61] It makes a claim about the just distribution of benefits and burdens across society and proposes the liability rule as the best method (of a bad bunch) of achieving that distribution. This is a holistic account: a claim where 'the justice of any particular assignment of benefits … depends—directly or indirectly—on the justice of the larger distribution of benefits and burdens in society.'[62] I return to such accounts shortly.

[58] ibid 122. See, too, EJ Weinrib, 'Correlativity and Personality' in *Corrective Justice* (OUP 2012) 17–18.

[59] I find Weinrib's own explanation of his claim puzzling. The crucial passages are obscure; a lot of the account is couched in terms of 'normative' losses and gains, mysterious concepts. I believe that my claims are consistent with Weinrib's but my exegetical difficulties mean I cannot be confident.

[60] On a similar theme in the law of unjust enrichment, see F Wilmot-Smith, 'Should the Payee Pay?' (2017) 37 OJLS 844, 845.

[61] There is an analogy in this respect with Strawson's 'optimist', who sees notions of responsibility as 'instruments of policy, as methods of individual treatment and social control': PF Strawson, 'Freedom and Resentment' in G Watson (ed), *Free Will* (OUP 1982) 76.

[62] Scheffler (n 18) 166.

Overview

The orthodox account of costs is individualist in nature. It says that the defendant should pay the plaintiff's costs because of factors local to their relationship. This means it lines up procedural rules on costs with rules on tort law (where individualist accounts have most plausibility). This faces serious objections; we should look for a better approach.[63] A holistic theory has more promise of providing a sound rationale for our rules on costs.

Holism in costs

I have already quoted a passage from Zuckerman which indicates that he is an individualist about costs. That may not be the right interpretation of his views. After the passage about indemnifying the plaintiff, he adds that

> The right of a successful party to be indemnified for his legal expenses is all the more important in a system, such as the English system, where litigation costs are high and could well exceed the value of the subject matter in dispute. In the absence of the possibility of recovering one's litigation costs, disputants might be deterred from going to court for fear that even favourable judgment may be more expensive than giving up the right in question. High and irrecoverable litigation costs may therefore amount to a denial of access to justice.[64]

This demonstrates Zuckerman's recurring concern with the construction of a just *system* of justice. The justification of the costs rule, the passage suggests, is its contribution to a legal system meeting some general criteria of assessment (such as 'access to justice'). On this account, indemnification is an instrument by which those criteria are met; it is not an end in itself.

This has some promise. Costs rules are one of the legal system's tools for designing a just justice system. Indemnification of the plaintiff and deterrence of the defendant can thus be seen as means, not ends.

Costs as controls

The individualistic account stressed indemnification. Another notion which echoes through the ages is costs' function as a deterrent of vexatious litigation.

[63] An anonymous reviewer and Rabeea Assy both suggest that I am too swift to reject individualism: a mixed theory might be the best justification. That is true in principle, but if my arguments are sound there is no individualistic reason to shift costs.

[64] Zuckerman (n 37) 27.48.

The 1175 Synod of Westminster (prescribing canon law) said that 'in . . . actions for the recovery of money . . ., the party who is the loser shall be condemned to pay costs to his opponent'.[65] The rule was implemented to 'put a check on litigation'.[66] Similarly, Reginald Heber Smith wrote that

> Costs have their place as a deterrent, but they should serve to discourage, not all litigation, but false litigation, specious pleas, vexatious proceedings taken for delay, and to ensure prompt compliance with court orders.[67]

And Hale LJ, who had claimed the right to costs is a matter of 'individual justice' ultimately justifies the loser's liability by pointing to the fact that 'the risk of an adverse costs order is seen as a deterrent to bringing bad claims or defending good ones'.[68]

These claims do not say that the costs rules are valuable because the defendant is responsible for the plaintiff's costs. Instead, the defendant is made responsible for costs because there are valuable consequences of making him so. This is a shift from individualism to holism: the value of the rule is sourced in the consequences of having it and those consequences are not local to the plaintiff and defendant.[69] On a holist's account of costs, the justice of the rules on costs—rules saying when one litigant must pay another for use of the procedure, and how much they must pay—depends on the justice of a wider distribution.

It follows that, for a holistic account of costs, the first question must be the distributive consequences which the law should promote. Only once that end-state is identified can the question of rule-design begin. To illustrate one possible analysis, recall Bentham's claim that we should aim to achieve 'the greatest happiness

[65] Roger of Hoveden, *The Annals of Roger de Hoveden: Comprising the history of England and of other countries of Europe from A.D. 732 to A.D. 1201* (HT Riley ed, HT Riley tr, first published 1201, HG Bohn 1853) 394. A helpful account of the early history of costs is found in Sir John Baker, *The Oxford History of the Laws of England, Volume VI: 1483–1558* (OUP 2003) 376–79. See, in particular, Baker's analysis of 3 Hen.VII, c.10 (confirmed by 19 Hen.VII, c.20): the purpose of the acts was to 'discourage vexatious litigants from delaying execution by means of unfounded writs of error'.

[66] Hoveden (n 65) 394. Those who cannot pay costs are liable 'to be punished at the discretion of his bishop'.

[67] RH Smith, *Justice and the Poor* (Charles Scribner 1919) 30.

[68] *Hamilton v Al Fayed (No 2)* (n 49) [74]. The case itself concerned third party costs orders, which are perhaps the clearest demonstration of my thesis. The rule in that context is that the third party funder is liable only to the extent of their own contribution to the litigation: *Arkin* (n 42). There is no principled explanation for that 'cap' save this: that the cap promotes the funding of litigation in a manner thought morally desirable. This is avowedly holistic.

[69] These claims are consistent with the view that the legal rule is justified by an accumulation of unilateral considerations. On this view, the moral imperative to make the plaintiff whole justifies her having a claim and the need to deter vexatious behaviour by the defendant justifies that claim being against the defendant. This justificatory analysis is most often seen in the law of tort and it is there that it receives its fullest response. See text to n 58.

of the greatest number'.[70] From this principle we can derive a claim about justice in costs: the justice of the rule depends on whether it contributes to this end state. Rules should be designed to further it.

Illustrative as it may be, Bentham's account is manifestly inadequate. Every claim about value, on that account, reduces to a claim about happiness. That is too reductive. It is a question for value theory what the proper statement is, a question clearly beyond the scope of this essay. Let me suggest, though, that we approach the question in a way local to costs. As the examples I have given—the Synod, Smith, Hale, and Zuckerman—demonstrate, accounts of costs tend to say that the justice of its rules depend on a quite specific distributional effect: their effect on the distribution of legal resources. That is the right place to start. So let me explore the idea in a little more depth.

Court time is a scarce resource the use of which must be rationed. One task of a justice system is to ration its own resources according to sound principles of justice. This rationing can only take place with rules in the system designed to achieve the desired end-state distribution, whatever that distribution might be. One desirable end-state, for example, is the exclusion from courts of those without substantive claims worthy of consideration. This is achieved in part by the power to strike claims out which disclose no reasonable grounds.[71]

The rules on costs also aim to assist; they are designed to channel cases not worthy of consideration out of courts. English law, for example, distinguishes between two bases of assessment of costs: standard and indemnity.[72] Indemnity costs are better for a plaintiff; they come closer to total indemnification. But the facts which determine whether a plaintiff obtains an indemnity award are not facts about *the plaintiff*. Instead, they are facts about a particular kind of defendant-sided misconduct, such as persistence with a hopeless case,[73] or failing adequately to particularize a case.[74] One reason to 'sanction' such behaviour is to deter individuals in future cases from similar actions, thus ensuring a more effective justice system.[75] The objection to the defendant's actions is that they have drained legal resources from other more deserving cases.

These cases are comparatively easy because they involve the deprivation of legal resources from those who have no underlying claim that requires resolution. More difficult to accept, but nonetheless vital, is the need for rules to allocate resources

[70] Bentham (n 20) 393 (emphasis removed).

[71] CPR r 3.4.

[72] CPR r 44.3.

[73] *Noorani v Calver (No 2) (Costs)* [2009] EWHC 592 (QB).

[74] *Select Healthcare (UK) Ltd v Cromptons Health Care Ltd* [2010] EWHC 3055 (Pat).

[75] The power to award indemnity costs is described as a sanction at Practice Direction (Pre-Action Conduct), paragraph 16(b). Simon Brown LJ has described indemnity orders as 'penal rather than exhortatory': *Kiam v MGN Ltd (Costs)* [2002] EWCA Civ 66, [2002] 1 WLR 2810 [12]. That is true to this extent: the *reason* for imposing costs on an indemnity basis is to sanction one who has acted unreasonably.

between *deserving* litigants. Not everyone for whom court time would be valuable can be assigned it; resources are scarce. This explains and partly justifies the impetus scholars and judges have had to incorporate ideas of proportionality and to promote settlement.[76] These concepts are used to try to allocate legal resources appropriately.

A basic picture of a holistic account of the law of costs begins to emerge. An individual's entitlement to costs does not arise because the losing defendant is responsible *for* those costs nor because plaintiffs are entitled *to* restoration. The rules on costs are a means of controlling the distribution of legal resources; the right created in the plaintiff is justified instrumentally, as a means of securing the preferred distribution of legal resources.[77] I will return to the precise distributional sphere in more detail below. Let us first consider an objection.

The justificatory structure

Holistic justifications of social institutions are haunted by the spectre of utilitarianism. But holism is not necessarily consequentialist in form, let alone utilitarian: that should be clear already from my invocation of Rawls as a holist; although Rawls's theory had interesting commonalities with utilitarianism, it is contractarian. In contemporary ethical theory, contractualism is distinguished from consequentialism in part by its requirement that rules be justifiable *to* affected individuals. Scanlon, for example, writes that

> An act is wrong if its performance under the circumstances would be disallowed by any set of principles for the general regulation of behaviour that no one could reasonably reject as a basis for informed, unforced, general agreement.[78]

How would a contractualist think about the law of costs? Suppose that contemporary costs rules happen to achieve the socially optimal outcome, whatever that may be. For the consequentialist, that concludes the inquiry. However, the contractualist thinks a further challenge remains. A defendant on whom the costs order is imposed gets to ask: 'why should I be the one used to achieve that outcome?' Any holist owes them an answer.

To develop that answer, we should begin by distinguishing between preinstitutional and institutional rights. Prior to entry into civil society, we have

[76] Compare O Fiss, 'Against Settlement' (1984) 93 Yale LJ 1073; H Genn, *Judging Civil Justice* (The Hamlyn Lectures, CUP 2009).

[77] Compare Richard Posner's claim that 'damages so assessed are paid over to the plaintiff (to be divided with his lawyer) as the price of enlisting their participation in the operation of the system': R Posner, 'A Theory of Negligence' (1972) 1 J Legal Stud 29, 33.

[78] TM Scanlon, *What We Owe To Each Other* (Belknap Press of Harvard University Press 1998) 153.

rights. We surrender some of those rights (such as the right to resist unjust punishment) by entry into civil society; others (such as the right not to be tortured or enslaved) remain. Part of the function of law is to codify and protect the rights we retain: it is a condition of state legitimacy that this is achieved. When we reason about these pre-institutional rights, individualism is the proper perspective. We have rights in virtue of our humanity and it is facts about that (such as our equality) which ground the rights. Nozick focussed on those rights, hence how his individualism gained what plausibility it has.

Rights can also derive from practices and institutions.[79] Humeans claim, for example, that there can be no proprietary or contractual rights prior to a practice. Procedural rights seem to be of this form. There is, for example, no right to have a claim form issued prior to the creation of an institution with the power to issue such a form. For reasons I will develop, individualism is an inappropriate perspective to take when considering institutional rights. Hence why John Rawls, who thought that justice was a virtue 'of social institutions', endorsed a holistic theory.[80]

Return now to the defendant who objects to the rules on costs. Costs concern not legal rights themselves but the conditions of their enforcement. Enforcement is achieved through a social institution, the justice system. The first challenge is demonstrating that the system is socially optimal. That challenge may be insurmountable. A regime which shifts costs has massive disadvantages, such as the inevitable ratcheting up of costs on both sides of litigation.

This is particularly objectionable within a system of privatized labour; the costs can be astronomical. Placed against a background of distributive inequality, one effect of the contemporary costs regime is to make access to legal procedures unaffordable. If the costs rule fails at this stage, it fails on holistic grounds: the allocation of the particular burden (the cost of suit) has damaging consequences for the justice of the wider sphere (the distribution of the benefits and burdens of a legal system).

Suppose, though, that the costs rules could be shown to be socially optimal. If pre-institutional rights were violated through the costs order, the defendant could object even to a socially optimal regime. This shows that there is a place, in a complete justification of a social institution, for individualistic perspectives. In this context, the most important pre-institutional right is to equal treatment, for example at the hands of institutions.[81] An arrangement violating that right could be rejected even if it were socially optimal *and* if there were no alternative arrangement which could achieve social optimality: the right, prior to the good, constrains the pursuit of optimality.

[79] In the realm of institutions, it is important to ensure that we talk of institutional rights rather than rights against institutions. Our basic human rights, such as the right not to be tortured, are exigible against institutions, but these are not institutional rights.

[80] Rawls (n 21) 3: 'Justice is the first virtue of social institutions, as truth is of systems of thought.'

[81] For a helpful treatment see TM Scanlon, *Why Does Inequality Matter?* (OUP 2018) ch 1. Another important consideration is the nature of the right on which the institution adjudicates. If the grounds

Working out the content of equal treatment in this context is a substantial challenge, made harder by the fact it has been ignored by most scholars. If the costs regime achieved optimality through the imposition of extraordinary burdens on one individual, that individual could reject the regime. But it does seem more obviously permissible for a class to be asked to bear greater costs if they are able to do so. Protective costs orders, for example, do not automatically violate the equal treatment constraint; the question is whether those protected from costs orders are less well able to bear the underlying burden.[82]

The demand of equal treatment requires that individuals be treated equally *overall* within the justice system. It is wrong, the holistic perspective shows, to focus only on one rule at a time. Instead, we need to ask whether the system as a whole unfairly prejudices some rather than others. It will do this, I have argued elsewhere, if some are less able than others to obtain justice when they suffer wrongs.[83] This shows a crucial point, one I have stressed throughout: the law on costs cannot be analysed in isolation from other features of the civil justice system.

So long as the costs regime applies equally, the pre-institutional constraints are satisfied. The socially optimal design within those constraints is one which, *ex hypothesi*, has minimized the net burdens on all actors within the institutional arrangement. Any objection of an individual to a burden incurred in that situation would unreasonably prioritize her interests above others.

Procedure and philosophy

I have argued that we should think of the rules on costs—rules about when and whether litigants are responsible for their own legal expenses, as well as rules which determine when they are responsible for others'—as part of the law's arsenal to manage the distribution of its valuable resources. If my argument is sound, civil procedure is a central mechanism by which we distribute one of the most important resources at the State disposal.

A corollary is that costs, and the law of civil procedure in general, is a lot harder than it is customarily thought. Before reforms can sensibly be undertaken we need an account of what the proper distributional end-state should be. What does a

of contractual and property rights are themselves holistic, in the manner Humeans claim, we might tolerate greater inaccuracy about their dispute resolution than the resolution of disputes concerning pre-institutional rights. Inaccuracies can be justified in the former case, for example, if they further the general practice. Not so in the latter case.

82 In correspondence, Andrew Higgins raises the case of QOCs as an instance where individuals' membership of a group may not match up with the reasons for treating groups differently. He also anticipates my own response to these cases, which is to invoke rule consequentialism.

83 F Wilmot-Smith, 'Equal Justice' in *Equal Justice: Fair Legal Systems in an Unfair World* (Harvard University Press 2019).

justice system distributing its resources fairly look like? That is a challenge few have sought to meet; it can be met only if the study of civil procedure is linked to wider debates in political philosophy, such as those concerning distributive justice.

Some may object that they *have* already been thinking about this task. Sir Rupert Jackson's foreword to his monumental report says that his reforms aim 'to control costs and promote access to justice'.[84] But this is a bromide. The phrase 'access to justice' occludes more than it illuminates in part because its meaning is rarely stated with any precision.[85] Everyone is in favour of access to justice—which, given the passionate disagreements at the level of concrete policy, implies that they are not all talking about the same thing.[86]

More perniciously, the bromide allows entrenched interests to maintain their position without radical challenge. Lawyers have escaped substantial regulation of their labour relations for generations. Perhaps that is because reforms limiting their conditions of work can always be met with the objection that this would 'limit access to justice'. Any measure, though, will inhibit access to justice in some way or another. Talk of 'access', thus, fails to grapple with basic questions: whose access? And at whose expense? We should dispense with the concept of 'access to justice'; it is too easy, under the cloak of that label, to avoid the hard questions: what is the desired distribution? And why?

The holist's next challenge is to make good any instrumental claims they have made. Once we have specified a desired end-state, the procedural rules must be shown to make a causal contribution to that end-state. Reforms are, therefore, not only the concern of the political philosopher but also of the economist. Notice who is left out: practicing lawyers should have, *qua* practicing lawyers, comparatively little voice in any reforms. They may supply data, helping to make models more reliable. But they have no particular expertise in the philosophical part or the instrumental part. And sound reforms may well be prejudicial to lawyers' interests; they may (even in good faith) defend bad rules for self-serving reasons.

Conclusion

Frederic Maitland began his first lecture on the forms of action at common law with a possible objection. 'Procedure', an imagined objector began,

[84] Sir Rupert Jackson, *Review of Civil Litigation Costs: Final Report* (2009) i. See, too, Sir Rupert Jackson, *Review of Civil Litigation Costs: Supplemental Report: Fixed Recoverable Costs* (2017) [1.9].

[85] For one game attempt see T Cornford, 'Access to Justice' in E Palmer and others (eds), *Access to Justice: Beyond the Policies and Politics of Austerity* (Hart 2016).

[86] Alan Paterson calls it a 'a feel-good concept—one that everyone can sign up to with uncritical examination.' A Paterson, *Lawyers and the Public Good: Democracy in Action?* (The Hamlyn Lectures, CUP 2011) 60.

> is not a good theme for academic discussion. Substantive law should come first—adjective law, procedural law, afterwards. The former may perhaps be studied in a University, the latter must be studied in chambers.[87]

Perceptions have not changed much since. Civil procedure is rarely taught in our universities. Many practitioners start their career having only learnt it through the vocational stage of the training course. That course is designed to teach students the rules; students are not required to consider whether those rules are coherent, or how such a body of law should be justified. The danger is that procedural rules are viewed as a list of arbitrary preconditions which determine whether some procedural benefit is unlocked.

Maitland was unimpressed: 'With this opinion I can not agree.'[88] Professor Zuckerman, likewise, saw the vitality of adjective law. He showed civil procedure to be a domain worthy of intellectual study and reflection; he has sought to render it coherent. There is, I have argued, a lot of work to do. But it will be a lot of fun.

[87] FW Maitland, in AH Chaytor and WJ Whittaker (eds), *Equity: Also, The Forms of Action at Common Law* (CUP 1910) 295.
[88] ibid.

PART V

HISTORY OF PROCEDURE AND PROCEDURAL POWERS

13

Does Procedural Mean Trans-substantive? A Historical and Normative Analysis of English Civil Procedure Rules

Carla Crifo

Introduction

In 2010, writing as General Editor of the Civil Justice Quarterly, Adrian Zuckerman bemoaned the 'Balkanisation' of English civil procedure anticipated by the proposed changes to the costs rules in the Jackson Report:[1]

> The one undoubtedly remarkable achievement of the great 19th century reforms was to make procedure trans-substantive. Under the old forms of action system there were different procedures for different types of claims. The procedure for action based on contract was different from that founded in tort. Even within each field of substantive law there were different forms for different types of claims. All this complexity was swept away by the reforms culminating in the Judicature Acts of 1875. The great variety of the forms of action gave way to a unified procedure usable for all types of claims—a trans-substantive procedure.
>
> This monumental achievement served the administration of justice well for over a century-and-a-half. This is now threatened because Jackson L.J. is recommending the implementation of many different costs regimes for different types of litigation. . . .
>
> It stands to reason that the greater the range of procedures, the greater the scope for process shopping and the greater the potential for dispute. Claimants would seek to bring their case under the costs regime that is most advantageous to them, and defendants would seek to pull the case towards the regime that benefits them more. Specialisation in the conduct of different types of proceedings would be even more critical than it already is; with the result that competition would be further impeded.

[1] A Zuckerman, 'The Jackson Final Report on Costs: Plastering the Cracks to Shore up a Dysfunctional System' (2010) 29 CJQ 263, 276.

Carla Crifo, *Does Procedural Mean Trans-substantive? A Historical and Normative Analysis of English Civil Procedure Rules* In: *Principles, Procedure, and Justice.* Edited by: Rabeea Assy and Andrew Higgins, Oxford University Press (2020). © The editors and several contributors. DOI: 10.1093/oso/9780198850410.003.0013

> A different costs regime for different types of proceedings or for different causes of action is a retrograde step which threatens to push civil litigation back to the dark ages from which it emerged in the middle 19th century.

Not everyone agreed that the introduction of a 'nuanced' set of costs rules for different cases—specifically depending on the nature of one of the parties or the subject matter of the case[2]—was problematic. Based on a critique of the rationale behind the different costs rules, for example, it was said that it is more, not less, responsive to justice concerns to tailor at least the costs rules to different situations.[3] Yet, if we take Zuckerman's point from a broader perspective than the admittedly always technical and precise costs rules, we can address some fundamental issues within the understanding of procedural rules systems, both in England and elsewhere. Zuckerman implicitly contrasts good procedural rules and bad ones, the former being the result of the nineteenth century reforms that led from the fragmented system of forms of action, commingling substance and procedure, to the unified, trans-substantive, and 'purely procedural' Rules of the Supreme Court. Bad rules—or perhaps, just rules leading to bad consequences—were those proposed by Jackson LJ, insofar as Zuckerman anticipated that they would lead to a return to the 'bad old days' in some way.

This calls for the identification of a criterion specific to civil procedure, which will allow us to assess the quality of its rules. Such a criterion may be what the proper role and scope of procedural rules is, as distinct from substantive rules. Additionally, we may consider whether it is possible to assess the legitimacy of purported procedural rules, that is, whether they flow from a legitimate exercise of the rule-making power. In some legal systems, the fundamental principles or qualitative requirements of civil procedure are explicit—for example in Constitutional articles. In others, of which the English system is one, it is up to the observer to identify any such principle by induction from the rules themselves or by analysis of how they came into being.

In light of this, this chapter has two purposes. Firstly, it considers the extent to which the English system of civil procedure, in light of its historical development, expects or requires that the rules of procedure must be trans-substantive ie, as Zuckerman puts it, 'procedure usable for all types of claims'. Secondly, it considers the extent to which rules that create separate procedural pathways (as do the Jackson costs rules) would indeed equate to a threat of Balkanization. The implied

2 Parts 44–48 CPR. See Part 2, Legal Aid, Sentencing and Punishment of Offenders Act 2012 for the enacted version of the proposals, and Lord Justice Jackson's speech at the first Costs Law Conference for an overview of his proposals and his assessment of the congruity of the Act with his proposals: <https://www.judiciary.uk/wp-content/uploads/2014/09/costsconfpaper.pdf> accessed 28 February 2019.

3 J Folkard, 'Extending Jackson's Patchwork Quilt: A Disintegrated Approach to the Costs-shifting Rule' (2015) 34 CJQ 172, criticized Zuckerman's position on Jackson's proposals to tailor the costs-shifting rule more specifically in different contexts, suggesting instead that different rationales (not just 'corrective justice') could apply better to a specific or specialized field.

assumption in Zuckerman's characterization is that the English system of civil procedure is 'a unified procedure', that its uniformity and the general applicability of its rules are desirable, and that any attempt to temper them, by carving off special procedures or directing processes into specialist pathways, is to be considered an inherently negative outcome. It deals with these issues through two separate approaches. Firstly, it considers whether, in the apparently inexorable march of 'progress' from the forms of action to the single court structure with a single set of rules, (with exceptions, most notably by maintaining some distinction of substantive jurisdiction in the Divisions of the Supreme Court of Judicature),[4] we can identify any ideology or philosophy, lato sensu, that establishes trans-substantivity or uniformity as positive, essential values of the post-Reform procedure. Section 2 attempts, so far as it is possible, to shine a light on the reasoning that lay behind the key procedural reforms of the nineteenth century, which for the most part can fairly be described as piecemeal and sometimes populist reactions to perceived technical problems (the length and cost of trials, for example, as publicized by pamphleteers and reformist writers to the general public in the nineteenth century), where the main driver for legislation was is the desire to avoid a set of unwelcome consequences, rather than the pursuit of any grand design. In section 3, particular attention is devoted to the cross-pollination of ideas across the Atlantic, especially with regards the then revolutionary possibility of fusion of (the procedures of) common law and equity. The American perspective on—and close following of—English procedural developments is particularly enlightening, and not just because the spectator sees more than the players in the heat of the game. US reformers were much more willing to engage in normative assessments of the validity of procedural rules: the very term 'trans-substantive' was first coined in reference to the Federal Code of Civil Procedure, and the transatlantic scholarship provides a rich seam of analysis of the essential requirements of procedure. Lastly, section 4 offers an attempt to draw together such theories and rationales as emerge for considering related issues, such as, for example, whether uniformity of process is a better means of providing access to justice than heterogeneity.

The historical progress from the forms of action to the Judicature Acts in England

Zuckerman's quote is a good starting point to isolate some of the core issues with regard to the creation of 'a unified procedure usable for all types of claims--a trans-substantive procedure'. The combined reforms of the nineteenth century are traditionally portrayed as a Good Thing because they removed the need to identify the

[4] S Rosenbaum, 'Studies in English Civil Procedure. II The Rule-Making Authority' (1915) 63 U Penn L Rev 151, 156–58.

'form of action' to be used for a specific claim. Under the forms of action system that had been in operation since medieval times, practice often followed artificial restrictions and pathways to adjudication in the definition of a case, based on the desire to use some procedural mechanisms only available to one type of claim (contract, tort, etc.), or restricting it in case of indeterminate or complex situations where the qualification of the case at hand was itself open to a drawn-out process of refinement of the issues at stake. At worst, it could mean a denial of adjudication where the 'wrong' form had been used. There were many points in litigation at common law where the choice of one action over another might affect the outcome: the competence of the court, the means of ensuring appearance, the procedure in absence of the defendant, the availability of default judgment, the differing pleading rules, the mode of trial, and the mode of execution, were all dependent on the form of action chosen,[5] and when some elements of the case could fit one or another form, the plaintiff's choice was irrevocable. As Maitland put it in 1909, '[i]n the Middle Ages discretion is entirely excluded; all is to be fixed by iron rules'.[6]

Maitland, in his charting of the dismantling of the old forms of action, brick by brick, viewed the procedural reforms of the nineteenth century as progress:[7]

> Now in 1833 the real and mixed actions were swept away at one fell swoop by the Real Property Limitation Act of that year, 3 and 4 Will. IV, c. 27, sec. 36....
>
> Meanwhile in 1832 a partial assault had been made on the personal forms.... By 2 Will. IV, c. 39 (1832) "Uniformity of Process Act"---the process in these personal actions was reduced to uniformity. The old original writs were abolished and a new form of writ provided. In this writ, however, the plaintiff had to insert a mention of one of the known forms of action. Another heavy blow was struck in 1852 by the Common Law Procedure Act, 15 and 16 Vic., c. 76. It was expressly provided (sec. 3) that it should not be necessary to mention any form or cause of action in any writ of summons. But still this blow was not heavy enough---the several personal forms were still considered as distinct.
>
> The final blow was struck by the Judicature Act of 1873 and the rules made thereunder, which came into force in 1875. This did much more than finally abolish the forms of actions known to the common law for it provided that equity and law should be administered concurrently. Since that time we have had what might fairly be called a Code of Civil Procedure. Of course we cannot here speak of the details of that Code; but you will not misunderstand me if I say that the procedure which it enjoins is comparatively formless ...

[5] See FW Maitland, *The Forms of Action at Common Law* (AH Chaytor and WJ Whittaker (eds) (CUP 1948) 2–3.

[6] ibid 4.

[7] ibid 7–8.

> Since the Judicature Acts there are, of course, differences of procedure arising out of the character of the various actions, whether for divorce, probate of a will, specific performance of a contract: such differences there must be, but they can now be regarded as mere variations of one general theme--procedure in an action in the High Court of Justice.

The narrative here is of as a sustained and determined attack on the judicial Ancien Régime, suggesting not of a series of opportunistic and coincidental changes but rather that the final result of half a century of reforms of procedure, enshrined in the Rules of the Supreme Court, was the intended goal all along. However, it is not at all clear from the contemporary evidence, or lack thereof, that this was the case at all. It is certainly true that the Commissioners charged in 1828 to consider practice and pleading at common law did so with a commendable overview of the entirety of the process, from start to finish.[8] The early reforms are made as rationalization of a system, but it does not seem that unification was sought as a goal in itself:[9] the criticisms tended to be of the various accretions and fictions in the forms of action, rather than of the entire system of forms. If trans-substantivity had been the goal then we might be forgiven for expecting to find, for example, idealistic drafts of potential codes of procedure offered up by law reformers to welcoming Commissioners and law makers. If we take the Judicature Acts to be the endpoint of such 'progress', then while they definitely put an end to the strict identification of the action in the originating process, and therefore the whole world-view of the forms of action (and extant Chancery) procedures, it is trite to note that they also led to the abandoning of a hitherto essential feature of English law: the existence of separate courts to administer common law and equity (and indeed, a plethora of other bodies of rules).[10] The question of the uniformity of process is thus, at least in England, intimately connected both to the centralization, simplification, and rationalization of the courts as institutions and to the rationalization of the substantive law. The question then is clearly political and, in a broader sense,

[8] Royal Commission on Practice and Proceedings of Superior Courts of Common Law, *First Report* (1829) HC Papers, 46 vol 9 XI,1.

[9] 'We shall have no hesitation in proposing the abolition, as far as practicable, of fictions, circuitous courses, and such matters of mere form, as by the progress-of time have ceased to be necessary to the purposes for which they were introduced, but which increase the length and consequently the cost of proceedings always keeping in view the condition mentioned by Lord Bacon, That the entire body and substance of the Law shall "remain, only discharged of idle and unprofitable or hurtful matter." We shall suggest the abridgment, in many cases, of the forms and language of pleading; some restraint upon the unlimited multiplication of counts and pleas, and an acceleration of every part of the suit, by allowing process to be returnable, pleadings to proceed, and final judgment, under certain restrictions, to be signed, not only upon default, but after verdict, and execution to be issued thereon, in Vacation as well as in Term.' ibid 7.

[10] Lord Brougham, in his famous speech on 'Reform of the courts' on 7 February 1828, mentioned the 'Courts of Civil Law', for example, encompassing the Court of Admiralty, Consistorial Courts, Court of Delegates, and even the Privy Council: J Eardly-Wilmot, *Lord Brougham's Law Reforms* (Longman 1860) 39–40.

constitutional. While the Judicature Acts led to today's uniform procedure, this seems to be mostly as a by-product of the fusion of the jurisdictions of common law and equity[11] rather than as an independent legislative goal.

It is simplification, and, at a pinch, uniformity within one type of action, that seems to be the main characteristic of the reforms. The further connotation of the resulting rules of procedure as 'trans-substantive', ie procedure that is applicable no matter what the subject matter of the dispute, is what completes the transition to the modern system whereby procedural rules must be able to deal with claims in all formerly separate areas of law. This is only conceptually acceptable because procedure and substantive law were de-coupled, and the latter took pre-eminence as an expression of legislative power, as opposed to practice, where process rule making could be left to the judiciary.[12] Our search of a holistic statement of an ideal procedure cannot but be drawn to Jeremy Bentham and his *Principles of Judicial Procedure, with the outline of a procedural code.*[13] On this point, Bentham was a pioneer, and his definitions of 'substantive law' and adjective law' led him to a very modern-sounding distinction between substantive and procedural rules:

> Here, then, comes the line of distinction-the distinction between that part of the proposed system of procedure, which may be given without the previous exhibition of any part of the system of substantive law, and that part which cannot. The means for coming at the truth, as to matters of fact, are the same in all cases; the means for obtaining and exercising the powers necessary to the giving execution and effect to the ordinances of substantive law, are the same in all cases. But of this general application of machinery, different ordinances of substantive law require the application of different engines or instruments to be brought into exercise. On which occasion, which instrument shall be brought into exercise, and how applied-this will depend upon the particular portion or article of substantive law, to which, for the purpose of giving effect to it, application is to be made of it.[14]

Even in Bentham's work, however, the focus does not seem to be on the qualities of procedural (or adjective) law per se, but rather by contrast to the more important substantive law and the even more important goal of judiciary and structural reform. When considering dispassionately the reforms, the evolution from the patchwork of courts administering a fragmented system, where substance and

[11] P Polden, 'Personalities, Politics and the Making of the Supreme Court of Judicature' (2002) 61(3) CLJ 575—with reference to contemporary and more critical modern commentary on that particular achievement, at fn 2.

[12] As expressly acknowledged through the Civil Procedure Act 1833, and subsequently the Judicature Act 1873.

[13] J Bentham, '*The Principles of Judicial Procedure*' in J Bowring (ed), *The Works of Jeremy Bentham* () (Tait Edinburgh 1838–1843) 1, 6 cited and discussed in the seminal article, GJ Postema, 'The Principle of Utility and the Law of Procedure: Bentham's Theory of Adjudication' (1977) 11 Ga L Rev 1393, 1401.

[14] Bentham (n 13) 15.

procedure were inextricably enmeshed, to the single High Court of Justice proceeding on the basis of a single set of rules is clearly about much more than the creation of a new set of simple procedural rules that minimize vexation and delay. In fact, it is as much a legal reform process as it is a political development entirely aimed at reconstructing the constitutional separation, or better the balance between the powers of the State under the supremacy of Parliament. This required the downgrading of the rules of procedure, and the neutralizing of their gatekeepers, the judiciary, which was done by removing those peculiarities of actions that could not be explained on the 'modern' basis of a simple appeal to the authority of the Court for a determination on the pre-existing substantive rights, while providing for basic 'fairness' (as understood in the adversarial sense of the word[15]). Such was also Bentham's vision—the democratic Parliament in charge of the creation of rights, and the judges in their courts cowed into mere application of the substantive law. Bentham found very little good in the court system he had been trained in: 'multiplication of the occasions of extracting fee; the cause of factitious complication, intricacy, obscurity, unintelligibility, uncognoscibility in the system of procedure'.[16] As a result, he considered that procedural rulemaking ought to be reduced to the minimum, with judges only retaining a residuary discretionary rulemaking power merely in order to regulate court processes.

The vagaries and inconsistencies of the forms of action or the Chancery procedures are mentioned time and again by politicians and Commissioners,[17] but merely as a means of garnering popular support for reforms that must have appeared complex even to the rarefied Victorian electorate. Brougham, in his celebrated 1828 speech to the House of Commons, had pleaded for a general reform of the whole system of courts, personnel, rules, etc but was not successful at marshalling it in his time.[18] As the reforms gathered pace, however, something interesting happened: as it took it upon itself to legislate about the courts and the judges—a task relatively new and which would perhaps have appeared repugnant to an earlier Parliament—Parliament officially 'delegated' the power to make rules of court to

[15] See eg L Fuller, 'The Adversary System' in H Berman (ed), *Talks on American Law* (Vintage Books 1961); A Zuckerman, *Zuckerman on Civil Procedure: Principles of Practice* (3rd edn, Sweet & Maxwell 2013) 72.

[16] J Bentham, 'Scotch Reform' in J Bowring (ed), *The Works of Jeremy Bentham* (William Tait 1843), 5: AJ Draper, '*Corruptions in the Administration of Justice*: Bentham's Critique of Civil Procedure, 1806–1811' (2004) 7 JBS 1; Postema (n 15). Bentham's position can be understood in the context of his criticism of the funding of administration of justice (though fees only), which created the deleterious incentive for (rulemaking) judges to increase complexity and litigation.

[17] The mostly political process leading to the reforms in Chancery and ultimately to the Judicature Act was the object of a thorough study by M Lobban, 'Preparing for Fusion: Reforming the Nineteenth-Century Court of Chancery, Part I' (2004) 22 Law & Hist Rev 389; 'Preparing for Fusion: Reforming the Nineteenth-Century Court of Chancery, Part II' (2004) 22 Law & Hist Rev 565, with comment by J Getzler, 'Chancery Reform and Law Reform' (2004) 22 Law & Hist Rev 601. Lobban notes that it is the court infrastructure—the institutions, the Judges, the Masters, and certain Lord Chancellors—that excites the reformist intent.

[18] Eardly-Wilmot (n 10) 62.

the judiciary, with the Civil Procedure Act 1833 (3 & 4 Will 4. C 42), 'An Act for the further Amendment of the Law, and the better Advancement of Justice'. The legislation merits citing in its entirety, both because it leads to a particular allocation of the power of rule-making—the judiciary's power now limited by being statutory rather than inherent—and because the formulation of the section is the model for all subsequent English enactments on the point, but also arguably it provides the inspiration for the US Rules Enabling Act:[19]

> WHEREAS it would greatly contribute to the diminishing of Expense in Suits in the Superior Courts of Common Law at Westminster if the Pleadings therein were in some respects altered, and the Questions to be tried by the Jury left less at large than they now are according to the Course and Practice of pleading in several Forms of Action; but *this cannot be conveniently done otherwise than by Rules or Orders of the Judges of the said Courts from Time to Time to be made, and Doubts may arise as to the Power of the said Judges to make such Alterations without the Authority of Parliament*:
>
> Be it therefore enacted . . . , That the Judges of the said Superior Courts, . . . shall and may, by any Rule or Order to be from Time to Time by them made, . . . make such Alterations in the Mode of pleading in the said Courts, and in the Mode of entering and transcribing Pleadings, Judgments, and other Proceedings in Actions at Law, and such Regulations as to the Payment of Costs, and otherwise for carrying into effect the said Alterations, as to them may seem expedient; and all such Rules, Orders, or Regulations shall be laid before both Houses of Parliament, . . . and no such Rule, Order, or Regulation shall have Effect until Six Weeks after the same shall have been so laid before both Houses of Parliament; and any Rule or Order so made shall, from and after such Time aforesaid be binding and obligatory on the said Courts, and all other Courts of Common Law, and on all Courts of Error into which the Judgments of the said Courts or any of them shall be carried by any Writ of Error, and be of the like Force and Effect as if the Provisions contained therein had been expressly enacted by Parliament: Provided always, that no such Rule or Order shall have the Effect of depriving any Person of the Power of pleading the General Issue, and giving the special Matter in Evidence, in any Case wherein he is now or hereafter shall be entitled to do so by Virtue of any Act of Parliament now or hereafter to be in force.
>
> [emphasis added]

Clearly a task as vast as the unification, harmonization, and rationalization of the various types of procedure within the two main systems of law, and then between those two systems when fusion becomes a real possibility,[20] could only be

[19] See below, n 33.

[20] S Rosenbaum, 'Studies in English Civil Procedure' (1914–15) 63 U Pa L Rev 105; 63 U Pa L Rev 151; 63 U Pa L Rev 273; 63 U Pa L Rev, 380; 63 U Pa L Rev 505 (and above n 5).

achieved by experts of the administration of those rules. This highlights the tension between the judicial power and the legislative power (which had for most of the century been of a political and constitutional nature rather than a strictly legal nature). There was a need to justify expressly why judges should be in charge of the rules of court—and eventually battle lines were drawn on the acceptable and appropriate object of judicial rule making. The first attempt to reform the rules of pleading, in 1834 in application of the 1833 Act,[21] backfired spectacularly in terms of increasing, rather than decreasing the complexity of applicable pleading rules.[22] However, the rule making process was well oiled by 1873, when section 68 of the 1873 Judicature Act[23] allowed judges to make rules for the sittings of the court, the duties of its officers, pleading, practice procedure, and costs of proceedings.[24] The new Rules Committees produced effectively a series of 'codes' of procedure, which with various amendments laid the basis for modern English procedure. Not all was plain sailing, however. When the product of the 1882 RC was put to Parliament, relatively late for amendments, as a schedule to the 1883 Act, a heated debate ensued.[25] Judges were accused of becoming 'despots in the Courts of law', going so far as abrogating whole Acts of Parliament by a mere prohibition of new writs on them, and effectively acting outwith the narrow power given in the Acts.[26] However, the Act (and its schedule) passed, the motion to annul the Rules was not carried and the rest is history.[27]

[21] W Holdsworth, 'The New Rules of Pleading of Hilary Term, 1834' (1923) 1 CLJ 261.

[22] ibid. Holdsworth actually poses the question of the effect on substantive law of the new rules of pleading, and concludes that there has been one, by forcing the litigants into being more precise with their claimed actions, the rules indirectly caused a return to forgotten lines of precedent.

[23] On which, see WB Perkins, 'The English Judicature Act of 1873' (1914) 12 Mich L Rev 277.

[24] Rosenbaum (n 5) fn 50.

[25] HC Debates, 11 August 1883, *Hansard* vol 283 cc 145–87.

[26] In his initial statement, the proposer of the motion to annul the Rules (Sir Hardinge Giffard) said:

> 'The power that had been given to the Judges … was to frame Rules for the regulation of the practice and procedure of the Courts …
>
> [T]hese rules had reference to matters most vitally affecting not merely practice—as the popular world would understand it— … of the Courts, but matters vitally affecting important political rights …
>
> Judges had done their best to increase and enlarge their jurisdiction, because in almost every case in which a question could arise under these Rules the Judge was to have the power of deciding it summarily.
>
> … […] would only refer to one example of what the Judges had done in the exercise of their power of making these Rules. By an Act, known as Sir Henry Keating's Act, no defence was permitted to be raised in certain circumstances in an action upon a bill of exchange; and the Judges by these Rules had, by a stroke of the pen, simply repealed that Act. They did not say in terms that the Act should be repealed—that would have been too scandalous— but they said that after the publication of these Rules no writ under Sir Henry Keating's Act should be issued. What was the meaning of that? In a certain sense it was procedure; but he did not think that under the powers conferred upon them by the Act they were authorized to repeal Acts of Parliament in this summary fashion …'

[27] J Sorabji, *English Civil Justice after the Woolf and Jackson Reforms* (CUP 2014) contains an important analysis of the ways in which the various procedural reforms since the mid-1800s attempted to deal with the problem of justice and its denial based on procedural reasons.

By 1883, the uniformity of the rules was a fait accompli. What exercised Parliamentary opposition was the sentiment that only Parliament may promulgate a rule that has the effect of abrogating Acts of Parliament, rather than judges. Effectively, the rules of 'adjective law', as promulgated by judges, could not be permitted to interfere with the higher level rules of 'substantive' law, despite being, technically, delegated legislation as a consequence of their mode of enactment. There was a visible sensitivity to legitimate and illegitimate rule making, rather than an intrinsic quality of any type of procedural rules.[28]

The reforms of the nineteenth century were an extraordinary achievement, which necessarily encompassed change at all levels of the administration of justice. However, while one of the many stated goals of the various reforming Committees was indeed to simplify procedure for the avoidance of vexation to the litigant, and this simplification became progressively more incisive until the point of fusion, there does not appear to be a broad theory of procedure guiding the reform process. Instead, the process appears to be overwhelmingly that of a rearrangement of the constitutional order, of which an integral part is constituted by the downgrading of the rules of court and of their gatekeepers, who maintain the power to make the rules but are policed against transgressions of the legislative primacy of Parliament.

The transatlantic dialogue: A digression

A particularly interesting point in the history of the making of modern procedure in England is the influence of the near-contemporaneous North American developments. Lobban in particular identifies the moment when the 1848 Field Code of procedure for New York State sparked enthusiasm in England, both for its procedural achievements and, for its successful fusion of common law and equity practices (with a marked prevalence of the equity procedure).[29] 'At the end of 1850', he writes, 'the society [for Promoting the Amendment of the Law] invited David Dudley Field to address them on these reforms and, having met the great reformer, set up a committee chaired by Robert Lowe to consider whether law and equity could be fused in England'.[30] Field's New York code was influential across

[28] It is no coincidence that Holdsworth's emphatic criticism of the Hilary Rules, which had essentially extended special pleading to all cases, began by asking, 'Did They Affect the Development of the Substantive Law?': Holdsworth (n 21).

[29] S Subrin, 'David Dudley Field and the Field Code: A Historical Analysis of an Earlier Procedural Vision' (1988) 6 Law & Hist Rev 311; S Subrin, 'How Equity Conquered Common Law: The Federal Rules of Civil Procedure in Historical Perspective' (1987) 135 U Pa L Rev 909. See also K Funk, 'Equity without Chancery: The Fusion of Law and Equity in the Field Code of Civil Procedure, New York 1846–76' (2015) 36 J Legal Hist 152.

[30] Lobban (n 19) 584.

the common law world, and its effects have long been debated. The code, with its reliance on equity-style procedure overall, was idealized in the USA by the later proponents of a Federal Code of Civil Procedure under the Rules Enabling Act of 1934.[31] To them it was an example of how it would be possible to have a code of civil procedure written under the authority of the Supreme Court in a way that was not only generally applicable to all claims of substantive law, ie, trans-substantive, but also was incapable of affecting substantively the outcome of the case. The terminology of the Act was interesting, as it very closely mirrored the English legislation. The current version[32] states:

(a) The Supreme Court shall have the power to prescribe general rules of practice and procedure and rules of evidence for cases in the United States district courts (including proceedings before magistrate judges thereof) and courts of appeals.
(b) Such rules shall not abridge, enlarge or modify any substantive right. All laws in conflict with such rules shall be of no further force or effect after such rules have taken effect.

In this text, the dichotomy between practice and procedure on the one hand, and substantive rights on the other is made explicit. This enabled the drafters to resolve the political problem of the allocation of law making power between Congress and the Supreme Court, under the umbrella of Article III of the US Constitution.[33] The requirement for procedure to be 'non-abridging' is the result of the importance in the American legal context of maintaining the constitutionally-mandated separation of powers. That is probably the reason why, despite its probable introduction as 'surplusage',[34] the second part of the article has taken on a life of its own in regard to the American concern with trans-substantive civil procedure. When the English reformers had looked at the Field code, however, they had seen firstly, a possible road to fusion of the jurisdictions, and secondly a series of potential mechanisms—equitable, thus steeped in a certain amount of discretionary power—to remove much of the rigidity of then existing rules and patterns of litigation. In a sense, the reformists on either side of the Atlantic looked to each other's progresses and may have learned from each others' mistakes.[35]

[31] On which see S Burbank, 'The Rules Enabling Act of 1934' (1982) 130 U Pa L Rev 1015 and PD Carrington 'Substance and Procedure in the Rules Enabling Act' (1989) 1989(2) Duke LJ 281.
[32] 28 USC § 2072. Rules of procedure and evidence; power to prescribe.
[33] Burbank (n 31) 1106.
[34] Burbank (n 31) 1107.
[35] Rosenbaum (n 5), for example, interestingly focuses on how non-problematic it is, in England, for the Rules Committee to be in charge of the workings of the courts.

The normative claim(s) as to the nature of Civil Procedure Rules: trans-substantivity, generality, and uniformity

One result of the dialogue across the Atlantic is that scholars of civil procedure in England have at their disposal, besides Parliamentary Papers and legal historians' efforts, a vast array of near-contemporary eye-witness accounts of the reform processes from a perspective more likely to notice general tendencies and normative fault lines than the self-referencing and often practice-led English literature of the time. Additionally, even in the midst of reforms of enormous import for civil procedure itself, the dismissive aspersions cast on 'adjective law' in English scholarship removed any incentive to analyse civil procedure rules as a set of rules, subject to the same philosophical rule-making principles as any other State rules. On the other hand, the constitutional notion of 'due process', the enormous influence of the US Supreme Court and the jurisprudence of the Federal courts in the USA, with the addition of academic Legal Realism, all gave American scholars many more criteria by which to describe and assess the rules of procedure as any other type of rules. Indeed, it is in the American literature that can be found a number of concepts, such as trans-substantivity, with which to proceed to an analysis of normative claims for procedure.

In nineteenth and twentieth century England, reforming the practice and procedure of the courts was an endeavour of such proportions that it did not allow much space for legal theory, even had there been more appetite for theory about 'mere' procedure. The historical emergence of a 'unified court, applying a single set of rules of procedure' was a revolution on several levels. Undoubtedly, fundamental changes were made to the way in which the court(s) processes are regulated, and the notion of civil procedure came to mean a lesser type of regulation, while still being the object of rule-making rather than mere administration. The public condemnation of the status quo included a very critical, but also very pragmatic view of procedural obstacles, and the new editions of Bentham's writings, with his dismissive categorization of substantive and adjective law must certainly have been an incentive for Parliamentary action. However, the historical record does not provide comfort for the assumption that the birth of the modern procedure, with its presumably positive qualities of uniformity and trans-substantivity, was the product of a deliberate and persistent ideology. Rather, it appears to have been a happy by-product of other forces at play.

Two concurrent strands of reformist intent can be thus identified. The first one targeted judicial officers and court structures, for not being objectively fit for the purpose of enabling the fair and efficient resolution of disputes. This was exemplified by Bentham's many writings and later in Brougham's exposure of the inefficiency and incoherence of such matters as the Law Terms or the appointment of judges. The second series of concerns, which coagulated in rationales for changes to the rules governing the process and the business of adjudication, referred to the variety of possible procedures with attendant risks of error, the inefficiency of over-specialism either in jurisdiction or in specific steps of the lawsuit, or again the costs and delay and general vexation. While similar issues arose on both sides of the Atlantic, they were given differing levels of emphasis.[36]

The English legislature was mostly guided by tendencies of the former type, rather than the latter. This is not to say that the reformists did not also believe that procedural changes could be instrumental to the eventual rationalization of the judicial 'power', or even of the whole of the substantive law. For example, the interest in the Field code and its equity-heavy type of procedural fusion could indicate an awareness of how to achieve substantive fusion, merely by operating on the processes, and of how a uniform procedure would lead, without need for further legislative effort, to a progressive rationalization of the substantive rules and systems, which would flow from reasoned arguments applying all relevant case-law and, in the case of conflict, 'the rules of equity should prevail'.[37] If that were the case, then the system of rules of civil procedure that emerged from reforms was not intended, teleologically, to have any general quality of trans-substantivity or uniformity. If today it does have those qualities, it is not because the reformers set out to create it in that way believing it to be qualitatively sounder.

At any rate, modern English procedure, as applauded by Zuckerman in the quote at the beginning of this chapter, ended up being uniform, ie with a clear expectation that the vast majority of cases would use a single set of rules and principles. Since the law that the courts were now expected to apply had not at this point been significantly amended, the structural uniformity of the process implied and required that the rules themselves be—by default—trans-substantive not only within the common law or the equity fields, but between the two. The historical development of the law, in response to real problems caused by the previous type of process, has led to a system which is generally uniform, tends to simplicity and aims at being economically efficient. But merely being the result of historical development does not confer a necessarily qualitative or normative superiority to the present-day procedure. The question is still open whether these attributes result in a process which is qualitatively better than rules which allow for fragmentation of the adjudicative processes, in other words, whether generally applicable procedures are always 'better' than specialized procedures. According to Sorabji, the Judicature Acts,[38] after the previous technical attempts to move from the dual system of a formalistic common law and a 'perfect—transubstantive—justice' in

[36] This might also be due to the timing of the individual steps towards reform: Funk (n 30) suggests that the Field code did not create the fusion of law and equity it is generally credited with, but merely originated in a fertile and conducive context where some fusion had already taken hold in New York State: at 154.

[37] Section 25(11) of the 1873 Act.

[38] Above, n 28. He identifies the change of attitude in the belief that a fault in procedure cannot defeat 'justice on the merits', only fully enshrined in the RSC (1965) Ord 2, r 1.

equity, finally alighted on a 'reformed equity procedure'.[39] However, he says, 'past experience of reform made it clear that merely adopting a simplified structure or set of procedural rules was not sufficient ... it needed a change in attitude, a cultural change'.[40] Thus, it needed the emphasis on the role of adjudication as needing to provide 'justice on the merits' seamlessly. There was to be no separate sense of procedural correctness, which might defeat that aim, although the position was only fully embraced in the system with the 1965 revision to the RSC. We now also know that this view of adjudication has undergone much criticism—not least by Zuckerman himself—and has certainly been at least qualified, if not abandoned, in the post-Woolf and post-Jackson reforms.

The question then is, whether trans-substantivity, or indeed uniformity of process, are or have ever been a normative ideal for a system of rules of civil procedure. It is necessary to delve a little deeper into their possible meanings, and separate the two, although they are partly synonyms, especially when presented as solutions to the various ills of complexity, delay, etc. As a matter of definitions, however, it ought to be possible to differentiate them and evaluate their desirability.

Trans-substantivity

Trans-substantivity, it thus seems, must be understood historically not as an end in itself but as part of a broader range of measures intended to ensure the supremacy of the legislature over the judiciary. This constitutional or political aspect flows openly though the American experience and less obviously—but still noticeably—in the English reforms. Utilitarianism, after all, is a political philosophy as much as anything, and Bentham's writings make a clear connection between the sovereignty of the legislature and the consequent restriction of the power of the judicial arm to 'make substantive law'.[41] Trans-substantivity is, rather counterintuitively, one quality of procedural rules that distinguishes them from substantive law: the quality not to affect—or 'abridge', in the American version—substantive outcomes.

The American analysis of trans-substantivity is very clearly dominated by its conception as a limit to judicial rule-making. The consequence of requiring it, is to make it inappropriate to articulate political or ideological values through the prism of 'procedural consequence' rather than the mere application of process rules and/or the imperative will of the legislature. If rules are best written by judges, who

[39] Sorabji (n 28) 57.

[40] ibid 65.

[41] This position is not universally accepted as starkly. Hart, for example, suggests a type of 'interstitial', residuary 'law creating powers', in cases that have been left 'partly unregulated', different from those of a legislature: not only are the judges' powers subject to many constraints *narrowing his choice* from which a legislature may be quite free, but since the judge's powers are exercised only to dispose of particular instant cases he cannot use these to introduce large-scale reforms or new codes. So his powers are *interstitial* as well as subject to many substantive constraints.' HLA Hart, *The Concept of Law* (2nd edn, OUP 1994) Postscript, 273.

are skilled in the law but suffer a democratic deficit, they must be neutral, and not outcome-determinative. Robert Cover, to whom some ascribe the first use of the term 'trans-substantive' in this field,[42] contrasted the hyper-realist disinclination to make any differentiation between primary rights and 'sanctioning consequences' of Supreme Court Justice Holmes, with a more nuanced view of what could be obtained by 'acceptable manipulations of process to further a substantive preference':[43]

> If by "law" one means a prediction as to what the courts will, in fact, do [OV Holmes, *The Path of the Law*, in Collected Legal Papers 167 (1897)], then adjective law, as much as substantive law, is a ground for the prediction …
>
> The perhaps naive view of Maine and Maitland in praising the Judicature Acts was that a neutral, segregated adjective law would render the substantive law the only proper ground for prediction: Procedure would reflect adjudicative values designed to serve the end of effective fact finding so that substantive law alone would become predictive of the incidence of public force …
>
> I accept the conclusion that procedure, broadly conceived, will inevitably shape substance; but I shall argue that there are proper and improper ways of structuring process with substantive ends in mind …

It might be worth remembering that in the US, the insistence in 1934–1938 (the year of the enactment of the FRCP) on withholding the power of making such manipulations from the court, especially the Supreme Court, was at a time when New Deal legislation was being thwarted in the Supreme Court by conservative judges.[44] In a sense, the constitutional / political significance of 'trans-substantive civil procedure' takes on a more intense role the wider the ideological gulf, real or perceived, between the legislature or the 'people' and the judiciary. It is the potential lack of democratic representativeness that makes it imperative that rules of procedure, where written (wholly or mostly) by judges, be neutral insofar as they can be seen to guide the process towards one outcome rather than another (or in Cover's version, only allow 'proper' manipulations of the process).

It appears to be a necessary character of civil procedure rules when all the following premises are correct:

1. Rules of procedure can and ought to be set down by those who are guided by them, which can be the judiciary, the professional legal world, or a combination of these and some lay or academic or political influences.

[42] SN Subrin, 'Federal Rules, Local Rules, and State Rules: Uniformity, Divergence, and Emerging Procedural Patterns' (1989) 137 U Pa L Rev 1999.

[43] Cover's article RM Cover, 'For James Wm. Moore: Some Reflections on a Reading of the Rules' (1975) 84 Yale LJ 718 was reprinted as part of an influential student textbook, RM Cover and OM Fiss, *The Structure of Procedure* (1st edn, Mineola NY The Foundation Press Inc 1979) 434.

[44] WE Leuchtenburg, 'The Origins of Franklin D. Roosevelt's "Court-Packing" Plan' [1966] Supreme Court Rev 347.

2. As the legal system (in the case of the USA, the Constitution; in England the guiding principle is the Diceyan conception of Parliament's sovereignty) requires 'the law' to be the product of the legislative arm, there must be no conflation of law-creation and procedure-setting.
3. Law creation is 'substantive law': rules that identify, eg, what a tort is or what the requirements for an enforceable contract are.
4. Procedure setting by the non-legislature, to be legitimate, cannot lead to an alteration of the outcome of the process beyond the application of the 'substantive' law (so, all that it can do is ensure that the conditions set down in substantive law are either satisfied or not satisfied by litigants).
5. Hence, procedural rules must be 'trans-substantive': they must apply and be applied no matter what the underlying cause of action is.

(There are, however, real-world limits. Any pragmatist would see that many procedural rules, no matter how outwardly trans-substantive, can be outcome-defining due to practical or financial reasons; or because of objective needs for additional or more specific procedural tools (generally connected to the acquisition of relevant evidence, though not necessarily falling within the category of rules of evidence) in some contexts. Taken to its logical and ideal conclusion, the requirement of pure trans-substantivity is impossible to satisfy in the real world, for any but the most basic, mechanistic rules of civil litigation (eg, the time for service, maybe). However, in a constitutional legal system based on the separation of powers, it is possible to accept a modified aspiration for trans-substantivity, as a democratic check on the rule-making authority.)

But is there an argument that trans-substantivity per se is necessary to proper civil procedure, even when the rule making power is not delegated? With his practitioner's hat on, Bentham conceded that, even should his criticisms of the administration of justice be translated into reform, the inevitable complexity of the rules of court remained and could best be dealt with on a case-by-case basis by judges. However, it should only be that level of rules that are 'part of the proposed system of procedure, which may be given without the previous exhibition of any part of the system of substantive law'.[45] On this analysis the rules of procedure are merely the guide book through the process of satisfying ones' rights. That would be true then for the method of initiating a claim if we make it sufficiently non-specific,[46] leaving the specification of the claim to the statement of case rather than using a particular claim form that, say, had an extra requirement for the presentation of additional, substance-specific evidence or plea. Taken without the attendant reforms of the judiciary and the court system, this manifestation of

[45] Above text to n 15.

[46] Such as a single claim form, Form N1 (https://assets.publishing.service.gov.uk/government/uploads/system/uploads/attachment_data/file/688390/n1-eng.pdf) accessed 3 March 2019.

trans-substantivity well describes the English procedure post-1875, at least in contrast with the forms of action and the various equity processes. Here the difference from substantive law is not based on the legitimacy of the rule-maker or giver, but on 'instrumental values of good system design, such as simplicity, flexibility and litigation efficiency (in the sense of eliminating obvious waste rather than minimizing social costs)'.[47]

But what does it mean to claim that a system of civil procedure that is trans-substantive, is better than one that is not, insofar as it can be a criterion for an assessment of any new proposed rules? The answer must lie either in 'instrumental values of good system design' or in external values placed on the function of the court, or the State, such as 'access to justice' for all on an equal footing.[48] The latter is best satisfied through a simple and accessible state-sponsored dispute resolution forum that does not require in-depth, professional-level knowledge of substantive law in order to claim that some right has been breached, some harm caused that can and ought to be compensated by someone else.[49] There is an element of circularity here, as clearly some inkling of 'legal need' must be present. However, where the ideal is that an individual citizen should be able to access the court system without recourse to professional advisors, or with such reduced recourse that may minimize her outgoings in money and time (cost and delay) without jeopardizing (too much) her likelihood of success 'on the merits', then a simple, general, accessible rule for all cases must be better than to expect or require specialization and/or the selection of a particular litigation pathway or even strategy from the beginning.

However, if the only assessment that can be made is whether the rules are of 'good design', this must be done by reference to more than one imperative, such as efficiency, or by minimizing costs, vexation, and delay. This means that there are several potentially conflicting pressures on the system. If we take as an example initiating process, and decide that a non-technical 'notice-pleading-style'[50] trans-substantive process best satisfies the external requirement of accessibility, we very quickly come across some problems, many of which are well known. Where the litigants don't have to work on finessing the claim, it is going to be down to the judicial officer or the sheer whittling due to back-and-forth of statements and denials

[47] RG Bone 'Improving Rule 1: A Master Rule for the Federal Rules' (2009–10) 87 Denv U L Rev 287, 290.

[48] Access to Justice was the title of Lord Woolf's Reports. The expression has a long pedigree in English law, see for all Zuckerman (above n 15) 81ff.

[49] See *Bremer Vulkan Schiffbau v South India Shipping Corp* [1981] 1 All ER 289, HL 295: 'Every civilized system of government requires that the state should make available to all its citizens a means for the just and peaceful settlement of disputes between them as to their respective legal rights. The means provided are courts of justice . . .' (Lord Diplock); Zuckerman (n 15) 81ff.

[50] On which see CB Whittier, 'Notice Pleading' (1918) 31 Harv L Rev 501. The Federal Rules were drafted with a rather liberal approach to pleading, but this has recently become a disputed area: KM Clermont and SC Yeazell, 'Inventing Tests, Destabilizing Systems' (2009–10) 95 Iowa L Rev 821.

to arrive at a justiciable issue (all at a cost, both to the litigant and to the 'taxpayer'). 'Good design' would balance the need for initial simplicity and accessibility with those for a threshold of allegation, that would make the process worth engaging with and would achieve efficiency by standardizing, as much as possible, initial procedural requirements. Additionally, once the process has started, it would be unreasonable (in terms of accessibility) to give too much (or any) weight to 'mere' procedural failings. The experiences of self-represented litigants are however indicative of the tension between the accessibility aspiration and the increased structural pressure 'downstream' through the litigation.[51]

A flexible procedure—which by definition is not very efficient at corralling unwilling participants—is the obvious companion to a liberal originating process.[52] However, the only way to conceive of a system allowing flexibility while being at the same time trans-substantive is by giving very little information and guidance in the rule itself, and leaving much of it to the discretion of the judge. Bentham would have approved, but this may then clash with trans-substantivity's historical raison d'etre, ie that the judge should not be given a free rein lest he 'manipulate', as Cover has it, the rule in relation to desirable substantive outcomes; and it may clash with the utility of the rules in general, if they do not allow the litigant to predict what the path is likely to be. To be trans-substantive by design a procedural system would contain few rules, articulated in general terms, with vast areas left to individual management by the judge. Any attempt to standardize processes would have to either carve out a sub-category of 'all substantive claims' where those standards were the norm, or risk inefficiencies through a blanket application of rules only 'mostly' applicable.

Can it be said that the CPR satisfy the requirement of a trans-substantive system of rules as they are? The rules for a claim—and for further process—following the Woolf reforms did not expect much precision at the beginning of the official process (the claim form). However, if the requirements of pre-action protocol compliance and the demands of case management (especially at case-management review level) were taken into account, considering that they led to increased and front-loaded costs,[53] there is an argument for suggesting that the open-endedness of the

[51] In the current climate of austerity and cost-cutting (including to Legal Aid provision, also effected with the LASPO Act 2012) the increase in unassisted litigants has become a matter of critical urgency: K Williams, *Litigants in person: a literature review* (Ministry of Justice 2011) <https://assets.publishing.service.gov.uk/government/uploads/system/uploads/attachment_data/file/217374/litigants-in-person-literature-review.pdf≥ accessed 3 March 2019.

[52] The imperative not to let procedural failings lead to a *non liquet*—in other words reliance on equitable powers to inject flexibility into the procedure—was central to the 'justice on the merits' approach which dominated the post-1875 Rules of the Supreme Court: Sorabji, text at n 28 above. Effectively, this was the debate on whether judges were to be the masters or the servants of the (procedural) law. Some of these issues are discussed in C Crifò, 'Enforcement of Process Requirements: A Search for Solid Grounds' (2010) 34(2) OJLS 325.

[53] J Peysner, 'A Blot on the Landscape' in D Dwyer (ed), *The Civil Procedure Rules Ten Years On* (OUP 2009).

initiating process rules was in relation to technical labelling only, not to the precision of facts still required. Additionally, from Woolf to Jackson it is now uncontroversial that the kind of procedural justice to be served by the CPR is clearly limited to providing an opportunity of access, rather than actual day in court, with all that that entails with regards to litigants who fail to take the opportunities offered. It is also the case that the rules—especially post-Jackson—now consist also of 'channeling',[54] semi-rigid consequential rules (timetables, case management, automatic and ad-hoc, and other directions on how to proceed, etc) which legitimately constrain the use of the 'service' by the litigant.[55]

What kind of argument, if any, can be made to assert that trans-substantivity is also an inherent requirement of procedure, by which current procedures such as the post-Jackson ones can be assessed? In the post-Woolf and post-Jackson landscape there is effectively now a complex conception of civil procedure: a layer of rules, the mechanic rules of process themselves, and, superimposed on this (whether by the Overriding Objective or by the implicit and explicit acceptance of a culture change by the primary legislator), a layer of 'super-rules', being a series of principles, factors, and considerations which are external to the process itself, and indeed often to an individual claim, but are not 'substantive law'. These are matters that affect the unequal financial position of the parties to litigation, but also the effect that allocating too many resources to one claim would have on any other on the court list, and issues such as cost, efficiency, time awareness, the effects of one instance of extended litigation or over-resourced litigation on the subsequent or surrounding cases on the court list,[56] etc. Viewed as part of a social and public phenomenon, litigation is an exercise of state power and use of state resources, and it is now impossible to allow that it happens in a 'bubble' untouched by external considerations. The presence of these considerations—taken into account under the blanket term of 'proportionality'—can easily lead to the conclusion that the rules are not purely trans-substantive (if they ever were) any more. This super-layer of procedural principles acts as a focusing filter, and in so doing, it does 'affect the substantive outcome' or prevent some rules from being applied in the same way to all claims.

In conclusion, there appears to be a small kernel of truth in the suggestion that trans-substantivity is an essential character of procedural rules, and in addition that it is a quality that must be defended. As a check on judicial overreach, it is an important aspiration that sets the boundaries of legitimacy of the rules. As a description of rules that 'apply to all claims regardless of the substantive law' it operates to reduce 'proper' procedure to its simplest, mechanic aspects. In terms of

[54] One of the functions of formalities, see Crifò (n 52).

[55] Sorabji (n 28) has an extensive analysis of the external factors now definitively part of the 'proportionate justice' approach at 165–99.

[56] ibid.

trans-substantivity as a positive quality, supposedly abandoned when 'special' features are attached to some, but not other types of claim, the question then becomes not whether any rules of civil procedure need to be applicable to all civil processes, but how and when any deviation from their uniformity, or general applicability, needs to be justified.

Generality and uniformity

The words trans-substantive, general, uniform, single can clearly overlap and refer to broadly similar aspirations or features of systems of civil procedure. Could it be that the essential requirement for a good system of procedure is not necessarily that it should be limited to mere mechanics of presentation of a claim and its supporting evidence, but rather, that it should be generally and uniformly applied to all citizens? A trans-substantive rule applies to all types of claims (a legal definition), whereas a general or uniform one applies to all individuals, or in all the courts of the land. The two characteristics are not the same.[57] The threat to the procedure that Zuckerman feared would come from the introduction of separate 'procedural streams' depending on which costs rule applies may not be simply to do with the content or applicability of those rules. It is not necessarily the provision of more specialized rules that is at issue—it is in the explicit raising of walls inhibiting the transition from one specialized 'stream' to another.

The generality of the law has long been held to be an essential requirement of the rule of law. Gardner makes the point that for Aristotle the fact that all law is universal means that some laws may lead to injustice by virtue of their over-generality.[58] The first of Fuller's eight requirements of the rule of law is that laws must be general (and the fourth is that they must be 'clear').[59] Perhaps the most important connection is that between the rule of law and the need for the law to be general, as made by Lord Bingham in *The Rule of Law* under the principle of equality of treatment: the laws of the land should apply equally to all, save to the extent that objective differences justify differentiation.[60]

Moreover, the existence of a general set of rules for process is the natural antithesis to the mosaic of courts and processes that so incensed the nineteenth century reformers. Where that was felt to be unsatisfactory, the opposite would have had

[57] See Subrin (n 40) 2006.

[58] Which will then require an equitable intervention to correct: J Gardner 'The Virtue of Justice and the Character of Law' (2000) 53 Curr Legal Probs 1, 17.

[59] LL Fuller, *The Morality of Law* (Yale University Press 1969) 39.

[60] T Bingham, *The Rule of Law* (Allen Lane 2010) ch 5.

enormous appeal. We can look to Montesquieu for an inkling of the desirability of generality in law, or lack thereof:[61]

> In governments where there are necessary distinctions of persons, there must likewise be privileges. This also diminishes the simplicity, and creates a thousand exceptions.
>
> One of the privileges least burdensome to society, and especially to him who confers it, is that of pleading in one court in preference to another. Here new difficulties arise, when it becomes a question before which court we shall plead.

The normative claim for uniformity of process is all there: in the eighteenth and nineteenth century socio-legal landscape, there were necessary distinctions of persons, and their right to be treated differently translated into the privilege of special courts and possibly special rules. Monarchies as a constitutional form led to a multiplicity of rules and 'very scrupulous enquiries'.[62] However, in a democratic system (Montesquieu talks of republics: but this is as much applicable to later constitutional monarchies, such as the post-Dicey landscape in England), the starting point is the equality of citizens, which correlates to the necessity of equality of treatment. The difference in personal status ceases to be a legitimate criterion for the 'privilege' of special courts, special rules, and special procedures. Other objective criteria are needed. Even more importantly, there exists an expectation, led by the equality principle, that the general rule is the 'default' mode and that any divergent rule will be the exception, properly justified.

Even if the single Supreme Court of Judicature was designed to provide the visuals of a central, rational, single forum, a number of jurisdictional specialisms have always remained, as did special procedures for particular substantive claims.[63] But the binary relationship between the 'general' process and the 'special' jurisdiction was well established. The reform of procedure led to a change that was typical of the transition to a modern state: the centralization and depersonalization of the exercise of the state's powers.

In addition, a modern interpretation of 'uniformity' goes further than application of the rule to all users (general) and to all claims (trans-substantive), though it overlaps with them in various ways. It is the quality of the specific set of rules to

[61] *Charles Louis de Secondat, Baron de Montesquieu The Spirit of Laws*, Book 6 Chapter 1; *The Complete Works of M. de Montesquieu* (London: T. Evans, 1777), 4 vols. Vol. 1. (accessed 24/03/2020). <https://oll.libertyfund.org/titles/837> 93.

[62] 'In republics, it is plain that as many formalities at least are necessary as in monarchies. In both governments they increase in proportion to the value which is set on the honour, fortune, liberty, and life of the subject.

In republican governments, men are all equal; equal they are also in despotic governments: in the former, because they are everything; in the latter, because they are nothing.' ibid.

[63] Both in the original Judicature Acts and in the many Administration of Justice Acts, and also in specific legislation attributing jurisdiction for disputes arising thereunder to a particular division of the High Court, or the County Courts, or to a tribunal.

be applied not only at inception in the same way and leading to similar outcomes ('like cases be treated alike'), but also not to be subjected to such stresses in interpretation and practice as to progressively change or multiply in variations. Thus, on the one hand, a set of rules, to apply uniformly to disparate contexts, must be sufficiently simple or general; on the other hand, the very generality of rules may require integration through interpretation that may by a process of accretion diverge until no vestige of generality remains. Uniformity ought to exist in order to allow everyone to utilize the same procedures in any forum and generally arrive, efficiently, at the same outcome.[64]

Conclusion: Cracks and interstices

It is unthinkable that in England civil procedure will not continue to be administered though generally uniform rules broadly laid down in a single framework by a statutory committee comprised of judiciary and non-judiciary expert members. The centralization and rationalization of structures and processes—though subjected to quite high stress—still has the weight of historical progress behind it, and few would accept in theory a fragmentation of that general single core of procedure, despite the fact that in reality any number of 'specialist' fora exist[65] and apply rules specifically designed for them.[66] The underlying assumption is still that these are exceptions to a general, trans-substantive core of procedural law. In many of the cases of specialized courts there are objective reasons for departing from the uniform default, and when it comes to allocation of jurisdiction it may be argued that it is a matter outside the proper province of the procedural regulation that is in the gift of the Rules Committee. Jurisdictional allocations are expressed in primary legislation and therefore on a par with substantive rules.

Additionally, with regards to the aspiration of trans-substantivity, certainly post-Woolf and post-Jackson, Sorabji has shown that it has been at the very least diluted by the introduction, in the interstices between 'mechanical' process and 'substantive law', of a set of considerations that are external to the process but are solely designed to either enhance it in terms of efficiency or to align it with socio-political concerns of allocation of public resources and trust in the administration of justice. In a sense, the pure principles of 'equality of treatment' for all has been overtaken by the additional considerations of efficiency and proportionality at the centre of

[64] As Subrin says, 'perhaps the most important type of uniformity [is] uniformity of result.... [A] major purpose of procedure is to help substantive law be applied in a constant fashion. Perhaps the primary goal of uniform rules in non-test case litigation should be to help similar cases end up with similar results in an efficient and economic manner.' Subrin (n 42) 2047.

[65] eg the Family Court, the Business and Property Courts (as of 2017: <https://www.judiciary.uk/wp-content/uploads/2017/03/bpc-explanatory-statement-final-20170518-v2.pdf> accessed 3 March 2019), the Patent Court, etc.

[66] eg, CPR 63 for the Patents Court, or the Chancery Code.

the Woolf and Jackson proposals, and of this the rules that raised Zuckerman's criticisms are only an example. The rules as introduced are the very opposite of trans-substantive, for they specifically predetermine the outcome of the costs determination depending on the substantive law or the nature of the applicant.

Although trans-substantivity may not be an absolute, general essential requirement of procedural law, without which the entire system of civil procedure is in some way undermined, it is helpful to ascertain the extent to which the rules are a legitimate exercise of rule-making power, or instead are deliberately subjected to an outcome preference, whether it comes from the substantive law or whether it comes from the intermediate layer of 'principles and goals of procedure' such as proportionality. The rules complained of by Zuckerman have been enacted (the costs rules that Jackson LJ recommended were implemented through primary legislation in LASPO Act, Part II), and have indeed created a distortion in the relative number of claims brought in one or the other pathway.[67]

English civil procedure is in a state of transition, in a situation not dissimilar to that described by Subrin, as a new 'non-trans-substantive era'.

> There are many questions in this developing new procedural era: i) what types of cases need some different procedures; ii) can the case types be determined in advance; iii) should the case be typed by the substantive law involved, the degree of complexity, the stakes involved, the nature of the litigants or their lawyers, or might these and other indicia all be used; iv) what should the procedural differences be, bearing in mind that the general procedural rules will cover most procedural steps unless and until modified; and v) who should make the decisions: legislators, the judiciary, the individual judge, or the litigants?[68]

Subrin identifies only two criticisms: the increase in transaction costs and the politicization of procedure. On the former, which does include satellite litigation, and the rules-shopping that Zuckerman foresaw, Subrin suggests that 'this misses the point' because this type of procedure is already a solution to other 'high transaction' scenarios. With regards to the risk that non-trans-substantive procedure may become too political, with real-world power being able to lobby for favourable changes, his answer is that the political dimension has always existed in the debates on procedure in the USA. This latter fear, however, is not as easily dismissed in the English context. There is no obvious political partisanship in the current makeup

67 'PI claim workload volumes decreased from 158K in the year pre LASPO to 137K at four years post LASPO. This is a reduction of 13 per cent (averaging 5K fewer claims per quarter, or 21K fewer per year). There is a noticeable upward spike in Q1 2013 at 42K claims, probably due to firms rushing to issue claims before the new regulations were introduced': MoJ *Post-implementation review of Part 2 of LASPO Act: initial assessment* (published 28 June 2018, <https://www.gov.uk/government/publications/post-implementation-review-of-part-2-of-laspo-act-initial-assessment> accessed 5 March 2019) 4.

68 Subrin (n 42) 2049.

of the Rules Committees who design the rules and their underlying culture, but if we look to the contributors to the various reviews, it is clear that the professional bodies and other 'stake-holders' are now contributing to reviews of the law in organized lobby groups, some of them with large interests riding on one or the other reform. It is impossible to avoid the fear that the traditional way of writing Rules of court is unprepared for sustained pressure by openly vested interests.

14

Inherent Jurisdiction and the Limits of Civil Procedure

Stuart Sime

Inherent jurisdiction is a characteristic feature of common law legal systems based on the English model. It forms part of procedural law in Scotland, Ireland, Canada, Australia, New Zealand, Cyprus, Singapore, and India, among others. It has sometimes been codified into the legal system, such as the Indian Code of Civil Procedure 1908, s 151, which provides: 'Nothing in this Code shall be deemed to limit or otherwise affect the inherent power of the Court to make such orders as may be necessary for the ends of justice or to prevent abuse of the process of the Court.' In contrast, civil law jurisdictions do not recognise the concept.[1]

Sir Jack IH Jacob in his seminal article on *The Inherent Jurisdiction of the Court* provided the best traditional definition for the inherent jurisdiction as '... the reserve or fund of powers, a residual source of powers, which the court may draw upon as necessary whenever it is just or equitable to do so, and in particular to observe the due process of law, to prevent improper vexation or oppression, to do justice between the parties and to secure a fair trial between them.'[2] These are all laudable aims that everyone would willingly sign up to.

While ensuring justice is achieved and preventing abuse of process are good things, these can and should be achieved through duly enacted procedural rules. Giving judges wide and undefined authority to make new procedural law is far more difficult to defend. It will not be suggested that any existing examples of the application of the inherent jurisdiction should be overturned. However, modern understanding of the rule of law[3] and the role of the courts under the separation of powers[4] both lead to the conclusion that in the twenty-first century judges

[1] JH Merryman and R Perez-Perdomo, *The Civil Law Tradition* (3rd edn, Stanford University Press 2007) 22–25. Particularly in France, the codification of the law in the Code Napoleon 1804 was intended to repeal all prior law in accordance with separation of powers theory, with the intention that only the legislature could make law (ibid at 23 and 28).

[2] Sir Jack IH Jacob 'The Inherent Jurisdiction of the Court' [1970] CLP 23. This definition has been approved in Canada in *Montreal Trust Co v Churchill Forest Industries (Manitoba) Ltd* [1971] 21 DLR 3rd 75 and in New Zealand in *Taylor v Attorney-General* [1975] 2 NZLR 675.

[3] Constitutional Reform Act 2005, s 1, and R Blackburn, *Halsbury's Law of England* (LexisNexis 2014) vol 20, para 6.

[4] *R v Home Secretary, ex p Fire Brigades Union* [1995] 2 AC 513, Lord Mustill at 567: 'It is a feature of the peculiarly British conception of the separation of powers that Parliament, the executive and the courts

Stuart Sime, *Inherent Jurisdiction and the Limits of Civil Procedure* In: *Principles, Procedure, and Justice.* Edited by: Rabeea Assy and Andrew Higgins, Oxford University Press (2020). © The editors and several contributors.
DOI: 10.1093/oso/9780198850410.003.0014

should stop legislating under the guise of exercising ill-defined powers under the inherent jurisdiction. Ongoing codification of civil procedure, combined with the arrangements for promulgating new procedural law following the Civil Procedure Act 1997 and the Constitutional Reform Act 2005, also mean there is little or no room for new procedural law to be generated by the judiciary under the inherent jurisdiction.

Part of the beauty of law is that it sets out clearly the rules that everyone has to follow, so everyone can be taken to know where they stand and what the consequences will be before they take any action. A danger of the current perception of the inherent jurisdiction is that it permits a judge to generate a new rule after the event, with no-one knowing in advance whether this is likely to happen, or what the scope or effect of the new application of the inherent jurisdiction might be. While that might have been acceptable in times past when the law was being formed, that is not the case today when in most common law jurisdictions civil procedure is laid down in mature and comprehensive codes based on statutes, rules of court, and duly authorized practice directions.[5] This, combined with the fact the existence of the inherent jurisdiction in a particular area is often evidenced by little more than a throw-away comment in the middle of a judgment, raises problems with the requirement of the rule of law that the law must be accessible, intelligible, clear, and predictable.[6]

Professor Adrian Zuckerman was the first to suggest the time has come to rein in at least parts of the generative aspects of the inherent jurisdiction. In an editorial[7] Professor Zuckerman closely examined the current statutory framework for the approval of new practice directions following the reforms made by the Constitutional Reform Act 2005. Under this Act the Lord Chancellor ceased being a member of judiciary in order to achieve a greater separation of powers. As part of this reform the power to make and revise practice directions was also put on a modern footing by replacing the former power to do this by substituting a new Civil Procedure Act 1997, s 5.[8] The Court of Appeal has insisted that it continues to be in the public

have each their distinct and largely exclusive domain. Parliament has a largely unchallengeable right to make whatever laws it thinks right. The executive carries on the administration of the country in accordance with the powers conferred on it by law. The courts interpret the laws, and see that they are obeyed.'

[5] Detailed codes of civil procedure can be found in almost all common law jurisdictions. The Australian Capital Territory Civil Procedures Rules 2006, SL2006-29, effective in 2018, extend to 1,372 pages. In the Republic of Trinidad and Tobago, the Consolidated Civil Procedure Rules 2016, which are heavily based on the English Civil Procedure Rules, run to 708 pages, and make extra provision for practice directions to be made by the Chief Justice (r 4.1).

[6] T Bingham, *The Rule of Law* (Penguin 2010) ch 3.

[7] A Zuckerman, 'Rule Making and Precedent under the Civil Procedure Rules 1998: Still an Unsettled Field' [2010] CJQ 1, discussing *Bovale Ltd v Secretary of State for Communities and Local Government* [2009] EWCA Civ 171, [2009] 1 WLR 2274.

[8] Constitutional Reform Act 2005, s 13 and sch 2, para 6. The County Courts Act 1984, s 74A, dealing with practice directions in the County Courts, which had been introduced by the Civil Procedure Act 1997, was repealed at the same time by the Constitutional Reform Act 2005, s 15 and sch 4, para 169.

interest that judges acting in their judicial capacity should be able to provide guidance for litigants, their legal representatives, and other judges who might need to deal with applications that are not be covered by the existing formal rules.[9] While no-one is suggesting that a court does not have the authority and indeed the duty to ensure suitable directions are made for the procedure to be followed in the actual case in hand,[10] laying down procedural requirements that purport to apply generally to all cases of a particular kind is legislating. As pointed out by Professor Zuckerman, just as the separation of powers meant the Lord Chancellor had to cease being a member of the judiciary, after the Constitutional Reform Act 2005 the judiciary had to stop legislating.[11]

Origin and nature of the inherent jurisdiction

Origin of the inherent jurisdiction

Contempt of court, wardship, abuse of process, and rule making are the four traditional areas covered by the court's inherent jurisdiction.[12] All of them can be traced back to before the Judicature Acts, and are well-established concepts. It is possible to trace the High Court's jurisdiction over contempt of court to the twelfth century, when it was known as contemptus curiae.[13] The High Court's wardship[14] jurisdiction is based on its role in acting on behalf of the sovereign as parens patriae.[15] In a widely quoted statement, Lord Blackburn has said that '... from early times (I rather think, though I have not looked at it enough to say, from the earliest times) the court had inherently the right to see that its process was not abused ...'.[16] Regarding the making of rules of court, Professor Zuckerman[17] relies on Samuel Rosenbaum's book on *The Rule-Making Authority in the English Supreme Court* where it is stated:

> Obviously, the methods and proceedings of the King's justices were not, in the beginning, matter for the supervision by Parliament. First by decisions and

[9] *Bovale Ltd v Secretary of State for Communities and Local Government* [2009] EWCA Civ 171, [2009] 1 WLR 2274 [42].

[10] A court has a duty to actively manage each case CPR, r 1.4(1), for which purpose it is given a wide range of case management powers by CPR, Parts 3 and 26–29.

[11] A Zuckerman, *Zuckerman on Civil Procedure* (3rd edn, Sweet & Maxwell 2013) para 2.22.

[12] Jacob (n 2) 25, 26; M Dockray, the author of the other leading article on this subject, 'The Inherent Jurisdiction to Regulate Civil Proceedings' [1997] LQR 120, at 120, 121.

[13] J Fox, *The History of Contempt of Court* (Clarendon Press 1927) p 1; N Lowe and B Sufrin, *Borrie & Lowe The Law of Contempt* (Butterworths 1996) 1.

[14] Wardship is an ancient concept. It pre-dates Magna Carta 1215: chapters 3, 4, and 5 of Magna Carta are devoted to wardship.

[15] Jacob (n 2) 46; *Re R (Infants)* [1967] 1 WLR 818; *Re M and N (Minors) (Wardship: Publication of Information)* [1990] Fam 211.

[16] *Metropolitan Bank v Pooley* (1885) 7 App Cas 210 at 220.

[17] Zuckerman (n 11) para 2.10.

> directions given in particular cases, and later by rules and orders, formulated for general use, the judges of each of the superior courts gradually built up a procedure suited to the character of the issues that came before them at trial. So well-established was this form of authority when Parliament set upon its career as law reformer about the middle of the nineteenth century, that rather than upset a useful and established custom, it clothed the custom with its sanction and elevated it into the dignity of statute law. Such is the character of the Rule Committee as constituted under the Judicature Acts.[18]

What may be more surprising is that the term 'inherent jurisdiction' appears to have been used in relation to contempt of court only from about 1810.[19] Professor Dockray points out that it began to be used in relation to procedural powers, costs, and the control of solicitors in about 1880, and in relation to trusts and children in about 1945.[20] This, together with the relatively recent vintage of many of the authorities on the inherent jurisdiction, point to the conclusion that outside of the four established areas, most of the other miscellaneous instances of the invocation of the inherent jurisdiction post-date the Judicature Acts.

Scope

Master Jacob was aware that his description of the court's inherent jurisdiction could be criticised as justifying the existence of what he described as an amplitude of amorphous powers which might be arbitrary in operation and which were without limit.[21] Part of the problem is that there is no systematic treatise on the full extent of the doctrine. Sir John Pennycuick has commented that it would be impossible to formulate the precise circumstances in which the court has an inherent jurisdiction, and wisely declined the attempt.[22] As mentioned above, its traditional scope covered the court's powers in relation to contempt of court, wardship of children, stays or dismissal for abuse of process, and laying down rules of practice and procedure. Slowly at first, but with increasing acceleration, after 1873 the ambit of the doctrine expanded into a wide and eclectic range of topics. Master Jacob described various examples over sixteen pages,[23] dividing the cases into three main classes: powers to control the court's process;[24] powers to exert control over

[18] S Rosenbaum, *The Rule-Making Authority in the English Supreme Court* (Boston 1917) 4–5.

[19] Dockray (n 12) at 122, citing the Report of the Select Committee of the House of Commons in *Sir Francis Burdett's Case* (1810) 8 Howell's St Tr 14.

[20] ibid at 121.

[21] Jacob (n 2) at 52.

[22] *Moore v Assignment Courier Ltd* [1977] 1 WLR 638.

[23] Without seeking to be comprehensive. Jacob (n 2) 31–46.

[24] Such as striking out, stays, rights of audience, and correcting an accidental slip in a judgment. Most of the examples have subsequently been codified by legislation or rules of court.

persons;[25] and the High Court's jurisdiction to exert control over inferior courts and tribunals.[26]

Professor Dockray noted that inherent jurisdiction concepts had featured in over forty reported cases in 1995.[27] His examples were wide and various, and different from those cited by Master Jacob. Professor Dockray asked rhetorically whether they were examples drawn from a single jurisdiction, or a cocktail of unrelated topics. The 2019 edition of the *White Book* has its own list of illustrations, which is different again.[28] Proliferation has been encouraged by various misconceptions of the doctrine, and in particular by over-reliance on the idea in Master Jacob's definition that the inherent jurisdiction can be resorted to 'whenever' it is just or equitable to do so.

Whenever just or equitable

It will be recalled that Master Jacob's definition of the inherent jurisdiction included the idea that it might be drawn upon as necessary whenever it is just or equitable to do so.[29] Master Jacob's use of the phrase 'just or equitable' initially looks like a reference to a discretion vested in the court to apply these reserve powers,[30] but is more probably a reference to their source as pre-Judicature Acts powers vested in the common law and chancery courts which survived the reforms of 1873.[31]

Professor Dockray exploded the idea that the phrase is to be taken literally, giving the court virtually despotic powers.[32] He pointed to a series of cases where the courts had refused to invent new procedures in purported exercise of

[25] Which included the High Court's wardship jurisdiction; what was originally the inherent jurisdiction to approve compromise agreements involving persons under a legal disability, and the High Court's summary jurisdiction over court officers including solicitors.

[26] Such as the summary contempt of court process to prevent interference with the processes of inferior courts (*R v Parke* [1903] 2 KB 432) and to render assistance to inferior courts, such as by issuing subpoenas (witness summonses) (*R v Judge, ex parte Isle of Ely Justices* [1931] 2 KB 442).

[27] Dockray (n 12) at 120–22. While preparing this chapter the current author found a similar number of cases raising inherent jurisdiction points in 2016–18.

[28] Sir Geoffrey Vos (editor-in-chief), *Civil Procedure* (Sweet & Maxwell 2019) ('the White Book'), vol 2 at para 9A-68.

[29] See Jacob (n 2).

[30] Dockray (n 12), points out that most of the identified inherent powers are exercised as a matter of judicial discretion (at p 121). This is not always the case. A principle that can be traced back to *Alaby v Praetorius* (1888) 20 QBD 764 was to the effect that a person affected by proceedings that were a nullity as opposed to merely irregular could apply to have them set aside ex debito justitiae in the inherent jurisdiction of the court without needing to have recourse to the rules of court that deal with discretionary setting aside orders for irregularity. See the Privy Council appeals from Sierra Leone in *MacFoy v United Africa Co Ltd* [1962] AC 152 (Lord Denning) and from St Vincent and the Grenadines in *Isaacs v Robertson* [1985] AC 97 (Lord Diplock). This particular application of the court's inherent jurisdiction was more recently rejected by the English Court of Appeal in *Raja v Van Hoogstraten (No 9)* [2008] EWCA Civ 1444, [2009] 1 WLR 1143 [78], [84].

[31] Judicature Act 1873 and Judicature Act 1875. Also known as the Supreme Court of Judicature Acts.

[32] Dockray (n 12) at 128–31.

the inherent jurisdiction[33] on topics such as security for costs, summary judgment, and interim payments. To take one example, in *Moore v Assignment Courier Ltd*[34] the Court of Appeal was confronted with a case where the defendant was not paying either rent or mesne profits although it was not in dispute that it was in continuing occupation of the property. There was a dispute over whether the lease was in continuing existence. Something was certainly payable for that occupation, but the dispute meant it was impossible to enter judgment until trial, and impossible to say at the interim stage whether the monies due were rent or mesne profits. There was legislation permitting orders for interim payments,[35] but rules made at that time were restricted to personal injuries claims.[36] Although invited to order an interim payment under the court's inherent jurisdiction, Sir John Pennycuick said the provisions that had been made at that time relating to interim payments meant '… the court has no general inherent jurisdiction to make interim payment orders whenever it thinks that it would be fair to do so.'

Juridical basis of the inherent jurisdiction

There are two competing, or possibly complementary, theories on the juridical basis of the inherent jurisdiction. These are:

(a) That the inherent jurisdiction stems from residuary powers that were vested in the High Court on the fusing of the common law and equity courts by the Judicature Acts ('the vesting theory'); and
(b) That the court needs to have inherent jurisdiction to control its own procedures and to prevent its process being abused ('the innate nature' of the court theory).

Both theories are supported by impressive authority. Both can be found in Master Jacob's article.[37] One consequence of the vesting theory is that it is the High Court alone that has inherent jurisdiction, because it is the High Court that inherited the jurisdiction of the pre-Judicature Act courts. Other courts, such as the County Court and the Court of Appeal, being creatures of statute, on this theory have no inherent jurisdiction.

In *Bremer Vulkan Schiffbau und Maschinenfabrik v South India Shipping Corporation Ltd* [1981] AC 909 Lord Diplock explained that the High Court has:

[33] ibid at 130.
[34] *Moore v Assignment Courier Ltd* [1977] 1 WLR 638.
[35] At that time, the Administration of Justice Act 1969, s 20. Now the Senior Courts Act 1981, s 32.
[36] At that time, RSC Ord 29, r 9. The present rules in CPR, rr 25.6–25.9 apply widely to money claims, with specific provision being made for claims in respect of use and occupation of land by r 25.7(1)(d).
[37] The vesting theory can be found in Jacob (n 2) 26, and the innate nature theory at 27.

> ... a general power to control its own procedure so as to prevent its being used to achieve injustice. Such a power is inherent in its constitution as a court of justice ... it would stultify the constitutional role of the High Court as a court of justice if it were not armed with power to prevent its process being misused in such a way as to diminish its capability of arriving at a just decision of the dispute.[38]

It will be noticed that Lord Diplock's rationale could apply to any court, given that all courts are there to dispense justice, and so supports the innate nature theory. At the same time the quotation only attaches this inherent power to the High Court, which would be consistent with the vesting theory. Further support for the innate nature theory can be found in Lord Morris's comment in *DPP v Connelly*[39] that: 'There can be no doubt that a court which is endowed with a particular jurisdiction has powers which are necessary to enable it to act effectively within such jurisdiction. I would regard them as powers which are inherent in its jurisdiction. A court must enjoy such powers in order to enforce its rules of practice and to suppress any abuses of process and to defeat any attempted thwarting of its process.' Lord Morris did not say that a court's inherent powers are derived from its inherent jurisdiction (which would be consistent with the vesting theory). Instead he used a slightly different phrase, that these powers are 'inherent in its jurisdiction', and so can apply to any court.

A lack of clarity at this point is the source of most of the confusion often found in discussions of the inherent jurisdiction. The better view is that the vesting theory means that only the High Court (and its equivalent in other jurisdictions) has 'inherent jurisdiction' properly so called. At the same time, the innate nature theory means that all courts of justice have lower level 'inherent powers' to prevent their procedures being abused. Further confusion is caused by the lax use of terminology, with the key concepts being inherent jurisdiction, general jurisdiction, inherent powers, judicial powers, administrative powers, and residual jurisdiction, which we will consider next.

Inherent jurisdiction and general jurisdiction

Almost the first point made in his article by Master Jacob was that the inherent jurisdiction was not to be confused with the High Court's general jurisdiction.[40] Its general jurisdiction is based on the Judicature Act 1873, which created the English

[38] *Bremer Vulkan Schiffbau und Maschinenfabrik v South India Shipping Corporation Ltd* [1981] AC 909 at 977.

[39] [1964] AC 1254 at 1301.

[40] Jacob (n 2) 23.

High Court as a superior court of record and vested it with all the jurisdiction previously exercised by the various common law and equity courts it replaced.[41] This general jurisdiction is now set out in almost identical terms in the Senior Courts Act 1981, s 19(1), (2). Over time the High Court's jurisdiction has been adjusted by legislation, as recognized by s 19(2). As a superior court of record, subject to any legislative restrictions, it enjoys an unrestricted and unlimited jurisdiction over all substantive law disputes.[42] Equivalent courts in other common law jurisdictions are also regarded as courts of unlimited jurisdiction.[43]

In relation to the inherent jurisdiction, s 19(2)(b) is the source of the vesting theory. Vested in the High Court is all the jurisdiction that was exercised by it (and previously, the pre-Judicature Acts superior courts) immediately before its commencement. There is an even more explicit reference in the Solicitors Act 1974, s 50(2) to the pre-Judicature Act courts in relation to the inherent jurisdiction over solicitors. This provides: 'Subject to the provisions of this Act, the High Court, the Crown Court and the Court of Appeal respectively, or any division or judge of those courts, may exercise the same jurisdiction in respect of solicitors as any one of the superior courts of law or equity from which the Senior Courts were constituted might have exercised immediately before the passing of the Supreme Court of Judicature Act 1873 in respect of any solicitor, attorney or proctor admitted to practise there.'

For Master Jacob, two main points emerge from this. First, the inherent jurisdiction is a part of the general jurisdiction, but is not the same as the general jurisdiction. Secondly, the inherent jurisdiction is restricted to questions of practice and procedure rather than substantive law.[44] There is no equivalent to s 19(2)(b) for any of the other courts in England and Wales. The result is that under the vesting theory it is only the High Court that has inherent jurisdiction.

Inherent jurisdiction and inherent powers

As Lord Bridge has said, defining the term 'jurisdiction' is difficult, because it has many shades of meaning in different contexts, with new meanings being acquired as the law develops.[45] A venerable working test is to examine three questions: in what actions does the court have jurisdiction; to what places is that jurisdiction confined; and to what persons does the jurisdiction extend?[46] In Singapore, jurisdiction has been defined as meaning the court's authority to hear and determine a

[41] Judicature Act 1873, s 16 as discussed in *Re Mill's Estate* (1886) 34 Ch D 24.
[42] *Peacock v Bell and Kendall* (1667) 1 Wm Saund 73.
[43] *Isaacs v Robertson* [1985] AC 97 (Lord Diplock).
[44] Jacob (n 2) 24.
[45] *Re McC (A Minor)* [1985] 1 AC 528 at 536.
[46] *Marshalsea Case* (1612) 10 Co Rep 68.

dispute brought before it.[47] For Professor Dockray, at its root jurisdiction means power, or the source of a court's powers.[48]

This similarity in meaning between jurisdiction and power has resulted in the terms being used almost interchangeably in this context. For example, adjacent headings in Master Jacob's article are 'Powers of the court under the inherent *jurisdiction*' and 'Inherent *powers* exercisable by summary process'.[49] In Singapore it has been held that the term inherent jurisdiction is a misnomer, with a better expression being simply that a court has certain inherent powers.[50] This view was expressed by the Singapore Court of Appeal, whose jurisdiction is defined by statute, so it is perfectly understandable that it would prefer the innate nature theory, which would enable it to exercise inherent powers. Under the vesting theory a court that is the creature of statute has no inherent jurisdiction.

In an interesting article[51] Chen Siyuan has drawn a distinction between a court's inherent power to control its own proceedings, and the inherent jurisdiction. Under the innate nature theory all courts will also have incidental case management powers to ensure the fair and efficient progress of proceedings within the court's express substantive jurisdiction. These could be described as inherent powers. At the extreme, adopting Lord Morris's approach from *DPP v Connelly*, all courts on this theory possess an inherent power to strike out for abuse of process.

Master Jacob divided inherent powers to control the court's process into administrative powers and judicial powers.[52] Administrative powers include the power to make rules of court. Judicial powers include what is now striking out for abuse of process. This distinction was recognised by the Privy Council,[53] where Lord Denning said: 'Some of the powers of the Chief Justice are clearly judicial powers, as when he sits in court to decide civil and criminal cases. Others are clearly administrative powers, as when he directs the times at which offices of the court shall be open, or appoints notaries public, or makes rules of court.' It is easy to see how any court of justice should be regarded as possessing everyday administrative powers of some of the kinds referred to by the Privy Council.

In contrast, inherent jurisdiction goes further than this, and refers to the court's authority to hear certain disputes or to grant certain remedies (interim or final) beyond those in the express statutory provisions defining the court's jurisdiction. The example given by Chen Siyuan is the inherent authority to reopen a dispute.[54]

47 *Muhd Munir v Noor Hidah* [1990] 2 SLR(R) 348 [19].
48 Dockray (n 12) 124.
49 Jacob (n 2) 28 and 29.
50 *Re Nalpon Zero Geraldo Mario* [2013] SGCA 28. Similar views have been expressed by Professor Pinsler, for example in J Pinsler 'The Inherent Powers of the Court' [1997] SJLS 1, and in cases such as *Wee Soon Kim Anthony v Law Society of Singapore* [2001] 2 SLR(R) 821.
51 C Siyuan, 'Is the Invocation of Inherent Jurisdiction the same as the exercise of Inherent Powers? *Re Nalpon Zero Geraldo Mario*' [2013] IJE&P 367.
52 Jacob (n 2) 33.
53 *Attorney-General of the Gambia v N'Jie* [1961] AC 617 at 630.
54 [2013] IJE&P 367 at 373. In England, see *Taylor v Lawrence* [2003] QB 528.

Other examples would be the first development of new forms of orders, such as *Norwich Pharmacal* orders,[55] freezing injunctions,[56] *Anton Piller* orders,[57] *Bankers Trust* orders,[58] and protective costs orders.[59] Inherent jurisdiction in this wider sense would only be available under the vesting theory. In England, that would mean that such jurisdiction is only exercisable by the High Court.

A similar distinction was identified in *Taylor v Lawrence*.[60] The way it was put by Lord Woolf CJ is that there is a distinction between the question whether a court has jurisdiction, and how it exercises the jurisdiction which it undoubtedly has. So, an appeal court cannot change the categories of appeals that it has jurisdiction to consider, but it has the power to lay down or change the procedures it will adopt in hearing those appeals. In this passage Lord Woolf CJ expressly refers to Master Jacob's article, which describes procedure making powers as part of the court's inherent jurisdiction (as opposed to a mere power), explaining that the term 'inherent jurisdiction' is used in a number of different senses.

[55] *Norwich Pharmacal Co v Commissioners of Customs and Excise* [1974] AC 133. This is an order typically for disclosure of the name and address of a potential defendant from someone who through no fault of their own has become mixed up in some wrongdoing in a way that facilitates the commission of the wrongdoing. These orders were first developed in *Norwich Pharmacal*, but based on the long forgotten chancery bill of discovery. They look like procedural orders, and so arguably are based on the High Court's inherent jurisdiction. Being based on the old chancery bill of discovery, another analysis is that they are part of the High Court's general jurisdiction. They are regarded as fitting within the scheme for disclosure laid down by the CPR by coming within r 31.18, which simply says other rules 'do not limit any other power the court may have to order ... disclosure against a person who is not a party to proceedings'.

[56] *Mareva Compania Naviera SA v International Bulkcarriers SA* [1980] 1 All ER 213. Lord Denning MR, who presided in the case in the Court of Appeal, described this case in *The Due Process of Law* (Butterworths 1980) at 134 as '... the greatest piece of judicial law reform in my time ...'. While initially thought of as an instance of the use of the inherent jurisdiction, the current consensus is that the court was simply making imaginative use of its existing statutory jurisdiction under what is now the Senior Courts Act 1981, s 37.

[57] *Anton Piller KG v Manufacturing Processes Ltd* [1976] Ch 55. Search orders are really a bundle of interim orders, but they have been put together to form a package that has even more invasive effects than a freezing injunction. To allay lingering concerns of judicial overstretch, statutory authority for this form of order is now provided by the Civil Procedure Act 1997, s 7.

[58] *Bankers Trust Co v Shapira* [1980] 1 WLR 1274. These are orders addressed to a bank, which is not a party to the case, to disclose details of the state of a customer's bank accounts and related relief. Typically used in tracing claims.

[59] *R (Buglife—The Invertebrate Conservation Trust) v Thurrock Thames Gateway Development Corporation* [2008] EWCA Civ 1209, [2009] 1 Costs LR 80.

[60] [2003] QB 528 [17]. The result in *Lawrence v Taylor* put reopening appeals in the category of powers rather than as an example of jurisdiction as suggested by Chen Siyuan. That reopening an appeal is only a power is supported by it being codified merely by rules (CPR, r 52.30 and PD 52A, paras 7.1–7.4) and the reasoning in the case itself, which included the Court of Appeal having no inherent jurisdiction. Support for reopening appeals being jurisdictional comes from *Patel v Mussa* [2015] EWCA Civ 434, [2015] 1 WLR 4788 and the exclusion of the County Court by r 52.30(3) on the basis the County Court has no inherent jurisdiction.

Residual jurisdiction

It will be recalled that Master Jacob's definition of the inherent jurisdiction referred to 'residual' powers. Starting from Lord Diplock's speech in *Bremer Vulkan Schiffbau und Maschinenfabrik v South India Shipping Corporation Ltd*,[61] Lord Woolf CJ in *Taylor v Lawrence*[62] argued that an appellate court has implicit or implied powers or jurisdiction to do what needs to be done to maintain its character as a court of justice.[63] Then, borrowing words from Master Jacob's definition, Lord Woolf CJ held that the Court of Appeal has a 'residual jurisdiction', outside the provisions of the CPR, to reopen an appeal in exceptional circumstances to avoid real injustice.[64]

This part of the judgment ended with the comment that in due course the Civil Procedure Rules Committee might wish to consider whether rules or a practice direction setting out the procedure should be introduced.[65] This has duly happened.[66] Rather like the wording of the Senior Courts Act 1981, s 49(3), the wording of the new provisions does not take the form of purporting to confer jurisdiction to reopen appeals, but rather recognizes the existing jurisdiction to do so by the Court of Appeal and the High Court.[67] It also says the rule does not apply to appeals to the County Court.[68]

Being a creature of statute, it was not open to the Court of Appeal on the vesting theory in *Taylor v Lawrence* to hold that it had inherent jurisdiction to reopen an appeal. On the innate nature theory it could have held it had an inherent power to do so, but that would have applied also to the County Court. Instead, it found it had a hybrid 'residual jurisdiction' to reopen an appeal, available in the Court of Appeal, but not in the County Court. This is stretching the Senior Courts Act 1981, the rule of law, and the separation of powers beyond breaking point.

One of the dangers of judicial law making as happened in *Taylor v Lawrence* is that it can quickly be applied in other situations, and even subvert primary legislation. There is a public interest in the finality of litigation, which is infringed if there are endless appeals combined with reopening of appeals after they are apparently completed. Reopening appeals was quickly extended to appeals to the High Court,[69] and the 'residual jurisdiction' to appeals in arbitration cases.

[61] [1981] AC 909 at 977.

[62] [2003] QB 528 [16].

[63] ibid [50]–[53].

[64] ibid [54].

[65] ibid [57].

[66] CPR, r 52.30 and PD 52A paras 7.1–7.4.

[67] CPR, r 52.30(1) provides negatively that; 'The Court of Appeal or the High Court will not reopen a final determination of any appeal unless . . .' three conditions are satisfied.

[68] CPR, r 52.30(3). The explanation is that the County Court has no inherent jurisdiction: *Patel v Mussa* [2015] EWCA Civ 434, [2015] 1 WLR 4788.

[69] *Seray-Wurie v Hackney London Borough Council* [2002] EWCA Civ 909, [2003] 1 WLR 257.

Regarding arbitration cases, convention obligations,[70] combined with the statutory general principle that the court should not intervene in arbitrations except as provided by the Arbitration Act 1996,[71] mean there are severe restrictions on judicial challenges to arbitral awards. This is augmented by provisions providing restrictions on any appeals from court decisions on such challenges.[72] Despite these restrictions, a number of cases have applied 'residual jurisdiction' concepts to such appeals, allowing reviews of court decisions that under the legislation should have been final.[73] While there may be some sympathy for allowing a further review in cases where there has been misconduct or unfairness,[74] there are wider policy issues at stake. Parties who have agreed to arbitrate have done so in the expectation there would be no more than light supervision by the court,[75] and an underlying policy of international arbitration is that the courts should uphold arbitral awards, and not subject them to repeated judicial scrutiny. Perhaps even more important is the primacy of Parliament. It is not for the courts to invent review mechanisms contrary to the legislative purpose of primary legislation.

Limits on inherent jurisdiction

Which courts have inherent jurisdiction?

The traditional distinction is between courts of unlimited jurisdiction, and courts that are commonly described as being the creatures of statute. In the first category is the English High Court, given it inherited the former jurisdiction of the pre-Judicature Act courts. Courts in this category possess a full inherent jurisdiction. In the second category are courts whose jurisdiction is conferred by statute. As creatures of statute, such courts on the vesting theory do not possess any inherent jurisdiction.

Master Jacob opened his article by stating that the High Court in England exercises what has been termed its inherent jurisdiction. Most of the discussion in the following thirty pages focussed on how the inherent jurisdiction applies in the High Court, with two paragraphs being devoted to the inherent jurisdiction of the inferior courts.[76] Although the article does refer to *DPP v Connelly* and the innate nature theory, the dominant premise is that under the vesting theory it is the High Court that is the guardian of the inherent jurisdiction.

70 New York Convention 1958, Art V.
71 Arbitration Act 1996, s 1(c).
72 See the Arbitration Act 1996, ss 67(4), 68(4), and 69(8).
73 *North Range Shipping Ltd v Seatrans Shipping Corporation* [2002] EWCA Civ 405, [2002] 1 WLR 2397 and subsequent cases.
74 Broadly, the basis on which this jurisdiction is exercised.
75 *Premium Nafta Products Ltd v Fili Shipping Co Ltd* [2007] UKHL 40, [2007] Bus LR 1719.
76 Jacob (n 2) 49 and 50.

The English County Court in what is recognizably its present form was established by the County Courts Act 1846,[77] and so is in the second category. Accordingly, the underlying problem with the County Court having any inherent jurisdiction is that it is the creature of statute.[78] Rather than having full inherent jurisdiction, Master Jacob ascribed only two areas of inherent jurisdiction to the County Court. One was the limited contempt of court jurisdiction of the County Court, and the other was in relation to abuse of process.

These two areas were justified by statute. Contempt of court has over the years been codified. At the time Master Jacob was writing this was by provisions in the County Courts Act 1959, and now by the Contempt of Court Act 1981. Section 14(4A) of the 1981 Act even provides that for this purpose the County Court shall be treated as a superior court and not as an inferior court. There is no need to engage any inherent jurisdiction for contempt of court powers expressly conferred by statute.

The second half of the discussion was on the County Court's power to stay or dismiss a claim for abuse of process. A statutory justification was also given for this, based on what is now the County Courts Act 1984, s 76.[79] Again, this sidesteps any direct problem with the County Court having no inherent jurisdiction. Section 76 provides that the general principles of practice of the High Court may be adopted and applied to proceedings in the County Court. Reliance was placed on *Williamson v Rider*[80] where Danckwerts LJ adopted what appeared to be common ground between the parties that what is now s 76 '... enables the County Court to exercise the inherent jurisdiction of the court to dispose of, for instance, actions which are an abuse of the process of the court.' In the event this was obiter, because the actual decision was that the County Court judge had no jurisdiction to make an order striking out the defence, because in the circumstances of the case the High Court would not have struck it out.

The argument based on s 76 cannot be right, because if it was there would be no or little restriction against applying all aspects of the inherent jurisdiction in the County Court, and this has never been the position. A better justification for the County Court possessing a power to deal with abuse of process before this was expressly incorporated into the applicable rules of court is under the innate nature theory. Just like the High Court, it is arguable that the County Court needs a power to dismiss or strike out proceedings which are an abuse of process to prevent its procedures being subverted.[81]

[77] Now the County Courts Act 1984, as amended. Post-1984 amendments include the reconstitution of the various local county courts into a unified national County Court by the Crime and Courts Act 2013, s 17.

[78] *Salekipour v Parmar* [2017] EWCA Civ 2141, [2018] QB 833 [70].

[79] At the time the equivalent provision was the County Courts Act 1959, s 103.

[80] [1962] 2 All ER 268 at 271.

[81] Support for this approach can be found in *R v Norwich Crown Court, ex parte Belsham* [1992] 1 WLR 54.

However, even this cannot be supported by *Williamson v Rider*, which is in fact typical of the dominant view that the County Court has no free-standing inherent jurisdiction. It is plain from the judgments in the Court of Appeal that the order by the County Court judge striking out the defence would have been upheld if that was allowed by the rules. There is a detailed analysis of the then current County Court Rules 1936,[82] but the conclusion was reached that there was no rule allowing a straight striking out for breach. All that was allowed under the rules was striking out following an 'unless order'.[83] Rather than opening up a wide-ranging use of the inherent powers in the County Court based on the innate nature theory, the case is an example of the vesting theory.

Perhaps the most controversial decision in relation to the inherent jurisdiction and the County Court is *Langley v North West Water Authority*.[84] A local practice direction had been issued by Liverpool County Court laying down requirements to be followed by both sides in personal injury claims in the court. A wasted costs order was made against the claimant's solicitor for failing to comply with the practice direction. At the time, the County Court Rules 1981, Ord 50, r 1, allowed practice directions to be made by the Lord Chancellor. The Court of Appeal dismissed an argument that the local practice direction had no effect, having been made only by the local judges. Without citing any authority, Lord Donaldson MR[85] simply said that although there was no statutory authority for making local practice directions, none was needed because every court has inherent jurisdiction to regulate its own procedures, save in so far as any such direction is inconsistent with statute law or statutory rules of court.

Professor Dockray regarded this case as part of the evidence that all courts have inherent power to regulate their own procedure under the innate nature theory, and that the authorities illustrating aspects of this were too numerous and consistent to ignore.[86] The better view is that it was an unprincipled departure from 120 years' understanding about the position of the County Court and the limits of the inherent jurisdiction. It caused a great deal of consternation. On its facts there seemed to be every reason to believe the lawyer directly involved, being from a firm in Liverpool specializing in personal injury claims, was well aware of the local practice direction. However, there were about 240 County Courts across the country at the time, and many practitioners dealt with cases all over the country. It was before the internet made communication easy. Lawyers litigating cases outside their local area were constantly worried they might be infringing unknown local practice directions. At a national level there was concern that different courts

[82] Which did not have an equivalent to the current CPR, r 3.4(2)(c), on striking out for breach of the rules, practice directions, or court orders.
[83] S Sime and D French (eds), *Blackstone's Civil Practice 2019* (OUP 2019) para 48.7.
[84] [1991] 1 WLR 697.
[85] With whom Woolf and Mann LJJ agreed.
[86] Dockray (n 12) 125–26.

would be making inconsistent practice directions, with different procedures being imposed in different parts of the country. The fear of local practice directions was one of the motivating forces behind the modern reform of the statutory provisions on the authorization of the rules of procedure, which will be considered below.

Given that the High Court is able to exercise an inherent jurisdiction by virtue of the Senior Courts Act 1981, s 19(2)(b), it may seem surprising that the same does not apply to the Court of Appeal. Like the High Court, the Court of Appeal is a superior court of record.[87] However, like the County Court it is a creature of statute, having been originally created by the Judicature Act 1873, and unlike the High Court, there is no equivalent of s 19(2)(b) in s 15, the provision conferring jurisdiction on the Court of Appeal.

Master Jacob relied on *Aviagents v Balstravest Investments Ltd*[88] for the proposition that the Court of Appeal exercises an inherent jurisdiction.[89] This is no longer sustainable. *Taylor v Lawrence*[90] recognized that its creation by statute meant the Court of Appeal has no inherent jurisdiction. This is reinforced by the fact that the Court of Appeal was established to exercise an appellate rather than an originating jurisdiction.[91]

Aviagents v Balstravest Investments Ltd was an appeal brought to the Court of Appeal from a decision of a County Court judge in a commercial rent valuation case on a question of fact. The relevant legislation at the time[92] only permitted appeals on a point of law. It was clear there was no jurisdiction to hear the appeal. The question was what form of order to make. Relying on a decision of the Divisional Court,[93] which of course does have inherent jurisdiction being part of the High Court, the court decided the Court of Appeal had an inherent power to strike out the notice of appeal. If the court meant 'inherent power' in the sense used above there is no conflict. However, Master Jacob relied on the case as an example of the use of the inherent jurisdiction. No reference was made in the case to what is now the Senior Courts Act 1981, s 49(3), which, as seen above, preserves what is described as the Court of Appeal's power to stay proceedings as it thinks fit. If the *White Book*'s interpretation of s 49(3) is right,[94] there are various possible conclusions:

(a) That s 49(3) recognizes and endorses the extension of the inherent jurisdiction (perhaps in full, but at least regarding stays and in relation to the inherent jurisdiction to discipline solicitors)[95] to the Court of Appeal.

[87] Senior Courts Act 1981, s 15(1).
[88] [1966] 1 WLR 150.
[89] Jacob (n 2) 23.
[90] [2003] QB 528.
[91] Lord Woolf CJ at [50].
[92] County Courts Act 1959, s 108.
[93] *Hives v Dawson* (1927) 138 LT 238.
[94] See n 28.
[95] By virtue of the Solicitors Act 1974, s 50(2), and the effect of *Harrison v Tew* [1990] 2 AC 523.

(b) That s 49(3) mentions the Court of Appeal in error, because it has no inherent jurisdiction to stay its own proceedings, being a creature of statute.

An alternative conclusion is that s 49(3) recognizes that the Court of Appeal has an inherent power to stay (and hence strike out or dismiss) any case where the court thinks fit. Being a power rather than a question of jurisdiction is consistent with the statutory foundation of the Court of Appeal. Today, *Aviagents v Balstravest Investments Ltd* is of no more than historical interest, because the English Court of Appeal now has an express power to strike out an appeal notice under CPR, r 52.18. What it has not done is to give birth to a free-ranging inherent jurisdiction vested in the Court of Appeal.

The United Kingdom Supreme Court and the European Union Court of Justice are in a similar situation to the Court of Appeal, and have no inherent jurisdiction. The Supreme Court was created by statute.[96] The European Union Court of Justice must act within the limits of the powers conferred upon it by the relevant Treaties.[97] There is no vesting provision giving either court any inherent jurisdiction. These courts might have inherent powers,[98] and less convincingly, residual jurisdiction.[99] While this may be the theory, in practice there appears to be a measure of gap-filling even in continental legal systems.[100]

The outcome applying the traditional view is what appears to be the illogical one that the only court in England and Wales with full inherent jurisdiction is the High Court. This is because it is the successor to the pre-Judicature Act courts (the vesting theory). This court sits in the middle of the court hierarchy, which is not where this enhanced jurisdiction would be placed in a logical system.

Codification

A recurrent theme in modern times is that once a particular application of the inherent jurisdiction becomes established, more often than not it will be incorporated into the civil code by the promulgation of rules of court or even by statute. Where the particular topic can be described as the exercise of an inherent jurisdiction,[101] codification is typically by primary legislation with procedural rules set out in rules of court. For example, in England and Wales primary legislation on contempt of court can be found in the Contempt of Court Act 1981, with procedural rules laid down in CPR, Part 81 and PD 81. Wardship remains largely uncodified,

[96] Constitutional Reform Act 2005.
[97] Known in civil law jurisdictions as competence d'attribution.
[98] See A Arnull, 'Does the Court of Justice have Inherent Jurisdiction' (1990) 27 CLR 683.
[99] These concepts are discussed above.
[100] See n 98.
[101] The distinction between inherent jurisdiction and inherent powers is considered below.

but there are statutory restrictions on the use of the wardship jurisdiction in the Children Act 1989, s 100. Relevant rules are to be found in PD 12D supporting the Family Proceedings Rules, which have the title 'Inherent Jurisdiction (Including Wardship) Proceedings'. Rule promulgation powers also come into this category, with the current legislation being found in the Civil Procedure Act 1997. We will consider the basis for generating new procedural rules and practice directions in more detail below.

In contrast, situations which may be regarded as merely the exercise of an inherent power may be codified simply by implementing changes to the rules of court without primary legislation. An example is the procedure on reopening appeals.[102] Abuse of process might be thought to be a typical example in this category, but it too has been codified in part by legislation in what is now the Senior Courts Act 1981, s 49(3), and in part by rules of court. This may not be obvious from a cursory look at s 49(3), which provides that; 'Nothing in this Act shall affect the power of the Court of Appeal or the High Court to stay any proceedings before it, where it thinks fit to do so . . .'. This wording does not in terms confer jurisdiction on the Court of Appeal and High Court to stay proceedings, but instead preserves and gives statutory recognition to the existing inherent power to do so.[103] Originally, a court exercising its inherent power to deal with an abuse of process would stay the proceedings. A distinction was drawn between absolute and conditional stays, and in this context it was an absolute stay that was imposed. The meaning has changed over time, and nowadays a 'stay' imposes a temporary halt on proceedings, which may be continued if the stay is lifted.[104] Today, s 49(3) continues to be the primary legislation codifying this aspect of the court's inherent powers, but it is implemented by using the striking out power now to be found in CPR, r 3.4(2)(b), which expressly includes abuse of the court's process as one of the grounds for striking out.

Codification and rule making powers

Starting with the Law Terms Act 1830,[105] and chronicled by Professor Jolowicz,[106] Parliament has taken an increasing role in the promulgation of rules of court in England and Wales. The current position is governed by the Civil Procedure Act

[102] CPR, r 52.30 and PD 52A paras 7.1–7.4.

[103] White Book (n 28) Vol 2 at para 9A-176.

[104] CPR Glossary. The modern approach is to confine the use of orders for stays to temporary halts in proceedings, and to make an order to strike out or to dismiss for a permanent end to proceedings. See *Rofa Sport Management AG v DHL International (UK) Ltd* [1989] 1 WLR 902. Various other statutes, such as the Civil Jurisdiction and Judgments Act 1982, the Insolvency Act 1986, and the Arbitration Act 1996 confer the courts with powers to impose stays, but these are often intended to be absolute stays.

[105] 1 wm 4, c 70, s 11.

[106] JA Jolowicz, 'Practice Directions and the Civil Procedure Rules' [2000] CLJ 53.

1997 as amended by the Constitutional Reform Act 2005, and has been carefully analysed by Professor Zuckerman.[107] Today, rules of court governing the practice and procedure in the English civil courts are made by the Civil Procedure Rule Committee.[108] These rules are made by statutory instrument[109] with a view to ensuring the civil justice system is accessible, fair, and efficient,[110] and are intended to be both simple and simply expressed.[111] An advisory body known as the Civil Justice Council was established under s 6 with duties among other things to keep the civil justice system under review and to refer proposals for changes to the Lord Chancellor and the Civil Procedure Rule Committee. By these means there is no longer any inherent jurisdiction vested in the judges to make actual civil procedure rules.

Current problems revolve around practice directions, less formal practice notes (by whatever name they may be called), and court guides. Prior to the commencement of the CPR judges, particularly the Heads of Division, but from time to time any judge, would issue a practice direction, practice statement, practice note, or other document[112] laying down procedural rules to be followed by all future cases in defined circumstances or in particular types of case. There were about 750 of these published in the All England Reports in the period between 1936 and 1999. In theory this was justified legally as being part of the court's inherent power to regulate its own procedures, and pragmatically as being a swift and efficient way of making beneficial changes to the way litigation was conducted. Most of them were swept away when the CPR came into force in 1999.

With the introduction of the CPR the broad scheme is that the various areas of civil procedure each has a designated Part in the CPR, usually with one of more practice directions issued by the Ministry of Justice. Up to date versions of these practice directions are made available on the Ministry of Justice website adjacent to the text of the relevant Part of the CPR. Technically the practice directions are made under the authority of the Civil Procedure Act 1997, s 5. The original iteration of s 5 proved to be somewhat obscure.[113] The post-2005 version of s 5 provides for two methods of making practice directions. Under s 5(1) they may be made by the Lord Chief Justice (or nominee) with the agreement of the Lord Chancellor, and under s 5(2) they may be made with the approval of both the Lord Chancellor and the Lord Chief Justice. There are slight modifications for practice directions consisting of guidance about the application or interpretation of the law, the making of judicial decisions, and the criteria for

[107] Zuckerman (n 7), looking at the ramifications of *Bovale Ltd v Secretary of State for Communities and Local Government* [2009] EWCA Civ 171, [2009] 1 WLR 2274.

[108] Civil Procedure Act 1997, ss 1(1) and 2(1).

[109] Section 3(1).

[110] Section 1(3).

[111] Section 2(7).

[112] In *Langley v North West Water Authority* [1991] 1 WLR 697 the practice direction was called 'an Explanatory Memorandum'.

[113] As discussed by Hale LJ in *Re C (Legal Aid: Preparation of Bill of Costs)* [2001] 1 FLR 602.

allocating judges to cases, all of which can be made without the approval of the Lord Chancellor.[114]

Changes to the Ministry of Justice practice directions have been made by periodic 'Updates', which now exceed 100. Since the Constitutional Reform Act 2005 came into force each Update has been signed off on behalf of the Lord Chief Justice and the Lord Chancellor. Relatively recently expressed ideas that these practice directions are made by the Heads of Division, and that they are made under the court's inherent jurisdiction,[115] are now consigned to history.

Bovale Ltd v Secretary of State for Communities and Local Government[116] is the most important recent decision on the authority to make practice directions. The actual decision was that Collins J did not have the power to make the practice direction under consideration in the case. However, the core idea as identified by Professor Zuckerman is at [39] to [41]. Under the Civil Procedure Act 1997, s 9(1), a practice direction is defined as meaning directions as to the practice and procedure within any court within the scope of the CPR. The majority agreed that at first sight a judgment in an individual case that includes directions of general application falls into this definition on a literal interpretation.[117] They could not accept that obtaining the approval of the Lord Chancellor (who is no longer a member of the judiciary) and the Lord Chief Justice before delivering such a judgment is what Parliament intended. Doing so would also interfere with the independence of the judiciary.[118] Consequently, the majority reasoned that Parliament simply did not intend to include judgments. Judges giving directions in individual judgments would, however, only be appropriate in 'gap' cases.[119]

With respect, Professor Zuckerman has to be right when he says the trouble with this reasoning is that it can equally point in the other direction.[120] While a judge is perfectly entitled to make directions in a case in a new area, the judge's role is to deal with that case, and that case alone. As soon as a judge purports to make directions that apply generally they have switched roles to legislating. After the Constitutional Reform Act 2005 it is plain that this is something a judge is not authorized to do. Rule making is for the legislature. The separation of powers applies to the judiciary as much as to other organs of government.

It is suggested that the right way for dealing with 'gap' cases is to use the structures set up by the Civil Procedure Act 1997. This should mean that it is for the

[114] Civil Procedure Act 1997, s 5(5) and (6). In relation to allocating judges, the Lord Chancellor should be consulted (s 5(6)(a)).

[115] Both of these ideas feature in *Bovale Ltd v Secretary of State for Communities and Local Government* [2009] EWCA Civ 171, [2009] 1 WLR 2274, eg at [28], but they are no longer the position.

[116] [2009] EWCA Civ 171, [2009] 1 WLR 2274.

[117] As was the view of Stanley Burnton LJ, who delivered a minority judgment.

[118] An important aspect of the separation of powers.

[119] The discussion in *Bovale* at [38] identified reopening appeal decisions following the decision in *Taylor v Lawrence* [2003] QB 528 and protective costs orders following *R (Buglife—The Invertebrate Conservation Trust) v Thurrock Thames Gateway Development Corporation* [2008] EWCA Civ 1209, [2009] 1 Costs LR 80 as examples of 'gap' cases.

[120] Zuckerman (n 7) 8.

Civil Justice Council to identify such areas as part of its review obligation, and to make proposals to the Civil Procedure Rule Committee.[121] Instead, the current position is that the Civil Procedure Rule Committee has announced the setting up of a new sub-committee to review possible gaps in the CPR. It is suggested it would be far better to use the system provided by the primary legislation.

Interface between inherent jurisdiction and Rules of Court

In his article, Master Jacob listed five features of the inherent jurisdiction.[122] The fifth was that the powers conferred by rules of court are in addition to, and not in substitution for, any established powers under the court's inherent jurisdiction. The words 'not in substitution for' are objectionable for reasons that will follow. What Master Jacob should be treated as meaning is that where there is an existing application of the inherent jurisdiction, and a later partial codification of that area, it is possible for the two jurisdictions to exist side by side. The effect being that on its facts one case would fall (only) into say the new rules of court, whereas another case, with different facts, would fall (only) to be considered under the established inherent jurisdiction. For example, in relation to stays, one case might fall to be decided under the principles in the Arbitration Act 1996, s 9, which provides for stays where parties have agreed to arbitrate, whereas another would only come into the inherent jurisdiction to stay.[123]

Ultimately, the extent to which an aspect of the inherent jurisdiction remains in operation after the enactment of primary or secondary legislation dealing with the same area is one of statutory interpretation.[124] For example, subsequent legislation may be in addition to the existing operation of the inherent jurisdiction, which in that situation remains in effect. At the opposite end of the spectrum, legislation may be expressly or impliedly negative in effect, in which case it ousts the previous inherent jurisdiction.[125] There is also a middle way where the inherent jurisdiction in an area remains in force to the extent to which it is not inconsistent with legislation.[126] What is clear is that the inherent jurisdiction cannot operate in ways that contradict or which are inconsistent with primary or secondary legislation.[127] What this means is that the reach of the inherent jurisdiction should be reducing as the extent of the rules of court increases. One of the problems is that this occurs

[121] Civil Procedure Act 1997, s 6(3)(a) and (d).

[122] Jacob (n 2) at 24–25.

[123] Assuming there is some remaining territory relating to stays not covered by any express provisions.

[124] *Harrison v Tew* [1990] 2 AC 523.

[125] This was the result in the actual appeal in *Harrison v Tew* [1990] 2 AC 523.

[126] Lord Lowry in *Harrison v Tew* [1990] 2 AC 523.

[127] *Raja v Van Hoogstraten (No 9)* [2008] EWCA Civ 1444, [2009] 1 WLR 1143 [76]; *Bovale Ltd v Secretary of State for Communities and Local Government* [2009] EWCA Civ 171, [2009] 1 WLR 2274.

in a patchy way, with potentially difficult points of statutory interpretation arising depending on how clear the relevant legislation happens to be.

Prior to the introduction of the Civil Procedure Rules in 1999 it was common for legal representatives to combine routine applications with grounds based on the rules of court and parallel grounds relying on the inherent jurisdiction. For example, it was common to combine striking out applications on grounds based on RSC Ord 18, r 19, with grounds alleging abuse of process under the inherent jurisdiction. At one level this may have been just to make the application look more intimidating. On another it potentially doubled the costs if the advocates decided to argue the application under both grounds. This is far from compliant with the overriding objective of dealing with cases justly and at proportionate cost.[128]

Making combined applications would be unnecessary if the implementation of a rule ousted the relevant aspect of the inherent jurisdiction. Part of the reasoning in *Harrison v Tew*[129] supporting the conclusion that the relevant rules had ousted the inherent jurisdiction was that the rules on the assessment (taxation) of solicitors' costs were a comprehensive statutory code. This has more general force in England today given the Civil Procedure Rules are a new procedural code.[130] Building on this in *Raja v Van Hoogstraten (No 9)*, Mummery LJ, giving the judgment of the court, said:

> In our judgment, therefore, where the subject matter of an application is governed by rules in the CPR, it should be dealt with by the court in accordance with the rules and not by exercising the court's inherent jurisdiction. There is no point in exercising the court's inherent jurisdiction if that would involve adopting the same approach and would lead to the same result as an application under the rules. And it would be wrong to exercise the inherent jurisdiction of the court to adopt a different approach and arrive at a different outcome from that which would result from an application of the rules....
>
> We would add that, if contrary to the view we have expressed above [the] application ... fell outside the scope of the CPR, and had to be dealt with under the inherent jurisdiction of the court, we would have held that the jurisdiction should be exercised conformably with the CPR. The CPR introduced a new code. It was intended to be comprehensive. If there is a lacuna, the omission should be made good in a way which is consistent with the rules. Our procedural regime would be incoherent if an application [made] pursuant to the CPR involved the exercise of a discretion in accordance with the overriding objective, but an application outside the rule involved the exercise of a narrower discretion or no discretion at all.[131]

[128] CPR, r 1.1(1).
[129] [1990] 2 AC 523.
[130] Also in CPR, r 1.1(1).
[131] *Raja v Van Hoogstraten (No 9)* [2008] EWCA Civ 1444, [2009] 1 WLR 1143 [78] and [85].

Conclusion

With the passage of time the legal landscape has changed. Back in 1970 Master Jacob was able to conclude that the inherent jurisdiction was a virile and viable doctrine that operated as a valuable weapon in the hands of the court to prevent clogging or obstruction of the stream of justice.[132] Developments in the 1970s proved him right. By 1997 a more cautious view was gaining ground, and Professor Dockray suggested that procedural revolutions should appear first in statutes or in the rules of court, not the law reports.[133]

Since then there has been substantial codification of the rules of civil procedure in many common law jurisdictions. As we have seen, the English Civil Procedure Rules 1998 have been described as intended to be a comprehensive code.[134] That leaves little room for an inherent jurisdiction capable of generating new procedural law. Combined with the restrictions on making new practice directions in the Civil Procedure Act 1997, s 5, the new constitutional position following the reforms of 2005, and the clearer differentiation between inherent jurisdiction and inherent or residual powers, a rethink is required on the continuing position of the inherent jurisdiction.

In these changed conditions it is suggested that while the established areas of inherent jurisdiction have proper legislative recognition, such as in the Senior Courts Act 1981, s 19, the constitutional reforms mean it is no longer acceptable for individual High Court judges to lay down new procedural law by resorting to the inherent jurisdiction. While it may have been acceptable in 1873 for the new High Court to be vested with an apparently wide-ranging inherent jurisdiction, today the right to legislate is vested in Parliament. Judges should restrict themselves to making decisions, whether procedural or on the merits, in the cases actually before them. Judges in all courts can make restrained use of their inherent powers to make suitable directions in the case in front of them,[135] but should avoid inventing new processes, and should avoid issuing practice directions (however described) outside the power provided by the Civil Procedure Act 1997, s 5.[136]

If a member of the judiciary has an idea for a development in civil procedure, the correct approach is to refer it to the Civil Justice Council. From there, proposals can be made to the Civil Procedure Rule Committee. That is the procedure laid down by Parliament, and it is designed so that innovations and their likely impact and ramifications can be properly considered, and with proper democratic scrutiny.

[132] Jacob (n 2) 52.

[133] Dockray (n 12) 131.

[134] *Raja v Van Hoogstraten (No 9)* [2008] EWCA Civ 1444, [2009] 1 WLR 1143 [85].

[135] As recognized by CPR, r 3.1(1), which in addition to the powers expressly given by the rules, practice directions, and primary legislation, preserves 'any other powers it may otherwise have.' Rule 3.1(1) extends to the County Court as well as the High Court and Court of Appeal.

[136] This is still happening. For example, the Practice Note: Business and Property claims in court, issued by Master Marsh on 3 December 2018.